Controlling Governments

This book studies the extent to which citizens control government. The chapters discuss what guides voters at election time, why governments survive, and how institutions modify the power of the people over politicians. The questions addressed include whether ideology or ethnic identity undermine the capacity of voters to assess the performance of incumbent politicians; how much information voters must have to select a politician for office or to hold a government accountable; whether parties in power can help voters to control their governments; how different institutional arrangements influence voters' control; why politicians choose particular electoral systems; and what economic and social conditions may undermine not only governments but also democracy.

The book combines analytical rigor with comparative analysis. Arguments are backed by vast macro- and micro-empirical evidence. There are cross-country comparisons and survey analyses of many countries. In every case, there has been an attempt to integrate analytical arguments and empirical research. The goal is to shed new light on perplexing questions of positive democratic theory.

José María Maravall is the Director of the Center for Advanced Studies in the Social Sciences, Juan March Institute (Madrid). He is also a Professor of Sociology at the Universidad Complutense (Madrid), an Honorary Fellow of St. Antony's College (Oxford University), and a Corresponding Fellow of the British Academy. He holds doctorates from the universities of Madrid and Oxford. He was a socialist member of parliament and Minister of Education and Science from 1982 to 1988. His previous publications include *Economic Reforms in New Democracies* (1993); *Regimes, Politics, and Markets* (1997); and (with A. Przeworski) *Democracy and the Rule of Law* (2003).

Ignacio Sánchez-Cuenca is Professor of Political Science at the Center for Advanced Studies in the Social Sciences, Juan March Institute (Madrid). He is also Associate Professor of Sociology at the Universidad Complutense (Madrid). He has been the Rice Visiting Associate Professor at Yale University and a Visiting Scholar at New York University and has held positions at Universidad Pompeu Fabra (Barcelona) and University of Salamanca. He has published four books in Spanish; articles in journals such as *Government & Opposition, Party Politics, European Union Politics*, and the *European Journal of Sociology*; as well as articles in several Spanish journals. He has authored chapters in several edited volumes, including *Democracy and the Rule of Law* (2003), edited by J. M. Maravall and A. Przeworski.

D0043669

CAMBRIDGE STUDIES IN THE THEORY OF DEMOCRACY

General Editor
ADAM PRZEWORSKI New York University

Controlling Governments

Voters, Institutions, and Accountability

Edited by

José María Maravall

Juan March Institute

Ignacio Sánchez-Cuenca

Juan March Institute

CAMBRIDGE
UNIVERSITY PRESS

CAMBRIDGE UNIVERSITY PRESS
Cambridge, New York, Melbourne, Madrid, Cape Town, Singapore, São Paulo, Delhi

Cambridge University Press
32 Avenue of the Americas, New York, NY 10013-2473, USA

www.cambridge.org
Information on this title: www.cambridge.org/9780521884105

© Cambridge University Press 2008

First published 2008

Printed in the United States of America

A catalog record for this publication is available from the British Library.

Library of Congress Cataloging in Publication Data

Controlling governments : voters, institutions, and accountability / edited by
José María Maravall, Ignacio Sánchez-Cuenca.
    p.   cm. – (Cambridge studies in the theory of democracy)
Includes bibliographical references and index.
ISBN 978-0-521-88410-5 (hardback) – ISBN 978-0-521-71110-4 (pbk.)
1. Voting – Case studies.   2. Elections – Case studies.   3. Political participation –
Case studies.   4. Comparative government.   5. Democracy.   I. Maravall, José María.
II. Sánchez-Cuenca, Ignacio.   III. Title.   IV. Series.
JF1001.C574   2008
321.8 – dc22   2007017745

ISBN   978-0-521-88410-5 hardback
ISBN   978-0-521-71110-4 paperback

Contents

Acknowledgments

This book is the product of a collective research project carried out within the Juan March Institute (JMI). Most of the authors are affiliated with this institution either as professors or as fellow doctors. The intellectual identity and the research facilities of the JMI help to explain this book. The academic community of the JMI, not a large one, shares similar backgrounds, research interests, and a commitment to theoretically oriented empirical analysis. Although there is significant variation in the research design of the chapters, they are all inspired by the necessity of combining good theory and detailed empirical analysis. The initial consensus and the intense interaction between the members of the project led to a collective book that was not intended to be a mere collection of chapters. Over three years, the authors discussed the original project, the construction of the data sets, and the successive drafts of the chapters. The interaction and cross-fertilization were strong. This should be reflected in the theoretical and methodological cohesiveness of the book as a whole.

The Scientific Council of the JMI supported the research project from the beginning. We thank the late Michael Wallerstein, as well as Gøsta Esping-Andersen, Yasemin Soysal, and Richard Breen. Adam Przeworski deserves our special gratitude for his help with the project and his comments to earlier drafts of most chapters. Finally, the two readers of Cambridge University Press provided stimulating and helpful observations.

Braulio Gómez provided competent research assistance and helped greatly in the construction of most of the data sets. Magdalena Nebreda edited the text and handled the administration of the project with great efficiency.

Contributors

ALICIA ADSERÀ, Visiting Associate Professor, Woodrow Wilson School of Public and International Affairs (Princeton University).

PALOMA AGUILAR, Doctora Miembro of the Instituto Juan March and Associate Professor of Sociology, Universidad Nacional de Educación a Distancia.

SONIA ALONSO, Doctora Miembro of the Instituto Juan March and Research Fellow, Wissenschaftszentrum Berlin für Sozialforschung.

BELÉN BARREIRO, Doctora Miembro of the Instituto Juan March and Advisor at the Cabinet of the Spanish Prime Minister.

CARLES BOIX, Professor of Political Science, Woodrow Wilson School of Public and International Affairs (Princeton University).

MARTA FRAILE, Doctora Miembro of the Instituto Juan March and Research Fellow at the Consejo Superior de Investigaciones Científicas (CSIC).

JOSÉ MARÍA MARAVALL, Professor of Sociology, Universidad Complutense de Madrid and Director, Centro de Estudios Avanzados en Ciencias Sociales (Instituto Juan March).

ALBERTO PENADÉS, Doctor Miembro of the Instituto Juan March and Associate Professor of Political Science, Universidad de Salamanca.

IGNACIO SÁNCHEZ-CUENCA, Doctor Miembro of the Instituto Juan March; Associate Professor of Sociology, Universidad Complutense de Madrid; and Professor of Political Science at the Centro de Estudios Avanzados en Ciencias Sociales (Instituto Juan March).

Controlling Governments

Introduction

José María Maravall and Ignacio Sánchez-Cuenca

We discuss in this book some core topics in the positive theory of democracy. We try to understand the relationship between citizens and politicians: what guides voters at election time, why governments survive and fall, and how institutions modify the power of the people over politicians. These are all relevant questions to determine the role of elections in democracy. Note, however, that elections can be analyzed from many other perspectives different from the representative dimension of democracy. Thus, elections can be also interpreted as an epistemic device to reach the right decision (Coleman 1989); as an exercise of self-government (Przeworski 2005); or as an opportunity for participation and deliberation (Elster 1998).

This book focuses on the representative side of democracy – how rule for the people and rule by the people are connected. Do elections (rule by the people) induce politicians to act in a representative way (rule for the people)? A common theme in all the contributions here included may sound commonsensical or even trivial: we need to combine some analytical rigor with empirical analysis. If we dare to say something so obvious, it is because the field is badly divided into formal analysis and empirical studies. We take seriously what we have learned from economic models of democracy, but we use these conclusions to organize the empirical research of cases that are far removed from the assumptions made in the formal literature.

The analytical approach to the study of representative government revolves around formal models on the control and selection of politicians through elections (for an introduction, see Persson and Tabellini 2000, ch. 4; Przeworski 2003, ch. 8). Control and selection respond to two logics. On one hand, control is associated with retrospective voting, and the main concern is how to induce politicians to behave in the interest of the electorate. More technically, the problem is how voters can avoid rent-seeking behavior by politicians (moral hazard). On the other hand, selection is associated with prospective voting. The problem is how to avoid the selection of bad types (adverse selection).

Although formal modeling has reinvigorated the theory of democracy and defined the relevant questions in a sharp and rigorous way, we still have some reservations about its empirical relevance. A brief reference to accountability models will help make the point. In purely retrospective models, all that matters is the past record of the incumbent. Voters set a particular threshold on the evaluation of their welfare between two elections: if it is achieved, they reelect the incumbent; otherwise, they throw him out. Pure accountability models (Ferejohn 1986) require several conditions for retrospective control to be possible: (1) citizens disregard promises and just observe outcomes; (2) they ignore differences between candidates because no selection is involved; (3) they do not differ in their distributive preferences over welfare that could be manipulated by the incumbent (i.e., the political space is unidimensional); and (4) they are able to coordinate on the voting rule that establishes the welfare threshold in virtue of which people vote for or against the incumbent.

Each of these conditions is crucial if citizens are to control the incumbent. These are not merely simplifying assumptions. They highlight how restrictive the conditions for electoral accountability are. It is rather obvious that in actual democracies, these conditions do not hold: there are various types of politicians; it is unlikely that voters will be able to coordinate on a voting rule; voters hear different promises; and politics tends to be run in more than one dimension.

Of course, later models have relaxed these conditions in various ways: for instance, allowing deviations from electoral promises (and not just unsatisfactory outcomes) to explain voters' reactions (Austen-Smith and Banks 1989), considering that candidates differ and have incentives to reveal in the campaign their true intentions (Harrington 1993), and introducing multiple agents that may provide information to the principal (Persson, Roland, and Tabellini 1997). Models of accountability also make important informational requirements: voters must be able to assess whether the incumbent is responsible for past outcomes. These may have been due to the actions of the government or to conditions beyond its control. If voters cannot know the causes of such outcomes, to establish a reelection threshold, and to reward or punish for past performance, becomes arbitrary.

Despite their more realistic assumptions, these models generally assume that representation can only be guaranteed via accountability. Elections, from this point of view, are little more than a mechanism to create rotation in office. As Riker (1982: 244) put it, "all elections do or have to do is to permit people to get rid of rulers." This view is echoed in Przeworski's (1999) minimalist conception of democracy.

Mackie (2003) has extensively shown that there seems to be some deep and unwarranted distrust in these models toward any function of elections that goes beyond kicking politicians out of office. Yet if elections are, after all, a punishment mechanism, it seems a rather inefficient one. Citizens have only one instrument, the paper ballot, to punish or reward the incumbent for the many decisions made during his or her time in office. Further, elections do not provide many opportunities for voters to coordinate on their judgments about the incumbent. Besides, as Fearon (1999) has argued, there are some resilient facts about the functioning of democracy that are scarcely compatible with the idea of retrospective control: (1) voters tend to dislike office-oriented candidates, (2) voters tend to reject politicians who follow too closely the shifts in public mood or who are too sensitive to surveys, and (3) some democracies work under term limits that eliminate the reelection incentive of the theory of accountability.

We have to provide a more realistic description of how the control of the incumbent is part of a wider democratic process. This is where we depart from the formal literature. But we try to stay close to the results of this literature to structure the empirical analysis. We do not believe that the alternative to formal models is running regressions, as is so often the case in the inexhaustible literature on economic voting. We hope to convince the reader that there is some middle ground between formalism and empiricism.

The chapters of the book focus on four themes that reveal the sort of complexities that emerge in the relationship between politicians and citizens. First, government survival does not depend entirely on electoral results. We must also take into account nonelectoral, parliamentary accountability. The mismatch between these two forms of accountability may have large implications for the calculations and strategies of the incumbent.

Second, voters make up their minds by combining judgments about incumbent performance with many other elements: these are not only retrospective and prospective considerations; voters may also vote for reasons that are unrelated to past or future performance.

Third, the relationship between governments and citizens is mediated by political parties. In the real world, the accountability relationship is a triangular one: the government is responsible to its voters but also to the party or parties that support it.

Finally, the extent of citizen control over politicians depends on institutions, but these institutions are endogenous, for they are designed by parties themselves. Parties, therefore, have certain latitude to decide to what extent they want to be constrained by citizens (Ferejohn 1999).

Note how distant we are with regard to pure accountability models. We have governments that can be controlled in more than one way, voters with varying degrees of sensitivity to government performance, parties that mediate between politicians and citizens, and endogenous institutions that enhance or reduce citizens' capacity for control. In each case, we have new problems that so far have received little attention in the positive theory of democracy.

Let us start with the survival of governments. We know that disconnections between loss of votes and loss of office exist in democratic systems. Such disconnections are particularly important under proportional representation and coalition governments. Cheibub and Przeworski (1999: 231–5) have shown that of 310 peaceful changes in prime ministers between 1950 and 1990, 48 percent were due to decisions made by politicians, either from their own party or from the ruling coalition. If we examine incumbents with majoritarian support in parliament and compare single-party and coalition governments in 23 parliamentary democracies from the end of the Second World War to 2003, 92.8 percent of prime ministers in single-party governments lost office through elections. This was the case for only 56.7 percent of prime ministers in coalition governments; the rest of losses were due to political conspiracies.[1] According to Maravall (2007), the criteria used by voters and politicians to sack a prime minister are antagonic. In 1,109 country/year observations for these democracies (which included 312 losses of office), when economic performance was bad, the probability of losing power at election time went up; when the performance was good, the probability of being thrown out of office by ambitious fellow politicians increased. This may explain why, on aggregate, the fate of prime ministers does not appear to depend on economic conditions.

---

[1] The countries are Australia, Austria, Belgium, Canada, Denmark, Finland, France, Germany, Greece, Iceland, Ireland, Israel, Italy, Japan, Luxembourg, the Netherlands, Norway, New Zealand, Portugal, Spain, Sweden, Turkey, and the United Kingdom.

If we focus only on elections and leave conspiracies aside, the bulk of the literature has concentrated on how the fate of governments depends on economic conditions, mainly because economic performance is an easy variable to assess. Yet the connection between economic performance and government survival is obscure. Many studies have indeed shown that past economic outcomes influence the support of governments (examples are Kramer 1971; Shaffer and Chressanthis 1991; Lanoue 1994; Monardi 1994; Svoboda 1995). This support also appears to depend on expectations about the future, however, not just on assessments about the past. Comparative evidence is also inconclusive: past economic performance seems to matter in some countries but not in others (Paldam 1991: 9). Further, economic conditions, even if they influence individual voting, do not seem to affect electoral outcomes and whether or not governments survive. Powell and Whitten (1993), after studying 102 elections in 19 countries between 1969 and 1988, conclude that economic growth, inflation, and unemployment have no consequences on the electoral support of governments. This is very much the conclusion of Cheibub and Przeworski (1999: 226–30): past economic conditions had no effect on the likelihood that prime ministers would survive in 99 democracies between 1950 and 1990, with 1,606 country/year observations.

Barreiro, in her contribution to this book, provides a more comprehensive picture. First, she takes into account other outcomes apart from the economic ones. Second, she contemplates the possibility that different governments are judged differently by voters. As she states in her chapter, "we know very little about how accountability works in different ideological and economic contexts." It has sometimes been argued that governments are more vulnerable to poor performance in policies at which they are assumed to be competent – as, for instance, the Republican Party in the United States over public spending (Lowry, Alt, and Ferree 1998). Other studies have stated, on the contrary, that this vulnerability is greater over policies at which they are assumed to be less adept – conservative governments over employment (Carlsen 2000; see also Warwick 1992).

Barreiro examines which criteria are used to punish or reward incumbents at election time, and whether they vary when right- or left-wing parties are in power and when the government corresponds to a rich or poor country. She studies 83 democracies between 1950 and 2000, looking at electoral gains and losses by incumbents. Governments in general tend to lose votes from election to election, with a mean loss of 3.9 percent. This tendency to *desgaste* is confirmed in Alonso's chapter, which shows that in multiethnic countries, class-based parties lose, on average, 1.40 percent of their vote between two consecutive elections, whereas ethnic parties lose 0.01 percent. Elsewhere, Maravall (2007) has shown that in parliamentary democracies, coalition governments lost, on average, 1.40 percent of their vote between elections, whereas single-party governments lost 2.50 percent. These findings contradict the hypothesis of an "incumbency advantage" – that is, the idea that holding office increases the likelihood of winning the next election because of the capacity to mobilize privileged resources.

Comparing the relative vulnerability of governments, Barreiro reaches two empirical conclusions: the first is that the criteria with which voters judge governments of left and right, and in rich and poor countries, do vary; the second, that the accountability of governments depends on the extent to which they can be held responsible for outcomes. Thus, although annual variations in per capita real income improve the electoral performance of all kinds of government, they matter somewhat more for governments of the left and in rich countries. Increases in total government expenditures as a percentage of GDP are beneficial for the vote for leftist parties in power (and indifferent for conservative ones). Further, if we accept that voters attribute more responsibility for outcomes the greater the share of seats in parliament of the party in power, this effect is greater in rich countries (i.e., as such share goes up, the greater the losses if performance is bad, and the greater the electoral rewards if performance is good).

Note that Barreiro studies accountability examining losses or gains of votes between two consecutive elections. She argues that "when incumbents lose or win votes for their outcomes, citizens are being sensitive to government performance. It is this sensitivity that may trigger the retrospective mechanism of accountability." Yet the loss of votes is not necessarily related to the loss of power. Electoral leaks may go on over a very long time before becoming a threat to survival; governments may react with fear or with phlegm. In Great Britain, Tony Blair lost 2.3 percent of Labour's share of total votes between the 1997 and the 2001 elections and 13.8 percent between the 2001 and the 2005 elections, but he preserved a majority of seats and stayed in power. It is only when votes lead to the loss of office that Friedrich's "law of anticipated reactions" (1963: 199–215) operates: that is, when politicians, fearing that voters at election time will throw them out, avoid shirking.

These arguments about democratic controls are retrospective: governments respond for their past actions. They abandon two crucial exigencies of pure accountability models, however: first, that all politicians in power are alike, so that elections involve no selection; second, that the electorate is homogeneous, so that incumbents cannot manipulate voters' distributional differences. The various contributors to this volume share a similar view of accountability. Sánchez-Cuenca's chapter combines both retrospective accountability and ideological differences among incumbents and voters.

A vast literature, from Downs (1957) onward, considers that elections are about selecting the best candidate for office and that this selection can be reproduced in a spatial "least distance" model. The "best" candidate is the one whose policies are closest to the voter's ideal position. Minimizing ideological distance is what guides both voters and parties. This is, of course, a prospective view of elections: no accountability is involved. In a different conception, elections are about holding governments accountable for their past record in office, and voters ignore differences between politicians. Very few consistent bridges have existed between these two distinct views of elections: what empirical studies have often done is simply juxtapose them – this has tended to be the case with the oceanic research on economic voting.

Sánchez-Cuenca shows why ideological voting and accountability can be combined. At election time, voters can assess the "ideological reliability" of a party – which depends on both the consistency of its policies and its political capacity. This assessment has to do with the past: "a government's performance provides plenty of evidence about its consistency and capacity." The "retentive power" of a party is then defined as the percentage of individuals who, being ideologically closer to that party, vote for it. Such percentage goes down as voters critically assess the capacity and consistency of the party despite its ideological proximity. Sánchez-Cuenca shows that a third of voters who were closer to the British Conservative Party or the German Christlich Demokratische Union/Christlich Soziale Union (CDU/CSU) than to any of their rivals did not vote following ideological proximity. The loss of retentive power was particularly important for the Spanish Socialist Party (PSOE): in 2000, only 52.3 percent of those voters who were closer to the PSOE than to any other party voted for it. Using conditional logit models, Sánchez-Cuenca demonstrates that such loss was first due to voters' attributions of inconsistency between ideology and policies (in the elections of 1986 and 1989) and later to their critical assessments of the party's capacity, mostly due to internecine struggles (in the elections of 1993, 1996, and 2000). This analysis therefore departs both from the simple logics of ideological proximity and of retrospective performance voting: it combines ideology and performance in an analysis of accountability where differences exist among parties and among voters.

Ideology can thus guide voters in several ways. It can contribute to assessments of the political reliability of a party; it can help to select the candidate closest to the voter's preferences; it can reduce information costs; it can also introduce biases in voters' judgments of performance. Maravall and Przeworski (2001) have shown that ideology influences voters' expectations about governments: when assessments of the past and expectations about the future are combined, voters can find intertemporal or exonerative arguments to rationalize their vote. Ideology can lead them to think that if the past was bad, it was a necessary pain for a brighter future; or that a bad past and a bleak future are caused by conditions beyond the control of the government. In both cases, voters go on supporting the incumbent. The reward–sanction mechanism of pure accountability models is thus thwarted.

We do not know to what extent nationalism operates as an extreme form of ideology. Strongly ideological voters may follow the dictum "my party, right or wrong" – they will consider no other alternative. In similar fashion, nationalist voters may only conceive voting for a party that responds to their conception of the demos. When a part of the electorate holds to a different national identity, how does this affect the democratic control of the government? Are nationalist governments electorally more immune to past performance? Is the nationalist vote less volatile and more subject to political blinkers? The chapters by Alonso and by Aguilar and Sánchez-Cuenca shed light on these largely unexplored questions.

As Alonso puts it, "if it is true that ethnic allegiances provide nationalist parties with a competitive electoral advantage over class-based parties, ceteris paribus (i.e., under similar institutional settings), ethnic parties should show lower fluctuation of votes, less electoral punishment, lengthier duration in office, and less political erosion with the passage of time than class-based parties." She studies five countries with fourteen ethnoregions (where ethnic and nonethnic parties compete), and 329 country/year observations. The analysis consists of a Weibull duration model in which the risk of losing office is assumed to vary as a function of time. She finds that the connection between government performance and survival in office is very different in majoritarian and proportional representation systems, both for ethnic and nonethnic parties. Because proportional representation facilitates party fragmentation, it also generates competition within the nationalist camp – that is, more shifts of votes within blocs than between the nationalist/nonnationalist blocs. On the contrary, in majoritarian systems, access to office requires parties to compete for votes beyond ethnicity barriers – thus, competition between blocs is greater.

Coalitions were the norm in ethnoregions: 85.5 percent of all observations against 73.0 percent in regions with no ethnic parties. Most of such coalitions were mixed – that is, they included nationalist and nonnationalist partners. Although the fluctuation of votes was greater in ethnoregions because of their more fragmented party systems, mixed coalitions had lower electoral losses than homogeneous coalitions. This was due to the greater stability of the vote of ethnic parties in systems of proportional representation. Here, ethnic parties could follow a conservative strategy: they could simply rely on their own nationalist constituency rather than compete for nonnationalist voters. So, in ethnoregions, nationalist parties did better in preserving their voters than class-based parties. Alonso concludes that "voters judge an ethnic party less severely when it shares office with other parties . . . than when it is in office alone. Governments made up of only one party are similarly judged by voters, irrespective of the type of party. An ethnic party in office alone will probably be judged not only by the defense of the ethnonationalist program, but also by its economic performance."

An intriguing question remains, as Alonso points out. The presence of nationalist politicians in mixed coalitions and the support given by nationalist voters to the collaboration with nonnationalist forces suggest a political pragmatism and a programmatic flexibility that contradicts the alleged rigidity of nationalist identities. So we need to move from a comparative analysis based on aggregate data on parties and governments to survey data on individual voters.

This is what Aguilar and Sánchez-Cuenca do in their chapter. They study the reactions of voters to the performance of a government in a complex scenario where, on one hand, nationalist parties enhance identity rather than performance, and, on the other hand, political decentralization increases voters' difficulties in attributing responsibility for past outcomes. The Spanish case provides an *experimentum crucis* to test the reaction of voters in a politically decentralized system where (1) the same party could hold the national and a regional government – it would thus be easier for voters to attribute responsibilities (the case in the chapter is Andalusia); (2) one party could hold power at the national level and be part of a coalition with nationalists at the regional level (the Basque Country);

or (3) different parties could be in office at the national and the regional levels – the regional government could be either nationalist (Catalonia) or nonnationalist (Castilla-León). The empirical analysis uses individual data from a 1992 survey with large national and regional samples.

Aguilar and Sánchez-Cuenca assess the relative influence of nationalism and ideology on the vote. They estimate the spatial distances between voters and parties both in a nationalist and an ideological dimension. What they find about the effect of such distances on the vote is the following:

1. The influence of ideology is stronger in general than that of nationalism. Both dimensions have a similar effect on nationalist voters, however. For nonnationalists, ideology matters much more.
2. There is coattail voting with respect to the central government. This is so particularly in nonnationalist regions, where the performance of the central government influences vote intentions for the regional governments.
3. In regions where nationalism is strong, the performance of regional governments has a greater effect on voters. This is particularly so for nonnationalist voters, who respond very much to the performance of the regional incumbent.
4. Nationalist voters tend to exonerate nationalist regional governments when the performance is poor. This is more the case with Basque than with Catalan nationalists: the former are much less sensitive to performance when deciding their vote. Nationalist voters also assess the performance of the central government much more critically than nonnationalist voters.

Therefore, the conclusion, which is based on comparative aggregate data, that nationalist governments survive longer in office than their nonnationalist counterparts under systems of proportional representation is coherent with the results of individual-level data. Nationalist voters tend to exonerate nationalist governments, their vote is less sensitive to performance, and their assessment of the central government is much more critical. So nationalists vote with political blinkers, and nationalist governments are more immune to performance.

So far, we have examined several aspects of the democratic control of governments, ignoring issues of information. However, citizens can hardly exercise such control if they do not know what is happening – that is, if they ignore political facts, if they cannot monitor the actions of the incumbent, if they cannot assign responsibilities for outcomes. If voting either consists of selecting the best candidates, generally on the basis of ideological proximity, or involves holding governments accountable for their past performance, voters need information on politicians and their actions. We do not know, however, whether information is more related to the logic of selection or the logic of accountability.

As Fraile points out in her chapter, arguments on this matter have been somewhat contradictory. Fearon (1999) defends that retrospective accountability requires more information than prospective selection. Zaller (1992, 2004), on the contrary, indicates that informed voters are more ideological (i.e., prospective). Fraile examines postelectoral survey data in Spain, Portugal, Hungary, and Poland – four multiparty systems in which she assumes that informational requirements will be comparatively more demanding. Her empirical conclusions appear to be consistent with Fearon's interpretation: "retrospective control depends more on citizens' political knowledge than if voters use ideology to select the incumbent." On the contrary, "low degrees of political knowledge lead voters to select politicians according to ideology." The logic of voting appears to follow clear criteria: when voters know more about the world of politics, they may better assess the performance of the government and vote accordingly; otherwise, ideology serves them as a compass in selecting the best candidate.

Voters may use all kinds of information to monitor and assess governments. Their information may typically come from the media, the opposition, or institutions of horizontal accountability. It may also be that the party in government serves voters, providing them with critical information – the internal accountability of incumbents (vis-à-vis party members) – would contribute to their external accountability. This is what Maravall discusses in his chapter. A strong argument for internal party democracy would exist if "discussion between party activists and leaders in public office might inform voters on the reasons for policy switches or on hidden actions of the government."

The government is conceived in this chapter as an agent with two principals – the party and the electorate. These are the interests of the three actors: (1) voters want a government that carries out policies close to their preferences but that is also capable of implementing them, (2) party members are interested in policies but also in holding office (differences in the relative relevance of these two interests distinguishes the *nomenklatura* of the party from rank-and-file members), and (3) the government wants the party to provide early warnings about electoral threats but also to persuade voters about its policies. So trade-offs might exist, both for the electorate and for the government, between information and capacity regarding the party.

Why would incumbent party members monitor the government better than voters? For one, their preferences over policy are stronger; this is why they militate in a party and do not just vote. Further, the political horizon of the party goes beyond that of leaders. Thus, party members will care about the ideological betrayals and the electoral costs of political U-turns or shirking. Even if the policy preferences of voters and party members do not overlap, the electoral program of the government is important for both: for the former, it is a set of promises on which the incumbent was elected; for the latter, a compromise between ideology and electoralism. Thus, open discussions within the party can be informative about what the government does, about whether or not it is implementing its program.

Yet debates can be ambiguous and carry too much noise. They can also undermine the capacity of the party in power. Survey data for Spain and the United Kingdom show that voters in two very different institutional contexts see such debates as factionalist disputes that undermine capacity. Consequently, they punish divided parties. An event-history analysis of twenty-two parliamentary democracies between 1975 and 1995, with 448 country/year observations, shows that parties last longer in office and the survival of prime ministers becomes more predictable when closed lists exist. If politicians believe that voters punish internal divisions, they will introduce discipline within their parties. This convergence of preferences between leaders and voters will be to the cost of party members and to the detriment of internal party democracy.

The last part of the book turns to explain the choice of institutions by politicians and their influence on the democratic game. Penadés's chapter provides an agent-based account of the choice of electoral institutions. As he puts it, such institutions "influence the manner in which governments can be made accountable. . . . Parties preferring the same rules behaved more similarly, under different electoral systems, than parties with opposite preferences competing in similar institutional environments." Preferences are explained by the consequences of electoral rules for government formation and by concerns about internal schisms and loss of votes.

Proportional representation (PR) generates incentives for party centralization, for conservative electoral strategies, and for postelectoral parliamentary alliances. On the contrary, in majoritarian systems, parties tend to be more decentralized, strategies try to expand the electorate, and winning elections entails more clearly assuming office. Institutional preferences will depend on the risk of losing former voters when trying to attract new ones, on the threat of divisions within the party, and on fears about governing. Penadés focuses on the preferences of socialist parties until the Second World War when, out of sixteen countries, fourteen turned to PR. Such preferences varied widely: this is why we cannot accept explanations according to which socialist parties should have systematically opposed PR (because it benefited their opponents) or, on the contrary, should have always supported it (because it led to greater income distribution). Neither did the preferences of socialists depend on the average size of their electorates: no significant differences existed between those who defended or opposed PR – before or after it was introduced.

Because internal schisms and loss of votes were the two main concerns of party leaders, they chose electoral institutions accordingly. The main explanation of the choice, according to Penadés, lies in the strength of the trade-union movement. His careful analysis of historical evidence leads to the conclusion that "the causal antecedent constraining the choice of strategy was set by the trade unions. At the time of institutional choice, it was union strength rather than party strength that could have predicted the preferences of socialist parties." Unions limited the threats of internal splits and of desertions by working-class voters. So leaders of union-based parties could opt for majoritarian representation, an expansive electoral strategy, and governmental responsibilities. On the contrary, parties related to weak unions were more vulnerable to organizational and electoral costs. Their choice was PR, thus transferring coalition games to the parliamentary arena, where entry into government was a decision that could be more quickly reversed.

These socialist politicians, when choosing the rules of representation, were anticipating the costs within their parties and their electorates. Their supporters' threat of exit was a democratic limit to institutional choices. The following chapter by Adserà and Boix studies nonelectoral constraints on politicians: these stem from the possibility of antidemocratic reactions. The chapter focuses in particular on the balance of forces between majorities and minorities, related to the level of available resources and their distribution. The control of material resources by a group sets limits on what governments can do in a democracy. When such assets are mobile, the threat of exit reduces the capacity of governments to tax or expropriate. When the assets are fixed, such threat of exit is not plausible: to avoid being taxed or expropriated, asset holders will turn to rejecting majority rule (and democracy).

Thus, either governments accept limits on their policies or democracy will be destabilized. The question is no longer what explains the survival of governments nor what influences voters' choices at election time; it is rather why would the losers in the democratic game accept the verdict of elections. What Adserà and Boix study in their chapter is the relative influence of institutional variables, compared with economic development and the distribution of wealth, on the incentives to comply with, or subvert, the rules of democracy. They assess the probability of democratic survival in all sovereign countries from the mid-nineteenth century to the end of the twentieth century.

Institutions have a comparatively minor influence on the stability of democracies. As Adserà and Boix point out, "within the strictures imposed by social and economic factors, constitutional structures play a relatively marginal role." Majoritarian systems produce greater instability but in underdeveloped countries. Federalism and parliamentarism lessen the stakes and thus the incentives to subvert. Adserà and Boix consider both to be the only institutional conditions that stabilize democracies: "the positive impact of federal parliamentarism is extremely powerful – to the point that it seems to be the only institutional mechanism that stabilizes democracy regardless of nonconstitutional conditions."

Democratic survival depends on the material conditions of electoral majorities and minorities. This is where the incentives to accept or reject the results of elections are rooted. Such a conclusion replicates previous results (Cheibub and Przeworski 1999; Przeworski et al. 2000; Boix 2003; Przeworski 2003). Adserà and Boix show that the likelihood of a democracy surviving for at least fifty years is under 10 percent if the country's per capita income is below $1,000; that it grows to 80 percent if the level reaches $8,000; and that democracies face no risk of collapsing if their economies reach $15,000 (at 1996 purchasing-power parities). An egalitarian distribution of wealth also decreases the threat to democracy. Levels of economic development make potential subverters risk-averse; economic egalitarianism reduces the distance between the preferences of minorities and the decisions of majorities. When these material conditions exist, the agendas of governments will be less restricted by antidemocratic constraints; incumbents will increase their autonomy vis-à-vis minorities with the capacity to veto the political process.

This is the string of arguments that this book presents. Arguments are backed by vast comparative evidence, at both the macro and micro levels. There are cross-country comparisons and survey analyses. In every case, there has been an attempt to integrate analytical arguments and empirical research. The goal was to shed new light on perplexing questions of positive democratic theory.

REFERENCES

Austen-Smith, David, and Jeffrey S. Banks. 1989. "Electoral Accountability and Incumbency." In Peter Ordeshook (ed.), *Models of Strategic Choices in Politics*. Ann Arbor: University of Michigan Press.

Boix, Carles. 2003. *Democracy and Redistribution*. New York: Cambridge University Press.

Carlsen, Fredrik. 2000. "Unemployment, Inflation, and Government Popularity: Are There Partisan Effects?" *Electoral Studies* 19 (2/3): 141–50.

Cheibub, José Antonio, and Adam Przeworski. 1999. "Democracy, Elections and Accountability for Economic Outcomes." In Adam Przeworski, Susan C. Stokes, and Bernard Manin (eds.), *Democracy, Accountability, and Representation*. Cambridge: Cambridge University Press.

Coleman, Jules. 1989. "Rationality and the Justification of Democracy." In Geoffrey Brennan and Loren E. Lomasky (eds.), *Politics and Process: New Essays in Democratic Thought*. Cambridge: Cambridge University Press.

Downs, Anthony. 1957. *An Economic Theory of Democracy*. New York: Harper Collins.

Elster, Jon (ed.). 1998. *Deliberative Democracy*. Cambridge: Cambridge University Press.

Fearon, James. 1999. "Electoral Accountability and the Control of Politicians: Selecting Good Types versus Sanctioning Poor Performance." In Adam Przeworski, Susan C. Stokes, and Bernard Manin (eds.), *Democracy, Accountability, and Representation*. Cambridge: Cambridge University Press.

Ferejohn, John. 1986. "Incumbent Performance and Electoral Control." *Public Choice* 50 (1/3): 5–25.

Ferejohn, John. 1999. "Accountability and Authority: Toward a Theory of Political Accountability." In Adam Przeworski, Susan C. Stokes, and Bernard Manin (eds.), *Democracy, Accountability, and Representation*. Cambridge: Cambridge University Press.

Friedrich, Carl J. 1963. *Man and His Government: An Empirical Theory of Politics*. New York: McGraw-Hill.

Harrington, Joseph. 1993. "The Impact of Reelection Pressures on the Fulfillment of Campaign Promises." *Games and Economic Behavior* 5 (1): 71–97.

Kramer, Gerald. 1971. "Short-term Fluctuations in US Voting Behavior. 1896–1964." *American Political Science Review* 65 (1): 131–43.

Lanoue, David. 1994. "Retrospective and Prospective Voting in Presidential-Year Elections." *Political Research Quarterly* 47 (1): 193–205.

Lowry, Robert, James Alt, and Karen Ferree. 1998. "Fiscal Policy Outcomes and Electoral Accountability in American States." *American Political Science Review* 92 (4): 759–74.

Mackie, Gerry. 2003. *Democracy Defended*. Cambridge: Cambridge University Press.

Maravall, José María. 2007. "Accountability and the Survival of Governments." In Carles Boix and Susan Stokes (eds.), *Oxford Handbook of Comparative Politics*. Oxford: Oxford University Press.

Maravall, José María, and Adam Przeworski. 2001. "Political Reactions to the Economy: The Spanish Experience." In Susan C. Stokes (ed.), *Public Support for Market Reforms in New Democracies*. Cambridge: Cambridge University Press.

Monardi, Fred. 1994. "Primary Voters as Retrospective Voters." *American Politics Quarterly* 22 (1): 88–103.

Paldam, Martin. 1991. "How Robust is the Vote Function? A Study of Seventeen Nations over Four Decades." In Helmut Norpoth, Michael Lewis-Beck, and Jean-Dominique Laffay (eds.), *Economics and Politics: The Calculus of Support*. Ann Arbor: University of Michigan Press.

Persson, Torsten, Gérard Roland, and Guido Tabellini. 1997. "Separation of Powers and Accountability." *Quarterly Journal of Economics* 112 (4): 1163–202.

Persson, Torsten, and Guido Tabellini. 2000. *Political Economics: Explaining Economic Policy*. Cambridge, MA: MIT Press.

Powell, G. Bingham, and Guy Whitten. 1993. "A Cross-National Analysis of Economic Voting: Taking Account of the Political Context." *American Journal of Political Science* 37 (2): 391–414.

Przeworski, Adam. 1999. "Minimalist Conception of Democracy: A Defense." In Ian Shapiro and Casiano Hacker-Cordón (eds.), *Democracy's Value*. Cambridge: Cambridge University Press.

Przeworski, Adam. 2003. *States and Markets: A Primer in Political Economy*. Cambridge: Cambridge University Press.

Przeworski, Adam. 2005. "The Possibility of Self-Government." Manuscript, New York University.

Przeworski, Adam, Mike Álvarez, José Antonio Cheibub, and Fernando Limongi. 2000. *Democracy and Development*. New York: Cambridge University Press.

Riker, William. 1982. *Liberalism against Populism*. Prospect Heights: Waveland Press.

Shaffer, Stephen, and George Chressanthis. 1991. "Accountability and U.S. Senate Elections: A Multivariate Analysis." *Western Political Quarterly* 44 (3): 625–39.

Svoboda, Craig. 1995. "Retrospective Voting in Gubernatorial Elections: 1982–1986." *Political Research Quarterly* 48 (1): 135–50.

Warwick, Paul. 1992. "Economic Trends and Government Survival in West European Parliamentary Democracies." *American Political Science Review* 86 (4): 875–87.

Zaller, John. 1992. *The Nature and Origins of Mass Opinion*. New York: Cambridge University Press.

Zaller, John. 2004. "Floating Voters in U.S. Presidential Elections: 1948–2000." In Willem Saris and Paul Sniderman (eds.), *Studies in Public Opinion: Attitudes, Nonattitudes, Measurement Error, and Change*. Princeton: Princeton University Press.

CHAPTER ONE

Explaining the Electoral Performance of Incumbents in Democracies

Belén Barreiro

Introduction

This chapter examines electoral performance for incumbents in democratic regimes. I explore whether parties in government lose and win votes for the outcomes produced under their mandates. In other words, the work investigates whether electoral support for incumbents depends on key economic, social, and political indicators. The study includes eighty-three democracies from the 1950s through 2000.

This chapter is structured as follows. I first discuss the state of the discipline, and I present the principal objectives of the research. Then I test three main hypotheses. First, electoral variations for ruling parties may not only depend on pure economic indicators, such as economic growth or inflation. Voters may also hold governments accountable for other policies. They may care about the role of the state in the economy, in particular the size of the state.[1] Second, right-wing governments may be judged differently from left-wing governments. Citizens may reward conservative parties for fostering economic freedom and left-wing parties for increasing the size of the state. Third, accountability may work differently in rich and poor democracies. Voters may be more demanding in rich democracies or they may not be.

Accountability and Electoral Performance

The analysis of electoral performance for parties in government contributes to our understanding of how accountability works. Rulers are

---

[1] The size of the state refers exclusively to central government expenditures, not to the state's regulation of economic activity or to the size of the public sector, which includes public enterprises.

accountable when voters sanction them for their actions, making the probability of survival in office depend on their performance (Przeworski, Stokes, and Manin 1999). We know that changes in government are not necessarily due to elections, but a fall in votes for the incumbent may easily produce its removal from cabinet. When incumbents lose or win votes for their outcomes, citizens are being sensitive to government performance. It is this sensitivity that may trigger the retrospective mechanism of accountability.

Results on whether democracies are accountable are not conclusive. A huge amount of empirical work has examined whether parties in government are punished when things go wrong, but conclusions are uncertain. Most of the research focuses on the impact of the economy on electoral support, showing that citizens punish the incumbent when economic indicators turn out to be bad (Lewis-Beck 1988).

Accountability is questioned in other studies. Cheibub and Przeworski (1999) have shown that governments are not accountable to voters for economic outcomes. Using a sample of 135 countries, which includes all democracies, covering the period 1950–90, they demonstrate that "the survival of prime ministers is slightly sensitive to the growth of employment, but this is all, and this result is weak. The survival of presidents appears to be completely independent of economic performance" (p. 229).

Findings on accountability are not conclusive. Variations in accountability have been attributed to the institutional design of democracies (Stein 1990; Powell and Whitten 1993; Atkeson and Partin 1995). If citizens are able to attribute responsibility for economic performance, they can punish or reward incumbents (Anderson 2000; Chappell and Veiga 2000; Kiewiet 2000). Voters should be able to clarify responsibility for voting for or against incumbents. Several political or institutional factors may reduce responsibility: minority governments, coalition cabinets, the lack of voting discipline of parties in government, or the opposition's control of the second house.[2] As Duch and Stevenson (2005) demonstrate, a party's administrative responsibility conditions its economic voting.

Accountability may also vary according to the heterogeneous nature of policies (Barreiro 2003). Three factors may alter representation across

---

[2] Accountability may be also conditioned by the endogeneity of economic perceptions. As Anderson, Mendes, and Tverdova (2004) show, people's evaluations of the economy is influenced by their own past electoral behavior.

policies: saliency (Miller and Stokes 1963; Erikson 1976; Page and Shapiro 1992; Monroe 1998), the amount of available information on a particular policy (Miller and Stokes 1963; Kuklinski 1978; Page and Shapiro 1983, 1992; Przeworski, Stokes, and Manin 1999), and the extent to which a policy is determined by exogenous conditions. Two main exogenous factors condition political decisions: international constraints and the state's financial capacity. When saliency is low, information is obscure, and issues are conditioned by exogenous events, policy representation and accountability are low.

Despite the number of studies that have been undertaken, the discipline still lacks a global account of whether democracies are accountable. Research in this field has two main limitations. On one hand, studies are usually based on small and biased samples. On the other hand, studies are normally limited to economic indicators. Obviously, any research on electoral performance has to confront a trade-off between the size of the sample and the range of governmental outcomes that explains the vote for the incumbent. Large samples restrict the number of indicators of governmental performance that can be considered because data are less available for poor democracies. Small samples allow the inclusion of more indicators, but conclusions will always be biased.

With one partial exception, there is not a single study that includes in its sample all democracies. The range varies from "one country, one election" studies to "cross-country (or area), cross-time" analyses. The most ambitious study is Cheibub and Przeworski's work (1999) on accountability for economic outcomes, which was based on a sample of 135 countries and includes all democracies. Nevertheless, the authors do not explain electoral performance; instead, they focus on the survival of heads of government. Yet we know that permanence in office is often independent of elections. As Cheibub and Przeworski show, 48 percent of changes of prime ministers in parliamentarism are not caused by elections.

Studies with limited samples may be useful, but they do not properly respond to the question of whether there is accountability in democracies, which should be answered irrespective of space and time. It is necessary to include if not all democracies, then at least an unbiased sample of them. This opens the possibility of comparing how accountability works in different political and economic contexts. The reward–punishment mechanism may or may not be different under right-wing and left-wing governments and in rich and poor democracies.

We know little about how accountability works in different ideological and economic contexts. On one hand, although an important amount of research focuses on how parties' ideology affect governmental outcomes (Budge, Roberston, and Hearl 1987; Hibbs 1987; Boix 1998), studies usually do not take into account the effect of the incumbent's ideology on accountability. However, there are some partial exceptions. Examining government survival, Warwick suggests that "governments are vulnerable only on the economic indicator they are generally less adept at handling" (1992: 884). Lowry, Alt, and Ferree (1998: 759) demonstrate that in the United States, "Republican gubernatorial candidates lose votes if their party is responsible for unanticipated increases in the size of the state budget; Democrats do not and indeed they may be rewarded for small increases." Carlsen (2000: 141) shows that government popularity depends on its ideology: "right governments are hurt by unemployment but not by moderate inflation. The results for left governments are less conclusive."

On the other hand, most of the economic voting research focuses on developed countries, and those studies that include in their sample less developed countries usually exclude Western democracies. For example, Pacek (1994) pays attention to national elections in four East Central European democracies, Bulgaria, the former Czech and Slovak Federated Republic, and Poland. Some analyses focus their attention exclusively on Latin America (Remmer 1991; Roberts and Wibbels 1999), whereas other studies are cross-continental but their sample only considers the underdeveloped world (Pacek and Radcliff 1995).

The second limitation is that most studies focus on the impact of economic outcomes on electoral losses, and they exclude others dimensions of governmental performance. But it may be the case, as Cheibub and Przeworski note, that voters "keep governments accountable for matters other than economic" (1999: 237). Assuming that accountability may not exclusively depend on the economy, some studies show that citizens also hold incumbents accountable for foreign policy (Nickelsburg and Norpoth 2000), fiscal policy (Kone and Winters 1993; Lowry, Alt, and Ferree 1998), corruption (Uslaner and Conway 1985; Fackler and Lin 1995), social policies (Fraile 2005), or abortion (Cook, Jelen, and Wilcox 1994; Abramowitz 1995). But none of these studies integrate more than two dimensions of governmental performance, and they are all limited in time and space.

This chapter provides a global explanation of how electoral performance works in democracies. It aims to fill two gaps in the literature on accountability and democratic theory: the effect of parties' ideology and of a country's economic development on electoral punishment. I explore whether right-wing governments are judged differently from left-wing governments. In general terms, citizens may expect *economic freedom* from conservative parties and *social equality* from left-wing parties. Voters support right-wing parties, in their conservative, liberal, or Christian democratic guise, both when they reject a strong involvement of the state in the economy and when they do not favor radical social equality programs. From socialist incumbents, people want policies oriented toward workers' protection and redistribution. Obviously, citizens, whether conservative or socialist, may also agree on certain matters. They may all attribute the same value to certain economic outcomes (economic growth). Consequently, governments may be accountable for some particular matters independently of their ideological position.

The chapter also analyzes whether accountability works differently in rich and poor democracies. The effect of governmental performance may differ in relation to the economic context. Bad outcomes may be more costly for citizens in poor economies: outcomes tend to be worse; variations in performance are more dramatic; and poorer countries have lower levels of welfare spending, exposing the population to less social protection. As Pacek and Radcliff (1995: 44) state, "the economy plays less of a role in states with high levels of spending, regardless of the direction of economic change."

Finally, another contribution of the chapter lies in its empirical scope. The analysis is based on a sample of nearly all democracies for a period of fifty years. Consequently, indicators on governmental performance have been inevitably restricted, even if not only pure economic outcomes are included. The explanation of electoral performance I offer is incomplete but relatively unbiased.

Electoral Performance in Democracies

Sample

The sample includes all countries that are actually democracies for which data on election results are available and that have had at least two successive elections. Therefore, countries that were democracies in the past but were dictatorships still in 2000 are not included (e.g., Peru, which became a dictatorship in 1990). A total of eighty-three democracies form the data set.[3] A maximum period of approximately fifty years, from the 1950s until 1999, is covered.

I have used the Alvarez/Cheibub/Limongi/Przeworski (ACLP) index (see Przeworski et al. 2000) for classifying a country as democratic. For my purposes, the ACLP index presents two principal advantages: first, it subscribes to a minimalist definition of democracy, which permits the inclusion in the analysis of a larger number of cases. The authors define democracy as "a regime in which those who govern are selected through contested elections" (2000, 15). Second, the index enables us to divide the world between dictatorships and democracies, facilitating in this way the decision of which countries to include. None of the other existing indices on regime type are categorical. In the other data sets, the measurement level is ordinal or interval (Munck and Verkuilen 2002).

Measuring Electoral Performance

My purpose is to explain electoral performance in democracies. Vote variation is measured by looking at the losses or gains of the incumbent between two successive elections.[4] For example, the Labour Party in the United Kingdom won the support of 30.9 percent of the electorate in 1997 and 24.2 percent in 2001. Therefore, the electoral loss for Labour is 6.7 percentage points. Note that electoral performance considers the percentage of vote of the electorate and not the percentage of vote of total voters. I assume that citizens may punish the incumbent not only by voting for another party but also by abstaining.

---

[3] For the following democracies, no data on election results have been found: Marshall Islands, Nauru, Micronesia, Solomon Islands, Thailand, Papua New Guinea, Suriname, and Mauritius. Moreover, for several particular elections of countries included, no data are available: Panama, 1989; Saint Kitts, 1993 and 1995; Bahamas, 1992 and 1997; Dominica, 1995; Dominican Republic, 1966 and 1970; El Salvador, 1984; India, 1997; Trinidad and Tobago, 1966 and 1971. For other reasons, the data set excludes the following elections: Portugal, 1976; Ecuador, 1996; Venezuela, 1998; Guatemala, 1991 and 1995; Armenia, 1995.

[4] Two alternatives for measuring electoral losses or gains may be used: the difference between the vote percentage for each party in two consecutive elections (Paldam 1991) or the vote percentage in the current election controlling for the vote percentage in the previous election (Powell and Whitten 1993). They both lead to the same result.

In the creation of this dependent variable, two problems had to be confronted: how to measure electoral performance in presidential systems and in coalition governments, particularly when parties are not the same for the whole legislature. The dependent variable computes losses and gains in parliamentary elections for parliamentary systems and vote fluctuations in presidential elections for presidential systems. Contrary to parliamentary systems, the constitution of governments under presidential systems depends entirely on the president, who can form a cabinet without the support of the legislature. The only exception to this rule is Bolivia, where the constitution establishes that when no candidate obtains a majority in presidential elections, Parliament selects the president through majority rule. Because in presidential systems it is up to the president to decide whether to form a coalition cabinet, I assume that it is the president who is truly responsible for the making of policies and therefore accountable for the whole incumbent's performance. Consequently, electoral performance only computes gains and losses for the president's party in presidential elections, leaving out electoral variations for other parties when they happen to be in government.

In parliamentary democracies, the electoral performance of coalition governments is measured by summing the variations of votes for all parties in the coalition. The simplest case is one in which all members of the coalition win or lose votes. In the 1998 German election, the two ruling parties, the Christian Democratic Union/Christian Social Union (CDU/CSU) and the Free Democratic Party (FDP), were punished: the former lost 3.7 percentage points and the latter 0.3. Therefore, for this observation, the value of the dependent variable is –4. However, in most cases, some members of the coalition are punished, whereas others are rewarded. Under such circumstances, electoral performance is still measured by summing variations in votes so that losses and gains may partially cancel each other out. Between 1998 and 2002, a coalition between the German Social Democratic Party (SPD) and the Greens ruled in Germany. In the last election, the SPD lost 3.1 percentage points of the electorate, whereas the Greens gained 1.3 percentage points. Consequently, in 2002 the total loss for the coalition was 1.8.

Computing electoral losses or gains is more complex when cabinets are unstable. I have followed several rules. If between two elections different governments are formed, the dependent variable takes the variations of votes of the parties that were in the last cabinet if its duration is of at least twelve months. When this is not the case, the variable computes the longest

Table 1.1. Description of Electoral Performance in Democracies

N	Mean	Standard deviation	Minimum value	Maximum value
477	−3.9	8.3	−49.49	31.20

government between two elections. If two governments have the same duration, the variable computes the last of the two governments with the same duration.

The dependent variable has a total of 477 observations. Table 1.1 describes the variable. The mean is −3.9, which indicates that the tendency for incumbents in democracies is to lose votes. The minimum value is −49.5 and the maximum is 31.2. The greatest loss corresponds to the 1992 Romanian election and the greatest gain to Jamaica in 1989. Extreme variations in votes for the incumbent are discussed in the next section.

Extreme Variations in Electoral Performance

Extreme losses are a combination of uncommon incidents and bad contexts. Huge electoral variations happen when certain extraordinary events take place in the context of bad economic and political conditions. Table 1.2 shows extreme electoral losses in democracies. Losses are above 20 percentage points in a total of sixteen elections in which different events occur: the resignation of the head of state or of government, the death of the head of state or his decision not to seek reelection, parties' internal struggles, and violations of democratic rules. Resignation of the head of state or government has taken place in seven cases. Corruption was the main cause of the resignation in three elections: Lithuania (1996), Venezuela (1993), and Brazil (1994). A financial crisis was the principal reason for the resignation of the Albanian prime minister before the 1997 elections, whereas a severe economic crisis and the failure to find a solution over the Quebec problem caused the dismissal of the Canadian head of government in 1993. Institutional conflicts led to resignations in Saint Tomé (1994) and Romania (1992); a general strike also contributed to the electoral failure in the latter case. Conflicts between the state's institutions were also the reason for the head of state's decision not to seek reelection in Ecuador (1988). In the Dominican Republic's election of 1996, the head of state did not seek reelection because he was accused of electoral fraud. In Grenada in 1990, the death of Herbert Blaize produced the electoral collapse. His

Table 1.2. Description of Extreme Electoral Losses in Democracies

		Cases		
Event	Country	Year	Electoral loss	Main cause
Resignation of Head of State or of Government				
	Lithuania[a]	1996	27	Corruption
	Venezuela[b]	1993	28.8	Corruption
	Brazil[c]	1994	42.3	Corruption
	Albania[d]	1997	32.1	Financial crisis
	Canada[e]	1993	21.1	Economic crisis and territorial conflict
	Saint Tome[f]	1994	30.6	Institutional conflicts
	Romania[g]	1992	49.5	General strike and institutional conflicts
Head of State Does Not Seek Reelection				
	Ecuador[h]	1988	26.8	Institutional conflicts
	Dominican Republic[i]	1996	27	Electoral fraud
Death of Head of State or of Government				
	Grenada[j]	1990	38	Authoritarian style of government
Parties' or Coalitions' Struggles				
	St. Lucia[k]	1982	26.5	Conflict over budgetary policy
	Ecuador[l]	1984	46.3	Coalition split
	Ecuador[m]	1992	31.5	Coalition split
Disturbances against Democratic Rules				
	Colombia[n]	1962	34.6	Arranged elections
	Jamaica[o]	1983	48.3	Electoral boycott
	Trinidad and Tobago[p]	1991	27.6	Attempted coup d'état

[a] Prime Minister Adolfas Slezevicius was dismissed on January 1996 after the legislature approved a decree calling for his resignation, when it had been known that he had withdrawn personal savings from the Lithuanian Incorporated Innovation Bank before its collapse, which froze the assets of many Lithuanians. Slezevicius also stood down as chairman of the Lithuanian Democratic Labour Party.

[b] Carlos Andrés Pérez was suspended from office on 21 May 1993 after he had to face corruption charges.

[c] Fernando Collor de Mello resigned two years before the election after he was found guilty of corruption.

[d] In March 1997, President Berisha ordered the resignation of Prime Minister Alexander Meksi. Violent demonstrations had taken place in January as a response to the collapse of several pyramid financial schemes.

[e] Brian Mulroney resigned as prime minister and as leader of the Progressive Conservative Party eight months before the election. With his resignation, he intended to improve the electoral support of his party. A severe economic recession and the failure to find a solution to the Quebec problem made him unpopular.

25

death gave citizens the opportunity to put an end to an authoritarian style of government.

Parties' or coalitions' internal struggles were the main reason for extreme electoral losses in Saint Lucia (1982) and Ecuador (1984 and 1992). Finally, disturbances against democratic rules caused the electoral failure of the incumbents in Colombia, Jamaica, and Trinidad and Tobago.

Although an extremely bad electoral performance is normally produced by extraordinary events, all these democracies have much in common.

Table 1.2. (*continued*)

f President Miguel Trovoada forced Norberto Costa Alegre's government to resign due to continuous conflicts between both institutions.

g Prime Minister Petre Roman, from the National Salvation Front (FSN), resigned after the violent general strike of 1991. Before the 1992 elections, President Ion Iliescu split from the FSN and founded the Democratic National Salvation Front (FDSN). Both parties competed separately in the 1992 election.

h President León Febres was kidnapped in January 1987 by air force paratroopers after he refused to promulgate a bill of amnesty for General Frank Vargas, approved by the left majority in Parliament. Vargas had been held in custody since 1986 following two attempted rebellions. Although in 1987 Congress failed to introduce impeachment measures against the president, the Congress passed a resolution accusing Febres of violating human rights and of aggression against the Congress.

i Joaquín Balaguer's presidential term was shortened to two years because of electoral fraud in the previous election (1994). Balaguer, who was not on the ballot, refused to support the candidate of the ruling Reformist Social Christian Party (PRSC), Jacinto Peynado. Many commentators believed that Balaguer supported the Dominican Liberation Party's (PLD) candidate Leonel Fernández in order to prevent the victory of the Dominican Revolutionary Party's candidate, Francisco Peña.

j Prime Minister Herbert Blaize died in December 1989. He had ruled with an authoritarian style since 1984.

k Allan F. L. Lousy resigned as prime minister on 30 April 1981 when the leader of the more radical faction of his Labour Party, George Odium, challenged him in Parliament by voting against budget proposals that were defeated. Odium broke with the ruling party to form the Progressive Labour Party, which competed in the 1982 general election.

l The coalition Popular Democracy–Cohort of the Popular Forces (DP–CFP), which allowed the electoral triumph of 1984, broke up during the legislature.

m The Popular Democracy–Christian Democratic Union (DP–UDC) broke the coalition with the president's party, Democratic Left (ID). Moreover, the president of the Congress, Averroes Bucaram, leader of the Popular Forces Concentration (CFP), began a campaign against the government, accusing several ministers and civil servants of corruption.

n Between 1958 and 1974, the Frente Nacional was in power, alternating between liberals and conservatives, independently of electoral results.

o The People's National Party (PNP) boycotted the 1983 elections, arguing that government broke its promise to update electoral registration and to implement antifraud measures. Therefore, the Jamaica Labour Party (JLP) won the total control of the House but with a turnout of 28.9 percent.

p Five months before the 1990 election, members of a Moslem sect attempted an unsuccessful coup d'état. The country was plunged into a severe and prolonged economic crisis.

Table 1.3. Political and Socioeconomic Indicators in Elections with Extreme Losses

	Extreme losses		Rest of observations	
	Mean	Percentage	Mean	Percentage
Political Indicators				
Years of democracy*	17.06		44.26	
Presidential systems*		43.75		17.35
Corruption*	3.31		4.53	
Variations in corruption	0		−0.2	
Socioeconomic Indicators				
Real GDP per capita*	4,647.37		7,903.02	
Variations in real GDP per capita*	−129.92		664.06	
Inflation	196.25		43.45	
Variations in inflation	21.83		−45.02	
Hyperinflation		31.2		23.4
Unemployment**	11.8		8.3	
Variations in unemployment	1.86		0.43	
Total central government expenditures as a total of GDP***	26.82		33.00	
Variations in total central government expenditures as a total of GDP	0.94		0.96	
Infant mortality**	32.94		20.77	

***Statistically significant at 0.01; **statistically significant at 0.05; *statistically significant at 0.10.

With the exception of Canada, none of these democracies belongs to the Organization for Economic Cooperation and Development (OECD). I have included in Table 1.3 a brief description of some political and socioeconomic indicators, comparing the context of extreme losses with the rest of the observations. The table has only an illustrative purpose.

With regard to political indicators, elections with extreme losses have taken place in countries with a shorter period of democracy: whereas the mean of democratic length is 44.3 years in elections that do not have an extremely bad electoral performance, it falls to 17.1 years in elections with losses over 20 percentage points. These elections are also more frequent in presidential systems, although the institutional design of democracy does not necessarily account for this finding. Presidential countries are economically and politically weaker. Only 4.8 percent of the elections for

OECD countries correspond to presidential systems, whereas among the non-OECD countries, 43.5 percent are presidential elections. Moreover, the length of democracy is shorter for presidential systems (23.4) than for parliamentary systems (41.4). Extreme losses have also occurred in generally more corrupt countries. In an indicator that goes from 1 (*more corruption*) to 6 (*less corruption*), the mean is 3.3 for democracies with extreme losses and 4.5 for the remaining observations.

Greater differences emerge if we look at some socioeconomic indicators. Data on real GDP per capita, inflation, and, to a lesser extent, unemployment show that extreme losses are associated with fragile economies. Whereas the mean real GDP per capita is 4,647.4 (1985 international prices) for the sample that includes only elections with extreme losses, it rises to 7,903 for the remaining observations. Inflation is more than four times bigger in democracies with extremely bad electoral performance, although much lesser differences (3.5 points) are found in unemployment.

Moreover, incumbents who lose more than 20 percentage points in the share of votes have a worse economic record, measured by variations between elections in economic indicators, than the other governments. The mean variation in real GDP per capita indicates that elections with extreme losses have been celebrated in a context of smaller economic growth than elections with "normal" losses. The same can be said about variations in inflation: large electoral losses coincide with a negative performance, something that does not take place in elections without extreme losses. Huge punishments are also more frequent when there is hyperinflation (i.e., an inflation rate of 100 percent or more).

Finally, total central government expenditures as a percentage of GDP are smaller in democracies with extreme electoral losses, but no differences are observed in the variations of this indicator. Infant mortality is also higher in unstable elections than in more stable ones.

What can be said about extreme electoral gains? Rewards above 20 percentage points are less frequent than extreme losses. Of a total of 477 elections, huge electoral gains took place only twice: in Jamaica in 1989 and in Uruguay in 1999. Incumbents in democracies are more often radically punished than rewarded.

Moreover, as Table 1.4 shows, extreme gains are the consequence of changes in the electoral arena. In Jamaica, the People's National Party boycotted the 1983 election, arguing that the government had broken its promise to update electoral registration and to implement antifraud

Table 1.4. Description of Extreme Electoral Gains in Democracies

Country	Year	Electoral gain	Main cause
Jamaica	1989	31.2	Previous electoral boycott
Uruguay	1999	20.8	Reform of the electoral system

measures. Consequently, the Jamaica Labour Party won all the seats in the low House with only 2.4 percent of the vote (of registered voters). The increase in votes in the next election was the result of a normal electoral turnout.

During the 1999 election in Uruguay, electoral law was reformed. Whereas with the previous system a plurality of votes was sufficient to win the election, with the new law the winner needed to reach an absolute majority in a second round to obtain the presidency. Therefore, the extreme gain was produced by the inevitable concentration of votes in the second round.

In sum, the general tendency for incumbents in democracies is to lose votes, moderately. Extreme losses, above 20 percentage points, have taken place in 16 of 477 observations, and extreme gains only twice. Huge electoral variations are produced by extraordinary events in bad economic and political contexts, whereas extreme gains respond to changes in how electoral competition is structured.

The Incumbent's Performance

My objective is to test whether governments are accountable for the outcomes they contribute to producing. Governmental performance does not only include economic results. Voters may also pay attention to the intervention of the state in the economy, the degree of economic freedom versus the size of the state. It is not, however, an easy task to look at other dimensions of governmental performance. Data on economic growth and inflation are easily available for most democracies since the 1950s, but other indicators of incumbents' performance are more difficult to find. For example, for the total of 477 observations of the dependent variable, we have data for 409 cases on per capita real income and 438 on inflation, but there are data on public spending on health for only 190 observations. Consequently, multivariate analysis has been inevitably restricted to those dimensions that did not reduce dramatically the sample. These are mainly per capita real income, inflation, and central government public expenditures.[5]

Per capita real income, inflation, and unemployment are usually included in studies on economic voting. I had to exclude unemployment because the data set contains information for only 228 observations.[6] Data on central government public expenditures are also scarce, but it is the variable with more observations among those that measure the role of the state in the economy. Moreover, its correlation with public expenditure on education (0.51) and on health (0.64) is relatively high. The variable, therefore, may be a good proxy of the dimension on economic freedom versus redistribution.

For each dimension of the incumbent's performance, I have constructed a variable that measures variations since the last election. I assume that at election times, citizens may look at how certain indicators have evolved since the last election. If things improve, incumbents win votes, and if they deteriorate, incumbents lose votes.

Next, I specify the independent variables considered in the regression models:

- Variations in per capita real income (measured at 1985 international prices). Data come from the ACLP data set. For example, in France, real GDP per capita was 13,663 in 1993 and 14,650 in 1997. Therefore, for

---

[5] The dimensions concerning universal social goods and the quality of politicians are excluded from the final regressions. However, indicators on universal social goods, such as infant mortality or life expectancy, do highly correlate with per capita real income. The Pearson coefficient of the logarithm of per capita real income and the logarithm of infant mortality is -0.83, and the coefficient is 0.79 for the correlation between the logarithm of per capita real income and the logarithm of life expectancy.

An index of corruption from the *International Country Risk Guide to Corruption in the Political System* may be used for testing whether voters care about the quality of politicians. But because this index starts in the 1980s, the variable reduces considerably the size of the sample. Previous multivariate regression analysis does, however, show that the variation of corruption does not have a statistically significant effect on electoral performance.

The possibility of including a dummy for elections with big electoral losses produced by scandals (suggested by an anonymous referee) is not a satisfactory solution because there could be many other scandals that do not produce big electoral losses. Therefore, this solution creates a clear selection bias. Because this study includes eighty-three democracies from 1950 to 2000, I have not been able to undertake a systematic search of scandals.

[6] I explored the possibility of using the increase of the labor force as a proxy of creation of employment, as Cheibub and Przeworski (1999) have done, but found no clear results. Variations in the labor force correlate with variations in population (0.6).

the 1997 election, variations in per capita real income were 987, which indicates economic growth.

- Variations in inflation, consumer prices (annual percent). Data come from the ACLP data set. In France, inflation was 2.1 in 1993 and 1.2 in 1997. For the 1997 election, the variable computes a decrease of –0.9.
- Variations in total central government expenditures as a percentage of GDP. Data come from the ACLP data set. Government expenditures represented 47.1 percent of GDP in 1993 in France and 46.6 percent four years later. Therefore, variations in total central government expenditure decreased 0.5 point in four years.

Control Variables

Five control variables are considered in the analysis. Three are related to the degree of responsibility that voters may attribute to incumbents for their performance, and the other two concern the conditions under which elections take place.

Electors have certain beliefs about the extent to which outcomes are the result of political actions or are rather the product of both policies and *exogenous conditions*. The consequences for electoral accountability are obvious: if voters do not blame governments for certain results, they should not automatically punish them for bad performance. Exogenous conditions include all those circumstances that may diffuse political power. Political circumstances are crucial: when there is a coalition cabinet, the implementation of their political program would be rather difficult. This circumstance is considered in the analysis.

Other factors may also interfere with political action. Consider a democracy in which a party wants to expand public expenditure by investing more economic resources in education or health. This party may be unable to implement its expansive policy if it has to confront a debt that absorbs a considerable part of public expenditure. A main function of the International Monetary Fund (IMF) is to provide loans to countries with balance-of-payments problems so that they can restore conditions for sustainable economic growth. In the database, 18.1 percent of the observations correspond to elections that took place under an agreement with the IMF. This agreement may not only prevent an expansion of public expenditure but also prevent current public expenditure from improving citizens' quality of life. Therefore, a dummy variable takes this circumstance into account.

Voters' reactions to governmental performance may vary according to certain political or economic conditions: the type of political system, presidentialism or parliamentarism; the percentage of seats that parties in government hold in the lower house; and the degree of economic development.

Presidential systems are frequently associated with weak and unstable democracies. This variable is included to check the effect of governmental performance when presidentialism is taken into account. But its inclusion will also tell us whether this type of political system makes democracies less accountable.

Incumbents' support in the lower house is introduced as a control for the size of the parties in power. I assume that the greater the support that a party or a coalition has in parliament, the greater the potential for electoral losses. A party that has 30 percent of the vote may easily lose 8 points, but this decrease is rather unlikely for a party that has the support of 9 percent of the electorate.

The inclusion in the model of economic development is necessary to identify the determinants of electoral performance, and it also tells us whether incumbents in richer democracies win more or fewer votes than in poorer ones. I list next the control variables included in the analysis:

- Number of parties in government
- Agreement with the IMF (Source: Vreeland 2002)
- Type of political system: presidential versus parliamentarian
- Incumbents' percentage of seats in the lower house
- Logarithm of per capita real income: real GDP per capita at 1985 international prices (Source: ACLP)

Multivariate Results

Two multivariate models are discussed in this section. The technique used is a robust regression because the sample has severe outliers, the high influence of which is set aside with this method. Although the database includes variables across time, no problems of autocorrelation have been detected in previous ordinary least square regression analyses. The dependent variable is electoral performance.[7] Table 1.5 specifies the descriptive statistics for the independent variables.

---

[7] The dependent variable has 477 observations, as described in Table 1.1. Extreme variations are included.

Table 1.5. Descriptive Statistics for Variables Entering Regression Models

Variable	N	Mean	SD	Minimum	Maximum
Variations in per capita real income	439	622.52	737.93	−2,596.86	5,263.4
Variations in inflation	360	−40.55	870.50	−11,734.5	7,450.05
Hyperinflation	438	0.04	0.19	0	1
Reduction of 100 in variations in inflation	360	0.03	0.17	0	1
Variations in central government public expenditures	247	0.93	5.3214	−39.19	14.18
Logarithm of per capita real income	509	8.64	0.7603	6.4118	10.0758
Agreement with the IMF	502	0.18	0.3856	0	1
Years of democracy	583	37.59	32.8932	1	130
Incumbents' percentage seats in lower house	483	57.36	15.18	11.17	100
Single government	589	0.50	0.50	0	1
Presidential system	583	0.21	0.40	0	1

Note: IMF = International Monetary Fund; SD = standard deviation.

A total of 215 observations enter the first model, as is shown in Table 1.6. Three variables have a statistically significant effect on the dependent variable: variations in per capita real income, the incumbent's percentage seats in the lower house, and per capita real income. Moreover, variations in central government public expenditures are statistically significant at 0.15. Signs are the expected ones. When there is economic growth between elections, the incumbent wins votes. The same is true for variations in the size of government: increases in public expenditure are rewarded.[8] Incumbents have a better electoral performance when there is economic growth and more public expenditure.

A greater percentage of the incumbent's seats in the lower house leads to a decrease in votes. Bigger parties or coalitions lose more votes than smaller ones. Finally, higher per capita real income produces an improvement in electoral performance. Incumbents lose more votes in poor

[8] Public expenditure reflects central public expenditure. It may be argued that this variable does not really reflect welfare spending because in federal or semifederal systems, public expenditure in education or health may be decentralized. The model should have introduced "federalism" as a control variable, but this has not been possible because the number of observations for this variable is too low, reducing dramatically the sample in regression analysis.

Table 1.6. Explaining Electoral Performance in Democracies

Dependent variable: electoral performance	Robust regression coefficients	
	Model 1	Model 2
	All incumbents	All incumbents
Variations in per capita real income	0.1672***	0.1515***
	(0.0367)	(0.0374)
Variations in inflation	−0.0001	0.0005
	(0.0003)	(0.0004)
Variations in central government public expenditures	0.0985	0.1321**
	(0.0680)	(0.0733)
Incumbents' percentage seats in lower house	−0.0868***	−0.0820***
	(0.0272)	(0.0269)
Single government	0.2492	0.3519
	(0.8176)	(0.8136)
Agreement with the IMF	−0.3854	−0.0366
	(1.1430)	(1.1284)
Presidential system	−0.8005	−0.6928
	(1.0721)	(1.0527)
Logarithm of per capita real income	1.1637**	1.1790**
	(0.7021)	(0.7048)
Hyperinflation (inflation of 100 or more)		−5.6844**
		(2.2168)
Anti-inflationary policy (reduction of inflation by 100 or more)		4.9395**
		(2.9365)
Constant	−11.0413	−11.3910
	(7.0467)*	(7.1130)
Number of observations	215	215
F	5.98***	6.28***

Note: Standard errors in parentheses.
***Statistically significant at 0.01; **statistically significant at 0.05; *statistically significant at 0.10.

countries. Variations in inflation and in the rest of the control variables do not affect the vote for parties in government. An agreement with the IMF is not statistically significant. Moreover, although in presidential systems the mean of electoral losses is double that in parliamentary systems (6.3 against 3.3), the institutional system does not account for this finding because the variable does not have a statistically significant effect. Finally, the type of government, single versus coalition cabinet, does not affect electoral variations. Electors do not seem to be sensitive to political responsibility.

To make sure that inflation is irrelevant to explaining electoral performance, the second model introduces the effect of both hyperinflation and a severe anti-inflationary policy. It is possible that small variations in inflation do not affect the vote for the incumbent, but it may be that extreme variations do have an influence. The hyperinflation variable includes those cases in which inflation is equal to or higher than 100 percentage points. There are eighteen in the sample, but only seven enter the regression: Israel 1981, Israel 1984, Argentina 1989, Nicaragua 1990, Romania 1992, Brazil 1994, and Bulgaria 1997. In two of these cases, losses were above 20 percentage points. Hyperinflation is, obviously, disruptive for the economy and for the lives of citizens.

Anti-inflationary policy reflects those cases in which reductions in inflation are equal to or higher than 100 percentage points. In the database, there is not a single case of anti-inflationary policy with hyperinflation: all incumbents who reduced inflation by more than 100 points have automatically taken their country out of hyperinflation. The sample has eleven cases of anti-inflationary policy: Albania in 1996, Argentina in 1995, Bolivia in 1989, Brazil in 1998, Bulgaria in 1994, Croatia in 1995, Israel in 1988, Lithuania in 1996, Macedonia in 1998, Nicaragua in 1996, and Romania in 1996. They all enter into the regression. In none of these cases have parties in government won votes, but in eight of them, the fall in votes was below the mean losses for all elections in each of these countries. Therefore, successful anti-inflationary measures reduce electoral losses.

When hyperinflation is introduced in the analysis, variations in inflation change its sign, but the variable does not yet have statistical significance. However, hyperinflation has a significant effect on electoral performance. It is when inflation is over 100 percent that incumbents lose votes. The model also shows that anti-inflationary policies have a positive and statistically significant effect on electoral performance. Incumbents are rewarded for fighting hyperinflation successfully. A look at regression coefficients shows that the effect of high inflation on electoral losses is strong, much greater than the effect of economic growth.

No other significant changes are detected in this second regression. The coefficient of the relative variations in public expenditure slightly increases and gains significance, but it is not significantly different from the coefficient of the previous model.

In sum, governments win votes when there is economic improvement and when public expenditure increases. Electoral performance also depends on the percentage of seats that the ruling parties have in parliament: a greater control of the house involves more punishment. Finally, the richer the country, the greater the electoral gains for the incumbent.

Electoral Performance of Different Ideological Governments

The Incumbent's Ideology

Now I want to test whether voters judge right-wing and left-wing governments differently. I assume that there is a main axis around which parties mobilize voters in democracies, the left–right cleavage. Other dimensions that may also structure political competition, such as nationalism, religion, or rural versus urban environments, are excluded. The left–right cleavage divides parties along a socioeconomic dimension, regarding principally the degree of state control of the economy.

Data on incumbents' ideology are taken from the Beck et al. (2001) data set of political institutions. Their categorization has three values, left (value 1), center (value 2), and left (value 3). Parties on the right are from the conservative and Christian democratic families, whereas left-wing parties include communists, socialists, or social democrats. In the center fall those political organizations that support both the strengthening of private enterprise and a certain redistribution by government. Parties are simply not categorized when it is impossible to place them on a left–right dimension.[9]

Parties, however, are not incumbents. When a party governs alone, the attribution of an ideological label to the executive presents no trouble: the government adopts the party's ideology. To give a unique value to ruling coalitions is more complex, however, particularly because it is often the case that the parties' share of governmental power is asymmetric. Let us look at the following example. In Sweden between 1952 and 1956, a coalition was formed by the Social Democrats (SDA) and the Agrarian Party (CP). In the database, ideology has value 1 for the SDA (left) and value 2 for the CP (right). If both parties had had the same weight in government, the ideology of the incumbent would have been the average of the ideology for the two parties. However, they did not. Therefore, it has been necessary to weight ideology by the party's governmental power.[10] Because the data set does

---

[9] For further explanations on how parties are coded ideologically, see the definition of variables in the *Database of Political Institutions* (http://econ.worldbank.org/).

[10] The assumption is that the impact of governmental performance is stronger for parties with more responsibilities (Hibbing and Alford 1981).

Table 1.7. Distribution of Incumbents by Their Ideology

	N	Percentage
Variable 1	412	100
Right wing and center	238	57.7
Left wing	174	42.2
Variable 2	412	100
Right wing	194	47.1
Left wing and center	218	52.9

not contain information on the number of ministries that each party holds, I have used as a proxy of their power in government the proportion of seats that each party has in the lower house. The formula is $\frac{\sum s_i i_i}{\sum s_i}$, where s_i is the proportion of seats of party i, and i_i stands for the ideology of party i.

In 1956, the SDA had 47.8 percent of seats and the CP 11.3 percent. Therefore, the ideology of the SDA–CP coalition is 1.2, which substantively means that the incumbent is close to the left but is not a totally left-wing government.

The obvious consequence of this procedure is that the ideology is transformed into a continuous variable that goes from 1 to 3. Because my purpose is to repeat the previous analysis for samples with left-wing and right-wing incumbents, the following step has been taken to convert ideology into a dichotomous variable. Two procedures have been followed. The first assumes that center parties are closer to right-wing parties on the socioeconomic dimension, whereas the second adheres to the opposite assumption. Consequently, both variables have two values: parties on the right and center versus parties on the left, and right-wing parties versus center and left-wing parties.

The first ideology variable has value 0 when the incumbent's ideology is between 2 and 3 (center and right) and has value 1 for the rest of the cases (left). The variable has 412 observations, which means that 166 incumbents do not have an ideology either because for a particular party no data are available or because it is not possible to place a party's ideology on a left–right dimension. As Table 1.7 reports, 42.2 percent of incumbents are left wing whereas 57.7 percent may be considered right-wing or center governments.

In the second variable, value 1 corresponds to left-wing and center governments (from value 1 to 2 of the original variable) and value 0 to

Table 1.8. Explaining Electoral Performance for Incumbents of Different Ideological Signs

	Robust regression coefficients			
	Model 1	Model 2	Model 3	Model 4
Dependent variable: electoral performance	Right wing/Center	Left wing	Right wing	Left wing/Center
Variations in per capita real income	0.1485*** (0.0548)	0.2071*** (0.0760)	0.1282** (0.0537)	0.2464*** (0.0750)
Variations in inflation	−0.0005 (0.0004)	0.0131 (0.0516)	−0.0007 (0.0007)	0.0008 (0.0010)
Variations in central government public expenditures	0.1616 (0.1400)	0.3698** (0.1470)	0.1820 (0.1362)	0.2996** (0.1474)
Incumbents' percentage seats in lower house	−0.0521 (0.0407)	−0.1691*** (0.0525)	−0.1078** (0.0414)	−0.0805** (0.0457)
Single government	0.1849 (1.3501)	0.4616 1.2771	0.0415 (1.3300)	1.2369 (1.2952)
Agreement with the IMF	−2.1192 (1.8987)	0.8756 (1.8966)	−2.1062 (2.332)	−0.5324 (1.5885)
Presidential system	−0.2825 (1.5712)	−0.8001 (1.9840)	−1.5332 (1.7675)	1.1333 (1.6305)
Logarithm of per capita real income	2.6362** (1.2716)	0.4627 (1.1853)	2.3484** (1.3440)	1.0855 (1.1257)
Constant	−26.3203** (12.9234)	−0.9470 (12.7486)	−20.4305 (13.4330)	−12.1791 (11.9786)
Number of observations	108	87	88	107
F	3.61***	3.29**	3.80***	3.11**

Notes: Standard errors in parentheses. IMF = International Monetary Fund.
***Statistically significant at 0.01; **statistically significant at 0.05; *statistically significant at 0.10.

right-wing incumbents (from value 2.09 to 3 of the original variable). Left-wing and center cabinets represent 52.9 percent of the sample, whereas right-wing cabinets represent 47.1 percent.

Multivariate Results

I present next a multivariate analysis for four samples that include different ideological types of incumbents: right wing and center, left wing, right wing, and left wing and center. Results are reported in Table 1.8.

The first model is restricted to right-wing and center governments. There are 108 observations. Two variables have a statistically significant effect on electoral performance: economic growth and economic development. They both have the expected signs. In the third model, the sample is right-wing and center governments (88 observations). Now the percentage of seats of the incumbent gains significance.

The second model includes left-wing governments (87 observations) and the fourth, left-wing and center cabinets (107 observations). In both models, economic growth and the incumbent's percentage of seats in the lower house have a statistically significant effect on the vote for the incumbent, but per capita real income does not affect the dependent variable. Economic wealth is relevant if conservatives are in power, but it is not when the country is ruled by the left. If we assume that conservatives have more aversion to reforms than leftists, it may be that in poor countries, the cost for citizens of a right-wing cabinet becomes too high. People in poor countries may believe that they deserve a better fate.

On the other hand, another variable becomes statistically significant: variations in central government expenditure. Whereas for right-wing and center cabinets the reward for an increase in public expenditure is not statistically significant, it becomes so for left-wing cabinets. A look at the fourth model reveals that when center cabinets join left-wing governments, the coefficient of the variations in central government expenditure remains significant, although it is lower than the coefficient for pure left-wing incumbents. Increases in public expenditure are then rewarded when parties in government are left-wing, although citizens do not punish conservative cabinets for increasing public expenditure.

In conclusion, right-wing incumbents are a little more frequent in democracies than left-wing governments. For both conservative and left-wing ruling parties, economic growth is rewarded. However, increases in public expenditure only win votes for leftist incumbents.

Electoral Performance of Governments in Rich and Poor Democracies

We already know that in poorer democracies, ruling parties lose more votes than in richer ones. But do voters react differently to governmental performance in rich and poor democracies? What explains electoral variations for ruling parties in rich and poor democracies?

Table 1.9. Explaining Electoral Performance for the Poorest and Richest Democracies

	Robust regression coefficients			
	Model 1	Model 2	Model 3	Model 4
Dependent variable: electoral performance	Poorest countries (below 75% of income level)	Richest countries (below 75% of income level)	Poorest countries (below 75% of income level)	Richest countries (below 75% of income level)
Variations in per capita real income	0.1587*** (0.0460)	0.2328*** (0.0731)	0.1767*** (0.0446)	0.2364*** (0.0744)
Variations in inflation	−0.0002 (0.0003)	0.0433 (0.0589)	−0.0002 (0.0003)	0.0431 (0.0597)
Variations in central government public expenditures	0.0502 (0.0810)	0.1464 (0.1517)	0.0386 (0.0784)	0.1464 (0.1534)
Incumbents' percentage seats in lower house	−0.0540 (0.0364)	−0.1291*** (0.0432)	−0.0325 (0.0354)	−0.1269*** (0.0440)
Single government	0.6789 (1.3475)	−0.3438 (1.0698)	1.0630 (1.3098)	−0.2567 (1.1008)
Agreement with the IMF	−0.2234 (1.2399)	Dropped	0.2977 (1.2243)	Dropped
Presidential system	−0.6281 (1.3414)	1.2579 (2.4406)	−0.0252 (1.3009)	0.8877 (2.5199)
Logarithm of per capita real income	1.9308* (1.0115)	−9.0043** (4.0603)	1.4613 (0.9952)	−9.5886** (4.3077)
Years of democracy			0.0890*** (0.0283)	0.0071 (0.0212)
Constant	−19.8525** (9.5634)	87.2019** (38.5167)	−20.4340** (9.2553)	92.0079 (40.2535)
Number of observations	112	103	112	103
F	3.80***	3.18**	4.91***	2.76***

Notes: Standard errors in parentheses. IMF = International Monetary Fund.
***Statistically significant at 0.01; **statistically significant at 0.05; *statistically significant at 0.10.

The sample is now divided according to economic development. The richer countries are those that have a per capita real income equal to or over the 75 percentile, which corresponds to Belgium in 1978, whereas the poorer are those under this percentile. Results are presented in Table 1.9.

The first model includes 112 observations for the poorer democracies and the second 103 cases for the richer ones. Increases in per capita real income and the percentage of seats in the legislature have a significant effect in both models, although coefficients are higher for richer democracies.

We know that the degree of economic development and the length of democracy keep a straight relationship. Weak democracies usually have weak economies (or the other way around). In the sample, the correlation between per capita real income and the years of democracy is 0.75. Therefore, it is possible that in the previous analysis, the variable of per capita income included the effect of the length of the democratic system.

The last two models check whether economic development has an impact on electoral performance when the length of democracy is taken into account. Model 3 shows that in richer countries, per capita real income is statistically significant but not so the length of democracy; in poorer countries, both variables have an effect on electoral performance. In poor countries, taking into account the effect of economic development, ruling parties win more votes if their democracy is older. In other words, the incumbent's electoral losses are bigger in newer democracies. The degree of institutionalization of parties may explain this finding. As Stokes points out (2001: 103–7): "When parties are uninstitutionalized and party discipline is weak, governments may have trouble dealing with legislatures, and may become immobile and unstable.... strong parties do make governments more responsive and predictable."

Conclusions

The principal findings of this chapter are the following:

1. Incumbents in democracies tend to lose votes, moderately. Extreme losses (above 20 percentage points) are normally the result of extraordinary events in countries with weak economies and a new democratic system. Extreme gains, much more unusual, are the consequence of changes in the conditions of electoral competition.

2. Governmental performance accounts for the vote for the incumbent. Voters care about the economy. They reward economic growth and a successful anti-inflationary policy, and they punish hyperinflation. But voters are also concerned about the role of the state in the economy. They care about the size of the state. Governments win votes when there is an increase in public expenditure.

3. Accountability varies according to political circumstances. When ruling parties hold more seats in parliament, they lose more votes. Citizens are able to clarify political responsibility.

4. Right-wing and left-wing ruling parties are both rewarded for economic growth, but, in one respect, accountability works differently for both types of governments. Voters clearly reward left-wing ruling parties for increases in public expenditure, whereas the effect (also positive) is not significant for right-wing parties.

5. Incumbents in poor democracies lose more votes than those in rich ones. An inferior electoral performance cannot, however, be attributed to certain institutional factors. Presidentialism, more frequent in poor democracies, does not have any influence on electoral variations. Moreover, results suggest that although in both rich and poor democracies voters reward economic growth, they are more sensitive to performance in the more wealthy democracies. Accountability works slightly better in rich countries. Finally, an important determinant of the vote for the incumbent in poor countries is the length of democracy: more time, more votes.

REFERENCES

Abramowitz, Alan I. 1995. "It's Abortion, Stupid: Policy Voting in the 1992 Presidential Election." *Journal of Politics* 57: 176–86.

Anderson, Christopher J. 2000. "Economic Voting and Political Context: A Comparative Perspective." *Electoral Studies* 19 (2/3): 151–70.

Anderson, Christopher J., Silvia M. Mendes, and Yuliya V. Tverdova. 2004. "Endogenous Economic Voting: Evidence from the 1997 British Election." *Electoral Studies* 23 (4): 683–708.

Atkeson, Lonna Rae, and Randall W. Partin. 1995. "Economic and Referendum Voting: A Comparison of Gubernatorial and Senatorial Elections." *American Political Science Review* 89 (1): 99–107.

Barreiro, Belén. 2003. "Political Representation and the Nature of Policies: The Effects of Citizens' Views on Abortion Policies in the World's Democracies." Unpublished manuscript.

Beck, Throsten, George Clarke, Alberto Groff, Philip Keefer, and Patrick Walsh. 2001. "New Tools in Comparative Political Economy: The Database of Political Institutions." *The World Bank Economic Review* 15: 165–76.

Boix, Carles. 1998. *Political Parties, Growth, and Equality: Conservative and Social Democratic Economic Strategies in the World Economy*. New York: Cambridge University Press.

Budge, Ian, David Robertson, and Derek Hearl. 1987. *Ideology, Strategy, and Party Change: Spatial Analysis of Post-War Election Programs in 19 Democracies*. New York: Cambridge University Press.

Carlsen, Fredrik. 2000. "Unemployment, Inflation, and Government Popularity: Are There Partisan Effects?" *Electoral Studies* 19 (2): 141–50.

Chappell, Henry W., and Linda Gonçalves Veiga. 2000. "Economics and Elections in Western Europe: 1960–1997." *Electoral Studies* 19 (2): 183–97.

Cheibub, José Antonio, and Adam Przeworski. 1999. "Democracy, Elections, and Accountability for Economic Outcomes." In Adam Przeworski, Susan C. Stokes, and Bernard Manin (eds.), *Democracy, Accountability, and Representation* (pp. 222–49). Cambridge: Cambridge University Press.

Cook, Elizabeth A., Ted G. Jelen, and Clyde Wilcox. 1994. "Issue Voting in Gubernatorial Elections: Abortion and Post-Webster Politcs." *Journal of Politics* 56: 187–99.

Duch, Raymond M., and Randy Stevenson. 2005. "Context and the Economic Voting: A Multilevel Analysis." *Political Analysis* 13 (4): 387–409.

Erikson, Robert S. 1976. "The Relationship between Public Opinion and State Policy: A New Look Based on Some Forgotten Data." *American Journal of Political Science* 20 (1): 25–36.

Fackler, Tim, and Tse-min Lin. 1995. "Political Corruption and Presidential Elections, 1929–1992." *Journal of Politics* 57 (4): 971–93.

Fraile, Marta. 2005. *Cuando la economía entra en el voto: el voto económico en España, 1979–1996*. Madrid: Centro de Investigaciones Sociológicas.

Hibbing, John R., and John R. Alford. 1981. "The Electoral Impact of Economic Conditions: Who Is Held Responsible?" *American Journal of Political Science* 25 (3): 423–39.

Hibbs, Douglas A. 1987. *The Political Economy of Industrial Democracies*. Cambridge, MA: Harvard University Press.

Kiewiet, Roderick D. 2000. "Economic Retrospective Voting and Incentives for Policymaking." *Electoral Studies* 19 (2/3): 427–44.

Kone, Susan L., and Richard F. Winters. 1993. "Taxes and Voting: Electoral Retribution in the American States." *Journal of Politics* 55 (1): 22–40.

Kuklinski, James H. 1978. "Representativeness and Elections: A Policy Analysis." *American Political Science Review* 72 (1): 165–77.

Lewis-Beck, Michael S. 1988. *Economics and Elections: The Major Western Democracies*. Ann Arbor: University of Michigan Press.

Lowry, Robert C., James E. Alt, and Karen E. Ferree. 1998. "Fiscal Policy Outcomes and Electoral Accountability in American States." *American Political Science Review* 92 (4): 759–74.

Miller, Warren E., and Donald E. Stokes. 1963. "Constituency Influence in Congress." *American Political Science Review* 57: 45–56.

Monroe, Alan D. 1998. "Public Opinion and Public Policy, 1980–1993." *Public Opinion Quarterly* 62: 6–28.

Munck, Gerardo L., and Jay Verkuilen. 2002. "Conceptualizing and Measuring Democracy." *Comparative Political Studies* 35 (1): 5–34.

Nickelsburg, Michael, and Helmut Norpoth. 2000. "Commander-in-chief or Chief Economist? The President in the Eye of the Public." *Electoral Studies* 19 (2/3): 313–32.

Pacek, Alexander. 1994. "Macroeconomic Conditions and Electoral Politics in East Central Europe." *American Journal of Political Science* 38 (3): 723–44.

Pacek, Alexander, and Benjamin Radcliff. 1995. "The Political Economy of Competitive Elections in the Developing World." *American Journal of Political Science* 39 (3): 745–59.

Page, Benjamin I., and Robert Y. Shapiro. 1992. *The Rational Public: Fifty Years of Trends in Americans' Policy Preferences*. Chicago: University of Chicago Press.

Paldam, Martin. 1991. "How Robust Is the Vote Function?: A Study of Seventeen Nations over Four Decades." In Helmut Norpoth, Michael Lewis-Beck, and Jean-Dominique Lafay (eds.), *Economic and Politics: The Calculus of Support*. Ann Arbor: University of Michigan Press.

Powell, G. Bingham, and Guy D. Whitten. 1993. "A Cross-National Analysis of Economic Voting: Taking Account of the Political Context." *American Journal of Political Science* 37 (2): 391–414.

Przeworski, Adam, Susan C. Stokes, and Bernard Manin (eds.) 1999. *Democracy, Accountability, and Representation*. Cambridge: Cambridge University Press.

Przeworski, Adam, Michael E. Alvarez, José Antonio Cheibub, and Fernando Limongi. 2000. *Democracy and Development. Political Institutions and Well-Being in the World, 1950–1990*. Cambridge: Cambridge University Press.

Remmer, Karen L. 1991. "The Political Impact of Economic Crisis in Latin America in the 1980s." *American Political Science Review* 85 (3): 777–800.

Roberts, Kenneth M., and Erik Wibbels. 1999. "Party Systems and Electoral Volatility in Latin America: A Test of Economic, Institutional, and Structural Explanations." *American Political Science Review* 93 (3): 575–90.

Stein, M. Robert. 1990. "Economic Voting for Governor and U.S. Senator: The Electoral Consequences of Federalism." *Journal of Politics* 52 (1): 29–53.

Stokes, Susan. 2001. *Mandates and Democracy*. New York: Cambridge University Press.

Uslaner, Eric M., and M. Margaret Conway. 1985. "The Responsible Congressional Electorate: Watergate, the Economy, and Vote Choice in 1974." *The American Political Science Review* 79 (3): 788–803.

Vreeland, James R. 2002. *The IMF and Economic Development*. Cambridge: Cambridge University Press.

Warwick, Paul. 1992. "Economic Trends and Government Survival in West European Parliamentary Democracies." *American Political Science Review* 86 (4): 875–87.

CHAPTER TWO

How Can Governments Be Accountable If Voters Vote Ideologically?

Ignacio Sánchez-Cuenca

Introduction

There are two very different logics of voting, the logic of ideology and the logic of the incumbent's performance. A citizen may vote out of ideological closeness to parties or candidates, but the citizen may also vote in an attempt to discipline and control the government. In the first case, only ideological closeness matters. In the second case, ideology does not play a role, and the voter only takes into account the government's performance. The underlying rule in each case is clear. For ideological voting, the voter follows a decision rule that is based on ideological closeness: vote for the party that minimizes ideological distance.[1] For performance voting, the voter follows a decision rule about reelection: vote for the incumbent if the utility produced by the government's policies is higher than a certain preestablished value; otherwise, punish the incumbent.

Of course, these two logics correspond roughly to the distinction between prospective and retrospective voting (Manin, Przeworski, and Stokes 1999). As Fearon (1999) has put it, under prospective voting, elections are a matter of selecting good types, whereas under retrospective voting, elections are a matter of sanctioning poor performance. This basic distinction can also be expressed in terms of the problem that each logic of voting produces: prospective voting is associated with adverse selection, retrospective voting with moral hazard (Ferejohn 1995).

Each logic of voting has been investigated by apparently self-contained literatures. Ideological voting is studied by spatial models, whereas

---

[1] If there are more than two parties, the decision rule is to minimize *expected* ideological distance.

I am grateful to Adam Przeworski and the late Michael Wallerstein for their comments. I also thank Braulio Gómez for his help as a research assistant.

performance voting is studied by accountability models. In pure spatial models, the incumbent's performance is just an irrelevant variable; in "impure" models, nonspatial factors (also called nonpolicy issues) are usually reduced to candidates' traits (Enelow and Hinich 1984: ch. 5). In pure accountability models, ideology is simply absent. Thus, according to Ferejohn's classical model (1986), ideology only matters insofar as it reduces the dimensionality of the policy space: accountability is possible when there is a single dimension in terms of which the government's performance can be assessed.

The somehow schizoid nature of the voting literature can hardly be extended to voters themselves. It seems odd to suppose that electorates are populated by such different creatures as the pure ideological and the pure performance voters. More likely, voters vote out of ideological considerations while being sensitive to the government's performance. How the combination of both factors works is the issue I analyze in this chapter. I try to show that accountability and ideological voting are not necessarily incompatible.

Concretely, I suggest that ideological factors interact with retrospective judgments about government performance in the following manner: ideology is not a good clue about future behavior when governments do not act consistently in ideological terms or when governments are unable to transform ideology into good policies. Parties in government that act in an erratic way from the point of view of ideology (e.g., making neoliberal economic policies when they run on a social democratic platform) or that show poor capacity to make policies (because of, e.g., corruption or internal quarreling) will not be ideologically reliable. Therefore, voters will take these features into consideration and will judge the incumbent party not only in terms of ideological positions but also in terms of consistency and capacity. To put it in another way, lack of consistency or capacity might weaken ideological voting. That is, prospective voting will be affected by past episodes of bad performance through the dilution of ideology as a criterion of party choice.

To flesh out the argument, I start with the spatial theory of voting. I assume that citizens vote according to the Downsian proximity model in a single-dimensional ideological space. Ideological preferences are determined by the distances between the voter's ideological position and the positions the voter attributes to the parties that compete in the elections. Yet the spatial theory is incomplete: it has nothing to say about how ideology is translated into policies or about how policies are related to observable outcomes. The first problem is that of ideological consistency – namely, whether policies are consistent with the ideological stance of the party. The second problem is the capacity of the party to produce the desired outcomes with the right policies. Various factors such as internal divisions, a weak leadership, shirking, and corruption may affect the party's capacity. In the spatial theory, it is assumed that these two problems are somehow solved.

The hypothesis that is explored here is simple: the voter's decision rule is purely based on ideological distance when there are no doubts about the parties' ideological consistency and capacity. However, when the spatial assumptions are not true, the decision rule becomes more complex, and a voter may end up voting for distant parties or abstaining. This implies that parties' performance is not irrelevant for ideological calculations. In other words: ideological voters may be sensitive to the incumbent's performance. Note that ideological consistency and capacity are features of parties. Thus, patterns of ideological voting may be party-relative; that is, people who are closer to a party with a strong image of consistency and capacity will vote for this party according to the spatial model, whereas people closer to another party whose consistency or capacity is questionable will not follow the proximity logic.

An in-depth analysis of the Spanish case, where we find dramatic variation in ideological voting compared with other countries, contributes to the testing of this hypothesis. I show how ideological voting for the Spanish Socialist Workers' Party (PSOE), the incumbent from 1982 to 1996, was progressively eroded first by charges of ideological inconsistency and later by charges of corrupt practices and quarreling within the party. An important group of voters who perceived such a loss of consistency and capacity and who were closer to the PSOE than to any other party did not vote following their ideological preferences. The proportion of those voting for the PSOE among those who were ideologically closer to the PSOE diminished election after election as a consequence of doubts about its capacity. Curiously, ideological voting for the right-wing party, the Popular Party (PP), was strong and stable for the whole period.

The second section contains an analytical discussion about the ideological spatial model and its relationship with the concepts of consistency and capacity. The third section is an empirical description of patterns of ideological voting in several European countries, with emphasis on Germany and Spain. The fourth section is devoted to a detailed analysis of the

Spanish experience in which ideological voting and accountability are combined in a single model.

Ideology, Consistency, and Capacity

In the spatial theory of voting, voters have ideal policy points for each of the issues that are part of the policy space, and voters know the positions of the parties (or candidates) on all these issues. The utility that a voter obtains from different parties being in power is a declining function of the distance between the voter and the party. Two complications arise at this point: first, how to define distance; and second, how to deal with the number of dimensions of the policy space.

Various proposals have been made about the measurement of distance: we have proximity, directional, and mixed models. Here, I limit myself to the Downsian proximity model in which distance is defined in Euclidean terms. It is not only the simplest and most intuitive model, it also works remarkably well in empirical terms.[2] If it is assumed, for the sake of simplicity, that all issues have the same weight in the voter's utility function, then we can simply express the quadratic utility function with regard to party π as

$$U(\pi) = -\|\pi - \mathbf{x}\|^2 = -\left(\sqrt{\sum_{i=1}^{n} (\pi_i - x_i)^2}\right)^2,$$

where π is a vector $\pi = (\pi_1, \pi_2, \ldots, \pi_n)$ containing the positions of party π in the n-dimensions and $\mathbf{x}$ is likewise a vector $\mathbf{x} = (x_1, x_2, \ldots, x_n)$ with voter's ideal points in the n-dimensions. The symbol $\|\mathbf{z}\|$ stands for the Euclidean distance of vector $\mathbf{z}$, as explained in the previous formula. The function reaches its maximum (zero value) when the voter's ideal points coincide with those of the party.[3] The greater the distance between the two vectors, the more negative the function becomes and the less utility the voter obtains.

With regard to the second complication, the dimensionality of the policy space, it is usually considered that voters do not make choices in this

---

[2] I have also tried directional models, but they do not work as well as proximity models in any case. For a systematic discussion of the various models, see Merrill and Grofman (1999).

[3] This function is specified as a quadratic one and therefore requires that voters are risk-averse. It is also common to use a linear function in which the voter is risk-neutral.

space but rather in an ideological one of lower dimensionality (Hinich and Munger 1996). It is often assumed that the ideological space is one-dimensional, but it is far from clear why it should be so (Ferejohn 1995).

An ideology is a summary of which policies parties would make if they remained in government for the whole set of issues. According to Downs (1957), ideologies exist because voters are unsure about parties. Voters may be uncertain of what parties will do once in office because of the costly nature of political information. It may be prohibitive to get informed about the positions of parties on all the issues in which the voter is interested. In this sense, ideologies are a cost-saving device. Because people cannot collect information about policies, they rely on ideologies.

Yet Downs does not justify why ideologies save so much information-gathering costs as to reduce the space to just a single dimension. More-over, there is something strange in the characterization of ideology as a cost-saving device, if only because ideology makes political information interesting. A person without ideological convictions will find little reason to invest time and effort in getting informed about politics: political infor-mation will be boring for him or her. Ideology provides the incentives to gather information about politics. This helps to explain the point already noted by Fiorina (1990: 337) that gathering political information must be understood not as an investment act but rather as a consumption one. Just as someone needs some passion for sports to enjoy the consumption of information about sports, in the political realm some kind of ideological passion is required to become knowledgeable about politics.[4]

If Downs's hypothesis about ideologies as cost-saving devices is not so convincing, it should not be chosen as the starting point for deriving an explanation about the single dimensionality of the ideological space. In a completely different line of reasoning, Ferejohn (1995) argues that there is a strategic basis for the existence of a single dimension: it is a necessary condition for governments to be accountable. However, this seems to be a functionalist rather than a strategic explanation: he says that "there is simply no purpose to using ideology at all unless it is essentially a sin-gle dimensional concept" (p. 122). Here, ideologies are developed because they serve the function of inducing accountability by reducing the dimen-sionality of the political space to a single one. Yet, even if ideology is useful

---

[4] Palfrey and Poole (1987) found that voters who occupy the extremes of the ideological space tend to be more informed about politics than those who occupy the center positions, who tend to be more indifferent.

for inducing accountability, it is doubtful that it creates a single dimension for this very reason.

A simpler case for the connection between ideology and single dimensionality can be made. Ideology, after all, has some encompassing aspiration: it provides a set of principles and values that help to make all kinds of political choices. Downs defines an ideology as "a verbal image of the good society and of the chief means of constructing such a society" (1957: 96). For Budge, ideology "provides politicians with a broad conceptual map of politics into which political events, current problems, electors' preferences and other parties' policies can all be fitted" (1994: 446). According to Hinich and Munger, ideology is "an internally consistent set of propositions that makes both proscriptive and prescriptive demands on human behavior" (1996: 11). Bawn says that "ideology is an enduring system of beliefs, prescribing what action to take in a variety of political circumstances" (1999: 305). What unifies these definitions is precisely the emphasis on the systematic, complete nature of ideology: it contains a potential answer to any conceivable political problem. Ideology tends to produce a single-dimensional space because of this capacity to create a view or image about how society should be organized. Once an ideology is formulated, it serves to infer ideal points in the whole array of policy issues. The political space is reduced to a single dimension because of the "organizing" power of ideology.

Note that ideologies not only create a single dimension by their very nature, they also contribute to solve the problem of incomplete contracts in democratic representation (although I am not suggesting that this is the reason people develop ideological beliefs because this would entail a functionalist explanation of the kind I have just criticized). Electoral platforms are clearly incomplete contracts. When a party is in office, it may face fully unexpected problems that were not contemplated in the original platform. The platform may not say a word about what the party should do under such circumstances, and yet the party in government has to act. An unexpected problem can even change the whole political agenda, as demonstrated, for instance, in the September 11 attacks of 2001: George Bush's electoral platform did not contain much information about how he would react to such a large-scale terrorist attack.

This problem is compounded by the hierarchical relationship of democratic representation: when a conflict arises between the principal (the people) and the agent (the government) that cannot be solved according to the terms contained in the representation contract (the electoral platform), the last word corresponds to the agent. The government is entitled to make policy as long as it remains in power.

Citizens are willing to delegate so much decision power to politicians because despite the incomplete nature of electoral platforms, politicians are predictable when unexpected problems arise: this predictability stems from the ideological principles to which politicians adhere. Ideology provides a focal point in this hierarchical setting in the sense that Kreps (1990) says that corporate culture creates focal points for unforeseen contingencies in the market. Hinch and Munger have applied Kreps's argument to political competition, concluding that ideology "implies a complete worldview that allows predictions about future actions" (1996: 101).

Now, the predictive power of ideologies suggests that ideological voting cannot be completely detached from parties' performance in office. If a party in office does not act according to the ideological principles that determine its position in the ideological space, or if the party is unable to make effective policies, voters will not be attracted to this party even if it is the closer party as defined by the proximity model. If we take seriously a spatial model of ideological behavior, we must conclude that ideological distances between voters and parties cannot be the only determinant of the vote. Ideological consistency, for instance, must be taken into account.

Generally speaking, standard spatial models are rather limited in the range of explanations that they usually produce to account for variations in the vote share of parties in elections. Votes change if parties move in the ideological space or if the distribution of voters' ideological ideal points changes (the latter can happen either because voters change their preferences or because the electorate changes with the entry of new voters and the exit of old ones). In this picture, government performance is just absent. Voters simply calculate ideological distances and vote for the party that minimizes expected distance.[5]

The hypothesis that voters vote for the party that minimizes expected ideological distance contains a crucial hidden assumption, namely: all parties that compete in elections are equal except for their spatial location. Ideological positions are all we need to explain voters' choices. At least two other variables should also be considered, however. The first, which I call

---

[5] In fact, spatial models sometimes make room for other variables. It is not uncommon to include a nonpolicy variable that refers to features of the candidates. The utility function becomes

$$U(\pi) = c_\pi - \|\pi - \mathbf{x}\|^2,$$

where c_π stands for the characteristics of the party's π candidate.

ideological consistency, is the degree of fit between ideology and policies: how well policies reflect the ideological stance of the party. When policies do not correspond to the party's ideological line, we have ideological inconsistency. The second variable, which I simply call capacity, measures the effectiveness of policies – that is, the extent to which policies produced some desired outcomes.[6] A party is more capable if it is internally united,[7] if it is able to reach agreements with other political and social forces, if its cadres and militants are honest and motivated people, and if it is not captured by interest groups. Voters conjecture on the consistency and capacity of parties by observing what parties say and do. This is particularly true for the incumbent: a government's performance provides plenty of evidence about its consistency and capacity.

Let us say that a party is reliable if it is both consistent and capable. There is no reason to suppose that all parties are equally reliable. If reliability is unevenly distributed, we should assume that when voters evaluate a party, they are making assessments of both its ideological position and its reliability. Voters who are closer to a party and who think that the party is reliable are going to vote for that party. Ideological distance will fully explain their behavior. However, as doubts about its reliability emerge, ideological distance will become less important. Thus, a voter who is closer to party π than to any other party may refrain from voting for π if π is perceived to be unreliable.

It follows, therefore, that patterns of ideological voting may be party-relative. People can make decisions with regard to some party based only on ideological distance to the party, whereas with regard to some other parties, ideological distance may be a less relevant variable because of some perception of inconsistency or bad performance regarding that party. This party-relative feature complicates somewhat the explanation about how many votes parties obtain. The vote share of parties may vary as a consequence of several factors: (i) changes in the ideological positions of parties that affect the number of voters who are closer to each party, (ii) changes in the distribution of voters' ideal points, and (iii) changes in the judgments about the consistency and capacity of parties. The introduction of (iii) means that, keeping constant an ideological distribution of voters

---

[6] There have been some partial attempts to introduce capacity into spatial models. See Adams and Merrill (1999); Enelow, Endersby, and Munger (1995); Enelow and Hinich (1982); Groseclose (2001); and Hinich and Munger (1997: 122–6).

[7] On the consequences of lack of internal unity, see Chapter 6 in this volume.

and parties, electoral results may vary considerably because of variations in reliability.

The general hypothesis can be put in the following terms: voting out of ideological proximity will wane as questions about the reliability of parties become more and more pressing. Issues of reliability do not have to affect all parties likewise: hence, we should observe patterns of ideological voting that are party-relative when some parties are seen as more reliable than others.

Patterns of Ideological Voting

To construct the kind of phenomenon about ideological voting that is to be explained, it is assumed that each voter votes for the party that produces higher utility as defined in a pure proximity model. Thus, we can calculate to what extent the data fit this assumption. Instead of using thermometer scores as proxies for utility, as is usually done in the spatial literature, I have constructed a categorical variable that establishes for each individual which party produces higher spatial utility. This variable simply determines to which party the individual is closer.[8] One of the attractive properties of this procedure is that it does not discard the possibility of a person having no ideological distance to parties, either because the individual is unable to establish an ideological bliss point or because he or she is unable to place parties in the ideological space. Thus, we can calculate the percentage of the sample to which ideological voting simply does not apply and how these people behave. Once we have such a variable, it can be cross-tabulated with vote intention or past vote: the kind of associations found among these variables will reflect the varying patterns of ideological voting.

The more technical details about the construction of the closeness variable are relegated to the Appendix. Basically, the building blocks of the variable are the self-placement of the respondent in the left–right scale and the positions the respondent attributes to the different parties in that scale.[9] Closeness to parties is then established through logical rules. Because the ideological scale is a discrete one, there can be voters who are equidistant

---

[8] A similar approach was used by Pierce (1995: 88–95) in his analysis of presidential elections in France and the United States.

[9] In the literature, it is common to infer the parties' positions from party manifestos or experts' opinions (see Gabel and Huber [2000] for a review and discussion). I think it is more consistent with the spatial theory to use purely subjective data.

between two parties. If there are n parties, at least n − 1 categories of being equidistant are possible.[10]

The variable cannot be applied to any party system. If there are too many parties, the number of categories of the closeness variable becomes unmanageable. Moreover, under such circumstances, it is difficult to make sense of the very idea of a voter being closer to some party because the voter may be rather close to several parties simultaneously. The variable is useful only for those countries with no more than, say, four relevant parties.[11]

A good indicator of the power of ideological voting is what I call parties' *retentive power*. The retentive power of a party can be defined as the percentage of individuals who, being ideologically closer to that party, vote for it. This indicator, therefore, shows the percentage of those voters who, according to the Downsian proximity model, should vote for the party and actually do so. Were the retentive power 100 percent, the proximity model would fully account for vote choices. All voters would vote for the party closer to their ideological ideal points; that is, parties would be able to retain all voters closer to them.[12]

Actually, the results of Table 2.1 show that small parties have lower retentive power than bigger parties. The table reproduces the retentive power of relevant parties in four European countries in 1994 with a roughly similar number of parties: Great Britain, Germany, Spain, and Portugal. That year, exceptionally, *Eurobarometer* included questions about the left–right placement of national parties in every member state, allowing a comparison of the functioning of the closeness variable. Small parties such as the Liberal Democrats in Great Britain, the Liberals and the Greens in Germany, and the right-wing coalition Social Democratic Center (CDS) in Portugal tend to have a low retentive power.[13] For instance, among those who are closer to the Liberals than to Conservatives or Labour in Great Britain, only 28 percent vote for the Liberals: 41 percent are willing to vote for Labour and 15 percent for Tories. The German Free Democratic

---

[10] There are only n − 1 categories if voters are able to order the parties correctly – for instance, if social democrats are always placed to the left of liberals or conservatives in the ideological scale.

[11] I consider that any party that obtains a vote share greater than 5 percent is a relevant one.

[12] I am assuming here that there is no strategic voting. A voter may vote for a more distant party for strategic reasons.

[13] This trend fits nicely with Adams's (2001: 42) model of partisan bias voting.

Table 2.1. Parties' Retentive Power in Four European Countries According to the Closeness Variable

Great Britain	Retentive power	Germany	Retentive power	Spain	Retentive power	Portugal	Retentive power
Conservative Party	72.1%	CDU/CSU	74.3%	PP	87.4%	CDS	38.5%
The Liberal Democrats	28.2%	FDP	11.8%	PSOE	37.8%	PSD	68.5%
Labour Party	84.5%	SPD	65.9%	IU	64.2%	PS	68.5%
		Greens	27.6%			CDU/PCP	64.9%

Data for Great Britain do not include Northern Ireland.
Retentive power has been computed by cross-tabulating vote intention and ideological closeness.
Parties in italics are small parties.
Source: Eurobarometer 44.1 (June–July 1994).

Party (FDP) has the lowest retentive power in this comparison, a mere 12 percent; 33 percent of those who are closer to the FDP want to vote for the Christian Democratic Union (CDU) and 26 percent for the German Social Democratic Party (SPD).[14]

I am interested here in the retentive power of big parties and, therefore, the issue of strategic voting is not relevant. In Great Britain, 72 percent of those who are closer to the Conservatives and 84 percent of those who are closer to Labour are willing to vote for these parties. In Portugal, the percentage is the same for the two main parties, the right-wing Social Democratic Party (PSD) and the left-wing Socialist Party (PS): 68.5 percent. Yet there is an astonishing figure for the Spanish socialists, PSOE: this party is able to retain only 38 percent of those who are closer to it. Although this is, as I show later, an underestimation of PSOE's retentive power, it points to a deviant case. In Spain, 1994 was at any rate a bad year for the socialist incumbent; economic conditions were bad and corruption scandals were flourishing at that time. This just makes the possibility of dwelling on the Spanish case more interesting, however.

The Spanish socialists won elections in 1982. PSOE had a majority in Parliament for the period 1982–93. From 1993 to 1996, it had a plurality and governed with the support of Catalan nationalist deputies. In 1996, the conservative party, PP, won elections and governed again with the support of nationalist parties. In 2000, the PP obtained a majority in Parliament. In 2004, three days after the Islamist bombings that killed 192 citizens in Madrid on March 11, the socialists, quite unexpectedly, won the elections.

PSOE and PP are the two main parties. United Left (IU), a leftist coalition dominated by the Communist Party, is a much smaller party, with a vote share below 10 percent.[15] In 1986 and 1989, there was a fourth party, CDS, a centrist party that was very much dependent on its leader, Adolfo Suárez, the former prime minister in the period 1977–81. The party collapsed in 1993, obtaining no representation in Parliament. These four parties

---

[14] The retentive capacity of the leftist coalition IU in Spain is clearly biased. As can be seen in a more detailed way in Table 2.4, elaborated with larger and more representative samples, the actual retentive capacity of IU is much lower. The *Eurobarometer* sample for each state member is really small (1,000) and provides distorting pictures of national politics. Thus, with regard to Spain, vote intention for PSOE and IU is the same in 1994, 16.5 percent, but PSOE usually gets three or four times more votes than IU.

[15] In 1986, IU received only a 3.8 percent of the vote, therefore not qualifying as a relevant party. However, I have included IU in 1986 for the sake of completeness.

together account for more than 80 percent of the vote. The rest corresponds to tiny nationalist and regionalist parties.[16]

The puzzling case of the Spanish socialists is clearly revealed when the vote in the last election variable is cross-tabulated with the closeness variable, as shown in Table 2.2. This table contains, among other things, the retentive power of Spanish parties for the six elections of the period 1986–2004. It provides much more detailed information than Table 2.1 about the retentive power of parties in various countries because we can reconstruct the choices of all those who do not vote according to the proximity model. Retentive power is signaled by percentages in bold. With regard to PP, it is difficult to discern any trend in its retentive power. It is greater than 80 percent in every year except 1989 and 2004. Ideological voting under the proximity model works well for this party. In contrast, in the case of PSOE, there is a progressive eroding of its retentive power that is only reversed in 2004. Whereas in 1986 retentive power was a reasonable 78 percent, in 2000 it declined to a mere 52 percent, meaning that only half of those who were closer to the socialist party voted for it.[17] This decline cannot be due exclusively to the onus of being in government and having to make difficult choices because it continued once the party left office.

Something similar is detected for IU: being a small party, the retentive power is lower, but it follows the same declining pattern as PSOE from 1989 onward. Unlike PSOE, the trend did not stop in 2004: if anything, the erosion became deeper in that year.

As would be expected from the previous discussion, patterns of ideological voting are party-relative. Ideological voting in Spain works for the right-wing party but not so much for the left-wing parties. The puzzle is how to explain this asymmetry.

Table 2.2 offers many other insights about the features of ideological voting in Spain. The signals of weakness of the left for mobilizing voters are evident everywhere in the table for the period 1993–2000. Among those equidistant between PP and PSOE, there is a huge increase since 1993 of the vote for PP and a sharp fall of the vote for PSOE, reversed only in 2004. Furthermore, there is an impressive increase in those who are closer to PSOE but vote for PP (i.e., from 0.5 percent in 1986 to 19 percent

---

[16] For the mean ideological positions of the main parties, see tables 2 and 3 in Torcal and Medina (2002).

[17] Note that the retentive capacity is in any case higher than that calculated from the 1994 *Eurobarometer* (see Table 2.1).

Table 2.2. Ideological Closeness and Past Vote in Spain, 1986–2004: Vertical Percentages

		Ideological closeness							
Vote	Election	PP	PP = CDS	CDS (86–89) PP = PSOE (93–04)	CDS = PSOE	PSOE	PSOE = IU	IU	Without ideological distance
PP	1986	**81.9%**	61.5%	12.8%	6.2%	0.5%	0.3%	0%	9.5%
	1989	**76.9%**	50.0%	20.0%	7.0%	1.9%	0%	0.4%	10.7%
	1993	**80.1%**		57.0%		11.4%	3.5%	3.4%	16.9%
	1996	**81.6%**		67.1%		17.8%	5.8%	4.7%	21.2%
	2000	**83.3%**		66.7%		18.9%	10.0%	5.9%	28.5%
	2004	**77.7%**		48.7%		9.0%	3.8%	2.2%	22.2%
CDS	1986	3.0%	9.4%	**38.7%**	11.6%	2.0%	1.3%	1.0%	5.4%
	1989	1.6%	9.5%	**31.9%**	8.5%	0.7%	0.8%	0.4%	1.6%
PSOE	1986	2.7%	5.1%	18.7%	55.1%	**78.4%**	72.4%	40.0%	30.6%
	1989	2.2%	9.5%	16.2%	43.7%	**72.8%**	62.0%	20.6%	29.8%
	1993	3.6%		13.4%		**66.1%**	64.2%	32.3%	28.9%
	1996	3.7%		8.8%		**56.8%**	59.4%	26.6%	24.9%
	2000	1.2%		5.8%		**52.3%**	59.9%	26.0%	14.9%
	2004	8.1%		19.9%		**70.8%**	68.6%	48.5%	28.4%

IU	1986	0.2%	0%	0.6%	1.6%	1.9%	7.4%	**32.5%**	1.7%
	1989	0%	0%	2.2%	4.2%	1.9%	12.4%	**53.4%**	2.5%
	1993	1.5%		1.4%		3.1%	9.5%	**42.5%**	3.1%
	1996	0.8%		2.4%		3.5%	13.2%	**43.5%**	2.8%
	2000	0.4%		0%		2.4%	7.1%	**33.0%**	1.2%
	2004	0.4%		0%		2.2%	7.6%	**26.4%**	1.2%
Abstention	1986	6.0%	14.5%	14.4%	10.5%	9.8%	13.0%	18.2%	25.0%
	1989	10.8%	11.9%	15.7%	16.9%	12.1%	15.7%	17.6%	25.8%
	1993	7.4%		12.0%		9.9%	13.0%	15.4%	24.2%
	1996	5.9%		8.8%		10.6%	11.7%	16.9%	19.2%
	2000	8.8%		13.2%		14.1%	16.4%	25.4%	24.8%
	2004	7.5%		8.4%		8.6%	8.1%	11.0%	21.7%
DK/DA	1986	6.3%	9.4%	14.9%	15.1%	7.4%	5.6%	8.3%	27.8%
	1989	8.6%	19.0%	14.1%	19.7%	10.4%	9.1%	7.6%	29.5%
	1993	7.3%		16.2%		9.5%	9.8%	6.4%	26.9%
	1996	8.0%		12.9%		11.4%	9.9%	8.4%	31.9%
	2000	6.3%		14.3%		12.4%	6.7%	9.6%	30.5%
	2004	6.3%		23.0%		9.4%	11.9%	11.9%	26.4%

Note: Bold percentages correspond to the retentive power of parties.
Source: Centro de Investigaciones Sociológicas (CIS), postelectoral surveys.

in 2000, going back to 9 percent in 2004). Nothing similar can be found in the other direction: among those who are closer to PP, the percentage of the vote for PSOE is insignificant and shows no trend, although in 2004, in the wake of the March 11 attacks, 8 percent of those closer to PP voted for PSOE. In addition, among the group of people without ideological distance, there is a dramatic fall of the vote for PSOE starting in 1993 (from 28.9 percent in 1993 to 14.9 percent in 2000), mirrored by an increase of support for PP (from 9.5 percent to 28.5 percent in the same period). Finally, the table also shows that people closer to PSOE have always abstained more than people closer to PP.[18] In 2000, this difference reached a peak of 5.3 points. Abstention is even higher among those closer to IU. In 2000, one in four abstained, helping to understand the process by which this party lost almost half of its votes between 1996 and 2000.

The mobilization deficit of the Spanish left was only overcome in 2004, most likely as a consequence of the terrorist attack that took place three days before the elections. Only in 2004 was the rate of participation similar for the right and left. Even under such circumstances, however, the retentive power of the PSOE was lower than that of PP. The overview provided by Table 2.2 shows that despite the terrorist attack, the elections were normal and comparable to those that took place before 1993 in Spain.[19]

The trends found for PSOE and IU are by no means universal. Moreover, it is not a matter of being the incumbent or being left wing. Using the same procedures as before, I have made a similar analysis for the German case. The contrast is interesting for various reasons. On one hand, there is a similar number of parties. I have started the analysis in 1976 and ended in 1994, covering two consecutive elections won by the SPD and four consecutive elections won by the CDU/CSU.[20] In this period, there were three relevant parties in 1976 and 1980 (CDU/CSU, FDP, and SPD) and four parties from 1983 onward with the appearance of the Greens. On the other hand, like Spain, the incumbency periods are indeed long: from 1969 to 1981 a SPD-FDP coalition was in office and from 1981 to 1998 a CDU/CSU-FDP one. Thus, we can check whether

---

[18] Barreiro (2002) analyzes the relationship between ideology and abstention in Spain.

[19] This is consistent with other studies about the 2004 elections concluding that the terrorist attack was not so crucial (Barreiro 2004; Lago and Montero 2005).

[20] For 1994, the German Election Study did not include questions about the placement of parties in the left–right scale. Hence, I have used data from *Eurobarometer* 44.1. I have not had access to the 1998 German Election Study.

the erosion of retentive power is intrinsically associated with being in government.

The retentive power has been calculated with vote intention (in Spain with past vote): vote intention tends to depress retentive power because some people have not yet made a decision. Nonetheless, Table 2.3 shows that the retentive power of the two big parties, CDU/CSU and SPD, is rather high every year. It could be argued that the CDU/CSU's retentive power went down since it started to govern in 1981, thus revealing that incumbency produces a weakening of ideological voting, but the decrease falls short of the one observed for PSOE in Spain. Moreover, unlike Spain, we do not observe differential patterns of abstention, and it does not seem to be the case that people closer to the two big parties vote for distant parties.

Comparison of Tables 2.2 and 2.3 shows that what has to be explained is precisely the mystery about PSOE's retentive power – its growing inability to mobilize the vote of those individuals who are closer to this party than to the rest of the parties.

Models of Ideological Voting in Spain

One of the more obvious lessons that can be drawn from Tables 2.2 and 2.3 in the previous section is that not everyone who is closer to a party votes for that party. According to the hypothesis of this chapter, the probability of voting for a party is a function both of the ideological distances between the voter and the parties and of some other independent variables related to consistency and capacity.

Next, I analyze various conditional logit models with vote intention (or past vote) as the dependent variable and ideological distances and indicators of consistency, capacity, and performance as independent ones. Conditional logit is a technique particularly well suited to the spatial analysis of voting in multiparty systems (Alvarez and Nagler 1998; Thurner 2000). In conditional logit, we can introduce alternative-specific variables, that is, variables with different values for each value of the dependent variable. This is precisely what we need for the spatial model in which each individual has a different distance with regard to each of the parties that forms part of the dependent variable. Thus, we get a single coefficient for the ideological distance variable that represents the overall influence of ideological voting. We can also add individual-specific variables (e.g., the opinion on government's performance), creating what is usually called a

Table 2.3. Ideological Closeness and Vote Intention in Germany, 1976–1994: Vertical Percentages

		Ideological closeness							
Vote	Election	CDU/CSU	CDU/CSU = FDP	FDP	FDP = SPD	SPD	SPD = GREENS	GREENS	Without distance
CDU/CSU	1976	**79.7%**	63.1%	28.9%	12.3%	5.9%			29.4%
	1980	**76.6%**	58.3%	20.8%	5.6%	5.3%			19.9%
	1983	**81.5%**	72.7%	44.1%	15.7%	6.4%	1.1%	7.3%	29.4%
	1987	**78.7%**	72.6%	36.7%	14.6%	5.8%	1.9%	3.1%	30.6%
	1990	**75.4%**	66.7%	37.6%	19.5%	3.7%	1.7%	4.8%	35.3%
	1994	*74.3%*	*62.5%*	*33.3%*	*22.6%*	*9.3%*	*5.3%*	*10.3%*	*20.9%*
FDP	1976	2.9%	8.2%	**16.4%**	9.7%	4.7%			7.2%
	1980	2.5%	5.4%	**14.8%**	7.8%	5.1%			2.1%
	1983	0%	1.4%	**6.8%**	1.4%	1.8%	1.1%	1.8%	2.4%
	1987	4.5%	8.0%	**18.0%**	1.2%	0.8%	0%	2.3%	5.6%
	1990	3.8%	9.1%	**12.0%**	8.0%	2.4%	0.9%	2.7%	4.4%
	1994	*3.2%*	*7.1%*	*11.8%*	*3.2%*	*2.3%*	*0.8%*	*2.5%*	*1.0%*
SPD	1976	4.9%	10.7%	37.7%	61.0%	**75.9%**			34.4%
	1980	9.9%	15.7%	44.9%	70.6%	**78.8%**			19.9%
	1983	5.3%	7.7%	25.0%	51.4%	**69.3%**	64.4%	45.5%	20.0%

1987	4.5%	5.9%	21.1%	57.3%	**68.3%**	56.3%	24.8%	13.9%
1990	6.1%	5.4%	26.4%	48.3%	**75.3%**	69.8%	40.1%	23.5%
1994	*5.9%*	*8.0%*	*25.8%*	*45.2%*	***65.9%***	*48.1%*	*35.5%*	*19.1%*
Greens **1983**	0.9%	0%	1.8%	5.7%	2.3%	15.6%	**23.0%**	8.2%
1987	1.7%	1.3%	1.0%	1.2%	8.6%	19.4%	**51.9%**	1.4%
1990	0%	1.6%	3.0%	4.6%	7.6%	12.1%	**29.9%**	1.5%
1994	*0.4%*	*0%*	*2.7%*	*4.8%*	*7.4%*	*26.3%*	***27.6%***	*4.1%*
Abstention **1976**	0.8%	1.6%	3.4%	2.6%	1.9%			10.0%
1980	2.5%	4.4%	5.3%	2.7%	2.9%			16.2%
1983	5.6%	6.3%	5.5%	7.1%	5.9%	4.4%	7.9%	10.6%
1987	2.6%	3.8%	8.3%	7.3%	5.6%	11.7%	6.2%	11.1%
1990	5.2%	5.4%	7.4%	5.7%	3.9%	6.9%	8.8%	13.2%
1994	*4.7%*	*2.7%*	*2.7%*	*1.6%*	*1.6%*	*4.5%*	*5.4%*	*11.0%*
DK/DA **1976**	11.7%	16.4%	13.6%	14.4%	11.8%			28.9%
1980	8.5%	16.2%	14.2%	14.4%	7.9%			41.9%
1983	6.6%	11.9%	16.8%	18.6%	14.2%	13.3%	14.5%	29.4%
1987	8.0%	8.4%	15.0%	18.3%	10.9%	10.7%	11.6%	37.5%
1990	9.5%	11.8%	13.6%	13.8%	7.1%	8.6%	13.6%	22.1%
1994	*11.5%*	*19.6%*	*23.7%*	*22.6%*	*13.6%*	*15.0%*	*18.7%*	*44.0%*

Note: Bold percentages correspond to the retentive power of parties.
Sources: 1976–1990 German Election Studies; *Eurobarometer* 1994: 44.1.

mixed conditional logit model.[21] The use of this technique is not without problems. We have to exclude both people without ideological distance and people who abstain. Abstention cannot be an outcome in the dependent variable simply because it is not possible to define a distance between the voter's ideal point and abstention.

From a methodological point of view, it is convenient to assume, as conditional logit does, that there is a single coefficient for ideological distance, so that the influence of ideological distance on voting is the same for all parties. Hence, party differences in the pattern of ideological voting must be due to some other variables, those that have to do with consistency and capacity. The party-relative patterns of ideological voting that were identified in the previous section are now explained by a common coefficient of ideological distance and differences in reliability.

To explain these party-relative patterns, it is necessary to introduce other factors apart from ideological distance. Variables related to capacity and performance enter here. Unfortunately, the lack of proper questions in Spanish surveys makes a systematic comparison along time impossible. For different election years, we have different questions. However, we can handle the problem if two broad periods are distinguished. During its long time in office, PSOE went through several episodes in which its reliability was openly discussed. Simplifying somewhat a complex story, it could be said that from 1982 to 1989, the party was often criticized for its conservative policy, which was considered improper for a socialist government. There was a charge of ideological inconsistency among important segments of the electorate. From 1989 to 2000, the party became increasingly divided, and corruption scandals affecting the government and the party

---

[21] In the pure conditional logit model, the probability that individual i makes the mth-choice is (Powers and Xie 2000: 239–43; Long and Freese 2001: 213–21)

$$\Pr(y_i = m \,|\, z_i) = \frac{\exp(z_{im}\gamma)}{\sum_{j=1}^{j} \exp(z_{ij}\gamma)},$$

where z_{ij} is a vector containing the values of independent variables with regard to outcome j of the dependent variable and γ is the vector of coefficients of the independent variables. Thus, there are J values for a single variable, but a single coefficient for each variable.

In the mixed model, we add a vector $\mathbf{x}_i$ with the values of the individual-specific variables and another vector β_m with their coefficients, assuming that $\beta_1 = 0$:

$$\Pr(y_i = m \,|\, z_i, x_i) = \frac{\exp(z_{im}\gamma + x_i\beta_m)}{\sum_{j=1}^{j} \exp(z_{ij}\gamma + x_i\beta_j)}.$$

If only individual-specific variables are included, conditional logit coincides with multinomial logit.

started to emerge, damaging the perception of its capacity. The internal crisis led to a historical defeat in 2000. After the elections, a new leadership was elected, and the party recovered its normal connection with voters in the 2004 elections. First, I deal with the problem of consistency, and then I move to the problem of capacity. I do not analyze the 2004 elections. They are a useful contrast to confirm that once these problems were removed, the party was able to regain its old retentive capacity.

Ideological Consistency

A party is ideologically inconsistent when it makes policy that is not congruent with its ideological stance. It could be argued that ideological inconsistency is just impossible: the inconsistency lies in voters' perceptions of the party. When voters observe policies made by the incumbent, they update their prior beliefs about the party's real ideological position. Therefore, there cannot be inconsistency because ideological positions are inferred from policy. Although this is to some extent correct, it tends to forget that ideological labels are not fully dependent on current actions: they represent also the history of the party, the position of the party as revealed in manifestos and in public statements, the kind of people recruited by the party, and so on. Moreover, voters may think that the party really holds the original ideological position but that the government is a bad agent of the party, perhaps because the government has been captured by interest groups or by experts. Here, I employ a purely subjective conception of policy inconsistency. It is just a perception shared by some voters, fair or not, grounded or not. I do not claim that the incumbent was really inconsistent.

The PSOE, particularly in its two first mandates (1982–6, 1986–9), suffered repeatedly the accusation of having made an economic policy that was too much to the right.[22] In foreign policy, the shift of the government in the NATO question in 1986, when it held a referendum defending the permanence of Spain within the organization, did not help to dissipate this accusation of ideological betrayal. The main problems were created by the brother union, General Workers' Union (UGT), that broke long-lasting links with the party and organized, together with other unions, the 14 December 1988 general strike. The general strike was a big success and

---

[22] Carabaña (2001: 43–4) argues that one of the main causes of the electoral loss of PSOE in the 1980s was a set of policies inconsistent with the ideology of its voters.

damaged enormously the image of the party.[23] Unions close to socialist parties, as shown in Chapter 7 of this volume, are crucial for the retentive power of these parties. The conflict between the union and the government must have put leftist workers in a state of confusion and anxiety: should they keep voting for the socialist incumbent, or was the conflict sufficiently serious to make them conclude the party was no longer representing the working class?[24]

Both in 1986 and in 1989, some preelection surveys included a question about ideological consistency. The respondent was asked to choose one of these statements regarding the incumbent's policy:

1. It has been too conservative, not proper for a socialist government.
2. Before all else, it has been realist, according to the circumstances.
3. It has been the proper policy of a socialist government.

I have conflated answers 2 and 3. There is inconsistency only if the respondent chooses 1. If the respondent chooses 2, there is a justification of possible policy deviations, and therefore the respondent will not regard these deviations as a signal of inconsistency: if the party has not acted as expected, it is because it had good reasons not to do so. In 1986, 23 percent of the whole sample said that PSOE was making a too conservative policy, 33 percent said that PSOE's policy was realist, and only 18 percent said it was truly socialist; 26 percent did not know or did not answer.[25] Three years later, in 1989, after the general strike, the percentage of those who thought that policy was inconsistent had risen to 32 percent, whereas 24 percent said that policy was realist and 14 percent said that it was truly socialist, and 30 percent did not know or did not answer.[26] The difference

---

[23] In a survey about the relationship between PSOE and UGT made in November 1987, people were asked whether the government should change its policy to make possible the reestablishment of good relations with UGT: 55 percent of the sample answered yes and only 13 percent said no (CIS 1711, n = 2,454). In the aftermath of the general strike, 23.5 percent said that their opinion about the government had worsened after the strike (only 6.5 percent said it had improved), whereas only 12 percent said their opinion about the UGT had worsened (and 26 percent said it had improved) (CIS 1780, December 1988, n = 2,498).

[24] This argument echoes part of the discussion in Chapter 6 of this volume about the government having two principals, the party and the voters. In this case, the union claimed to be another principal. The general secretary of the UGT often treated the prime minister as if he were an agent of the union.

[25] CIS 1526, April–May 1986, n = 25,667.

[26] CIS 1789, January–February 1989, n = 27,287.

between 1986 and 1989 is interesting. In its first term, the government had to face a deep economic crisis that provoked a dramatic rise in the unemployment rate (from 16.2 percent in 1982 to 21.5 percent in 1986, an increase of 5.3 points). In contrast, during the second term, the economy was booming, and the creation of employment was indeed impressive (the unemployment rate went down from 21.5 percent in 1986 to 17.3 percent in 1989, a decrease of 4.2 points). Under good economic conditions, there were fewer reasons to exonerate ideological inconsistency by appealing to the circumstances; thus, the percentage of those who said that the incumbent's policy was realistic decreased 9 points between 1986 and 1989. Despite the difference in economic conditions, the party lost more or less the same amount of vote share (4 percentage points) in the first two terms, neglecting the relevance of the economic cycle.[27]

Although the perception of ideological inconsistency was prevalent to the left of PSOE (72 percent of those closer to IU thought so in 1989), it was also common within the right (43 percent of those closer to PP in 1989). For right-wing people, this opinion might be a sincere impression of what PSOE was doing, but it could simply be another means to express their rejection of the government. The variable could present, then, some measurement problems.[28] However, if the variable measures to some extent ideological inconsistency, the prediction is that the effect of inconsistency on a left incumbent should be more noticeable for left-wing than for right-wing voters. As shown subsequently, this prediction is born out by the statistical analysis.

If we focus on those who were closer to PSOE according to the ideological closeness variable, we find that 18 percent in 1986 and 29 percent in 1989 still thought that policy was inconsistent. This means that in 1989, more than one in four among those closer to PSOE than to any other party thought that the socialist government was too conservative. That year, vote intention for PSOE and the intention to abstain among those who thought that PSOE's policy was realist or socialist were 73 percent and 4 percent,

---

[27] If percentages are calculated from the whole electorate, the party lost 7 points during the first term and 3 during the second (see Carabaña 2001). Participation fell 9 points in 1986 compared with 1982. Thus, PSOE lost 7 points, but PP, being the opposition party, lost almost 3 points.

[28] Yet it is worth noting that, as Table 2.2 reveals, people closer to PSOE started to vote for PP to a significant extent in 1993, not before. Thus, in 1989, only 2 percent of those closer to PSOE voted for PP, whereas in 1993, this percentage increased to 11.4 percent.

respectively. Among those who thought that PSOE's policy was too conservative, the corresponding percentages were 34 percent and 16 percent. Vote intention was reduced by more than half, and abstention increased four times as a consequence of ideological inconsistency. This kind of effect is clearly crucial to understand the decline of PSOE's retentive power in the 1980s.

I have estimated a conditional logit model for 1986 and 1989 in which the spatial variable of proximity is combined with a variable of capacity or performance, ideological inconsistency, adding some demographic controls.[29] The underlying hypothesis is that the perception of a party's inconsistency should decrease the probability of voting for that party keeping constant ideological proximity. Table 2.4 shows the results. The coefficient of ideological inconsistency for PSOE is, as expected, negative. However, it is confirmed that the influence of the consistency variable is much stronger among those to the left of PSOE than among those to the right. It is true that inconsistency increases the probability of voting for CDS or PP, but the increase is much higher for the probability of voting for IU. The fact that the impact is greater on the left than on the right shows that ideological inconsistency is something more than generic criticism of the incumbent.[30]

Because the interpretation of conditional logit coefficients is not easy, I have included in Table 2.5 the effect of ideological inconsistency on the probability of voting for each party for three spatial scenarios in 1989.[31] In the first (Table 2.5-1), the respondent's ideal point coincides with PSOE's point, he is equidistant between IU and CDS (2 points away from each) and 4 points to the left of PP. The probability of voting for PSOE decreases

[29] The proximity variable measures the quadratic distance between the respondent and the parties (from 0 to 81). Ideological consistency is a dummy variable (0 = *Consistent*, 1 = *Inconsistent*). The demographic control variables are education (1 = *No education*, 2 = *Primary school*, 3 = *High school*, 4 = *University studies*), sex (1 = *Male*, 2 = *Female*), and age.

[30] I have tried other specifications. The more important change is produced when the evaluation of parties' leaders is included as an alternative-specific variable. The coefficient of ideological consistency is weakened, although it is still highly significant. But this has to do with the fact that the evaluation of leaders is related to their performance. Thus, those who think badly of the prime minister tend also to think that his government has made a too conservative policy. The effects of leadership are enormous in the models, but I have not included them to allow pure performance variables to enter into the analysis.

[31] The age and education variables are kept constant at their means. Sex has value 1 (*Male* category).

Table 2.4. Conditional Logit Models for 1986 and 1989

	1986			1989		
	CDS/PP	PSOE/PP	IU/PP	CDS/PP	PSOE/PP	IU/PP
Ideological proximity		−0.1686**			−0.1918**	
		(0.0039)			(0.0041)	
Intercept	−1.0314**	2.7856**	0.2398	−0.0404	2.1507**	−0.2149
	(0.3407)	(0.2751)	(0.3779)	(0.2828)	(0.2775)	(0.3709)
Ideological inconsistency	0.4296**	−0.7779**	1.4454**	0.5192**	−0.9011**	1.3031**
	(0.1222)	(0.1046)	(0.1384)	(0.0959)	(0.0949)	(0.1325)
Education	−0.3589**	−0.5201**	−0.4879**	−0.2596**	−0.5341**	−0.1549
	(0.0686)	(0.0549)	(0.0775)	(0.0652)	(0.0637)	(0.0840)
Age	−0.0107**	−0.0235**	−0.0305**	−0.0173**	−0.0137**	−0.0378**
	(0.0048)	(0.0031)	(0.0045)	(0.0031)	(0.0030)	(0.0044)
Sex	0.2850*	0.0175	−0.1333	0.0621	0.0309	−0.2519
	(0.1174)	(0.0959)	(0.1332)	(0.0959)	(0.0938)	(0.1305)
Pseudo R²		0.61			0.54	
N		8,368			8,302	

Notes: Standard errors are in parentheses. Dependent variable: vote intention (base category: PP).
**Significant at 1%; *significant at 5%.
Sources: 1986: CIS 1526; 1989: CIS 1789.

Table 2.5 Probabilities of Voting According to Different Spatial Locations and Ideological Consistency (1989)

Table 2.5-1

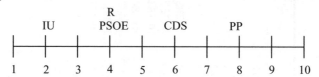

Note: R stands for the respondent's ideal position. 1 is the more leftist position, 10 is the more rightist one.

	Pr (Vote for IU)	Pr (Vote for PSOE)	Pr (Vote for CDS)	Pr (Vote for PP)
Ideologically consistent	0.02	0.88	0.07	0.03
Ideologically inconsistent	0.15	0.60	0.21	0.05

Table 2.5-2

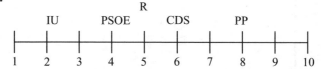

Note: R stands for the respondent's ideal position. 1 is the more leftist position, 10 is the more rightist one.

	Pr (Vote for IU)	Pr (Vote for PSOE)	Pr (Vote for CDS)	Pr (Vote for PP)
Ideologically consistent	0.01	0.75	0.13	0.11
Ideologically inconsistent	0.05	0.45	0.34	0.16

Table 2.5-3

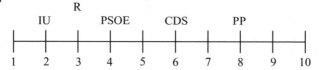

Note: R stands for the respondent's ideal position. 1 is the more leftist position, 10 is the more rightist one.

	Pr (Vote for IU)	Pr (Vote for PSOE)	Pr (Vote for CDS)	Pr (Vote for PP)
Ideologically consistent	0.05	0.91	0.03	0.01
Ideologically inconsistent	0.31	0.59	0.09	0.01

28 points because of inconsistency. The probability of voting for IU increases 13 points and that of CDS 14 points. In the second scenario (Table 2.5-2), the respondent is more centrist: he is equidistant between PSOE and CDS (1 point away from each) and equidistant between IU and PP (3 points away from each). Now the probability of voting for PSOE is lower, both for consistency (75 percent) and for inconsistency (45 percent), a reduction of 30 points. The probability of voting for IU does not change greatly, but it changes for PP and particularly for CDS. Finally, in the third scenario (Table 2.5-3), we have a more leftist respondent, equidistant between IU and PSOE (1 point away from each), 3 points away from CDS, and 5 from PP. If that respondent thinks that the incumbent has been consistent, the probability of voting for it is indeed high – 91 percent – but it goes down to 59 percent if the respondent thinks policy has been inconsistent. Now we observe a huge increase in the probability of voting for IU.

Table 2.5 reveals that there is significant punishment for ideological inconsistency even among those who have an ideological position that coincides with that of PSOE. Ideological convictions are not powerful enough to neutralize completely the effects of a negative perception of government's performance. The consequence of the reduction in the probability of voting for the incumbent in the spatial configurations I have examined is an increase in the probability of voting for the small parties close to PSOE, not greatly affecting the main opposition party, PP.

Party Unity and Corruption

In the 1990s, new problems emerged for the incumbent. First, all kinds of corruption scandals occurred – some related to the party, some related to members of the government. The scandals varied in substance: abuse of power, illegal financing of the party, and personal enrichment. To this, the dirty-war issue must be added, a dark episode in the fight against Basque Homeland and Freedom (ETA) from the period 1983–6 that resurfaced judicially in 1994. Second, the party was divided into two opposed factions and became increasingly isolated from other social forces. Problems of leadership worsened after the 1996 defeat. The surprising resignation of Felipe Gonzalez in 1997, the general secretary since 1974 and prime minister for the entire 1982–96 period, started a phase of internal turmoil and introspection in which the party was unable to solve its own organizational problems. This period lasted until July 2000. That month, after the great loss of vote share in the general elections, a new team of young people replaced the old leadership.[32]

Both the scandals and the internal divisions had some impact on the capacity of the party – that is, the capacity to make and to implement policies leading to the desired outcomes. The idea is that a divided party may lead to paralysis or deadlock, and corruption may signal that policies are inefficient, or more simply that politicians do not have the proper motivations to make the right policy. The problem lies in how to measure capacity. I have used two different measures for 1993 and 1996. It was impossible to construct a capacity index for 2000. In 1993, respondents were asked about six dimensions of the three main parties: PP, PSOE and IU. The dimensions were responsiveness, trustworthiness, able leaders, internal unity, the honesty of the militants, and respect for the law in the finances of the party.[33] Not all of them have to do with capacity. More concretely, the first two, responsiveness and trustworthiness, are in a sense preconditions for capacity. A voter will not value the capacity of a party if the party is considered unresponsive or untrustworthy. I have not tried to separate these dimensions because a principal component analysis showed that there is a single underlying component.

The mean values are reported in Table 2.6. Some interesting comparisons can be made. The three parties obtain similar means in responsiveness, trustworthiness, and leadership. Yet there are big differences in terms of unity and honesty. PP is seen as a much more united party than PSOE or IU. Although the more honest party is IU, both with regard to militants and to the party's financing, there are still important differences between PP and PSOE in favor of PP. The socialists obtain low scores in these two dimensions.

The index for 1996 is less fine-grained. Respondents were asked to name the party that best fit each of five statements: the party that better represents the ideas of the respondent, the more trustworthy party, the

---

[32] For the reaction of PSOE to corruption scandals, see Maravall (1999: 172–6). On how public opinion reacted to these scandals, see Caínzos and Jiménez (2000); Sánchez-Cuenca and Barreiro (2000: ch. 4). On the internal problems of PSOE, see Almunia (2001: ch. 15–19) and Chapter 6 in this volume.

[33] The variables have five values, from the most negative opinion (−2) to the most positive (+2). Although originally there was not a median value, the DK/DA (don't know/don't answer) answers have been given a 0 value, being therefore the median value. I have calculated the mean value for each party for each individual, creating later an alternative-specific variable for conditional logit.

Table 2.6. Party Means in Six Dimensions of Capacity
(1993)

	PP	PSOE	IU
Responsiveness	−0.49	−0.53	−0.49
Trustworthiness	−0.67	−0.68	−0.74
Able leaders	−0.17	−0.20	−0.33
Internal unity	+0.25	−0.09	−0.05
Honesty	−0.10	−0.26	−0.01
Legal financing	−0.30	−0.57	−0.22

Note: The mean can vary between –2 (*most negative view*) and +2
(*most positive view*).
Source: 1993: CIS 2048.

party with better leaders, the more capable party to govern, and the party
that can better solve the problems of Spain.[34] Again, the first two statements are the ones that have less to do with capacity.

Apart from these indexes, I have also included a generic variable of government's performance for the three elections and another variable about
the job of the main opposition party in 1993 and 2000.[35] As for corruption,
there were not adequate questions in the surveys employed.[36] In fact, a
good deal of information about corruption is incorporated in the capacity
index for 1993. An indirect indicator on corruption has nonetheless been
used for that year: it is a 0–10 scale about how worried the respondent is
about political corruption.

Conditional logit estimates appear in Table 2.7. Unlike the models of
Table 2.4, those of Table 2.7 are not so easily comparable because for each
election, there are different independent variables. First, the capacity variable is extremely powerful both in 1993 and in 1996, although more so in
1993, probably due to the fact that the variable is more accurately measured in that year. Second, the opinion on government's performance is
much more important than the opinion on the job made by the opposition,
both in 1993 and in 2000. The opposition is probably judged prospectively

---

[34] Again, this enters as an alternative-specific variable in the statistical analysis. Each individual has a score from 0 to 5 for each party, representing the number of times that the
party has been chosen as the answer to any of the five questions.

[35] The question about the opposition's performance was not included in 1996. Both variables
are measured from 1 to 5, 1 being the most positive opinion and 5 the most negative one.
Because there is a median value, I have eliminated from the sample the DK/DA answers.

[36] The good questions are included in more specialized surveys about corruption in which
ideological distances cannot be calculated. See Sánchez-Cuenca and Barreiro (2000: ch. 4).

Table 2.7. Conditional Logit Models for 1993, 1996, and 2000

	1993		1996		2000	
Ideological proximity	-0.1062** (0.0121)		-0.0716** (0.0074)		-0.1124** (0.0031)	
Capacity	2.0998** (0.1875)		0.9197** (0.0431)		–	
	PSOE/PP	IU/PP	PSOE/PP	IU/PP	PSOE/PP	IU/PP
Intercept	5.8465** (1.4631)	1.8264 (1.6541)	4.0894** (1.0883)	1.9663* (0.9986)	-2.8328** (0.3129)	-5.8658** (0.4079)
Government's performance	-1.3367** (0.2586)	-0.4943* (0.2525)	-1.5915** (0.2382)	-0.6101** (0.1903)	2.5293** (0.0714)	2.0984** (0.0820)
Opposition performance	0.4488 (0.2428)	0.6414* (0.2617)	–	–	-1.3540** (0.0593)	-0.3091** (0.0713)
Corruption	-0.1376* (0.0704)	-0.1184 (0.0769)	–	–	–	–
Education	-0.6081* (0.2450)	-0.2796 (0.2798)	-0.5045** (0.1788)	-0.0842 (0.1687)	-0.1306** (0.0501)	0.1393* (0.0630)
Age	-0.0076 (0.0113)	-0.0450** (0.0146)	-0.0068 (0.0093)	-0.0270** (0.0098)	0.0013 (0.0025)	-0.0134** (0.0035)
Sex	0.0875 (0.3394)	-0.0215 (0.3826)	0.6545** (0.2795)	0.2018 (0.2705)	-0.1357 (0.0792)	-0.3066** (0.1046)
Pseudo R²	0.77		0.82		0.63	
N	954		2,951		9,510	

Notes: Standard errors in parentheses. Dependent variable: vote intention (base category: PP).
**Significant at 1%; *significant at 5%.
Sources: 1993: CIS 2048; 1996: CIS 2207; 2000: CIS 2382.

rather than retrospectively. Third, in the only year in which we have a separate question on corruption, 1993, the variable is not so important, and it matters only for the comparison PSOE/PP, but not for IU/PP. The more worried a person is about corruption, the more likely he or she is to vote for PP.

To understand the crucial effect of capacity and how capacity accounts for the party-relative patterns of ideological voting, I have calculated probabilities of voting for the three parties according to various configurations of values in capacity and distance in the 1993 model.

Let us suppose first a spatial configuration like the one described in Table 2.5-1 (i.e., someone who coincides with PSOE and is 4 points away from PP and 2 from IU). All the independent variables except capacity are held constant at their means. Capacity is an alternative-specific variable: hence, each individual has a different value for each party. The values of capacity for PP and IU are again held constant at their means. Now, if the individual attributes a capacity of +0.5 to PSOE, the probability of voting for this party is 0.93; if capacity is −0.5, the probability goes down to 0.63, a reduction of 0.30 points (the variable ranges from −2 to +2). Variations in capacity provoke huge changes in the probability of voting for parties, keeping constant the ideological positions and all other independent variables.

If we want to explain the asymmetry between PP and PSOE in terms of ideological voting, as reflected in Table 2.2, we must then find differences in the distribution of opinions about capacity according to party. In other words, if ideological distance is powerful in predicting the vote for PP and less so for PSOE, it must be because people closer to PP attribute high capacity to this party, whereas people closer to PSOE have a worse opinion of PSOE's capacity. This is precisely what the data show. Using the ideological closeness variable of the previous section, it turns out that among those closer to PP, the mean values of capacity are +0.50 for PP, −0.98 for PSOE, and −0.40 for IU; among those closer to PSOE, the mean values are −0.07 for PSOE (note that it is a negative value), −0.38 for PP, and −0.33 for IU. Thus, people closer to PP have more positive views about their preferred party than people closer to PSOE about PSOE; moreover, people closer to PP have more negative views about PSOE than people closer to PSOE about PP.

It seems likely that the progressive loss of retentive power by PSOE was a consequence of a growing perception, even among people very close to the party, that its capacity was low. The fact that the party kept losing retentive power in 2000, after four years of being in opposition, shows that the incumbent's performance was not the only variable that could affect ideological voting. The internal disarray in the party, which actually was aggravated in the period 1996–2000, was equally important to account for the weakening of the ideological vote for this party. After the 2000 debacle, the party decided to renovate its leadership with a young team of people who had not participated in the long period of government (1982–96). The fact that in the 2004 elections the PSOE's retentive power increased by almost 20 percentage points (see Table 2.2) confirms how damaging internal quarrels and corruption had been for the capacity of the party.

In summary, the explanation of temporal variation in the vote share of parties has to do with two factors: first, the spatial distribution of voters and parties; second, judgments about the capacity and performance of parties, as reflected in their retentive power. The electoral decay of PSOE in the period 1986–2000 is a consequence of its loss of reliability.[37] In other words, this implies that a pure spatial model is not always sufficient to reconstruct the evolution of electoral results. When a party suffers internal problems or when a party in office is making ideologically inconsistent policy, it is necessary to add opinions about the party's reliability.

Conclusions

How can governments be accountable if voters vote ideologically? In the pure ideological spatial model, governments are not accountable: voters simply vote for the closer party. Closeness to parties is all that matters. Thus, parties are equal except for their ideological positions. There is little reason to suppose, however, that voters follow such a mechanical decision rule. Ideological considerations cannot be fully independent of considerations about how ideology is transformed into policies (party's ideological consistency) and how policies produce certain outcomes (party's capacity).

I have argued that ideological voting might be compatible with accountability when these two problems, ideological consistency and capacity, are taken into account. Unlike the standard spatial model in which these two problems are solved by assumption, I have shown that if a government makes decisions that lead voters to conclude that the government is ideologically inconsistent or that the government has low capacity, the decision rule of voting for the closer party can be violated, at least for the incumbent.

---

[37] For a different explanation of the role of ideology in the evolution of Spanish parties' vote share, see Torcal and Medina (2002).

People closer to the incumbent party than to any other party will not necessarily vote for it.

Ideological voting is not universal. It is instead a party-relative behavior.
Voters who think that the party in office is making inconsistent policy or
that the party is not capable because of its internal divisions will tend to
punish the incumbent, even if they are closer to it than to any other party.
The retentive power of parties, defined as the percentage of people who,
being ideologically closer to the party, vote for it, depends on consistency
and capacity.

The analysis of the Spanish case reveals that to understand the electoral
trend in the 1980s and 1990s, it is not enough to know the evolution of the
ideological distribution of voters. We also need to incorporate the effects
of consistency and capacity on ideological voting.

APPENDIX. THE IDEOLOGICAL CLOSENESS VARIABLE

The aim of constructing a closeness variable is to classify individuals in
terms of ideological distances. To calculate distances, I have used the
respondent's self-placement in the ideological scale (usually a 0–10 or 1–
10 scale) and the ideological positions that the respondent attributes to
the parties. There is some consensus in the spatial literature that using
respondents' subjective positions of parties is more reasonable and more
consistent with the underlying theory than using parties' mean position;
moreover, it seems that mean placements create a favorable bias for the
directional model (see Merrill and Grofman 1999: appendix 4.3).[38]

Not every party is introduced in the analysis. Irrelevant parties (i.e.,
parties with a vote share under 5 percent) are discarded. First, we know
that tiny parties do not attract voters regardless of their closeness. Second,
many small parties defend a single issue or compete in dimensions that
are not the left–right dimension I am studying here. In the case of Spain,
for instance, all regionalist or nationalist parties are not considered. This
means two things: distances to irrelevant parties are not calculated, and all
the voters who vote for irrelevant parties are eliminated from the sample.

---

[38] I have replicated the calculus of the retentive power of Spanish parties in 1996 (postelection
survey) using mean party placements. Some significant distortions emerge. For instance,
the retentive power of PSOE goes down to 37.2 percent (compared with 55.6 percent in
Table 2.4). Another consequence of using mean party placements is that it is no longer
possible to be equidistant because mean positions are not integers.

Let us represent the ideological distance to party P for individual i (the difference between i's ideal point and the placement of P by i) as d_i^P. Now, let $C_i(P_j)$ stand for the fact that individual i is closer to party j than to any other party, and $C_i(P_j = P_k)$ that individual i is equidistant between parties j and k and closer to j and k than to any other party. If we have four parties, P_1, P_2, P_3, and P_4, such that their order in the ideological scale is $P_1 < P_2 < P_3 < P_4$, then ideological closeness is calculated according to the following logical rules:[39]

$$C_i\left(P_1\right) \leftrightarrow \left(d_i^{P_1} < d_i^{P_2}\right) \& \left(d_i^{P_1} < d_i^{P_3}\right) \& \left(d_i^{P_1} < d_i^{P_4}\right)$$

$$C_i\left(P_1 = P_2\right) \leftrightarrow \left(d_i^{P_1} = d_i^{P_2}\right) \& \left(d_i^{P_1} < d_i^{P_3}\right) \& \left(d_i^{P_1} < d_i^{P_4}\right)$$

$$C_i\left(P_2\right) \leftrightarrow \left(d_i^{P_2} < d_i^{P_1}\right) \& \left(d_i^{P_2} < d_i^{P_3}\right) \& \left(d_i^{P_2} < d_i^{P_4}\right)$$

$$C_i\left(P_2 = P_3\right) \leftrightarrow \left(d_i^{P_2} = d_i^{P_3}\right) \& \left(d_i^{P_2} < d_i^{P_3}\right) \& \left(d_i^{P_2} < d_i^{P_4}\right)$$

$$C_i\left(P_3\right) \leftrightarrow \left(d_i^{P_3} < d_i^{P_1}\right) \& \left(d_i^{P_3} < d_i^{P_2}\right) \& \left(d_i^{P_3} < d_i^{P_4}\right)$$

$$C_i\left(P_3 = P_4\right) \leftrightarrow \left(d_i^{P_3} = d_i^{P_4}\right) \& \left(d_i^{P_3} < d_i^{P_1}\right) \& \left(d_i^{P_3} < d_i^{P_2}\right)$$

$$C_i\left(P_4\right) \leftrightarrow \left(d_i^{P_4} < d_i^{P_1}\right) \& \left(d_i^{P_4} < d_i^{P_2}\right) \& \left(d_i^{P_4} < d_i^{P_3}\right)$$

Note that if an individual does not answer either about his or her own ideological placement or about any party's placement, that person is excluded from the sample. This person is not acting according to the decision rule of the spatial model given that not all the relevant ideological distances can be calculated. The closeness variable includes a value for all those who do not have ideological distances to the relevant parties.

It is important to stress that ideological distances cannot be identified with party identification. It is one thing to "feel" close to a party and quite another to *be* close to it. The Spanish postelection survey of 2000 contained a question about feeling close to parties; 57 percent of respondents did not feel close to any party, but more than half of these people had values in the ideological closeness variable. However, for the 37 percent of the sample for whom ideological distance cannot be determined, 21.5 percent felt close to some party. The feeling of closeness has a much stronger relationship with past vote than ideological closeness. Hence, ideological closeness does not measure party identification: it is something else.

[39] Note that I only calculate equidistant values consistent with the initial ordering $P_1 < P_2 < P_3 < P_4$. Thus, I disregard the possibility of someone being equidistant between, say, PP and IU, because this implies that PSOE is not placed between PP and IU.

Because of the subjective nature of the ideological closeness variable, it could contain what is called in the literature a "projection effect"; that is, people tend to place preferred parties closer to their ideal points. Empirical studies show that the projection effect is small, however. I have recalculated the ideological closeness variable for the Spanish 1996 postelection survey, making an adjustment for the projection effect (see the procedure described in Merrill and Grofman 1999: appendix 5.1), but differences between the new and the original variables were negligible.

REFERENCES

Adams, James. 2001. *Party Competition and Responsible Party Government*. Ann Arbor: University of Michigan Press.

Adams, James, and Samuel Merrill, III. 1999. "Modeling Party Strategies and Policy Representation in Multiparty Elections: Why Are Strategies So Extreme?" *American Journal of Political Science* 43 (3): 765–91.

Almunia, Joaquín. 2001. *Memorias políticas*. Madrid: Aguilar.

Alvarez, R. Michael, and Jonathan Nagler. 1998. "When Politics and Models Collide: Estimating Models of Multiparty Elections." *American Journal of Political Science* 42 (1): 55–96.

Barreiro, Belén. 2002. "La progresiva desmovilización de la izquierda en España: un análisis de la abstención en las elecciones generales de 1986 a 2000." *Revista Española de Ciencia Política* 6: 183–205.

Barreiro, Belén. 2004. "14-M: Elecciones a la sombra del terrorismo." *Claves de la Razón Práctica* 141: 14–23.

Bawn, Kathleen. 1999. "Constructing 'Us': Ideology, Coalition Politics, and False Consciousness." *American Journal of Political Science* 43 (2): 303–34.

Budge, Ian. 1994. "A New Spatial Theory of Party Competition: Uncertainty, Ideology, and Policy Equilibria Viewed Comparatively and Temporally." *British Journal of Political Science* 24 (4): 443–67.

Caínzos, Miguel, and Fernando Jiménez. 2000. "El impacto de los escándalos de corrupción sobre el voto en las elecciones generales de 1996." *Historia y Política* 4: 93–133.

Carabaña, Julio. 2001. "Clase, voto y políticas sociales en España, 1982–2000." *Zona Abierta* 96: 7–55.

Downs, Anthony. 1957. *An Economic Theory of Democracy*. New York: Harper & Row.

Enelow, James M., and Melvin J. Hinich. 1982. "Nonspatial Candidate Characteristics and Electoral Competition." *Journal of Politics* 44 (1): 115–30.

Enelow, James M., and Melvin J. Hinich. 1984. *The Spatial Theory of Voting. An Introduction*. Cambridge: Cambridge University Press.

Enelow, James M., James W. Endersby, and Michael C. Munger. 1995. "A Revised Probabilistic Model of Elections: Theory and Evidence." In Bernard Grofman (ed.), *Information, Participation, and Choice* (pp. 125–40). Ann Arbor: University of Michigan Press.

Fearon, James D. 1999. "Electoral Accountability and the Control of Politicians: Selecting Good Types Versus Sanctioning Poor Performance." In Bernard Manin, Adam Przeworski, and Susan Stokes (eds.), *Democracy, Accountability, and Representation* (pp. 55–97). Cambridge: Cambridge University Press.

Ferejohn, John. 1986. "Incumbent Performance and Electoral Control." *Public Choice* 50 (1–1): 5–25.

Ferejohn, John. 1995. "The Spatial Model and Elections." In Bernard Grofman (ed.), *Information, Participation, and Choice* (pp. 107–24). Ann Arbor: University of Michigan Press.

Fiorina, Morris P. 1990. "Information and Rationality in Elections." In John A. Ferejohn and James H. Kuklinsky (eds.), *Information and Democratic Processes* (pp. 329–42). Urbana: University of Illinois Press.

Gabel, Matthew J., and John D. Huber. 2000. "Putting Parties in Their Place: Inferring Party Left–Right Ideological Positions from Party Manifestos Data." *American Journal of Political Science* 44 (1): 94–103.

Groseclose, Tim. 2001. "A Model of Candidate Location When One Candidate Has a Valence Advantage." *American Journal of Political Science* 45 (4): 862–86.

Hinich, Melvin J., and Michael C. Munger. 1996. *Ideology and the Theory of Political Choice*. Ann Arbor: University of Michigan Press.

Hinich, Melvin J., and Michael C. Munger. 1997. *Analytical Politics*. Cambridge: Cambridge University Press.

Kreps, David. 1990. "Corporate Culture and Economic Theory." In James E. Alt and Kenneth A. Shepsle (eds.), *Perspectives on Positive Political Economy* (pp. 90–143). Cambridge: Cambridge University Press.

Lago, Ignacio, and José Ramón Montero. 2005. "Del 11-M al 14-M: los mecanismos del cambio electoral." *Claves de la Razón Práctica* 149: 36–45.

Long, J. Scott, and Jeremy Freese. 2001. *Regression Models for Categorical Dependent Variables Using Stata*. College Station, TX: Stata Press.

Manin, Bernard, Adam Przeworski, and Susan Stokes. 1999. "Elections and Representation." In Bernard Manin, Adam Przeworski, and Susan Stokes (eds.), *Democracy, Accountability, and Representation* (pp. 29–54). Cambridge: Cambridge University Press.

Maravall, José María. 1999. "Accountability and Manipulation." In Bernard Manin, Adam Przeworski, and Susan Stokes (eds.), *Democracy, Accountability, and Representation* (pp. 154–96). Cambridge: Cambridge University Press.

Merrill III, Samuel, and Bernard Grofman. 1999. *A Unified Theory of Voting. Directional and Proximity Spatial Models*. Cambridge: Cambridge University Press.

Palfrey, Thomas R., and Keith T. Poole. 1987. "The Relationship between Information, Ideology, and Voting Behavior." *American Journal of Political Science* 31 (3): 511–30.

Pierce, Roy. 1995. *Choosing the Chief. Presidential Elections in France and the United States*. Ann Arbor: University of Michigan Press.

Powers, Daniel A., and Yu Xie. 2000. *Statistical Methods for Categorical Data Analysis*. San Diego, CA: Academic Press.

Sánchez-Cuenca, Ignacio, and Belén Barreiro. 2000. *Los efectos de la acción de gobierno en el voto durante la etapa socialista (1982–1996)*. Madrid: Centro de Investigaciones Sociológicas.

Thurner, Paul W. 2000. "The Empirical Application of the Spatial Theory of Voting in Multiparty Systems with Random Utility Models." *Electoral Studies* 19 (4): 493–517.

Torcal, Mariano y Lucía Medina. 2002. "Ideología y voto en España 1979–2000: los procesos de reconstrucción racional de la identificación ideológica." *Revista Española de Ciencia Política* 6: 17–56.

CHAPTER THREE

Enduring Ethnicity: The Political Survival of Incumbent Ethnic Parties in Western Democracies

Sonia Alonso

Introduction

Ethnonationalist parties have been successful in mobilizing voters within Western parliamentary democracies. In their century-long existence, these parties have helped foster ethnic identities as well as voter loyalty and electoral support. In so doing, they have drawn supporters away from parties on the left and the right; they have pushed their agendas for autonomy and devolution, for cultural protection, revival, and assertion; they have built stable and, in many cases, large and enduring constituencies; their numbers have mushroomed in the multiethnic political systems of the West. One might even claim that ethnonationalist parties in Western parliamentary democracies have done better than class-based parties. For example, at the start of the twenty-first century, they continue to increase their electoral support while class-based parties have difficulties maintaining their past electoral records. The saliency of the ethnic cleavage not only endures but is growing stronger as class seems to fade in Western postindustrial societies (Table 3.1). Why have ethnonationalist parties been comparatively successful?

One possible answer could be that ethnic identities, once created, tend to be stable. Ethnic voters are more rigid in their loyalties than other types of voters, and ethnonationalist parties transform this rigidity into an electoral advantage. There is no agreement among social scientists about how strongly individuals are tied to their ethnic identities. *Primordialists* would say that people think about ethnicity in primordial terms and, therefore, individual ethnic identities, once constructed, are highly perdurable (Geertz 1973; Gellner 1983; Horowitz 1985; Gil-White 1999; Van Evera 2001). When voting is mainly based on ethnic membership, an ethnonationalist party's electoral performance is expected to be stable

Table 3.1. Average Shares of the Vote of the Largest Ethnonationalist Party and the Total Ethnic Group Parties in Subnational Elections (Western Parliamentary Democracies, 1948–2004)

Region	Ethnic group	Largest nationalist party		Total nationalist parties	
		1948–1976	1977–2004	1948–1976	1977–2004
Basque Country	Basques	–	33.9	–	60.0
Catalonia	Catalans	–	39.8	–	48.4
Navarre	Basques	–	11.4	–	16.6
Galicia	Gallegos	–	14.2	–	17.0
Valle d'Aosta	Francophones	15.2	33.2	15.2	33.4
South Tyrol	Austrians	62.7	57.9	64.5	64.1
Faeroe Islands	Faeroese	24.4	20.2	47.8	57.1
Greenland	Inuit	–	38.1	–	53.9
N. Ireland	Irish Protestants	33.8	24.5	43.2	53.8
N. Ireland	Irish Catholics	23.0	19.8	12.5	36.5
Quebec	Francophones	31.6	41.5	31.6	41.5
Flanders	Flemish	13.3	11.7	13.3	17.3

election after election as a straightforward reflection of ethnic demography (Horowitz 1985: 326). Incumbent ethnonationalist parties would then be highly immune to electoral punishment. In contrast, *constructivists* would say that individual ethnic identities are easily changeable and highly malleable by political entrepreneurs[1] (Brass 1997; Fearon and Laitin 2000b; Chandra 2001, 2004; Brubaker 2004). Therefore, we should not expect a priori more stable support for ethnonationalist parties than for any other type of party. A lot would depend on the parties' strategies of mobilization given particular institutional and sociodemographic conditions. Parties do not simply mirror society; therefore, the electoral performances of ethnonationalist parties are not mere reflections of ethnic demography. Yet why, then, do ethnonationalist parties seem to do better than class-based parties? What is special about them that class-based parties do not possess and therefore cannot use to their advantage?

---

[1] For a good discussion of the ongoing academic debate between primordialists and constructivists, see Hale (2004).

Let us suppose that ethnic and class-based parties are indistinguishable from one another in terms of voters' loyalties but they are judged by voters using different criteria. Ethnonationalist parties are judged according to their defense of the ethnonationalist program of national independence and ethnic hegemony. Thus, they are *relatively* immune to electoral punishment stemming from government performance as conventionally defined in economic terms. Class-based parties, on the contrary, are judged sensitively by voters on economic matters. This supposition is not merely theoretical; it has empirical substance. There is some evidence that ethnonationalist parties are not judged by voters according to government performance. In their contribution to this volume, Aguilar and Sánchez-Cuenca show how nationalist voters tend to exonerate nationalist regional governments when the performance is poor. This is so because, again following Aguilar and Sánchez-Cuenca, voters decide "not so much in terms of outcomes or government performance but in terms of the capacity of the government to represent the group that considers itself to have a national identity different from the rest" (see Chapter 4).

If this difference in the way voters judge the two types of parties were so, it could then become a competitive advantage for ethnonationalist parties. Economic policies are usually, although not necessarily, easier to judge by voters than cultural, linguistic, or any other type of nation-building policies, if only for the facility to observe them and quantify their consequences. The impact of economic policies is measured in figures. The impact of nation-building policies, and of assertive nationalist policies vis-à-vis the state, is rarely quantified in such manner (except, perhaps, language policies), given their nature.[2] Economic policies have an immediate impact in the lives of citizens; nation-building policies are only felt in the medium and long term. Finally, economic policies are more prone to crises and failures than nation-building policies because they depend not only on the government's actions but also on factors outside government control. Moreover, governments are sometimes forced to implement unpopular economic policies to avoid a deterioration of the economy that could jeopardize their hold to power. Incumbent ethnonationalist parties, however, do not need

---

[2] Think, for example, of a typical, direct, and effective way to apply a nation-building policy – namely, changing the content of history books in schools. This type of action is of a more subtle nature than, say, an increase in the price of electricity or in the level of unemployment. The perception of the first policy is not immediately available. The perception of the second not only is available, but it is also easily quantifiable in figures everybody understands, and, moreover, its consequences are felt immediately.

to implement nation-building policies that are known to be highly unpopular. They can wait for a better moment.

To evaluate whether ethnonationalist parties have a competitive advantage over class parties and, if so, to what extent, one must first answer a number of questions. First, is the support for ethnonationalist parties more stable than for class-based parties? Second, are ethnonationalist parties more successful in holding on to office? Third, are ethnic and class parties punished differently by voters?

This chapter focuses on parties and governments at the substate level of federal or quasi-federal states. It examines aggregate data, relying on three principal empirical measures dealing with electoral performance, fluctuation in voter support, and duration in office. It is structured as follows. The next section lays out a theoretical perspective on ethnonationalist parties and pays particular attention to their strategies and the institutional context within which these strategies fail or succeed. Some hypotheses concerning the differences between class-based parties and ethnonationalist parties with respect to electoral performance and political survival are stated. The third section describes the variables and the way they have been measured. Sections four and five then turn to an empirical evaluation of the connection between the type of party and the prospects of electoral success and long incumbencies. Finally, some conclusions are presented.

Ethnonationalist Parties and the Institutional Context

Nationalism is a political doctrine according to which there has to be congruence between nation and state. A nationalist political agenda aims at rendering the boundaries of the nation congruent with those of the state (Hechter 2000). Common to all nationalisms is an assertion of the primacy of national identity over the claims of class, religion, or humanity in general. Ethnonationalism, however, makes ethnicity the stuff of which the national identity is made. An ethnic group is "a group larger than a family, for which membership is reckoned primarily by descent, is conceptually autonomous, and has a conventionally recognized 'natural history' as a group" (Fearon and Laitin 2000a: 20). For ethnonationalists, the natural history of the ethnic group is the natural history of the nation.

An ethnonationalist party is one that pursues the maximalist political program of independent statehood for the nation it claims to represent and ethnic homogeneity within the territory of this nation.[3] This constitutes the ethnic party's long-term political and policy program, its raison d'être. In the short term, however, an ethnic party may engage in moderate and accommodating action strategies and policy agendas to push forward its long-term political program. This difference between the short-term and the long-term objectives of ethnic parties clearly indicates that what is recognized as primordially given, and thus "ethnic," is a matter of political negotiation and convention. Ethnic identities are malleable, and nationalist parties make of this malleability a centerpiece of their political and electoral strategies. Indeed, they have moved historically from "ethnicity by birth" to "ethnicity by choice" as a strategic move away from the straitjacket of sociodemographic constraints in those regions where ethnic demography was not an asset but an obstacle.

Ethnic parties must craft a constituency large enough to get them in government and loyal enough to keep them in office to pursue their long-term political and policy programs. This, in turn, depends on the successful construction and mobilization of an ethnic political identity. There is no structural limit to this activity. Ethnic demography may constrain or facilitate this endeavor, but it certainly does not determine the maximum number of voters that ethnic parties can aspire to mobilize.[4] The only limit to the construction and mobilization of ethnic identities by nationalist parties comes from the competition for votes and power with other parties.[5]

Historically, ethnic parties in Western democracies have had to compete with parties based on other social cleavages, such as religion and class, for voters' support. The saliency of the ethnic cleavage has thus been tempered by its coexistence with other ideological allegiances. The political relevance of social cleavages is not exogenous to the mobilization strategies of political parties. The weakening of the class cleavage in postindustrial Western countries is in part connected to the leftist parties' strategy of gaining electoral support by extending their appeal beyond the working

---

[3] From this point on, I refer to ethnonationalist parties as ethnic parties or nationalist parties without distinction for the sake of language simplicity.

[4] Applying Przeworski and Sprague's thesis on socialist parties to ethnonationalist parties, "the voting behaviour of individuals is an effect of the activities of political parties. More precisely, the relative salience of class [*ethnicity*] as a determinant of individual voting behaviour is a cumulative consequence of the strategies pursued by [*ethno-nationalist*] political parties" (Przeworski and Sprague 1986: 9).

[5] "A sociological theory of preference formation can identify the clienteles. . . . It is insufficient, however, for predicting the rise of parties . . . because their emergence depends on the strategic interaction of existing parties in the competitive system" (Kitschelt and McGann 1997:14).

class (Przeworski and Sprague 1986). Similarly, changes in the influence of the ethnic cleavage are partly due to the nationalist parties' strategy of gaining electoral support by redefining the concept of ethnicity. The ethnic group has been redefined to include all those who share the nationalist program, irrespective of ethnic origin. It is paradoxical that the same type of party strategy – expanding the electoral appeal beyond the core group – has led to diverging processes for class parties and ethnic parties: a weakening of class and a strengthening of ethnonationalism.

However, the structure of party competition is determined not only by the number of cleavages but also by the electoral system (Powell 1982; Amorim Neto and Cox 1997). Electoral systems, like any institutional structure, afford actors different incentives and at the same time pose different constraints. As the saliency of ethnonational identities increases, so does electoral competition for the nationalist cause. Ethnonationalist parties are, in consequence, liable to being preempted either by other, nonethnic parties or by their own radical flanks.

Under proportional electoral arrangements (PR), party systems are usually fragmented, and electoral majorities are difficult to achieve. However, such majorities are not indispensable for participation in government. PR ensures the biggest parties at least a share of the regional government. This, in turn, offers these parties the chance to pursue long-term policy objectives, something extremely important for a nationalist party. Therefore, the incentive to become the biggest party in the region, even if not the majoritarian one, is strong. At the same time, PR makes it possible for more radical groups to survive as separate political forces, allowing the major nationalist parties to appeal more effectively to a larger group of more moderate voters. As a result, there is always more than one nationalist party competing for votes. Thus, although the nationalist camp may be electorally reinforced as a whole, the major nationalist party loses potential voters, and the electoral competition extends beyond the nationalist–nonnationalist bloc to the nationalist bloc itself. Indeed, the tendency everywhere in the last decades has been toward an increased fragmentation within the nationalist bloc toward more and smaller parties.[6]

Hence, PR encourages "within-bloc" shifts of allegiance rather than movements "between blocs." Dissatisfied voters will not need to change their ideological allegiances if they want to change their vote. They can

---

[6] Increased fragmentation of the ethnonationalist bloc, in contrast, brings about increased levels of regional assertiveness (Van Houten 2000).

always turn to another party within the same bloc. This will make party loyalty more difficult to maintain, especially for the larger parties. In a PR setting with its various encapsulated electorates, the fluctuation in party fortunes can be high. This may induce conservative electoral strategies on the part of parties, and perhaps greater cooperation between parties rather than greater competition for votes (Ware 1987: 69).

The fragmentation of the nationalist bloc benefits parties of the non-nationalist bloc, offering them increased opportunities to control the regional government and, in extreme cases, to remain in it for long periods. However, if the nonnationalist bloc is itself fragmented, a likely event under PR, these advantages disappear.

Majoritarian winner-takes-all electoral arrangements lead to two-party systems.[7] Such a situation is usually marked by alternating control of the government by one of the two parties. Nationalist parties are unlikely to face competition within the nationalist bloc, but they may have difficulties reaching office if they are small. In addition, they need to rely on vote-maximizing electoral strategies, targeting the clienteles of the other major party. As a consequence, competition is fiercer between nonnationalist and nationalist parties.

Winner-take-all systems, therefore, encourage "between-bloc" shifts of allegiance rather than "within-bloc" shifts. Dissatisfied voters must change their ideological allegiances if they want to change their vote. This encourages party loyalty to a greater extent than is the case in PR systems. The fluctuation in the electoral fortunes of parties will then be lower.

The connection between electoral performance and survival in office is mostly an institutional artifact: it arises out of the electoral rules and the structure of the party system. Governing parties that lose votes do not always lose control of government. Therefore, survival in office only partly depends on voters' decisions regarding government's performance. In majoritarian bipartisan systems, loss of votes is more likely to bring about loss of office than in proportional multiparty systems. This is because in fragmented party systems, the formation of governments depends on postelectoral negotiations. An incumbent party in a coalition government that has lost votes may still be a necessary partner to form a new government. It is possible to find examples of coalition partners whose vote shares

---

[7] I do not exclude the possibility that there may be more than two parties in the system. For all intents and purposes, however, there are two major parties that can win the election and a number of minor parties.

move in opposite directions and whose aggregate vote support remains the same, thereby allowing all of them to remain in government. Thus, the connection between government performance and survival in office differs in majoritarian and PR systems. One might anticipate, then, that party duration in government is longer in PR systems.

If in PR fragmented party systems coalition governments are the norm, the programs offered by parties will not be implemented intact. The policies will be subject to bargaining inside the coalition. The connection between electoral promises and policy implementation will be weak (Ware 1987; Powell 2000). Therefore, the parties' elites know that they will not be expected to deliver their promises to get reelected. A wide literature suggests that the electoral costs of incumbency for parties in coalition governments are smaller, such governments do better in elections than single-party ones, and majority governments are more likely to lose office (King, Alt, Burns, and Laver 1990; Alt and King 1994; Diermeier and Stevenson 1999; Sáez Lozano 2002). Responsibility is more difficult to assign to particular parties, and, when in doubt, voters generally exonerate their own party.

The duration of parties in office is dependent on the passage of time. There are two hypotheses concerning this effect of time (Rose and Mackie 1983). According to the first, incumbency is a liability: the longer the time a party stays in office, the higher the likelihood that it will fall. This is so because parties will increasingly suffer the political erosion of mistakes, failures, political crises, and negative changes in the national and international context. This is why Rose and Mackie (1983: 119) write that "opposition is said to be the best position for a party to be in if it wishes to win the next election." According to the second hypothesis, incumbency gives parties considerable resources compared with those of the opposition: the control of the bureaucracy, patronage networks, privileged information, and so on. Therefore, the longer a party stays in government, the more resources it has at its disposal to stay even longer. Whether and under what circumstances incumbency is an asset or a liability for a party's electoral support and survival in power is an empirical question.

To summarize, if it is true that ethnic allegiances provide nationalist parties with a competitive electoral advantage over class-based parties, ceteris paribus (i.e., under similar institutional settings), ethnic parties should show lower fluctuation of votes, less electoral punishment, lengthier durations in office, and less political erosion with the passage of time than class-based parties.

Measuring the Variables

This chapter deals with two main questions: first, what are the effects of incumbency on ethnic parties, and, second, are these effects significantly different from those that arise for class-based parties? The analysis concentrates on the subnational governments of Canada (provinces), Spain (autonomous communities), Italy (regions), United Kingdom (only Northern Ireland),[8] and Denmark (special-status territories) during the last twenty to fifty-five years, depending on the country. All these countries contain ethnic minorities geographically concentrated and organized around ethnic parties. The subnational territories take two forms. The *ethnoregions* are those subnational territories that are home to an ethnic minority. As a consequence, they are assigned a special institutional status by the state constitution.[9] The *ordinary regions* are the rest of the subnational territories in which the state is divided. All the subnational territories included in the analysis have their own parliamentary and governmental structures with ample powers assigned to them.[10] However, ethnoregions have, by definition, wider competencies and a greater degree of political autonomy than ordinary regions.

In the ethnoregions, the number of social cleavages is higher and the party systems are more fragmented. As a general rule, this fragmentation, together with a PR system, makes single-party governments a rarity. Coalition governments are the norm in ethnoregions, except in Quebec where, because of the majoritarian electoral arrangement, the region is closer to a two-party system than any other ethnoregion and governments are

---

[8] This is so because in the other two special regions of the United Kingdom, Wales and Scotland, there have been only two elections to their respective regional assemblies, and this does not allow a long enough time span for the analysis of duration. In Northern Ireland, however, there have been elections to the regional assembly for forty-eight years between 1921 and 1969 (besides the two following devolution).

[9] These regions are Basque Country, South Tyrol, Catalonia, Faeroe Islands, Friuli-Venezia Giulia, Galicia, Greenland, Navarre, Quebec, Sardinia, Sicily, Trentino–Alto Adige, Trento, and Valle d'Aosta. In several ordinary regions in Spain (Aragon, Andalusia, Canary Islands, Valencia, and Balearic Islands), there are regional parties that compete with left–right parties for votes. However, these regions are not defined by constitution as having a qualitatively different procedure to achieve increased levels of autonomy from the rest. Also, these regional parties are more the result of the particular institutional setting of the Spanish autonomous communities than the product of a long historical process of mobilization of culturally distinctive groups.

[10] In Denmark and the United Kingdom, only the special-status territories are included in the analysis. This is because the rest of the state is organized in a unitary form, and there are no ordinary regions with subnational parliaments and governments.

usually single party. The incidence of coalition governments in is in fact high for the two types of regions: they represent 78.4 percent of governments overall. They are even more common within ethnoregions, where they contribute 86.5 percent of all observations as opposed to 73 percent in ordinary regions. Under majoritarian electoral systems, single-party governments are the norm. In proportional systems, single-party governments exist only if the opposition is highly fragmented – the party in government, even if small, is the biggest party in terms of votes and seats. Political parties are classified as ethnic and class-based. For purposes of this analysis, ethnic parties are to be found only in ethnoregions.

The analysis focuses on three main variables: electoral performance, vote fluctuation, and survival in office. The *electoral performance of incumbent parties* is measured as the average percentage of gains or losses of votes by a party during its period in office. A positive value would indicate a positive incumbency effect.[11] The electoral performance variable ranges from –13.21 for the party whose incumbency costs have been greatest to 8.94 for the party whose incumbency gain has been highest. The *fluctuation of votes* is measured as the coefficient of variation of the percentage of votes for one party during one *episode*. The coefficient of variation (the standard deviation divided by the mean) is calculated: $V = \frac{s}{\bar{x}}$. This coefficient provides a relative measure of variability – in this case, of vote fluctuation. The closer the coefficient is to 0, the lower the level of fluctuation. Coefficients over 1 represent high levels of fluctuation. This variable ranges from 0.005 for the lowest values to 1.2 for the highest. The coefficients are related to parties that rely to a greater extent on stable electoral clienteles or whose support comes, to a greater extent, from floating voters. The *survival (or duration) in office* is measured as the number of consecutive years that a political party stays in government. It ranges from 0.5 year for the shortest duration to 54 years for the longest.

The data set has 329 observations, or *episodes*. Each episode is a continuous period of time in which a party is in office. Of the 329 cases, 33 are right-censored; that is, the parties were still in office (or, in terms of duration data, the *event* – out of office – had not yet taken place). Therefore, the data set contains 296 events (i.e., completed episodes) and 33 "incomplete" episodes. Each complete episode is defined by a starting date – the

---

[11] For a similar application of this variable, see Rose and Mackie (1983) and Narud and Valen (2001).

date the party arrives to office – and an ending date – the date the party leaves office.[12] One party can be in office for two or more consecutive electoral periods. This implies that during one episode (one observation), a party may have been part of different governments, sometimes in coalition, sometimes alone. The duration variable, therefore, only gives us one piece of information – the number of consecutive years in office (or part of a year) – and the rest is captured by a list of independent variables such as "number of coalition governments in one episode" or "number of legislative periods in one episode."

The type of party is a dummy variable with a value of 1 for the ethnic parties and 0 for the class-based ones. The type of region is also a dummy variable, with a value of 1 for the ethnoregions and 0 for ordinary regions. The type of government to which the incumbent parties belong is a dummy variable called "single" with a value of 1 for those parties that have been in single-party governments during the whole episode. The value 0 is used for those parties that have been in coalition governments, or changed from coalition to single-party ones and vice versa, during their episodes in office. The size of the party is measured as the average percentage of votes during one episode. This indicator is an indirect way of measuring the level of fragmentation of the party system. The higher the level of fragmentation, the smaller the average size of parties within the system.

The analysis proceeds in the following way. First, I provide a description of the data on the three indicators. This is followed by the presentation of results related to estimates of the parameters of a hazard function for the likelihood of parties losing office. The aim of this analysis is to gain some insight into how survival in office is related to ethnicity, type of government (whether coalition or single-party), and the electoral performance of incumbent parties in government.

Description of the Data

According to the information presented in Table 3.2, in 61 percent of the subnational elections held in Canada, Spain, Italy, Denmark, and the United Kingdom since 1948, the vote share of incumbent parties has decreased. Incumbent ethnic parties have increased their vote share

---

[12] I have used the dates of elections as the times of entry and exit in and out of office. I am therefore assuming that the time a party remains in office as part of an interim government (i.e., between the dissolution of parliament and the formation of a new one) belongs to the same duration or episode.

Table 3.2. Electoral Performance of Incumbent Parties in Regional
Governments (1948–2001)

	Incumbent parties gaining votes at election time		Incumbent parties losing votes at election time		Total	
	N	%	N	%	N	%
Class-based parties	235	38.5%	376	61.5%	611	100%
Ethnic parties	52	41.9%	72	58.1%	124	100%
All	287	38.7%	448	61.3%	742	100%

42 percent of the time, as opposed to 38 percent of the time in the case of class-based parties. This difference does not seem large, although it still holds if we restrict the analysis to coalition governments, which are supposed to do better in elections than are single-party governments.[13]

If we look at the overall percentage of electoral losses and gains that incumbent parties have experienced during their time in office, we find that, on average, incumbent parties lost 1.2 percent of votes during their period in office (Table 3.3). The difference between ethnic and class-based parties is significant. On average, class-based parties lost 1.4 percent of votes during their period in office, as opposed to 0.01 percent in the case of ethnic parties. This difference still holds when we take into account only the ethnoregions. Here, the average electoral losses are 1.3 percent and 0.01 percent, respectively. In single-party governments, the average electoral losses are the same for ethnic and class-based parties. In coalition governments, however, ethnic parties gain more votes than they lose: 0.37 percent on average, as opposed to class-based parties, which lost 0.92 percent.

The evidence suggests that within the ethnoregions and within coalition governments, ethnic parties do better than class-based parties in terms of electoral performance. These differences in electoral performance suggest that ethnic parties and class-based parties have been judged differently: ethnic parties have been less severely treated than class-based parties.

---

[13] If we only analyze coalition governments, incumbent ethnic parties increase their vote share 42 percent of the time compared with 39 percent in the case of class-based parties.

Table 3.3. Electoral Performance, Fluctuation of Votes, and Survival in Office for Different Subsamples: Descriptive Statistics

	Electoral performance (average percent losses/gains)	Fluctuation of votes (coefficient of variation)	Duration in office (average number of years)
Ethnic parties	**−0.01**	0.23	8.2
Class-based parties	**−1.4**	0.21	8.4
Ethnic regions	−0.8	**0.25**	7.8
Ethnic parties	−0.01	0.26	7.4
Class-based parties	−1.31	0.22	8.6
Ordinary regions (class parties)	−1.5	**0.18**	8.8
Coalition govs.	**−0.7**	**0.22**	**7.8**
Ethnic parties	**0.37**	0.23	7.16
Class-based parties	**−0.92**	0.22	7.96
Single-party govs.	**−2.8**	**0.17**	**10.0**
Ethnic parties	−2.09	0.20	10.03[a]
Class-based parties	−2.83	0.16	10.05
All	−1.2	0.21	7.6

Note: Bold figures indicate that the comparison of means test is statistically significant at least at the 0.05 level.

[a] The case of the Unionists in Northern Ireland, who were in office alone for a total of 47 years, has been excluded, because, as an extreme outlier, it has a disproportionate effect over the average. With the Unionists included in the calculation, the average duration of ethnic parties in single-party governments is 16.02 years.

Let us look more closely into the coalition governments in ethnoregions, where class parties compete for voters with ethnic parties. Most coalitions are mixed, that is, formed by a combination of ethnic and class parties. There are only eight observations that correspond to coalitions composed exclusively of ethnic parties. Mixed coalitions have a lower average loss of votes than homogeneous ones (either exclusively nonethnic or exclusively ethnic). At the same time, the maximum electoral gain achieved is considerably higher in mixed coalitions than in homogeneous ones (Table 3.4). Ethnic parties' voters are happy to reward nationalist politicians who show flexibility in their alliances. This is prima facie evidence against the rigidity of nationalist voters and nationalist parties.[14]

[14] Nor do mixed coalitions seem an impediment for longer durations in power. The mean duration of parties in office in homogeneous coalitions is 6.3 as opposed to 7.6 in mixed coalitions. The ethnic party that has lasted longer as part of an exclusively ethnic coalition

Table 3.4. The Electoral Performance of Parties in Homogeneous and Mixed Coalitions

	N	Min.	Max.	Median	S
Homogeneous coalitions	90	−11.8	2.8	−0.8	1.89
Mixed coalitions	87	−9.6	8.94	−0.55	3.34

Electoral costs are more severe for parties in single-party governments. Here, ethnic parties and class-based parties are equally punished. This is probably related to the fact that the clarity of responsibility is higher among single-party governments. The basic argument in the literature is that coalition governments obscure accountability and, as a consequence, the ability of the electorate to assign responsibilities is reduced. Therefore, voters will be less able to target electoral punishments and rewards. The empirical evidence confirms that coalition parties do better in elections.

The mean level of vote fluctuation for the data set as a whole is 0.21 (see Table 3.3). Parties with a very high level (coefficient of variation over 1) are a minority (4.25 percent). Levels of fluctuation over 1 are generally related to an electoral debacle. Therefore, it is not so much an indication of an unstable electorate but of the loss of both floating voters and long-term party identifiers. A majority of the parties (70.8 percent) have levels of vote fluctuation under the mean value. This stability of votes can be due to the strength of the voters' ideological and ethnic ties.

For ethnic and class-based parties, the fluctuation in their share of the vote is equally low. Although there is no evidence of higher vote stability for ethnic parties, a significant difference exists between parties in ethnoregions and ordinary regions. The fluctuation of votes in ethnoregions is, on average, 30 percent higher than the fluctuation that takes place in ordinary regions: 0.25 and 0.18, respectively. This is probably due to the differences in the structure of party competition. Fragmented party systems bring about higher levels of electoral volatility.[15] In the fragmented party systems of the ethnoregions, voters with strong ethnic or ideological ties

has been in office for 15.8 years. The ethnic party that has lasted longer as part of a mixed coalition has been in office for 54 years.

[15] There has been a historical tendency toward increased fragmentation of the nationalist bloc, as shown in Table 3.1, if one compares the differences in votes shares between the largest nationalist party and all the nationalist parties considered together.

who are dissatisfied do not need to change their ethnic or ideological allegiances when changing their votes. They can always turn to another party within the same ideological or ethnic bloc. However, voters with multiple identities can change more easily between blocs. This wider choice provides them the opportunity to switch their vote to or from incumbent parties, rewarding or punishing them. Consequently, the reason for the higher level of vote fluctuation in ethnoregions may simply be that the fragmentation of the party system yields greater choice for the voters – that is, greater opportunities to express their satisfaction or dissatisfaction with the party they had previously supported. The fluctuation of votes, therefore, is not only a function of ideological preferences but also of what else is on offer.[16]

The mean duration of incumbent parties in regional governments is 7.6 years. Only 14.5 percent of all episodes in the data set are four or more legislative periods long. The duration in office of ethnic and class-based parties is similar: 8.2 and 8.4 years, respectively (see Table 3.3). Incumbent parties in ordinary regions stay, on average, one year longer in office than parties in ethnoregions. This difference is statistically insignificant.

To sum up, ethnic and class parties are indistinguishable in terms of vote fluctuation and time length in office. However, the electoral performance of ethnic parties seems to be better than that of class parties, especially when both types of party are in office together forming a coalition government.

The Likelihood of Ethnic Parties Losing Office

The duration model of Table 3.5 shows how long it takes for an *event* to happen. This is the dependent variable – the occurrence of an event. Falling from office is the event, a transition from being in office to being out of office. The time interval between entry to and exit from a specific state is

---

[16] The fluctuation of votes may also be capturing long-term processes. High levels of vote fluctuation could indicate a process of continuous loss of support for an incumbent party election after election, as is the case of the Christian Democrats in Italy. It could also result from the formation of new parties, either as a consequence of an internal split (as is the case of the Basque Nationalist Party and Eusko Alkartasuna in Spain) or as a consequence of a new cleavage entering the competition between parties (as in Quebec in the 1960s, when a party defending the cause of French Canadians appeared, after decades in which the French–English cleavage was part of the liberal–conservative party competition). For a discussion of the Quebec case during the decades previous to the formation of the Parti Québécois, see Filley (1956).

Table 3.5. Likelihood of Parties Losing Office (Weibull Distribution)

	All	Ethnic parties	Class-based parties
Event	220	31	189
Censored	24	8	16
Total	244	39	205
	Coefficient	Coefficient	Coefficient
Ethnic party	−0.039	−	−
	(0.224)		
Ethnoregion	0.462***	−	0.418***
	(0.159)		(0.160)
Party size (% avg. vote)	−0.045***	−0.111***	−0.039***
	(0.006)	(0.027)	(0.007)
Electoral performance	−0.106***	−0.009	−0.133***
	(0.031)	(0.055)	(0.033)
Single-party governments	0.057	0.610	0.260
	(0.297)	(0.812)	(0.335)
PR electoral system	−0.556*	−1.875**	−0.132
	(0.321)	(0.879)	(0.354)
Constant	−2.340***	0.035	−2.989
	(0.370)	(0.895)	(0.440)
p parameter [h(t) > 1]	1.34***	1.44***	1.38**
	(0.067)	(0.212)	(0.077)
$\chi 2$	68.43***	29.82***	49.39***
Log likelihood	−300.29	−44.82	−247.34

Note: Standard errors are in parentheses.*Significant at 10%; **significant at 5%; ***significant at 1%.

defined as an episode or duration. Therefore, the time an incumbent party persists in office is a duration.[17]

Hazard functions tell us the risk that the event (losing office) takes place at a point in time, given that it has not occurred before during this episode. There are different ways to fit a duration model. The parametric models,

---

[17] The most restricted duration model is based on a process with only a *single episode* and *two states* (one *origin* and one *destination* state). This is the form used here. For simplicity, I have treated the data as if they were single episodes, although the same party can be in and out of office more than once. This does not affect the results because the object of the research is not the trajectory of the unit of analysis in and out of a particular state across time. My interest lies in the general pattern of the transition rate from the incumbency state to the out-of-office state. If for each unit of analysis only one episode is considered, as is the case here, then the number of records in the data file corresponds to the number of units.

such as the exponential and the Weibull models, define a specific functional form for the baseline hazard function (the effect of time on the transition rate). All the regressions I present here are Weibull regressions, which assume that the hazard rate increases (h(t) >1) or decreases (h(t) <1) monotonically over time; in other words, the risk of losing office increases or decreases as a function of time. This model best tests whether the passage of time has an erosion effect over incumbent parties. The estimated p parameter must be positive and higher than 1 if the assumption of increasing risks of losing office is correct. When the p parameter is lower than 1, the risk of losing office decreases with time. The estimation of a Weibull model for different subsamples of the data set will allow us to see whether the effects of incumbency vary for different types of parties.

The results in Table 3.5 show that the likelihood of losing office decreases with party size, a good electoral performance, and a PR system; the likelihood is greater for those parties that are located in ethnoregions. With respect to the time dependency of the transition rate, the estimations of the p parameter are always higher than 1; this implies that the assumption of increasing risks of losing office over time holds. In sum, the results confirm the existence of a negative incumbency effect: with the passage of time, incumbent parties suffer the political erosion of office.

Other things being equal, the ethnic- or class-based character of parties does not seem to be connected to survival in office. The coefficient for the ethnic party term is not statistically significant. Given that ethnic parties, on average, do slightly better at the polls than class-based parties (see Table 3.3), this shows a weak connection between electoral performance and survival in office in the case of incumbent ethnic parties. In fact, this is confirmed if one looks at the separate regressions for ethnic and class-based parties. The political survival of class-based parties is sensitive to electoral gains and losses. For ethnic parties, however, electoral performance is unrelated to losing office. The reasons for losing incumbency probably differ between both types of party. Ethnic parties' survival in office depends less on voters' decisions and more on coalition politics and on the institutional structure in which they operate. Proportional electoral systems seem to benefit ethnic parties more than they do class-based parties. The presence of a PR system is associated with a large reduction in the likelihood of losing office for ethnic parties.

Given that there is only one ethnic party that competes in elections in a majoritarian electoral system, the Parti Québécois, the PR coefficient is mainly capturing the damage that the absence of proportionality can inflict on the electoral prospects and the political survival of ethnic parties competing for votes with class-based parties. An ethnic party in a winner-takes-all electoral system, such as the Parti Québécois in Quebec, has to engage in vote-maximizing strategies to a far greater extent than a similar party in a PR system. Therefore, when competing with class-based parties, it will try to appeal to voters beyond its "natural" electorate, the pool of ethnic voters. This requires broadening the policy program to emphasize socioeconomic issues not directly related to the maximalist nationalist program of independence and ethnic hegemony. It also requires moving away from extreme positions and appealing to the median voter. Emphasizing socioeconomic issues encourages voters to be more attentive to the performance of the ethnic party in office. One could say that the institutional incentives to appeal to a broadened electorate push ethnic parties to bring on themselves more severe voters' judgments in terms of performance. Moving away from the maximalist nationalist program dilutes the saliency of the ethnonationalist cleavage in the eyes of voters and may eventually reduce the rigidity and intensity of these voters' ethnic allegiances.

For an ethnic party in a PR fragmented party system, the opposite holds. Ethnic parties in fragmented systems have incentives to engage in conservative electoral strategies. Their principal objective is to maintain their vote share to remain a necessary coalition partner. These parties do not need to dilute the saliency of the ethnonational cleavage nor emphasize socioeconomic issues to attract voters from class-based parties. This would only be necessary when the competition for votes within the nationalist bloc is fierce. Voters are therefore encouraged to judge ethnic parties according to their defense of the nationalist program, maximalist or not, rather than according to the government's performance on socioeconomic issues.[18] One can conclude that the encapsulated electorates of fragmented party systems judge ethnic parties' government performance less severely than class-based parties' performance. This seems to be indirectly confirmed by

[18] Fernández-Albertos (2002) has shown that the saliency of the ethnic cleavage as the basis for voters' decisions increased in the Basque Country since 1979. During the first half of the 1990s, the left–right dimension was more relevant than the nationalist dimension in the electoral calculus of all voters from the Basque Country, both in national and regional elections. After the mid-1990s, however, this was reversed. This tendency was in part the result of the electoral strategies pursued by the Basque Nationalist Party, using the advantages of incumbency to encourage voters to vote according to their nationalist allegiances more than to the class-based ones.

Table 3.6. Electoral Performance, Fluctuation of Votes, and Duration in Office among Big Parties (Average Vote Share over 25 Percent)

Type of party	Electoral performance (average percent losses/gains)	Fluctuation of votes (coefficient of variation)	Duration in office (average number of years)	N
Ethnic parties	−0.55	0.16	16.4	15
Class-based parties	−2.17	0.14	12.3	97
PR system	−1.37	0.12	13.9	70
Majoritarian system	−2.9	0.17	11.1	42

the empirical results. The survival analysis shows that class-based parties in ethnoregions do worse than ethnic parties.[19] Class-based parties' likelihood of losing office increases considerably if these parties are situated in an ethnoregion and, therefore, if they are competing for votes with ethnic parties. As shown in Table 3.3, they receive larger electoral punishments than ethnic parties because they are judged more severely in terms of performance.

The size of parties seems to be more important for ethnic parties than for class-based parties. Clearly, large ethnic parties do better at the polls than large class-based parties. Also, large ethnic parties tend to remain in office for longer periods of time (Table 3.6). The difference between large ethnic and class parties may, again, be institutionally rooted. The largest ethnic parties are all situated in PR systems. Large parties in proportional systems may indicate that the opposition is highly fragmented. If this is so, an ethnic party is more likely to be resilient in office despite poor government performance than is a class-based party. They will be able to implement their long-term nationalist program and deemphasize the relevance of socioeconomic issues and of government's economic performance. As a result, voters will judge them less on the basis of performance as conventionally understood and more on the basis of the defense of the nationalist program. Class-based parties, by the very nature of their ideological stance, cannot do so.

---

[19] Remember that ethnic parties are only to be found in ethnoregions, whereas class-based parties exist in both ethnoregions and ordinary regions.

Conclusions: Ethnic Parties and Political Accountability

The ability of citizens to change their government when they do not approve of its actions is the sharpest difference between dictatorship and democracy. It is the behavior of voters at the polls that ensures democratic representation. Politicians know that to remain in office, they need to look after citizens' interests rather than their own. Otherwise, they can lose their offices and the perquisites that go with them. In blunt terms, the better they look after the interests of citizens, the longer they will stay in power.

Even when governments act in the best interest of citizens, however, they make mistakes and are liable to policy failures. If politicians are truly accountable to citizens, political parties will rotate in office. After all, "[a] democracy predicated on the ability to 'throw the rascals out' is far less convincing when it exists only in the abstract than when it is backed up by periodic examples of rascals actually flying through the doors" (Pempel 1990: 7).

The evidence presented in this chapter makes two points clear. First, not all incumbent parties are equally punished and rewarded at election time by citizens. Second, even if citizens punish politicians, alternation in office does not immediately follow. Certain institutional contexts make the relationship between electoral performance and survival in office a weak one.

The empirical evidence presented in the chapter suggests that class-based parties are more severely punished than ethnonationalist parties when they fail in the pursuit of the citizens' interests. So voters use different criteria for judging class and ethnic parties. The interests of citizens are highly heterogeneous, and political parties tend to specialize in one coherent set of interests among all the possible sets available. Class-based parties, by their very nature, specialize in those interests related to the individual's position in the class structure. Ethnic parties specialize in those interests related to the cultural and ethnic identity of individuals. When citizens judge how well an incumbent party has defended their interests, the criteria they use for class-based parties and ethnic parties differ. Ethnic parties tend to be judged by their furtherance of the ethnonationalist program of national independence and ethnic homogeneity. Class-based parties tend to be judged according to the economic benefits they produce and the protection of the material interests of particular social strata.

101

Economic interests are more prone to failures, mistakes, and criticisms than any other set of interests if only because of the facility to observe them in the everyday lives of citizens. Cultural and ethnic interests, in contrast, are less tangible and have a less direct impact on the everyday well-being of citizens. Thus, voters' judgments will be less severe and frequent in those policy realms where failures can be disguised and setbacks can be presented as advances, as happens with nationalist policies.

Under particular institutional circumstances, the difference in the way that voters judge the two types of parties becomes a competitive advantage for ethnic parties. Voters judge an ethnic party less severely when it shares office with other parties, especially with class-based parties, than when it is in office alone. Governments made up of only one party are similarly judged by voters, irrespective of the type of party. An ethnic party in office alone will probably be judged not only by its defense of the ethnonationalist program but also by its economic performance. How much of the voters' judgment will rely on one aspect or the other is, of course, an empirical question. In any case, an ethnic party in a single-party government cannot expect to be exonerated as easily as an ethnic party in a coalition.[20]

In the case of mixed coalitions, where the ethnic party shares power with a class-based party, it is the class party that is punished more severely by voters. The class party will be judged according to the government's economic performance. In the case of homogeneous coalitions, ethnic parties are also less severely punished than class parties. A homogeneous class coalition will focus its policies on socioeconomic matters and will be judged with more demanding criteria. In sum, proportional electoral systems offer ethnic parties a competitive advantage over class-based parties because they make coalition governments a much more likely occurrence than majoritarian electoral systems.

Little evidence can be shown to support the argument that ethnic voters are more rigid than class voters in their allegiances. The fluctuation in the vote shares for political parties is low in all cases, irrespective of the type of party. It is only the ideological proximity between parties that increases vote fluctuation. This is so because voters do not have to change their ethnic or class allegiances to change their vote. Moreover, ethnic voters seem willing to reward nationalist politicians who show flexibility in

---

[20] The only exception would be that of a single-party government in a region where, for historical reasons, the saliency of the ethnonational cleavage is overwhelming. This would explain why the Südtiroler Volks Partei in South Tyrol has managed to remain in government for fifty-three years, irrespective of the evolution of the economy.

their political alliances. The abundance of ethnic parties that take part in mixed coalitions and are rewarded by voters at election time suggests that nationalist politicians and nationalist voters are more flexible than the alleged rigidity of ethnic identities would predict them to be. The fragmentation of the nationalist bloc suggests, in turn, that ethnic voters can be highly heterogeneous in their interests and preferences.

REFERENCES

Alt, James E., and Gary King. 1994. "Transfer of Governmental Power. The Meaning of Time Dependence." *Comparative Political Studies* 27: 190–210.

Amorim Neto, Octavio, and Gary W. Cox. 1997. "Electoral Institutions, Cleavage Structures, and the Number of Parties." *American Journal of Political Science* 41 (1): 149–74.

Brass, Paul R. 1997. *Theft of an Idol: Text and Context in the Representation of Collective Violence*. Princeton: Princeton University Press.

Brubaker, Rogers. 2004. *Ethnicity without Groups*. Cambridge, MA, and London: Harvard University Press.

Chandra, Kanchan. 2001. "Constructivist Findings and Their Non-incorporation." *American Political Science Association-Comparative Politics* 12(1): 7–11.

Chandra, Kanchan. 2004. *Why Ethnic Parties Succeed*. Cambridge: Cambridge University Press.

Diermeier, Daniel, and Randolph T. Stevenson. 1999. "Cabinet Survival and Competing Risks." *American Journal of Political Science* 43:1051–68.

Fearon, James, and David D. Laitin. 2000a. "Ordinary Language and External Validity: Specifying Concepts in the Study of Ethnicity." Paper presented at the Laboratory in Comparative Ethnic Processes meetings, University of Pennsylvania, October 20–22.

Fearon, James, and David D. Laitin. 2000b. "Violence and the Social Construction of Ethnic Identity." *International Organization* 54 (4): 845–77.

Fernández-Albertos, José. 2002. "Votar en dos dimensiones. El peso del nacionalismo y la ideología en el comportamiento electoral vasco: 1993–2001." *Revista Española de Ciencia Política* 5: 153–81.

Filley, Walter O. 1956. "Social Structure and Canadian Political Parties: The Quebec Case." *Western Political Quarterly* 9 (4): 900–14.

Geertz, Clifford. 1973. *The Interpretation of Cultures: Selected Essays*. New York: Basic Books.

Gellner, Ernst. 1983. *Nations and Nationalism*. Ithaca: Cornell University Press.

Gil-White, F. J. 1999. "How Thick Is Blood?" *Ethnic & Racial Studies* 22 (5): 789–820.

Hale, Henry. 2004. "Explaining Ethnicity." *Comparative Political Studies* 37 (4): 458–85.

Hechter, Michael. 2000. *Containing Nationalism*. Oxford: Oxford University Press.

Hinich, Melvin J., and Walker Pollard. 1981. "A New Approach to the Spatial Theory of Electoral Competition." *American Journal of Political Science* 25 (2): 323–41.

Horowitz, D. L. 1985. *Ethnic Groups in Conflict.* Berkeley: University of California Press.

King, Gary, James Alt, Nancy Burns, and Michael Laver. 1990. "A Unified Model of Cabinet Dissolution in Parliamentary Democracies." *American Journal of Political Science* 34: 846–71.

Kitschelt, Herbert, and Anthony McGann. 1997. *The Radical Right in Western Europe. A Comparative Analysis.* University of Michigan Press.

Narud, Hanne M., and Henry Valen. 2001. "Coalition Membership and Electoral Performance in Western Europe." Paper presented at the 2001 Annual Meeting of the American Political Science Association, San Francisco, August 30–September 2.

Pempel, T. J. (ed.). 1990. *Uncommon Democracies. The One-Party Dominant Regimes.* New York: Cornell University Press.

Powell, G. Bingham. 1982. *Contemporary Democracies: Participation, Stability, and Violence.* Cambridge, MA: Harvard University Press.

Powell, G. Bingham. 2000. *Elections as Instruments of Democracy: Majoritarian and Proportional Visions.* New Haven: Yale University Press.

Przeworski, Adam, and John Sprague. 1986. *Paper Stones. A History of Electoral Socialism.* Chicago and London: University of Chicago Press.

Przeworski, Adam, Susan Stokes, and Bernard Manin (eds.). 1999. *Democracy, Accountability, and Representation.* Cambridge: Cambridge University Press.

Rose, Richard, and Thomas T. Mackie. 1983. "Incumbency in Government: Asset or Liability?" In Hans Daalder and Peter Mair (eds.), *Western European Party Systems.* London and Beverly Hills: Sage Publications.

Sáez Lozano, José Luis. 2002. "Economía y política en la duración de los Gobiernos: el caso de España." *Hacienda Pública Española/Revista de Economía Pública* 161 (2): 69–96.

Van Evera, Stephen. 2001. "Primordialism Lives!" *American Political Science Association-Comparative Politics* 12 (1): 20–2.

Van Houten, Pieter. 2000. *Regional Assertiveness in Western Europe. Political Constraints and the Role of Party Competition.* Doctoral dissertation, University of Chicago.

Ware, Alan. 1987. *Citizens, Parties and the State.* Cambridge: Polity Press.

CHAPTER FOUR

Performance or Representation? The Determinants of Voting in Complex Political Contexts

Paloma Aguilar and Ignacio Sánchez-Cuenca

Introduction

It may seem somewhat obvious to state that citizens, when voting, take government performance into consideration. However, it is one of the most fundamental ingredients of democracy that citizens may use their vote to reward good governments and punish bad ones (Przeworski, Stokes, and Manin 1999). This notion that voting is linked to government performance has been argued extensively (e.g., Fiorina 1981; Key 1966).

Nevertheless, in practice it is clear that there are numerous obstacles to the vote being a mechanism by which rewards and punishments are issued. To begin with, the vote is far from being a perfect evaluation tool because of what is often called "policy bundling" (Besley and Coate 2000) in which voters are forced to include in one single decision their evaluations of many widely different aspects of government performance. Moreover, it may be the case that these same evaluations are biased by voters' political and ideological preferences (Maravall and Przeworski 2001) or simply that voters find it difficult to gauge the extent to which the government is responsible for policy results (Powell and Whitten 1993; Barreiro 1999; Anderson 2000; Powell 2000; Rudolph 2003).

The aim of this chapter is to determine how voters respond to government performance when two simultaneous circumstances that obstruct the simple application of the vote as a reward and punishment tool are at play. On one hand, the voters are faced with a government that is vertically divided (there are both a central government and regional governments). When evaluating policy results, it is not clear to the voter whether these results are due to the behavior of the central government, the regional

We are grateful to José Fernández-Albertos, Héctor Cebolla, Luis de la Calle, and Leire Salazar for comments and suggestions.

government, or both (Anderson 2006). On the other hand, in those areas in which nationalism has a dominant presence in society, citizens may cast their votes not so much in terms of outcomes or government performance but in terms of the capacity of the government to represent the group that considers itself to have a national identity different from the rest.

Clearly, these two circumstances are not completely independent of each other because it is often the case that vertical divisions in power exist where there are ethnic or religious divisions and where such divisions are concentrated in a geographical area, generating problems between the center and the periphery. Our aim is to understand the distortions that the combination of a vertically divided government and widespread nationalism may produce.

First of all, nationalism can make the political arena more complex than usual by adding a further dimension to the traditional left–right dimension, which largely reflects the various positions of parties and voters with regard to the redistribution of wealth. In addition, nationalism questions the very premise of democratic decision making because it begs the question of who in fact has the right to make such decisions. When a group feels that it is not represented by its government and wants to take its own decisions independently of the state to which it belongs, its main demand will not concern proposed policies but rather the need to defend and represent its own interests against those of the rest of the state. In such cases, it may be that voters cast their votes not on the basis of what a government does but on the basis of who they feel the government represents. We consider that the fundamental question underlying nationalism, and exclusive nationalism especially,[1] is centered around the representation capacity of those in power. Carl Friedrich offers several examples in which nationalist or ethnic representation has been the basis for voting:

> In Switzerland, for example, it is a matter of course that the French-speaking cantons elect French-speaking representatives, the Italian-speaking cantons

---

[1] The distinction between inclusive and exclusive nationalism can be found in classical theory of nationalism, although there are varying definitions. A number of studies have distinguished between "civic" and "ethnic" nationalism (e.g., Smith 1991), with the most inclusive features being found in the former and the most exclusive ones in the latter. According to one study of both types of nationalism, "the civic type consists of a territorial or spatial approach to the nation. There is an emphasis in common interests, and a strong sense of a legal, political community." By contrast, in the ethnic type, the emphasis is put on "a community based on birth," where "the idea of the nation is a sort of 'supra-familiy,'" centred on the myth of a 'common descent'" (Serrano 1998: 98–9).

Italian-speaking representatives, and the German-speaking cantons German.... Again, in prewar Germany, the Poles elected Polish representatives. Czechoslovakia offered another interesting political arena of a similar sort, where the antipathy of nationalities toward each other was at times so profound as to make election of a representative of the other nationality utterly inconceivable. (1937/1968: 324)

The importance that representation acquires in the context of nationalism may introduce several distortions into the classical model of democratic control, and these we must bear in mind. For instance, it is possible that those who do not feel part of the dominant demos in a country will have a negative bias in the evaluation of the performance of the central government and a positive bias in the evaluation of that of the regional government. It may also be the case that the more intense the notion of demos is and the more exclusive the terms on which it is based, the greater the importance of representation and the lesser that of performance.

In the previous chapter, Sonia Alonso demonstrated by means of aggregate data that nonnationalist parties lose more votes than nationalist parties in regions where there is nationalist conflict. Given that our study looks at the vote from a micro-perspective, we are able to show in detail the decision-making process that voters go through, that is, how voters combine their evaluations of both central and regional government management with nationalist considerations. This should let us understand how voters punish nonnationalist parties more than nationalist ones.

In this chapter, we analyze by means of survey data the voting patterns in four Autonomous Regions in Spain. A comparison of the four regions will allow us to isolate the specific effects of nationalism in contexts in which power is vertically divided. In section 2, we justify the relevance of the case of Spain and explain the criteria followed in selecting the four regions. In section 3, we analyze the bidimensional structure of the political space in the chosen regions. In section 4, we examine the relationships among voting, the evaluation of central and regional government performance, and nationalist identity. Section 5 contains the conclusions reached.

Research Design

In our opinion, Spain is an excellent case study for a number of reasons. The regional power structure in Spain is highly decentralized, and there are some regions where there is strong nationalist conflict. This combination can be found in few places. In addition, there are detailed public opinion surveys regarding this question with sufficiently large samples as to allow us to focus at a regional level.

The Spanish State is an especially complex one, which contributes to voters' confusion when they must attribute responsibility for performance; alongside the central government, there are regional governments, local governments (not considered in this study because they have no legislative power), and also directives from the European Union that by law must be implemented by the Autonomous Regions. In the Basque Country, there are other local bodies (*instituciones forales*) that are also democratically elected and have substantial political clout. Furthermore, in 1992 (the year the survey being analyzed was carried out), the Autonomous Regions in Spain still had very different levels of autonomy.[2] Finally, although the Spanish State has exclusive jurisdiction in certain areas and the regions in others, there are yet other areas in which the State and the regions have equal power and yet others still where they share power. Wherever we encounter this institutional complexity, "the difficulty of assigning responsibility is greater, given the ignorance shown by public opinion about what level of government should be held accountable in different areas" (Font 1999: 147).

Such a complex institutional structure offers a wide variety of distinct political circumstances. In particular, in this study, we examine only those circumstances that were present during the year of our study, 1992. There are three:

1. The same party ruling in both the central and the regional governments[3]
2. One party ruling in the central government, and this same party being part of a coalition government in the Autonomous Region[4]
3. One party ruling in the central government and another in the regional government[5]

In situation 1, there is either little or no conflict between the two levels of government and, as such, voters should not find it particularly difficult to include in their voting decisions evaluation of government performance

---

[2] Regarding public expenditure, at the beginning of the 1990s, approximately 70 percent corresponded to the central level, 20 percent to the regional level, and 10 percent to the local level.

[3] Andalusia, Asturias, Castilla-La Mancha, Valencia, Extremadura, Madrid, and Murcia.

[4] The Canary Islands, the Basque Country, and La Rioja.

[5] Aragón, the Balearic Islands, Cantabria, Castilla-León, Catalonia, Galicia, and Navarre.

(whether regional or central). However, in situation 3, voters are faced with a rather complex problem. Because there are parties of different political persuasions in each level of government, they must separate the effect of each one and form a different evaluation for each. Finally, situation 2 is the intermediate case, with a lower degree of complexity than situation 3 but of greater complexity than situation 1.

The fact that there are two levels of government allows us to ascertain whether the central government produces *coattail voting*, that is, a certain contagious effect that can occur between levels of government (Calvert and Ferejohn 1983; Campbell and Summers 1990). In a number of cases, it has been demonstrated that there is a causal relationship between the popularity of the president of a country (and other factors, such as a healthy national economy) and the likelihood of candidates of the same party in other levels of government being voted: "If presidential approval is high and/or the economy is performing well, candidates of the incumbent party are expected to benefit at all levels of government" (Remmer and Gélineau 2003: 801).

The Autonomous Regions in Spain, as well as being heterogeneous in terms of the political composition of their governments, vary in terms of the question of nationalism. In some regions, such as in the Basque Country and Catalonia, nationalism is powerful, so much so that the party system in these regions is significantly different from the Spanish system in general.[6] In others, there is a considerable level of regionalism, such as in Andalusia, Navarre, and Valencia. Hence, the assumption of a one-dimensional space of political competition based on the left–right axis does not hold in these cases.

We also have variation among various types of nationalism. In the Basque Country, national identity has historically been of a much more exclusive and ethnic nature than in Catalonia.[7] As such, an analysis of the

---

[6] For a more detailed description of the Basque and Catalan political systems, as well as the voting patterns in each up to the date of this study, see Llera (1998) and Pallarés and Font (1994), respectively.

[7] The "civic" and "ethnic" nationalism dichotomy has been applied to the Catalan and Basque nationalisms, respectively (Conversi 2000; Serrano 1998). In the Basque Country, "Race and nation were founded on the immutable decision of blood and biological kinship. A Basque could never be Spanish and a Spaniard could never be Basque. These were permanently mutually exclusive categories. Since race was a matter of blood, the stamp of a member of a race was to be found in the surname. A Basque was a person with Basque surnames – a proof of Basque descent even though he spoke only Spanish. . . . For Arana and the Basque nationalists in general surnames took on an overwhelming importance" (Heiberg 1989: 52). In contrast to the Basque nationalists, "'Catalanists' remained faithful to the definition

Basque and Catalan cases allows us to test the hypothesis that the more exclusive national identity is, the more likely the voter is to consider the question of demos, which may weaken the punishment administered to an incumbent with a poor record if the party in power is thought to represent the same demos.

Our dependent variable is vote intention in regional elections. In the survey being used, vote intention in the general elections and the regional elections is similar, perhaps because this survey was not carried out at the time of either general or regional elections, meaning that the interviewee, in the absence of any electoral or preelectoral campaign, considered casting the same vote in both types of elections.

Given that we aim to explain voting and that the party system in a number of regions varies, in part because of the presence of nationalism, we cannot analyze the Spanish sample as a whole. Thus, we have selected various regions and analyze each one separately, later comparing the results obtained. Because the Spanish case contains considerable variety, we have chosen four regions where the differences are greatest. More specifically, we have used a double criterion: regions in which the same or different parties are in both levels of government, which allows us to test our hypothesis about the role of government performance when the government is vertically divided, and nationalist and nonnationalist regions, which allows us to determine the specific effects of nationalism.

Table 4.1 shows the regions chosen: two regions with a strong nationalist presence, Catalonia and the Basque Country, and two regions with no nationalist presence, Andalusia and Castilla-León.[8] In the latter regions, we can expect a certain level of regionalism, especially in Andalusia. Equally, we have chosen two regions in which the party in the regional government is not the same as the party in the central government, Catalonia (governed by the nationalist party *Convergencia i Unió*, CiU) and

of citizenship as articulated in the ancient laws of the medieval principality, the origins of which dated back to the thirteenth century. These had a rather typical civic and ethnic ring, paralleled those regimes in existence in much of Western Europe, and contained the well-known combination of *jus sanguinis* and *jus soli*. Not only were children and grandchildren of Catalans to be considered Catalan, but so were long-term residents, regardless of the surnames and birthplaces of their parents. In short, the naturalization of immigrants was legally possible and even desirable" (Jacobson 2006: 223).

[8] In 1992, the year in which the survey was carried out, the Basque Country, Catalonia, and Andalusia (together with Galicia) enjoyed a far greater level of autonomy than the other regions. As such, comparatively, Castilla-León had little autonomy. In fact, it was in 1992 that the Pactos Autonómicos were signed that, in time, would help to balance, although with a number of exceptions, the level of autonomy within the different regions.

Table 4.1. Case Selection

	Nationalism	
	Yes	No
Party in power		
Same (totally or partially)	The Basque Country	Andalusia
Different	Catalonia	Castilla-León

Castilla-León (governed by the conservative Popular Party, PP), and two regions in which the governing party is the same in both or shares power at a regional level: in the case of Andalusia, the party is the same, and in the case of the Basque Country, the Socialist Workers Party of Spain, the PSOE, was a minority member of the coalition government with the Basque Nationalist Party, the PNV. Besides the aforementioned selection criteria, the number of observations in each region was also an important factor. Accordingly, Andalusia was a much more suitable case than Extremadura or Valencia, as was the case of Castilla-León with regard to the Balearic Islands or Cantabria.

With regard to the data, we analyze a unique survey carried out by the *Centro de Investigaciones Sociológicas* (CIS) in 1992:[9] the same questionnaire was used in all seventeen of the Autonomous Regions using large samples in each. The questionnaire is particularly rich in content and includes questions regarding the positioning of voters and parties on both ideological and nationalist scales, which permits us to carry out a spatial analysis of the data.

The Political Space

The majority of empirical studies that test spatial models do so assuming a one-dimensional space consisting of the left–right dimension alone (or a liberal–conservative one, in the case of the United States). Given that there is a nationalist dimension in some of the regions in Spain, we ought to consider the possibility of there being two dimensions in these regions. In the nonnationalist regions, the question of regionalism still remains, although naturally of a different nature and nuance than the nationalism of Catalonia and the Basque Country; therefore, it is important to know whether these regionalisms have the same effect as nationalism. For the sake of brevity, when the context permits, we refer to this dimension as

[9] Surveys 2025–2041 (CIS).

the nationalist dimension. The fact that the party system in the nationalist regions differs from that of the other regions, in the sense that the strongest parties in both the Basque Country and Catalonia are the nationalist parties that compete in these regions alone, might lead us to think that the regionalism of Andalusia and Castilla-León is of lesser importance in explaining the vote than the nationalism of the Basque Country and Catalonia.

By means of a spatial analysis of the vote, we wish to determine the relative importance of nationalism and regionalism with respect to the left–right ideological dimension. To do so, we have calculated the absolute distances between the ideological position of the voter and the positions she ascribes to the parties in the ideological dimension. The same has been done with the distances on the nationalism scale (for Catalonia and the Basque Country) and the regionalism scale (for Andalusia and Castilla-León). In all cases, the distances have been measured on a scale of 1 (*on the extreme left, minimum regionalism/nationalism*) to 10 (*on the extreme right, maximum regionalism/nationalism*).

We find that all the parties hold more extreme positions in the nationalist dimension than in the ideological one with respect to their voters, there being greater average distances in all cases.[10] Similarly, these distances show a greater standard deviation in the nationalist dimension than in the ideological one.[11] Given that we want to determine the relative weight of each dimension of electoral competition on the vote, we have standardized all the distance variables to be able to compare them.

Each individual has a distance (whether ideological or nationalist/regionalist) with regard to every party competing in the region. The only way of collecting all this information and estimating the effect of these distances on the vote is by using conditional logit models (Alvarez and Nagler 1998; Merrill and Grofman 1999), with which we can include independent

---

[10] Consequently, when quadratic distances are calculated, instead of the absolute distances used here, the effect of nationalism is reduced with regard to that of ideology.

[11] The greatest standard deviations could be because the positions of the voters in the nationalist dimension are not as fixed as those in the ideological dimension, perhaps indicating that the political elite assume that these positions can be modified and that it is worth employing persuasion tactics to change the preferences of the electorate, which would help to explain the greater averages in this dimension. Parties would have incentives to adopt more extreme positions in an attempt to pull its electorate with it. Fernández-Albertos (2002) shows that in the Basque Country in the 1990s, the nationalist parties managed to ensure that the nationalist dimension gained importance with regard to the ideological dimension.

variables with different values for each value of the dependent variable (i.e., a different distance for each individual with regard to each party in terms of ideology and nationalism).

A first approximation to the political space of the four Autonomous Regions consists of analyzing the effect of the distances on the vote. The first model (M1) of Table 4.2 shows these results. We have included the constants of the parties, which reflect the punishments and rewards usually issued to the small and large parties, respectively, beyond spatial considerations. That done, it is clear that there are two dimensions of competition, although the ideological dimension is stronger than the nationalist/regionalist one, even in the nationalist regions. This coincides in part with the findings of Fernández-Albertos (2002) in his groundbreaking study on the influence of nationalism and ideology on the vote in the Basque Country.[12] Comparing the effects of both distances, the nationalist distance is especially important in Catalonia (the nationalism coefficient is almost 80 percent with respect to the ideology coefficient). Curiously, the weight of regionalism in Andalusia (62 percent with respect to ideology) is greater than the weight of nationalism in the Basque Country (58 percent with respect to ideology). This shows the importance of regionalism in Andalusia. Regionalism, however, is rather weak in Castilla-León (32 percent with respect to ideology), the only region where no regionalist or nationalist party was represented in the regional parliament at the time the survey was carried out.[13]

This analysis, however, is based on a double assumption that is not entirely convincing. In spatial models of more than one dimension, it is necessary to take into consideration the possible relationships between the dimensions of competition under analysis (Hinich and Munger 1997: ch. 4). On one hand, the two dimensions may or may not be separable. If we identify distances with preferences, it is possible to separate the preferences when distances in one dimension do not affect distances in the other. On the other hand, each of the dimensions may or may not have the same salience for the voters. If the dimensions do not have the same salience, the resulting indifference curves will be elliptical and not

---

[12] Fernández-Albertos (2002) does not standardize the distances; therefore, the coefficients he presents are not directly comparable.

[13] One notable difference between Catalonia and the Basque Country on one hand, and Andalusia and Castilla-León on the other, is that in the latter group there are a lot more people who do not know where to place themselves or the parties in the regionalist dimension than there are in the Basque Country and Catalonia in the nationalist dimension.

Table 4.2. Conditional Logit Models: The Bidimensional Nature of the Political Space

	The Basque Country		Catalonia		Andalusia		Castilla-León	
	M1	M2	M1	M2	M1	M2	M1	M2
Ideological distance	-1.595*	-1.564*	-1.159*	-1.167*	-1.359*	-1.354*	-1.138*	-1.128*
	(0.115)	(0.116)	(0.067)	(0.068)	(0.074)	(0.075)	(0.067)	(0.067)
Nationalist distance	-0.932*	-0.594*	-0.922*	-0.614*	-0.853*	-0.471*	-0.366*	-0.014
	(0.086)	(0.117)	(0.066)	(0.091)	(0.083)	(0.132)	(0.083)	(0.124)
Nationalism* nationalist distance		-0.817*		-0.711*		-0.603*		-0.635*
		(0.206)		(0.152)		(0.174)		(0.172)
Constants								
IU	-2.466*	-2.145*	-2.581*	-2.467*	-1.688*	-1.706*	-1.841*	-1.876*
	(0.248)	(0.258)	(0.162)	(0.165)	(0.134)	(0.135)	(0.145)	(0.147)
PP	-3.933*	-3.514*	-3.380*	-3.061*	-1.540*	-1.476*		
	(0.381)	(0.384)	(0.214)	(0.219)	(0.140)	(0.141)		
PSOE	-1.364*	-1.055*	-1.356*	-1.166*			-0.069	-0.092
	(0.177)	(0.192)	(0.114)	(0.121)			(0.096)	(0.096)
EA	-1.565*	-1.547*						
	(0.176)	(0.179)						
EE	-1.879*	-1.790*						
	(0.202)	(0.204)						
HB	-1.265*	-1.377*						
	(0.178)	(0.187)						
ERC			-1.556*	-1.683*				
			(0.119)	(0.125)				
PA					-1.163*	-1.240*		
					(0.116)	(0.119)		
Pseudo R²	0.49	0.50	0.49	0.50	0.43	0.44	0.42	0.43
N	3,553	3,553	4,714	4,714	3,311	3,311	2,600	2,600

Notes: Standard errors in parentheses. *p < 0.01. Political parties of a national level (PSOE and IU are left wing; PP is right wing); political parties of a regional level (in the Basque Country: EA, EE, PNV, and HB; the first three are nationalist; the last, separatist; in Catalan: CiU and ERC; the first nationalist and the second separatist; in Andalusia: PA, regionalist).

Parties in the Basque Country: IU, PP, PSOE, PNV, EA, EE, HB.

Parties in Catalonia: PP, PSOE, IC, CiU, ERC.

Parties in Andalusia: PP, PSOE, IU, PA.

Parties in Castilla-León: PP, PSOE, IU.

circular. These results (models M1 in Table 4.2) assume that the dimensions considered are separable and that the salience of each dimension is the same for all the individuals in the sample.

In terms of the dimensions being separable or not, when we analyze the correlations between the nationalism/regionalism scale and that of ideology, we can see that the relationship between both is very low in Catalonia, Andalusia, and Castilla-León; it is always below |0.2|. Only in the Basque Country is there a correlation of certain importance ($r = -0.24$). Indeed, the data for this region show that there is no correlation at all for the nonnationalists (those that fall between 1 and 5 on the 1–10 nationalism scale) but that the correlation for the nationalists is considerable ($r = -0.36$). Among nationalists, being leftist is associated with stronger nationalism. Given that the supposition is not held in only one group of one of the four regions, we consider that ideological and nationalist preferences are separable.

The issue of salience is a more complex one. Having standardized the variables, the distance coefficients of the models M1 in Table 4.2 are directly comparable and their differences indicate that the relevance of the two dimensions is different in the sample as a whole. In general, voters attach greater importance to ideological distance than they do to a nationalist one. However, in our opinion, ideological and nationalist distances are not, strictly speaking, comparable; it may be that nationalist distance is more important for the nationalists than it is for the nonnationalists. Nationalists will be sensitive to nationalist distances with respect to the parties; however, nonnationalists will attach little or no importance to such distances. There is no justification for presenting a similar argument for ideology. This will be of equal importance to both right-wing and left-wing sympathizers.

To test this hypothesis, we have divided the sample of each region into two groups: voters that place themselves in positions 1 through 5 on the nationalism/regionalism scale and those that place themselves in positions 6 through 10. If we are correct in our assumption, the distance in the nationalist dimension will be greater for the second group than for the first. In Table 4.2, in the second model (M2) of each region, we can see the effect of the interaction between the nationalists/regionalists and the nationalist/regionalist distance. In every case, the interaction term is very significant and in the expected direction. Consequently, the effect of the nationalist distance on the vote is not the same for all voters. It is more important for the nationalists than it is for the nonnationalists. Here, we

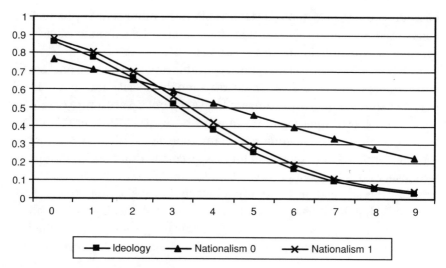

Figure 4.1. The probability of voting CiU in Catalonia based on the distances noted in model M2 in Table 4.2.

have a differential effect of great relevance that clearly qualifies the original finding that ideology is of greater importance to the vote than the nationalist question.

In Figure 4.1, we can see an example of the effect of distances. We have chosen the vote for the CiU in Catalonia. We have calculated how the probability of voting for this party changes when the distance in one dimension to the CiU increases and the remaining distances to the other parties (in both dimensions) remain unchanged. Thus, we have one curve for ideology and two for nationalism (i.e., when the person is not nationalist – "nationalism 0" – and when the person is nationalist – "nationalism 1"). The curves that show greater variations in the probability of vote are the ideological distance and the nationalist distance for the nationalists, which are almost identical. Finally, the nationalist distance for the nonnationalists has a lesser effect on the vote for the party in the regional government, it being the flattest curve of the three.

Taking interaction into consideration, we can see that there is a clear and logical contrast between the two nationalist regions and the two nonnationalist ones. The coefficient of the interaction term is stronger in the Basque Country and Catalonia than it is in Andalusia and Castilla-León. In the case of the Catalan nationalists, the nationalist distance is more important than the ideological one. In the nonnationalist regions, ideology

Table 4.3. Descriptive Statistics of Management Variables

	Mean	SD	Min	Max	N
Evaluation of regional government performance					
The Basque Country	2.96	0.83	1	5	2,873
Catalonia	2.54	0.76	1	5	4,659
Andalusia	3.01	0.83	1	5	3,249
Castilla-León	2.89	0.71	1	5	2,468
Evaluation of central government performance					
The Basque Country	3.47	0.88	1	5	2,873
Catalonia	3.23	0.85	1	5	4,659
Andalusia	3.09	0.91	1	5	3,249
Castilla-León	3.07	0.80	1	5	2,468

is clearly more important than regionalism. We can also see that regionalism in Andalusia is more important than in Castilla-León.

The results of model 2 reflect the complexity of the political arena of the Spanish Autonomous Regions where the nationalist question is of central importance. Whereas for the nationalists, the nationalist dimension is fundamental (and for the Catalans more so than ideology), for the rest, the clearly dominant dimension is ideology. In the nonnationalist regions, regionalism is important above all in Andalusia, but its importance, even among those of a strong regionalist persuasion, is less than ideology.

The Evaluation of Government Performance and Nationalism

Having characterized the nature of the political space in the four regions, we may now include the factors relative to the evaluation of government performance. These evaluations of the regional and central governments in both cases are measured as follows: from 1 (*very good*) to 5 (*very bad*). The descriptive statistics of the variables appear in Table 4.3. Although all four of the regions award greater values to the regional government than they do to central government, the greatest differences between the evaluations of both types of performance are to be found in the nationalist regions. The Catalans are especially satisfied with the CiU's government performance. The nationalist regions are those that have the worst opinion of the central government, worse even than that of Castilla-León, the only region of the four that is ruled by a right-wing party, whereas central government is ruled by a left-wing party.

The introduction of the performance variables improves the fit of the models in Table 4.2. In the four models in Table 4.4, the reference category is always the ruling party in the regional government: the CiU in Catalonia, the PP in Castilla-León, the PSOE in Andalusia, and the PNV in the Basque Country. Although the PSOE was part of a coalition government with the PNV, it is convenient to leave this aside for reasons we now explain below. When the party in the regional government receives a bad evaluation, the probability of voting other parties in the four regions increases. As such, it would appear that voters, even in regions where nationalism is a dominant force and the party in power is nationalist, punish or reward regional governments on the basis of their performance of the government.

That said, there are a number of important results that deviate considerably from a simple model of rewards and punishments issued on the basis of performance evaluation. We concentrate on two types of effects: those relative to the vertical division of power and those relative to the presence of nationalism. In terms of the first type, Table 4.4 shows that when the ruling party in central government receives a bad evaluation, this party is always punished at the regional level. Moreover, in the nationalist regions, a bad evaluation of the PSOE at a central level increases the probability of voting for nationalist parties at a regional level.[14] It would seem, then, that there is a transfer of responsibilities from one level of government to another: when the PSOE is viewed negatively at a central level, there is a clear reduction in its probabilities of being voted at a regional level, whereas the probabilities of the other parties being voted increases. This same argument could be presented in another way: a good evaluation of the PSOE at a central level benefits the PSOE at a regional level. As such, the data indicate that there is coattails voting with regard to the party governing at a central level, given that the probability of this party winning votes in regional elections depends on the evaluation it receives for its performance of central government.

There are several reasons why coattails voting might occur. It could come about quite simply because the voters value the impact of central

---

[14] This is not the only consequence. We also observe that when the PSOE receives a bad performance evaluation at a central level, the coefficients of all the nonnationalist parties are negative (except in the case of IU in Catalonia), whereas those of all the nationalist parties are positive. Although a number of these coefficients are not significant, we believe that the very fact that they have the same sign indicates that, in some way or another, the bad evaluation of the central government has a negative effect on the probabilities of people voting for nonnationalist parties and a positive effect on the nationalist parties.

Table 4.4. Conditional Logit Models: Spatial and Nonspatial Variables

Regional vote	The Basque Country	Catalonia	Andalusia	Castilla-León
Ideological distance	−1.436*** (0.122)	−1.076*** (0.073)	−1.286*** (0.082)	−1.025*** (0.035)
Nationalist distance	−0.527*** (0.126)	−0.538*** (0.099)	−0.380*** (0.140)	0.005 (0.139)
Nationalist distance* nationalist identity	−0.709*** (0.220)	−0.742*** (0.166)	−0.529*** (0.184)	−0.603*** (0.186)
Regional performance × PSOE[a]	1.043*** (0.364)	1.716*** (0.210)		0.914*** (0.176)
Regional performance × IU	0.565 (0.383)	1.479*** (0.242)	0.848*** (0.316)	0.667*** (0.230)
Regional performance × PP	1.479** (0.701)	1.331*** (0.309)	0.831*** (0.303)	
Regional performance × ERC		0.920*** (0.187)		
Regional performance × EA	0.801*** (0.302)			
Regional performance × EE	0.873** (0.348)			
Regional performance × HB	1.016*** (0.322)			
Regional performance × PA			0.822*** (0.275)	
Central performance × PSOE	−1.696*** (0.371)	−1.202*** (0.196)		−1.225*** (0.166)
Central performance × IU	−0.036 (0.377)	0.065 (0.208)	1.295*** (0.283)	−0.019 (0.205)
Central performance × PP	−0.115 (0.661)	−0.166 (0.269)	1.233*** (0.278)	
Central performance × ERC		0.546*** (0.153)		
Central performance × EA	0.512* (0.310)			
Central performance × EE	0.180 (0.327)			
Central performance × HB	0.909*** (0.316)			
Central performance × PA			1.126*** (0.251)	
Constants				
PSOE	1.043 (0.827)	−2.185*** (0.631)		0.946* (0.548)

(*continued*)

119

Table 4.4. (*continued*)

Regional vote	The Basque Country	Catalonia	Andalusia	Castilla-León
IU	−3.433***	−6.392***	−7.849***	−3.589***
	(1.174)	(0.861)	(0.721)	(0.815)
PP	−7.415***	−5.910***	−7.598***	
	(2.376)	(1.123)	(0.798)	
ERC		−5.691***		
		(0.697)		
EA	−5.555***			
	(1.099)			
EE	−4.821***			
	(1.133)			
HB	−7.688***			
	(1.235)			
CiU				
PA			−6.778***	
			(0.656)	
Pseudo R^2	0.55	0.56	0.52	0.48
Number of observations	3,519	4,659	3,249	2,468

[a] All the coefficients that are multiplied by a political party must be interpreted as if they were logit multinomial coefficients; as such, they must be compared with the reference category – in this case, the governing party. So the regional performance × PSOE coefficient shows how the evaluation of regional government performance affects the vote for the PSOE compared with the PNV in the Basque Country, the CiU in Catalonia, and so on.

Level of significance: $*p < 0.1$; $**p < 0.05$; $***p < 0.01$.

Note: The reference category is the party in the regional government: the PNV in the Basque Country; the CiU in Catalonia; the PSOE in Andalusia; the PP in Castilla-León.

government performance on the country as a whole. However, it could also be that the reasons for being satisfied with central government performance are related to target investments made by the central government in certain regions for electoral ends.[15]

In terms of the effects of nationalism, it is interesting to note, first of all, the case of the Basque Country, where a good evaluation of the regional government reduces the probability of voting for the PSOE, despite the

[15] The related literature offers two forms of reasoning: that central government invests more in those regions where it also governs at a regional level (Ansolabehere and Snyder 2003; Dasgupta, Dhillon, and Dutta 2004; Remmer and Gélineau 2003) or that it invests more in those regions where it has strong electoral competition and where electoral success depends on the decision of a small number of swing voters (Dixit and Londregan 1995). For the case of Spain, see De la Calle (2005).

fact that the PSOE formed part of the coalition government. Conversely, a bad evaluation increases the probability of voting for the socialists.[16] Figure 4.2 shows these results by means of a simulation in which the evaluation of the regional government of the nonnationalists varies whereas all the other variables remain constant.[17] Here, it would seem that the voters do not see this party as being responsible for the performance of the regional government.[18] In fact, the thing that really affects the PSOE vote in the Basque Country is the evaluation of central government and not that of the regional government, which in fact proves the existence of coattails voting: the PSOE is voted for not because of its management of the Basque government but because of its management of central government. This result is in accordance with the findings of Sonia Alonso in the previous chapter: in coalition governments formed by nationalists and nonnationalists, nonnationalists suffer greater electoral losses than nationalists.

It is not that voters are confused as to how to evaluate the regional government because of problems of how to assign responsibilities in coalition governments (Powell and Whitten 1993) but that they follow a clear rule: they reward the PNV for the good results of the coalition to the detriment of the PSOE.[19] In our opinion, this result is a consequence of the debate surrounding nationalism. The PNV manages to give the impression that

[16] During the previous legislature (1986–90), the PNV and the PSOE had already governed in coalition (as was also the case during 1985–6). At that time, although the PSOE had won two seats more than the PNV, both parties agreed to share the regional ministries in equal parts, and the PNV also occupied the presidency of the regional government. In the legislature under consideration here (1990–4), after an initial failed attempt to create an entirely nationalist coalition (PNV, EA, and Euskadiko Eskerra [EE]) that only lasted until September 1991, a stable government was formed between the PNV and the PSOE (and from 1993 with the coallegiance of EE), where the division of regional ministries, although not symmetric (the relationship between the different forces no longer being the same), did reserve a number of important government responsibilities for the socialists; they were in charge of areas such as the judiciary, economy, housing, and education, among other entities.

[17] We have also carried out this simulation with the nationalists, and the results are the same.

[18] Indeed, even when the evaluation of regional government performance is "very bad," the probabilities of voting for the PSOE are slightly higher than those of the PNV.

[19] Joan Font, who studied whether the mere fact of governing wore out governments by analyzing what has happened in the Autonomous Regions and the Spanish local governments since 1979, observed that in coalition governments, the majority member was the one who usually benefited from the experience of government and, in particular, illustrated his argument with the negative repercussions that participation in the Basque government as a minority member of the coalition had for the PSOE (Font 1999: 159). In our analysis, we find that the majority partner is the one who capitalizes on the effects of the evaluation of the regional management, whether this is positive or negative, whereas the minority member seems to be much more immune to them.

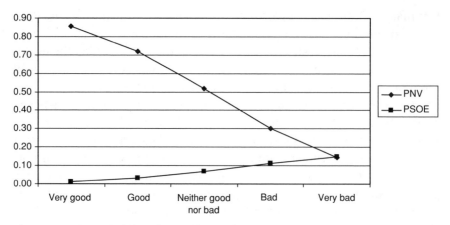

Figure 4.2. The probability of nonnationalists voting the PNV or the PSOE in the regional elections based on the evaluation of the performance of the Basque government.

its government is that of the Basque nationalists and, consequently, that the role of the PSOE is secondary. In other words, the nationalists manage to achieve the goal of the Basque government being judged more for its representative capacity than for its capacity to produce good outcomes. The PNV has managed to transfer, from the very beginnings of devolution, all of its party symbolism to the institutions of the Basque government, to the extent that it is difficult to distinguish between them both.

Ramón Jáuregui, the socialist *vice-lehendakari* (vice president) of the first Basque coalition government, mentions in his memoirs that the PNV never recognized the PSOE "as a legitimate representation of the country.... They never accepted us. Their aim was always to govern Euskadi (the Basque Country) alone." Further on, he mentions how he himself began to worry

> when it became obvious that the public was unable to distinguish the players in the team.... The fact is that people, particularly those who did not pay much attention (the vast majority), did not separate what each of the parties within the government were doing.... Even if we controlled the main economic resources of the Basque administration, and the policies with higher social impact..., it was becoming painfully evident that people did not identify all this with the Socialists.... Because symbols, flag colors, and even letter font in every internal or external communication of the Basque government were, or resembled, those of the nationalists. (Jáuregui, 1994: 278–9)

In addition to this effect in the Basque Country, the models in Table 4.4 show that the evaluation of regional performance, compared with that of the central government, is more important in nationalist regions than it is in nonnationalist ones. The coefficients of regional performance are higher in Catalonia and the Basque Country than in Andalusia and Castilla-León (even if Andalusia had the same competences as Catalonia or the Basque Country). In regions where nationalism is intense, voters generally attach more importance to regional government performance in deciding how they are going to vote. This effect is particularly noticeable in Catalonia, the only region where the coefficients of regional government evaluation are always higher than those of the central government. The opposite case is that of Andalusia. Despite the importance that regionalism has there, the influence that central government performance has on the vote is more important than that of the regional government. Remember that this is the only case in which the party of the central government, the PSOE, is also the ruling party in the region.

The joint impact of these two types of effects, vertical division of power and nationalism, may be analyzed by means of probability simulations based on the results of the models in Table 4.4. We have centered on the Basque Country and Catalonia because these are the two regions where nationalism is present. We have considered three criteria when calculating the probability of voting for the party in government (i.e., PNV in the Basque Country and CiU in Catalonia): (i) if the interviewee claims to be a nationalist or not, (ii) his or her evaluation of regional performance, and (iii) variations in the distance between the interviewee and the regional government party in the nationalist dimension.

By comparing the Basque Country and Catalonia in Table 4.5, not only are we able to analyze the global effect of nationalism on the vote but also to detect differences in the type of nationalism present in each region. First of all, if we focus on the contrast between nationalists and nonnationalists in these regions, we can see that, generally speaking, nonnationalists are more sensitive to variations in the evaluation of regional government performance than nationalists are. This is especially so in the Basque case. The Basque nationalists who are very close to the PNV on the nationalist scale have a high probability of voting for the PNV regardless of their evaluation of the Basque government, whereas those nationalists who are distant from the PNV on the same scale have a very low probability of voting for the PNV, again regardless of their evaluation of government

Table 4.5. Simulations of Voting Probabilities Based on the Models in Table 4.4

Evaluation of regional performance	Distances regarding the party in government in the nationalist dimension											
	0				2				4			
	Nationalists		Non-nationalists		Nationalists		Non-nationalists		Nationalists		Non-nationalists	
	Basque Country	Cat	Basque Country	Cat	Basque Country	Cat	Basque Country	Cat	Basque Country	Cat	Basque Country	Cat
Very good	0.96	0.87	0.92	0.86	0.69	0.89	0.79	0.87	0.16	0.73	0.57	0.81
Good	0.92	0.75	0.83	0.73	0.49	0.78	0.62	0.74	0.08	0.54	0.37	0.64
Regular	0.83	0.55	0.67	0.53	0.29	0.59	0.41	0.54	0.03	0.33	0.19	0.43
Bad	0.66	0.33	0.45	0.31	0.14	0.37	0.22	0.33	0.01	0.16	0.09	0.23
Very bad	0.43	0.16	0.24	0.15	0.06	0.18	0.10	0.16	0.00	0.07	0.04	0.11

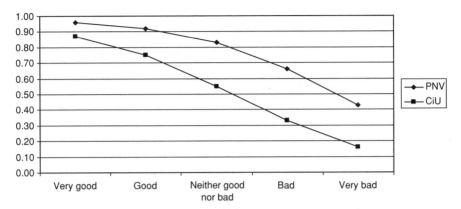

Figure 4.3. The probability of Basque and Catalan nationalists voting for the governing party based on the evaluation of regional performance (if they are zero units distance from this party in the nationalist dimension).

performance at the regional level. In Table 4.5 we can see that among the nationalists who have a zero distance, the probability of voting for the PNV falls no lower than 0.43 (when the evaluation of the Basque government is very bad). However, among those nationalists who have a distance of four units, the probability of voting for the PNV goes no higher than 0.16 (when the evaluation of the Basque government is very good). Nonnationalist Basques, however, are sensitive to the performance of the PNV regardless of how near or how far they are to this party on the nationalist scale. Such pronounced differences do not exist in Catalonia. There, nationalists and nonnationalists alike are equally sensitive to the evaluation of government management in their region.

Let us now compare only Basque and Catalan nationalists. Figure 4.3 shows clearly that when both occupy the same position on the nationalist scale as the ruling regional party, the Catalan nationalists are considerably more sensitive than the Basque nationalists to regional government evaluation.

The difference between Basque nationalism and Catalan nationalism is also clear when we analyze the effect of distances on the nationalist scale. In the Basque Country, such distances produce much greater variations in the vote than in Catalonia. When Basque nationalists position themselves at a four-unit distance from the PNV, the probability of voting for this party is minimal (regardless of regional performance evaluation); however, Catalan nationalists at a four-unit distance from the CiU have a high probability of voting for this party if their evaluation of this party's performance is good.

Why is the effect of nationalist distance so different in these two regions? The somewhat puzzling pattern in the probability of voting for the PNV in the Basque Country is largely due to the presence of Herri Batasuna (HB), the political branch of ETA, the Basque terrorist organization. The vast majority of nationalists at a four-unit distance from the PNV vote HB: few of them have a good opinion of the Basque government, and among the few who do, the probability of voting for the PNV is still extremely low. This is not the case in Catalonia. In the year of the survey, 1992, Esquerra Republicana de Catalunya (ERC), a separatist, nonviolent nationalist party, had a totally marginal presence compared with that of the CiU, the dominant party.

The fact that nationalist distance is so important in the Basque Country (and of such little importance in Catalonia) indicates that the question of representation is valued more than that of regional performance. For Basque nationalists, representation, understood to be some kind of defense of Basque identity, is crucial; it is more important than judgments about government performance. Conversely, Catalan nationalism better combines representation and judgments about regional government performance.

These differences between the Basque and Catalan cases are probably related to the fact that, historically, Basque nationalism has been more exclusivist than that of Catalonia, it having being based, at least until the mid-1930s, on racial criteria, which is much less susceptible to negotiation than linguistic criteria, that which Catalan nationalism has traditionally been based on.

Conclusions

The statistical analysis carried out allows us to form a number of conclusions. First, there is coattails voting. The worse the evaluation of the party in central government is, the more likely the vote will go to other parties at a regional level, and vice versa. This relationship is especially complex in the Basque Country, where the same party that governs the central government is in coalition in the regional government, yet it alone is punished when the regional government receives a good evaluation – the other member of the coalition, the PNV, being the only beneficiary.

Second, over and above the spatial effects of ideological and nationalist/regionalist distances on the vote are the clear effects of regional government evaluation. Voting is sensitive to such evaluations, especially in those regions where nationalism is dominant. Only in Andalusia, the one region where the ruling party is the same as that of the central government, central government evaluation is more important than regional government evaluation.

Third, nationalist voters forgive a bad regional government evaluation more than nonnationalist voters do. This effect, besides, is more pronounced in the Basque Country than it is in Catalonia. It would seem that the type of nationalism is a relevant factor because more exclusivist blends of nationalism manage to ensure to a greater extent that negative perceptions of government performance are not converted into punishment votes.

We think that our findings about the effects of decentralization and particularly of nationalism are important. Regarding the first of these, a similar phenomenon to that found in other highly decentralized countries can also be found in Spain: there is coattail voting between both levels of government. Remmer and Gélineau (2003) have highlighted the difficulties of democratic control at a regional level when the vote depends on what happens at a central level; they also argue, along the same lines, that decentralization may fail to achieve its principal aim, which is to obtain greater congruence between citizens' preferences and the assignation of public resources at a regional level.

In the study presented here, although it is true that the evaluation of the party in central government always has a certain influence on the regional vote, this influence is not the same for all the cases analyzed, it being greater in those regions where there is no nationalist conflict. Where nationalist conflict does exist, the evaluation of regional performance is more important in explaining the vote than the evaluation of central performance. However, to coattails voting, we must add another effect distorting democratic control, that which is derived of a bidimensional political arena. Nationalism, as we have seen, is a dimension of political competition independent of the left–right dimension. What has not as yet been considered in the literature is that the former dimension works in a different way from ideology given that it has a different salience for nationalists than it does for nonnationalists. Whereas for nonnationalists, the fundamental factor is the ideological distance that separates them from parties, for nationalists both distances are fundamental to their vote decision. This is not simply a question of nationalists operating in a more complex political space. Nationalists value central government evaluation more negatively than nonnationalists do and value regional government evaluation more positively.

In our opinion, these effects are derived of the very essence of nationalism, that is, the fact that nationalists in principle believe that politicians who share their national identity will better represent them. It is not that government evaluation is irrelevant to nationalists but rather that nationalists mix government evaluation with other factors that either soften or intensify its effect. Such factors originate in the idea that nationalist voters perceive the nationalist party in power at a regional level as affirmation of the existence of a distinct demos.

REFERENCES

Alvarez, R. Michael, and Jonathan Nagler. 1998. "When Politics and Models Collide: Estimating Models of Multicandidate Elections." *American Journal of Political Science* 42 (1): 55–96.

Anderson, Cameron D. 2006. "Economic Voting and Multilevel Governance: A Comparative Individual-Level Analysis." *American Political Science Review* 50 (2): 449–63.

Anderson, Christopher J. 2000. "Economic Voting and Political Context: A Comparative Perspective." *Electoral Studies* 19 (2): 151–70.

Ansolabehere, Stephen, and James M. Snyder. 2003. "Party Control of State Government and the Distribution of Public Expenditures." Unpublished manuscript.

Barreiro, Belén. 1999. "Justificaciones, responsabilidades y cumplimiento de promesas electorales." *Revista Española de Ciencia Política* 1:149–69.

Besley, Timothy, and Stephen Coate (2000). "Issue Unbundling via Citizens' Initiatives." National Bureau of Economic Research, Working Paper 8036. Cambridge, MA, December.

Calvert, Randall L., and John A. Ferejohn. 1983. "Coattail Voting in Recent Presidential Elections." *American Political Science Review* 77 (2): 407–19.

Campbell, James E., and Joe E. Summers. 1990. "Presidential Coattails in Senate Elections." *American Political Science Review* 84 (2): 513–24.

Conversi, Daniele. 2000. *The Basques, The Catalans, and Spain: Alternative Routes to Nationalist Mobilization*. London: Hurst.

Dasgupta, Sugato, Amrita Dhillon, and Bhaskar Dutta. 2004. "Electoral Goals and Center-State Transfers: A Theoretical Model and Empirical Evidence from India." Unpublished manuscript.

De la Calle, Luis. 2005. "Carreteras y votos: el PSOE y las políticas territoriales de apoyo, 1982–1996." *Revista de Investigaciones Políticas y Sociológicas* 4 (1): 65–95.

Dixit, Avinash, and John Londregan. 1995. "Redistributive Politics and Economic Efficiency." *American Political Science Review* 89 (4): 856–66.

Fernández-Albertos, José. 2002. "Votar en dos dimensiones: el peso del nacional-ismo y la ideología en el comportamiento electoral vasco, 1993–2001." *Revista Española de Ciencia Política* 6: 153–81.

Fiorina, Morris P. 1981. *Retrospective Voting in American National Elections*. New Haven: Yale University Press.

Font, Joan. 1999. "El pez grande se come al chico: las consecuencias electorales de gobernar en las CC. AA. y municipios españoles." *Revista Española de Investigaciones Sociológicas* 87: 145–76.

Friedrich, Carl J. [1937] 1968. *Constitutional Government and Democracy: Theory and Practice in Europe and America*. Waltham, MA: Blaisdell.

Heiberg, Marianne. 1989. *The Making of the Basque Nation*. Cambridge: Cambridge University Press.

Hinich, Melvin J., and Michael C. Munger. 1997. *Analytical Politics*. New York: Cambridge University Press.

Jacobson, Stephen. 2006. "Spain: The Iberian Mosaic." In Mark Hewitson and Tim Baycroft (eds.), *What Is a Nation? Europe 1789–1914*. Oxford: Oxford University Press.

Jáuregui, Ramón. 1994. *El país que yo quiero: memoria y ambición de Euskadi*. Barcelona: Planeta.

Key, V. O. 1966. *The Responsible Electorate: Rationality in Presidential Voting, 1936–1960*. Cambridge, MA: Belknap Press of Harvard University Press.

Llera, Francisco. 1998. "Pluralismo y gobernabilidad en Euskadi (1980–1994)." In Manuel Alcántara and Antonia Martínez (eds.), *Las elecciones autonómicas en España, 1980–1997* (pp. 413–43). Madrid: Centro de Investigaciones Sociológicas.

Maravall, José María, and Adam Przeworski. 2001. "Political Reactions to the Economy: The Spanish Experience." In Susan C. Stokes (ed.), *Democracy, Accountability, and Representation* (pp. 35–76). Cambridge: Cambridge University Press.

Merrill, Samuel III, and Bernard Grofman. 1999. *A Unified Theory of Voting: Directional and Proximity Spatial Models*. Cambridge: Cambridge University Press.

Pallarés, Francesc, and Joan Font. 1994. "Las elecciones autonómicas en Cataluña: 1980–1992." In Pilar del Castillo (ed.), *Comportamiento político y electoral* (pp. 221–73). Madrid: Centro de Investigaciones Sociológicas.

Powell, G. Bingham, and Guy D. Whitten. 1993. "A Cross-National Analysis of Economic Voting: Taking Account of the Political Context." *American Journal of Political Science* 37 (2): 391–414.

Powell, G. Bingham. 2000. *Elections as Instruments of Democracy: Majoritarian and Proportional Visions*. New Haven: Yale University Press.

Przeworski, Adam, Susan C. Stokes, and Bernard Manin (eds.). 1999. *Democracy, Accountability, and Representation*. Cambridge: Cambridge University Press.

Remmer, Karen L., and François Gélineau. 2003. "Subnational Electoral Choice: Economic and Referendum Voting in Argentina, 1983–1999." *Comparative Political Studies* 36 (7): 801–21.

Rudolph, Thomas J. 2003. "Who's Responsible for the Economy? The Formation and Consequences of Responsibility Attributions." *American Journal of Political Science* 47 (4): 689–713.

Serrano, Araceli. 1998. "Manifestaciones étnicas y cívico-territoriales de los nacionalismos." *Revista Española de Investigaciones Sociológicas* 82: 97–125.

Smith, Anthony D. 1991. *Nationalism: Theory, Ideology, History*. Cambridge: Polity.

CHAPTER FIVE

Political Knowledge and the Logic of Voting: A Comparative Study

Marta Fraile

Introduction

This chapter examines the decision-making process by which individual voters cast their ballots. In particular, it discusses two traditional explanations of electoral behavior: *ideological voting* and *performance voting*. These explanations of voting share a common assumption: electors' decisions are based on what they expect to get from their choice. Each potential outcome has a benefit or a cost, and citizens might choose the one benefiting them most or costing them least. That is, voters will maximize the utility of their electoral decision. To maximize the utility of a given decision, an individual needs to have a certain amount of information at hand.

Previous research has explained the simple and straightforward decision rule at work in both ideological and performance voting. In the case of ideological voting, citizens vote for the party that is perceived to be closer to their ideal position on the left–right dimension. Given the lack of perfect information for the electorate, Downs conceived ideology as an information-saving device – that is, a perceptual cue that helps ordinary citizens gain a general idea about the policy positions of the main parties of their political system. In the case of performance voting, citizens decide on a standard of what they consider good performance and reward the incumbent if this standard has been achieved; otherwise, they punish the incumbent. Again, governments' performance is often considered as a particular low-cost indicator that any given citizen can use as a heuristic tool to decide her or his vote in place of more costly and less salient information (e.g., electoral manifestos or policies).

Yet to be able to judge incumbent governments by their performance or by their ideologies, voters must have a certain degree of information and factual knowledge on matters such as the state of the economy, international politics, or the ideological positions of each of the policies included in parties' manifestos. However, research on public opinion and voting behavior from Converse (1964, 1970) onward often indicates that the overall level of information, knowledge, and comprehension of politics among the average citizen is relatively poor. We therefore need to consider systematically the degree of information and factual political knowledge citizens have at their disposal. *Does political knowledge mediate the logic of ideological or performance voting?*[1]

Although models of ideological or performance voting generally assume that all citizens are similarly informed and equally guided by the same considerations or motives (Downs 1957; Kramer 1971, 1983; Kiewiet 1983; Kinder and Kiewiet 1979, 1981), in this chapter I analyze the extent to which the electors' degree of factual political knowledge influences their decision rules when casting their ballot. Previous literature has provided contradictory answers to this question. For instance, Krause (1997) finds that uninformed citizens are less likely to vote on the basis of government's performance, but Zaller (1992, 2004) argues the opposite. According to Zaller, poorly informed citizens are more likely to vote on the basis of performance or other currently salient issues, whereas informed electors use an ideological logic when deciding their vote. This is very much the opposite of Fearon's views about retrospective voting on the grounds of performance. As he puts it,

> There can be no doubt that formidable problems are involved in monitoring and evaluating incumbent behavior to make informed judgements about whether to reelect.... Voters have neither the time to follow policy debates... nor the training and skill to evaluate conflict "expert" arguments about what is best. (Fearon 1999: 68).

Performance voting thus requires a considerable amount of political knowledge. Rational voters would only use the logic of performance if they are well informed; therefore, the conclusion would be that political knowledge is positively related to performance voting and negatively related to ideological voting.

---

[1] In this chapter, I use the concept of political knowledge to refer to citizens' factual political knowledge (Delli Carpini and Keeter 1996). This implies knowledge about rules, actors, and the relevant political issues of the polities, as well as the capacity of individual citizens to influence the political outcome. Other scholars use different terms to refer to the same topic, such as "political awareness" (Zaller 1992) or "political sophistication" (Luskin 1990).

We thus have contradictory arguments about the relationship between political knowledge on one hand and performance and ideological voting on the other. To answer these questions, I provide empirical evidence from postelectoral survey data for parliamentary elections held in four polities: Spain, Hungary, Poland, and Portugal. The data come from the Comparative Study of Electoral Systems (CSES) Module 2 third advance release data set (June 2005) from which comparable information about citizens' degree of political knowledge is available across countries. By selecting countries with diverse political structures, I am able to test whether the effect of political knowledge on the logic of voting is common across individuals in different polities.

I proceed in four parts. First, I review the literature on the logic of ideological and performance voting and discuss the critical assumption that both theories share: that this logic of voting can be used to the same extent by all citizens, independently of their degree of political expertise. I present specific hypotheses regarding the likelihood of citizens to rely on this logic depending on their level of political knowledge. I follow this with a section discussing issues of data and case selection. After testing my hypotheses, I conclude that although the influence of political knowledge is clear on performance voting across polities, the effect is less conclusive on ideological voting. I finally discuss the broader implications of these empirical results for the theories on ideological and performance voting.

The Argument: Why Political Knowledge?

The ideological logic of voting was initially proposed by Downs (1957). His departure point was that voting decisions can be explained as rational behavior. When faced with a decision that affects one's interests, the individual will choose the most cost-effective means of maximizing her or his gains. An action that maximizes utility is rational. For citizens to take such rational action, however, they need to rank their preferences in transitive order and choose their most preferred alternative. Citizens will then always make the same decision if presented with the same set of alternatives in different points in time (Downs 1957: 6). These criteria assume that citizens have information at hand that allows them to make their choices.

However, individuals do not always have a clear notion of what they want as an outcome of their actions, of how the alternatives relate to such outcome, or of how the different outcomes relate to their own interests. Therefore, Downs assumed that citizens do not take their political decisions under conditions of perfect information. Rather, they live in a world of uncertainty in which they search for information before coming to a decision. Information gathering, and the processing of that information, is, however, a costly action. Hence, some voters might be able and motivated to invest time and resources to collect information, whereas others might not. Under these conditions, parties' ideologies appear to be information shortcuts for voters who cannot judge politics expertly. The ideological labels of parties then guide nonexpert citizens about the general political intentions of parties. More specifically, ideologies can order the programs of political parties on a single policy dimension. Downs's main assumption is that the majority of policy issues are related and can be included in this single political dimension. In sum, ideology appears as an information-saving device or heuristic (Popkin 1991; Sniderman, Brody, and Tetlock 1991) that citizens use to guide their political decisions.

Nevertheless, some electors might encounter difficulties both in defining their own preferences in the ideological dimension and in placing the political parties' policies. In fact, survey research on citizens' attitudes has shown that the public in general presents low levels of factual political knowledge. Moreover, the competencies needed to form and express consistent opinions appear to be limited (Converse 1970; Bennet 1988, 1989; Delli Carpini and Keeter 1996; Althaus 2003). If citizens are politically ignorant, they may not be able to organize consistently their opinions by their ideology. In this case, the ideological labels of parties would not work as a shortcut for ignorant citizens to decide their vote. Previous research has shown that there are significant differences in the structure and stability of political attitudes and ideology among knowledgeable and ignorant citizens (Delli Carpini and Keeter 1996; Bartle 1997; Sinnott 2000): the former have more consistent political ideologies, opinions, and attitudes. Therefore, to use ideology as a criterion for voting, electors need some amount of information. Voters with little information about candidates' positions on important issues will use ideology to cast their votes to a lesser extent than knowledgeable citizens.

There is, however, another possible argument about the role of factual political knowledge on ideological voting. For ideology to work as an information-saving device, citizens should know something about politics but not to the extent that they become experts. If this were the case, the effect of political knowledge on ideological voting would be nonlinear. Moderately knowledgeable citizens might rely on the ideological logic of voting to a greater extent than either ill-informed citizens or perfectly well-informed citizens. Studying the influence of political knowledge on information diffusion and opinion change, Zaller (1992) finds a nonmonotonic relationship between political knowledge and opinion change in response to messages from the mass media. Well-informed citizens are more likely than poorly informed citizens to receive and to understand such messages but, at the same time, they are less likely to change their opinions. Moderately well-informed citizens show the greatest levels of media-induced opinion change compared with both ill-informed and well-informed citizens.

Therefore, empirical evidence shows that some people tend to be more informed than others. This variance is unevenly distributed because the highest degree of political knowledge is concentrated among the politically and socially advantaged. Much of the empirical variation in the propensity to know about politics is explained by individual differences in motivation, ability, and opportunity (Bennet 1995; Delli Carpini and Keeter 1996; Althaus 2003).[2] The main question that I examine here is the extent to which variations in factual political knowledge influence voters' propensity to use ideology when casting their ballots. More informed voters will have a consistent, ideologically sophisticated interpretation of the world. I expect to find that the likelihood of using ideology as a criterion to decide which party to vote for will be higher among voters with medium or high levels of political expertise than among those with a low level of political knowledge.

The logic of performance voting is apparently simple. When deciding how to vote, electors seek to maximize their utility from the outcomes of the policies implemented by the incumbent. Hence, according to the logic of performance voting, citizens are guided by outcomes rather than policies. They calculate a threshold of general welfare and, if they believe that the incumbent has achieved this, they reelect the candidate or party. For the logic of performance voting to work, however, electors need political information. They need to know which party is (or are, in the case of coalition governments) in government; what changes have taken place during

---

[2] The discussion about the sources of differences in the levels of citizens' factual political knowledge is beyond the scope of this chapter but, according to Althaus (2003), motivation to become informed seems to depend on interest in politics and sense of civic duty. The ability to process political information is enhanced by education and by routine exposure to daily news, whereas opportunities to become informed depends on the content of available news coverage, geographic location of the citizen, and some other contextual characteristics of the place where the individual lives (see also Bennet 1995; Delli Carpini and Keeter 1996).

the mandate in economic conditions, international politics, or whatever outcomes they consider relevant; and the extent to which the incumbent government is responsible for such outcomes.

When voters are poorly informed about politics, these three conditions might not be present. If this is the case, citizens will not decide their vote on the basis of an informed evaluation of government's performance. Factual political knowledge helps people to assess more accurately their interests as individuals and as members of groups. It is a key determinant of instrumental rationality (Delli Carpini and Keeter 1996). The more knowledgeable citizens are, the better will they understand the impact of public policies on their own interests, and the more likely they are to vote on the basis of performance. Studies about voting as a response to the economic performance of government have often treated the electorate as undifferentiated, ignoring systematic heterogeneity among voters (exceptions are Krause 1997; Gómez and Wilson 2001, 2006; Althaus 2003). My claim here is that we need to test the extent to which performance voting is influenced by the degree of factual political knowledge of citizens. The theoretical expectations to be tested in this chapter are summarized in Table 5.1.

To summarize, both ideological and performance voting explain individual voting as the product of a rational decision. For a decision to be rational, a certain amount of information is needed. I expect the likelihood of ideological and performance voting to increase as the level of factual political knowledge grows. Studies that explore the influence of political knowledge on voting decisions are scarce (but see Bartels 1996; Krause 1997; Andersen, Heath, and Sinnot 2001; Gómez and Wilson 2001; Zaller 1992, 2004). I now analyze postelectoral survey data from four polities.

Data and Cases

I want to test the comparative effect of political expertise on ideological and performance voting in the European multiparty systems. In such systems, voters will find more difficulty in selecting which party is ideologically closer to their position than in two-party systems. In addition, multiparty systems are often related to coalition governments in which performance voting requires greater political knowledge for voters to hold the government responsible for outcomes. Thus, both ideological and

Table 5.1. A Summary of Theoretical Expectations

	The influence of factual political knowledge
Authors	Hypotheses
Ideological voting	
Downs 1957; Popkin 1991	No effect of citizens' factual political knowledge on the propensity to vote according to ideology. ⇒ Ideology operates as an information-saving device or heuristic that citizens use to guide their political decisions. Therefore, the propensity to vote ideologically will be homogeneous across citizens independent of their political expertise.
A refutation of the assumptions of Downs and others	The propensity to vote ideologically will be heterogeneous across citizens, depending on their political expertise. ⇒ *The likelihood of using ideology will be higher among voters with medium or high levels of political knowledge.*
The logic of performance voting	
Key 1966 and later interpretations: Kramer 1971, 1983; Kiewiet 1983; Kinder and Kiewiet 1979, 1981	No influence of citizens' factual political knowledge on their propensity to vote according to performance. ⇒ Performance constitutes a heuristic that citizens use to guide their political decisions. Therefore, the propensity to vote looking at the performance of the government will be homogeneous across citizens independent of their political expertise.
A refutation of the assumption of Key 1966: heterogeneous economic voting behavior (Krause 1997; Gómez and Wilson 2001, 2006; Althaus 2003)	The propensity to vote according to the performance of the government will be heterogeneous across citizens, depending on their political expertise. ⇒ *As citizens become more knowledgeable about politics, their propensity to vote on the basis of performance will increase.*

Source: My own elaboration. The hypotheses to be tested in this chapter are in italics.

performance voting require comparatively more information for rational voters who want to cast their vote according to ideological proximity or retrospective assessments of performance.

The CSES project provides comparable postelectoral survey data for different countries. In each country, national probability samples of the adult population were interviewed shortly after a national election. A problem with postelectoral surveys is that levels of political knowledge might be overestimated: during electoral campaigns, voters receive the highest degree of political information about the whole legislature. Acquiring information at these times is less costly than in the middle of a mandate. Political knowledge can also be higher when elections are competitive and political tension is high.[3]

Nevertheless, this bias in the level of political knowledge goes in the same direction across countries. Moreover, overestimation of citizens' political knowledge goes against my main hypothesis – that both ideological and performance voting are influenced by variations in voters' political knowledge. Political knowledge some weeks after an election should be more uniformly distributed than in the middle of a mandate.

I have chosen four polities from the CSES Module 2 (June 2005). I use this comparative design to examine the robustness of the hypotheses proposed in Table 5.1 – that is, whether ideological or performance voting is mediated by citizens' political knowledge across different polities. The countries present considerable variations – on their democratic history, the complexity of their multiparty systems, the level of competition of the campaigns, the extent of electoral participation, the type of government, and the performance of the economy. Table 5.2 summarizes all these features. It classifies each election according to the degree of competitiveness and the level of turnout. It also provides information on the political systems: which was the incumbent party at the time of election, whether the government was a coalition, whether the government had majoritarian support in parliament. All of the elections resulted in a government change. Economic performance was particularly bad in Portugal and Poland. In the latter, the government was also accused of corruption. In contrast, the economic performance in Hungary and Spain was relatively good, although policies implemented by the governments were unpopular (e.g., the Spanish

[3] Levels of political knowledge estimated in postelectoral surveys are especially high for Poland compared with the rest of the countries included in the analysis (see descriptive statistics in the Appendix: Tables A5.1 and A5.2).

military participation in the Iraq war[4]), and the Hungarian government was accused of corruption.

Table 5.2 also classifies the electoral campaigns carried out in each country on the basis of ideology or performance.[5] The campaign was clearly dominated by performance in Hungary, Poland, and Portugal. In the case of Hungary, this was mixed up with the nationalist agenda of the conservative Fidesz-MPP government. In Poland, the dominant topic was the rise of unemployment, the public budget deficit, and the increasing differences in living conditions between rural and urban areas (CSES 2005). In Portugal, the deep economic crisis as well as the public deficit were the main issues of the electoral campaign (Costa, Magalhaes, and Freire 2004). The Spanish campaign was mixed: the conservative government emphasized economic performance and "Spanish nationalism" against Basque demands. The opposition focused the campaign on unpopular policies such as the participation in the Iraq war and social and educational reforms.

The four polities present institutional differences that might influence the results. For instance, the translation of individual votes into aggregate electoral results is mediated by electoral laws that specify the degree of proportionality of the electoral system. This is influenced by the number of electoral districts, the electoral formula used to distribute the votes, or the electoral threshold. All these features vary across the four polities compared here.[6] The explanation for the way in which differences in the institutional context of elections might influence voters' decision rules lies

---

[4] There were a number of other controversial or unpopular policies implemented by the conservatives in Spain, such as the territorial organization of the Spanish state or the Ebro water transfer. The conservative government also had to face a national-level general strike (Torcal and Rico, 2004).

[5] This classification is based on reports about each election in *Electoral Studies* (2002–4), as well as on documentation from the Comparative Study of Electoral Systems (CSES) project. The CSES is a collaborative program of cross-national research among election studies conducted in over fifty states. See http://www.cses.org/.

[6] For instance, the number of electoral districts varies from 41 (Poland) to 176 (Hungary), 21 (Portugal), and 52 (Spain), being all primary electoral districts except in Hungary, where there is one secondary nationwide district. The electoral formulas are all variants of D'Hondt except for Poland, where a modified Sainte-Laguë formula is used. The D'Hondt method is a highest averages method for allocating seats in party-list proportional representation. This system is less proportional than the other popular divisor method, Sainte-Laguë, because D'Hondt slightly favors large parties and coalitions over scattered small parties, whereas Sainte-Laguë is neutral. The electoral thresholds are 5 percent in Poland and Hungary (only in the regional multimember districts or at the national level) and 3 percent in Spain. In contrast, there is no electoral threshold in Portugal. Finally, the electoral lists are closed in all countries except in Poland, where the lists are almost open (Macro-reports of CSES, 2005; http://www.parties-and-elections.de).

Table 5.2. The Political Context of Elections in the Four Countries

	Spain	Portugal	Poland	Hungary
Incumbent party	PP (conservative)	PS (social democratic)	AWSP (conservative)	Fidesz-MPP (conservative)
Support and composition of the incumbent	Majority	Majority	Coalition	Coalition
Change of government	Yes (PSOE, social democratic)	Yes (PSD, center-right)	Yes (social democratic coalition: SLD+UP)	Yes (social democratic coalition: MSZP+SZDSZ)
Performance previous to elections	Middling	Bad	Bad	Middling
Degree of competitiveness	High	High	Low	High
Main opposition parties	PSOE	PSD	Fragmented	MSZP
Dominant topic in the electoral campaign	Mixed campaign	Performance campaign	Performance campaign	Performance campaign
Turnout	70%	62.3%	43.6%	70.5%
Date of election	March 2004	March 2002	September 2001	April 2002

AWSP: Solidarity Electoral Action of the Right; Fidesz-MPP: Hungarian Civic Union; MSZP: Popular Party; PS: Socialist Party; PSD: Social Democratic Party; PSOE: Spanish Socialist Party; SLD: Democratic Left; SZDSZ: Union of Free Democrats; UP: Labour Union

Source: My own elaboration based on http://www.parties-and-elections.de and on the documentation (macro-reports) of the Comparative Study of Electoral Systems, Module 2 (June 2005).

well beyond the scope of this chapter. Accordingly, I have not considered these issues when commenting on the results in the following section. On the contrary, I have emphasized the similarities across the four polities given that the scope of the comparative design adopted in this chapter is to test the robustness of the findings about the influence of political knowledge on ideological or performance voting.

Empirical Results

I test the hypothesis about the influence of political knowledge on ideological and performance voting with a multinomial logit equation. Declared vote is the dependent variable. To contrast the vote for the incumbent and the main opposition party across countries, the results from the multinomial logit estimations correspond only to this dichotomy. Each equation indicates the propensity to vote for the incumbent party versus its main challenger.

The two variables concerning performance and ideological voting are specified as follows. First, retrospective judgments of performance are a dichotomous variable taking the value 0 (for *bad* and *very bad opinion*) and 1 (for *good* and *very good opinion*).[7] Second, ideological voting is tested through two variables measuring the quadratic distance of each voter's ideological position with respect to the ideological position attributed by the respondent to both the incumbent party and the main opposition party.[8]

Other independent variables in the voting equations across countries have been specified as follows. Age varies from 18 to 99 years. Gender is a dummy variable, taking the value 1 for female and 0 for male. Education takes the values 1 (*low education*), 2 (*medium education*), and 3 (*maximum education*) in the case of Hungary and ordinal values in Poland, Portugal, and Spain (ranging from *no education* to *university education*).[9] The last

---

[7] The question was the following: "Now thinking about the performance of the government in general, how good or bad a job do you think the government did over the past [number of years between the previous and the present election or change in government] years. Has it done a very good job? A good job? A bad job? A very bad job?"

[8] More specifically, the ideological distance is specified as follows: $(x_i^* - x_i^G)^2$, where x_i^* is voter i ideological position in a scale that goes from 0 (*extreme left*) to 10 (*extreme right*) and x_i^G is the ideology attributed to the incumbent party (and its main challenger) by the same voter i.

[9] For Hungary, education has been specified in the equations as a categorical variable taking the intermediate value as the reference category, whereas for Poland, Portugal, and Spain, the variable has been specified in the voting equations as ordinal variables.

variable indicates the labor-market position of respondents.[10] Descriptive statistics of all the variables are given in the Appendix (Table 5A.1).[11]

Political knowledge is based on three answers to the CSES questionnaire. Table 5.3 reproduces the questions used in each of the countries, showing the percentages of correct answers. Although the questions are different across countries, they were specifically designed to allow for cross-national comparison.

To create the variable, the number of correct responses were added (taking the values from 0 = *all responses incorrect* to 3 = *all responses correct*). I consider no responses as incorrect answers. The resulting score was recoded from 0 to 1.[12] Additional information on political knowledge would have improved the analysis, but this proxy was the best that could be done with the data available – moreover, a similar variable has already been used in comparative political analyses (see, e.g., Millner 2002; Toka 2003).

Tables 5.4 through 5.7 present the results of the logic of voting for each country. The columns of equation 1 in each of the four tables confirm the existence of both ideological and performance voting across countries. Moreover, the coefficients that show the effect of ideological distance from both the incumbent and the opposition parties are all statistically significant. The sign is also correct across countries: coefficients are negative for ideological distance from the incumbent and positive for ideological distance from the main opposition party (what the tables show is the effect of each independent variable on the propensity to vote for the incumbent versus the main opposition party). The coefficients that indicate the effect of retrospective evaluations of performance are also statistically significant,

---

[10] The categories of this variable are the following: 1 = employed, 2 = home duties, 3 = unemployed, 4 = students, and 5 = retired. I have specified this variable in the equations as categorical, taking "retired" as the category of reference.

[11] I also used the class scheme of Erikson and Goldthorpe (1992), collapsing it in six different classes: 1 (*service class*), 2 (*middle class*), 3 (*urban bourgeoisie*), 4 (*rural bourgeoisie*), 5 (*skilled and semiskilled workers*), and 6 (*nonskilled workers*). However, none of these categories turned out to be statistically significant in the voting equations; consequently, this class variable was excluded from the equation. The results with the effect of the six categories' class variable are available to the interested reader. Recall that the occupational codes included in the CSES module employ only the first two digits of 1988 ISCO/ILO International Standard Classification of Occupations. This does not provide satisfactory information to classify properly the individuals' class position. Hence, I do not discard the possibility that this variable did not turn out to be significant across the equations, given the lack of detailed information.

[12] Through the following metric transformation of the variable: $K = \frac{X - X_{min}}{X_{max} - X_{min}}$.

Table 5.3. Survey Questions of Political Knowledge; Percentage of Correct Responses to Each of the Questions

Degree of difficulty of the question	Spain (2004)	Portugal (2002)	Poland (2001)	Hungary (2002)
Item 1 (easy)	Do you happen to remember the name of the first president of government in our democracy? 70%	Do you happen to remember the name of the Portuguese prime minister before António Guterres? 92%	Who is the chairman of the SLD? 77%	Do you know who presides over the Constitutional Court? 67%
Item 2 (medium)	In what year was the Spanish Constitution approved? 40%	Do you happen to remember the number of European Union member-states? 40%	Who currently is the president of Russia? 75%	Do you know what percentage of the votes a party must get in order to have some of its candidates sent to the new parliament? 65%
Item 3 (difficult)	Do you know how many countries are members of the European Union at the present time? 31%	Number of district-level candidates correctly identified by respondents (at least one or more). 19%	Could you please name the military alliance of which Poland is currently a member? 75%	Number of politicians correctly identified (at least one or more). 13%

Source: Comparative Study of Electoral Systems, Module 2 (June 2005). My own elaboration.

Table 5.4. Voting for the Incumbent in Hungary (Only Coefficients of the Comparison among the Incumbent and the Main Opposition Party Are Given)

Independent variables	Equation 1 Coef	Equation 1 SE	Equation 2 Coef	Equation 2 SE	Equation 3 Coef	Equation 3 SE	Equation 4 Coef	Equation 4 SE
Ideological distance from the incumbent	−0.06**	0.01	−0.07**	0.03	−0.06**	0.01	−0.06**	0.01
Ideological distance from the challenger	0.04**	0.01	0.04**	0.01	0.02+	0.01	0.04**	0.01
Performance (1 = *good*)	3.17**	0.31	3.19**	0.31	3.15**	0.31	2.34**	0.54
Index of Political Knowledge	1.30**	0.49	1.17*	0.61	0.59	0.64	−0.02	1.05
Ideological distance from the incumbent × PolKnowledge			0.02	0.03				
Ideological distance from the challenger × PolKnowledge					0.07**	0.02		
Performance × PolKnowledge							2.17*	1.11
Age	0.01	0.01	0.01	0.01	0.01	0.01	0.01	0.01
Gender	0.11	0.26	0.11	0.26	0.13	0.26	0.08	0.26
Education (reference category: 2. Intermediate level)								
1. Minimum level	1.06**	0.33	1.07**	0.33	1.11**	0.33	1.02**	0.33
3. Maximum level	0.34	0.38	0.35	0.38	0.41	0.38	0.35	0.39
Labor market position (reference category: 5. Retired)								
1. Employed	0.54	0.45	0.53	0.45	0.48	0.45	0.49	0.45
2. Home duties	3.28**	0.89	3.29**	0.88	3.24**	0.89	3.26**	0.89
3. Unemployed	0.31	0.62	0.32	0.62	0.21	0.62	0.26	0.62
4. Students	0.15	0.87	0.15	0.87	0.05	0.87	0.07	0.87
Constant	−3.94**	0.90	−3.88**	0.90	−3.55**	0.92	−3.28**	0.98
Number of cases	872		872		872		872	
LR χ^2	756.26**		757.07**		763.94**		766.51**	
Pseudo R^2	0.438		0.438		0.442		0.446	

Note: Entries are logit maximum-likelihood estimates and their associated standard errors.

**Statistically significant at the level of 0.01; *at the level of 0.05; +at the level of 0.10.

Table 5.5. Voting for the Incumbent in Poland (Only Coefficients of the Comparison among the Incumbent and the Main Opposition Party Are Given)

Independent variables	Equation 1 Coef	SE	Equation 2 Coef	SE	Equation 3 Coef	SE	Equation 4 Coef	SE
Ideological distance from the incumbent	−0.04**	0.01	−0.08*	0.04	−0.04	0.01	−0.04**	0.01
Ideological distance from the challenger	0.06**	0.01	0.06**	0.01	0.04	0.03	0.06**	0.01
Performance (1 = *good*)	0.84*	0.39	0.88*	0.40	0.85*	0.39	−3.22	1.99
Index of Political Knowledge	0.16	0.30	0.22	0.91	0.65	0.92	0.24	0.66
Ideological distance from the incumbent × PolKnowledge			0.04	0.04				
Ideological distance from the challenger × PolKnowledge					0.02	0.03		
Performance × PolKnowledge							4.58**	1.09
Age	0.00	0.01	0.00	0.01	0.00	0.01	0.00	0.01
Gender	−0.14	0.24	−0.15	0.24	−0.15	0.24	−0.16	0.24
Education	0.21*	0.09	0.20*	0.09	0.20*	0.09	0.20*	0.09
Labor market position (reference category: 5. Retired)								
1. Employed	−0.10	0.39	−0.13	0.39	−0.12	0.39	−0.14	0.39
2. Home duties	0.52	0.54	0.50	0.54	0.50	0.54	0.50	0.54
3. Unemployed	−0.47	0.59	−0.44	0.58	−0.46	0.59	−0.48	0.59
4. Students	0.18	0.74	0.15	0.74	0.17	0.74	0.15	0.75
Constant	−1.67*	0.97	−1.64	1.22	−2.10+	1.21	−1.64	1.09
Number of cases	733		733		733		733	
LR χ^2	472.49**		476.15**		474.69**		481.88**	
Pseudo R^2	0.254		0.258		0.257		0.271	

Note: Entries are logit maximum-likelihood estimates and their associated standard errors.

**Statistically significant at the level of 0.01; *at the level of 0.05; +at the level of 0.10.

Table 5.6. Voting for the Incumbent in Portugal (Only Coefficients of the Comparison among the Incumbent and the Main Opposition Party Are Given)

Independent variables	Equation 1		Equation 2		Equation 3		Equation 4	
	Coef	SE	Coef	SE	Coef	SE	Coef	SE
Ideological distance from the incumbent	−0.13**	0.02	−0.15**	0.03	−0.13**	0.02	−0.13**	0.02
Ideological distance from the challenger	0.11**	0.01	0.11**	0.01	0.09**	0.03	0.11**	0.01
Performance (1 = *good*)	1.77**	0.26	1.77**	0.26	1.76**	0.26	0.70	0.53
Index of Political Knowledge	−0.15	0.44	−0.31	0.50	−0.27	0.53	−0.69	0.49
Ideological distance from the incumbent × PolKnowledge			0.03	0.06				
Ideological distance from the challenger × PolKnowledge					0.04	0.05		
Performance × PolKnowledge							2.82**	1.01
Age	−0.01	0.01	−0.01	0.01	−0.01	0.01	−0.01	0.01
Gender	−0.37	0.24	−0.38	0.24	−0.37	0.24	−0.36	0.24
Education	−0.08	0.08	−0.08	0.08	−0.08	0.08	−0.06	0.08
Labor market position (reference category: 5. Retired)								
1. Employed	−0.20	0.37	−0.20	0.38	−0.23	0.38	−0.18	0.38
2. Home duties	−0.63	0.45	−0.63	0.45	−0.64	0.45	−0.62	0.45
3. Unemployed	−0.08	0.69	−0.08	0.69	−0.09	0.68	−0.04	0.69
4. Students	−0.79	0.86	−0.81	0.85	−0.80	0.86	−0.67	0.86
Constant	0.85	0.87	0.96	0.89	0.94	0.89	0.93	0.87
Number of cases	662		662		662		662	
LR χ^2	399.79**		400.89**		401.62**		408.55**	
Pseudo R²	0.286		0.287		0.288		0.298	

Note: Entries are logit maximum-likelihood estimates and their associated standard errors.
**Statistically significant at the level of 0.01; *at the level of 0.05; +at the level of 0.10.

Table 5.7. Voting for the Incumbent in Spain (Only Coefficients of the Comparison among the Incumbent and the Main Opposition Party Are Given)

Independent variables	Equation 1 Coef	Equation 1 SE	Equation 2 Coef	Equation 2 SE	Equation 3 Coef	Equation 3 SE	Equation 4 Coef	Equation 4 SE
Ideological distance from the incumbent	−0.11**	0.02	−0.09**	0.02	−0.11**	0.02	−0.12**	0.02
Ideological distance from the challenger	0.12**	0.02	0.12**	0.02	0.14**	0.04	0.12**	0.02
Performance (1 = *good*)	2.85**	0.35	2.87**	0.35	2.85**	0.35	1.84*	0.65
Index of Political Knowledge	−0.07	0.45	0.28	0.57	0.16	0.55	−1.26	0.81
Ideological distance from the incumbent × PolKnowledge			−0.07	0.04				
Ideological distance from the challenger × PolKnowledge					−0.04	0.05		
Performance × PolKnowledge							2.17**	0.95
Age	0.02	0.01	0.02	0.01	0.02	0.01	0.02	0.01
Gender	0.56+	0.34	0.59+	0.34	0.55+	0.34	0.56+	0.34
Education	0.25*	0.10	0.25*	0.10	0.25*	0.10	0.27**	0.10
Labor market position (reference category: 5. Retired)								
1. Employed	0.53	0.50	0.53	0.50	0.52	0.50	0.55	0.50
2. Home duties	1.01*	0.48	1.03*	0.48	1.00*	0.48	1.05*	0.48
3. Unemployed	0.73	0.68	0.84	0.68	0.74	0.68	0.75	0.68
4. Students	0.65	0.92	0.64	0.93	0.62	0.92	0.64	0.93
Constant	−4.43**	1.14	−4.65**	1.16	−4.51**	1.14	−3.96**	1.17
Number of cases	794		794		794		794	
LR χ^2 (33)	713.88		719.66		713.88		739.21	
Pseudo R^2	0.410		0.413		0.410		0.428	

Note: Entries are logit maximum-likelihood estimates and their associated standard errors.
**Statistically significant at the level of 0.01; *at the level of 0.05; +at the level of 0.10.

with positive signs in all the countries. Positive assessments about governmental performance increase the likelihood to vote for the incumbent. In sum, there is clear evidence of both ideological and performance voting across countries.

I turn now to analyze the influence of political knowledge on the propensity to vote according to performance and to ideology. To assess such an influence, I specify an interaction term between political knowledge and each of the three variables for ideological and performance voting. That is, an interaction term between political knowledge and ideological distance from the incumbent (equation 2 in each of the tables); another interaction term between political knowledge and ideological distance from the main opposition party in equation 3; and, finally, an interaction term between political knowledge and assessments of government performance in equation 4.

The results of Tables 5.4 through 5.7 suggest that political knowledge conditions performance voting but has much less effect on ideological voting. This is reflected in the statistically significant coefficients for the interaction term of political knowledge and performance of equation 4 in Tables 5.4 through 5.7. These coefficients indicate that the effect of a good evaluation of performance in the chances to vote for the incumbent versus the main opposition party increases with political knowledge.

In contrast, the interaction term of political knowledge and ideological distance both from the incumbent and from the main opposition party is not statistically significant. Nevertheless, caution is needed in interpreting interaction terms (Brambor, Clark, and Golder 2005): it is possible that the marginal effect of X (in this case, ideological distance) on Y (in this case, the vote) is statistically significant for relevant values of Z (in this case, political knowledge) even if the coefficient for the interaction term is not. To include an interaction term or not in an equation cannot be decided only on the grounds of the statistical significance of the coefficient.[13]

This empirical problem is dealt with as follows. I calculate the coefficients for ideological distance from the incumbent party conditioned by the minimum (0), low medium (0.33), high medium (0.66), and maximum (1) values of the index of political knowledge in each of the country samples. In this way, the conditioned coefficients for ideological distance have a

---

[13] This is what Brambor et al. (2005) criticize about many articles in which interaction terms were dropped because the coefficient was not statistically significant. In so doing, they missed important conditional relationships among the variables specified in their equations.

Table 5.8. Coefficients of Ideological Distance from the Incumbent Conditioned to Different Values of Political Knowledge

Levels of political knowledge	Hungary	Poland	Portugal	Spain
Nonconditioned (see Tables 5.4 through 5.7: equation 1)	−0.06** (0.01)	−0.04* (0.01)	−0.13** (0.02)	−0.11** (0.02)
Lowest (see Tables 5.4 through 5.7: equation 2)	−0.07* (0.03)	−0.08* (0.04)	−0.15** (0.03)	−0.09** (0.02)
Medium-low	−0.66** (0.01)	−0.06** (0.02)	−0.13** (0.02)	−0.10** (0.01)
Medium-high	−0.58** (0.01)	−0.05** (0.01)	−0.12** (0.01)	−0.13** (0.01)
Highest	−0.05** (0.02)	−0.03** (0.006)	−0.11** (0.03)	−0.15** (0.03)

Note: This table shows only the "ideological distance from the incumbent" coefficients conditioned to the different values of political knowledge. The rest of the coefficients for the other independent variables remain the same as in the third column of Tables 5.4 through 5.7. Entries are logit maximum-likelihood estimates and their associated standard errors. **Statistically significant at the level of 0.01; *at the level of 0.05; +at the level of 0.10.

substantive meaning when the interaction term is specified in each of the four equations. In addition, the corresponding standard errors associated with each of the conditioned coefficients are reported so that the statistical significance of each of the conditioned coefficients can be better appreciated. This is done through a linear transformation of one of the variables included in the interaction term across countries. For example, when calculating the coefficient conditioned on the maximum value of the index of political knowledge, I take the old value of this index minus its maximum value and then specify the interaction term between this transformed index and the ideological distance from the incumbent. Hence, the coefficient corresponding to this ideological distance indicates its incidence on the chances of voting for the incumbent versus its main challenger for the highest value of political knowledge. I used the same logic for the other three calculations of Table 5.8 (i.e., the calculations of the coefficients conditioned on the minimum, low-medium, and high-medium values of political knowledge).

The first two sets of coefficients of Table 5.8 replicate the coefficients of Tables 5.4 through 5.7: they correspond to the nonconditioned coefficients of ideological distance from the incumbent for equation 1 and to the same coefficients conditioned to the minimum value of political knowledge (i.e., value 0) for equation 2. The other three sets of coefficients and their

Table 5.9. Coefficients of Ideological Distance from the Main Opposition Party Conditioned to Different Values of Political Knowledge

Levels of political knowledge	Hungary	Poland	Portugal	Spain
Nonconditioned (see Tables 5.4 through 5.7: equation 1)	0.04** (0.01)	0.06* (0.01)	0.11** (0.01)	0.12** (0.02)
Lowest (see Tables 5.4 through 5.7: equation 3)	0.02+ (0.01)	0.04 (0.03)	0.09** (0.03)	0.14** (0.04)
Medium-low	0.04** (0.01)	0.04* (0.01)	0.10** (0.01)	0.13** (0.02)
Medium-high	0.06** (0.01)	0.05** (0.01)	0.12** (0.01)	0.11** (0.01)
Highest	0.08** (0.02)	0.06** (0.01)	0.12** (0.02)	0.10** (0.03)

Note: This table shows only the "ideological distance from the incumbent" coefficients conditioned to the different values of political knowledge. The rest of the coefficients for the other independent variables remain the same as in the third column of Tables 5.4 through 5.7. Entries are logit maximum-likelihood estimates and their associated standard errors.
**Statistically significant at the level of 0.01; *at the level of 0.05; +at the level of 0.10.

associated standard errors are conditioned to the other three values of political knowledge (i.e., medium-low, medium-high, and highest). As can be seen in Table 5.8, the magnitudes of the conditioned coefficients are slightly higher in the intermediate categories of political knowledge in all the polities analyzed here – the exception is Poland, where the magnitude is higher in the medium-high and maximum levels of political knowledge.[14]

Table 5.9 presents the conditioned coefficients for the ideological distance from the main opposition party. The results are exactly the same: differences in the magnitude of the coefficients are slight, and the highest coefficients are those conditioned to the intermediate values of political knowledge – the exception is again Poland, where the highest coefficients are those for the highest level of political knowledge.

This evidence provides limited support for my initial hypothesis on the influence of political knowledge on the propensity to use ideology when voting. Nevertheless, this effect on ideological voting appears to be non-linear and, in any case, very moderate. It might also be the case that the influence of political knowledge on ideological voting depends on a previous causal mechanism: voters unable to position themselves (or the two

[14] In comparing the magnitude of the conditioned coefficients, I consider not only the coefficient themselves but also their associated standard errors.

main parties) in the ideological scale cannot use the logic of ideological voting. These voters are also those who more frequently do not answer questions on political knowledge. The data, however, do not allow us to distinguish nonrespondents who are politically ignorant from those who do not want to answer for some other reason.[15]

In contrast, the influence of political knowledge on performance voting is more conclusive in Tables 5.4 through 5.7. The interaction terms are statistically significant in the four countries. The results of Table 5.10 show with no exception that the magnitudes of the coefficients corresponding to assessments of governmental performance are higher as the level of political knowledge increases. For instance, if we consider the lowest level of political knowledge, the coefficient is not statistically significant in Portugal. In Poland, the effect of governmental performance is statistically significant only for the highest level of political knowledge.[16] I now conclude this chapter with a brief discussion of the implications of these empirical findings.

Conclusions

This chapter set out to assess the effects of political knowledge on political choices. The empirical analysis has shown such effects on voting decisions. For performance voting, the results are conclusive: the influence of performance on the vote is of greater magnitude as the level of political knowledge increases. There are no exceptions to this. Moreover, in two of the four polities (Portugal and Poland), performance does not influence voting among the less knowledgeable citizens. This suggests that

[15] I have done a bivariate analysis of those respondents who do not position themselves in the ideological scale and the political knowledge index. The relationship is not especially relevant for Spain and Portugal (with V Cramer equal to 0.23 and 0.21, respectively); it is higher for Hungary and especially Poland (with V Cramer equal to 0.32 and 0.39, respectively). In these two countries, those who do not respond to the ideological questions are also those presenting the lowest levels of political knowledge.

In contrast, the relationship between those respondents who do not answer the performance question and the political knowledge index is of smaller magnitude across countries: V Cramer of 0.11 in Hungary, 0.13 both in Spain and Portugal, and 0.22 in Poland. These results are available to the interested reader. Cramer's V is the most popular of the chi-square-based measures of association among two nominal variables. It ranges from 0 (no association) to 1 (perfect association).

[16] Again, in comparing the magnitude of the conditioned coefficients, I consider not only the coefficients themselves but also their associated standard errors.

Table 5.10. Coefficients of Performance Voting Conditioned to Different Values of Political Knowledge

Levels of political knowledge	Hungary	Poland	Portugal	Spain
Nonconditioned (see Tables 5.4 through 5.7: equation 1)	3.17** (0.31)	0.84* (0.39)	1.77** (0.26)	2.85** (0.35)
Lowest (see Tables 5.4 through 5.7: equation 4)	2.34** (0.54)	−3.22 (1.99)	0.7 (0.53)	1.84** (0.65)
Medium-low	3.06** (0.31)	−1.69 (1.19)	1.5** (0.30)	2.5** (0.36)
Medium-high	3.79** (0.47)	−0.16 (0.62)	2.31** (0.38)	3.28** (0.40)
Highest	4.51** (0.68)	1.36** (0.45)	3.11** (0.58)	4.02** (0.48)

Note: This table shows only the "ideological distance from the incumbent" coefficients conditioned to the different values of political knowledge. The rest of the coefficients for the other independent variables remain the same as in the third column of Tables 5.4 through 5.7. Entries are logit maximum-likelihood estimates and their associated standard errors.
**Statistically significant at the level of 0.01; *at the level of 0.05; +at the level of 0.10.

a politically informed citizenry is a necessary (although not sufficient) condition for a democratic control of governments based on their past performance.

In addition, this evidence contradicts the mainstream view of the literature on economic voting, which states the empirical predominance of retrospective over prospective voting. According to this view, retrospective voting would involve far lower decision-making costs than prospective voting. The informational demands required to vote on the basis of performance appear to be modest in comparison to those required to vote on the basis of promises for the future. However, the results of this chapter suggest that the retrospective mechanism of reasoning is not as simple as the literature tends to suggest. On one hand, the process by which voters attribute responsibility to the incumbent for political outcomes is a complex one. On the other hand, voters' calculation of the minimum standard of general welfare expected from the incumbent may be mediated by contextual conditions, individual subjective biases, and levels of political knowledge. In short, the empirical results shown in this chapter suggest that voting on the basis of the government's performance might depend on political expertise, therefore confirming the hypothesis given in Table 5.1.

In contrast, for the case of ideological voting, the results are less conclusive. There is some evidence that the likelihood of using ideology to decide which party to vote for is higher among voters with intermediate levels of political knowledge than among those presenting the lowest level of political expertise. This evidence is fairly limited, however. Thus, my empirical conclusions do not appear to support Zaller's (1992, 2004) thesis that well-informed voters use ideological proximity as a criterion for voting, whereas poorly informed ones use assessments of past performance. The conclusions, on the contrary, are congruent with Fearon's views about the strong informative requirements of performance voting. When "the electorate's ability to monitor what politicians do is poor, then the force of the electoral sanction is weak" (Fearon 1999: 82). Low degrees of political knowledge lead voters to select politicians according to ideology.

This evidence indicates that voters require a sufficient level of political expertise to control governments. This is not an unexpected discovery: political scientists have long argued about the importance for democracy of an informed and knowledgeable citizenry (Key 1966; Pitkin 1967; Mayhew 1974; Manin, Przeworski, and Stokes 1999). Although relatively few empirical studies have tested the effects of political knowledge on voting decisions, they have shown that election outcomes could be considerably different if the electorate as a whole was generally well informed about politics (Bartels 1996). The main contribution of this chapter, therefore, is that the effect of political knowledge on voting is not homogeneous: it varies according to the different logics of voting. If rewards and sanctions for past performance are crucial for governments to be representative, this chapter provides evidence that this retrospective control depends more on citizens' political knowledge than if voters use ideology to select the incumbent.

APPENDIX

Table 5A.1. Descriptive Statistics of All the Variables Included in Each Equation

Variables	Hungary					Poland				
	N	Mean	SD	Min	Max	N	Mean	SD	Min	Max
Declared vote	990	1.72	0.68	1	3	982	2.01	1.10	1	4
Ideological distance from the incumbent	1,042	22.80	29.73	0	100	1283	28.50	29.80	0	100
Ideological distance from the challenger	1,050	20.19	28.46	0	100	1329	21.61	26.96	0	100
Performance	1,165	0.51	0.50	0	1	1649	0.10	0.30	0	1
Level of Polknowledge	1,200	0.38	0.29	0	1	1794	0.76	0.35	0	1
Age	1,198	50.32	17.36	18	92	1794	47.28	17.49	18	98
Gender	1,199	0.39	0.49	0	1	1794	0.43	0.49	0	1
Education	1,199	1.81	0.63	1	3	1794	4.36	1.34	1	7
Employed	1,184	0.47	0.50	0	1	1655	0.42	0.49	0	1
Home duties	1,184	0.04	0.19	0	1	1655	0.10	0.30	0	1
Unemployed	1,184	0.05	0.21	0	1	1655	0.13	0.33	0	1
Students	1184	0.03	0.18	0	1	1655	0.05	0.21	0	1
Retired	1184	0.42	0.49	0	1	1655	0.31	0.46	0	1

Table 5A.2. Descriptive Statistics of All the Variables Included in Each Equation

Variables	Portugal					Spain				
	N	Mean	SD	Min	Max	N	Mean	SD	Min	Max
Declared vote	784	1.78	0.74	1	3	942	1.98	0.91	1	4
Ideological distance from the incumbent	1,092	8.23	14.24	0	100	1044	24.18	26.25	0	100
Ideological distance from the challenger	1,091	11.87	18.53	0	100	1044	6.83	13.11	0	100
Performance	1,193	0.20	0.40	0	1	1044	0.44	0.50	0	1
Level of Polknowledge	1,303	0.47	0.29	0	1	1212	0.47	0.35	0	1
Age	1,303	45.26	16.62	18	80	1212	46.09	17.89	18	94
Gender	1,303	0.44	0.50	0	1	1212	0.49	0.50	0	1
Education	1,295	4.41	2.04	1	8	1206	4.45	1.81	1	8
Employed	1,293	0.60	0.49	0	1	1193	0.44	0.50	0	1
Home duties	1,293	0.11	0.32	0	1	1193	0.21	0.41	0	1
Unemployed	1,293	0.04	0.20	0	1	1193	0.09	0.28	0	1
Students	1,293	0.03	0.18	0	1	1193	0.06	0.24	0	1
Retired	1,293	0.21	0.41	0	1	1193	0.20	0.40	0	1

REFERENCES

Althaus, Scott. 2003. *Collective Preferences in Democratic Politics*. Cambridge: Cambridge University Press.

Andersen, Robert, Anthony Heath, and Richard Sinnot. 2001. "Political Knowledge and Electoral Choices." *CREST* Working Paper No. 87.

Bartels, Larry. 1996. "Uninformed Votes: Information Effects in Presidential Elections." *American Journal of Political Science* 40 (1): 194–230.

Bartle, John. 1997. "Political Awareness and Heterogeneity in Models of Voting: Some Evidence from the Recent British Election Studies." In Charles Pattie, David Denver, Justin Fisher, and Steve Ludlam (eds.), *British Elections and Parties Review*, vol. 7 (pp. 1–24). London: Frank Cass.

Bennet, Stephen. 1988. "Know-nothing Revisited: The Meaning of Political Ignorance Today." *Social Science Quarterly* 69: 476–90.

Bennet, Stephen. 1989. "Trends in Americans' Political Information, 1967–1987." *American Politics Quarterly* 17: 422–35.

Bennet, Stephen. 1995. "Americas' Knowledge of Ideology, 1980–1992." *American Politics Quarterly* 23: 259–78.

Brambor, Thomas, William Roberts Clark, and Matt Golder. 2005. "Understanding Interaction Models: Improving Empirical Analyses." *Political Analysis* 13: 1–20.

Comparative Study of Electoral Systems. 2005. CSES Module 2 Third Advance Release [data set]. Ann Arbor: University of Michigan, Center for Political Studies. June 29 (see http://www.cses.org).

Converse, Philip. 1964. "The Nature of Belief Systems in Mass Publics." In David Apter (ed.), *Ideology and Discontent* (pp. 206–61). New York: Free Press.

Converse, Philip. 1970. "Attitudes and Non-Attitudes: Continuation of a Dialogue." In Edward Tufte (ed.), *The Quantitative Analysis of Social Problems* (pp. 168–89). Reading, PA: Addison-Wesley.

Costa Lobo, Marina, Pedro Magalhaes, and André Freire. 2004. "Introduçao." In André Freire, Marina Costa Lobo, and Pedro Magalhaes (eds.), *Portugal a Votos: As Eleiçoes Legislativas de 2002* (pp. 25–34). Lisbon: Imprensa de Ciencias Sociais.

Delli Carpini, Michael, and Scott Keeter. 1996. *What Americans Know about Politics and Why It Matters*. New Haven: Yale University Press.

Downs, Anthony. 1957. *An Economic Theory of Democracy*. New York: Harper and Row.

Erikson, Robert, and John Goldthorpe. 1992. *The Constant Flux: A Study of Class Mobility in Industrial Societies*. Oxford: Clarendon.

Fearon, James. 1999. "Electoral Accountability and the Control of Politicians: Selecting Good Types versus Sanctioning Poor Performance." In Adam Przeworski, Susan C. Stokes, and Bernard Manin (eds.), *Democracy, Accountability, and Representation* (pp. 55–97). New York: Cambridge University Press.

Gómez, Brad, and Matthew Wilson. 2001. "Political Sophistication and Economic Voting in the American Electorate: A Theory of Heterogeneous Attribution." *American Journal of Political Science* 45 (4): 899–914.

Gómez, Brad, and Matthew Wilson. 2006. "Cognitive Heterogeneity and Economic Voting: A Comparative Analysis of Four Democratic Electorates." *American Journal of Political Science* 50 (1): 127–45.

155

Key, V. O., Jr. 1966. *The Responsible Electorate: Rationality in Presidential Voting: 1936–1960*. Cambridge, MA: Harvard University Press.

Kiewiet, D. Roderick. 1983. *Macro-economics and Micro-politics: The Electoral Effects of Economic Issues*. Chicago: University of Chicago Press.

Kinder, Donald R., and Roderick Kiewiet. 1979. "Economic Discontent and Political Behavior: The Role of Personal Grievances and Collective Economic Judgements in Congressional Voting." *American Journal of Political Science* 23: 495–517.

Kinder, Donald R., and Roderick Kiewiet. 1981. "Sociotropic Politics." *British Journal of Political Science* 11: 129–61.

Kramer, Gerald H. 1971. "Short-Term Fluctuations in U.S. Voting Behavior, 1896–1964." *American Political Science Review* 65: 131–43.

Kramer, Gerald H. 1983. "The Ecological Fallacy Revisited: Aggregate versus Individual Level Findings on Economics and Elections, and Sociotropic Voting." *American Political Science Review* 77: 92–111.

Krause, George A. 1997. "Voters, Information Heterogeneity, and the Dynamics of Aggregate Economic Expectations." *American Journal of Political Science* 41: 1170–200.

Luskin, Robert. 1990. "Explaining Political Sophistication." *Political Behavior* 12: 331–61.

Manin, Bernard, Adam Przeworski, and Susan Stokes. 1999. "Elections and Representation." In Adam Przeworski, Susan Stokes, and Bernard Manin (eds.), *Democracy, Accountability, and Representation* (pp. 29–54). New York: Cambridge University Press.

Mayhew, David R. 1974. *Congress: The Electoral Connection*. New Haven: Yale University Press.

Millner, Henry. 2002. *Civic Literacy: How Informed Citizens Make Democracy Work*. Tufts University: University Press of New England.

Pitkin, Hanna F. 1967. *The Concept of Representation*. Berkeley: University of California Press.

Popkin, Samuel L. 1991. *The Reasoning Voter*. Chicago: University of Chicago Press.

Sinnot, Richard. 2000. "Knowledge and the Position of Attitudes to a European Foreign Policy on the Real-to-Random Continuum." *International Journal of Public Opinion Research* 12: 113–37.

Sniderman, Paul M., Richard A. Brody, and Philip E. Tetlock. 1991. *Reasoning and Choice. Explorations in Political Psychology*. New York: Cambridge University Press.

Toka, Gabor. 2003. "Can Voters Be Equal? A Cross-National Analysis. Part 1." *The Review of Sociology* 9: 51–72.

Torcal, Mariano, and Guillem Rico. 2004. "The 2004 Spanish General Election: In the Shadow of Al-Qaeda?" *South European Society & Politics* 9 (3): 107–21.

Zaller, John R. 1992. *The Nature and Origins of Mass Opinion*. New York: Cambridge University Press.

Zaller, John R. 2004. "Floating Voters in US Presidential Elections: 1948–2000." In Willem Saris and Paul Sniderman (eds.), *Studies in Public Opinion: Attitudes, Nonattitudes, Measurement Error, and Change*. Princeton: Princeton University Press.

CHAPTER SIX

The Political Consequences of Internal Party Democracy

José María Maravall

Introduction

My purpose is to explore whether democracy within the incumbent party can help citizens to monitor the government, that is, if the internal accountability of party leaders facilitates their external accountability as public office holders. On one hand, voters might reward parties in which internal monitoring provides information needed to control ruling politicians. On the other hand, internal partisan debates may carry too much noise for citizens and entail costs for the political capacity of the government. Voters might, in this case, reward disciplined parties and punish undisciplined ones; this would reinforce the position of leaders at the expense of critical activists. External electoral considerations would then be detrimental to the internal accountability within the party. I examine parliamentary democracies only. The reason is not that parties are different under presidentialism and parliamentarism, but rather that the relationship of the governing party with the executive is not the same.

Let us start with some clarifications on who's who. Think first of voters. Citizens elect for office that party whose promises are closer to their own political preferences, and they want the elected government to be democratically accountable and politically capable. Such a government would provide information about its actions and answer for them at election time. However, it would also need to be able to implement its promises, and this ability could be undermined by internal dissent and factionalism. Voters will face trade-offs if accountability were to hamper capacity, or vice versa.

I wish to thank Andrew Richards, Covadonga Meseguer, Henar Criado, Adam Przeworski, and Margaret Levi for their comments.

157

Consider now the government. Incumbents expect their party to fulfill two tasks: on one hand, to serve as an early warning instrument, that is, to provide information on electoral risks. This early warning requires internal democracy: it can only be reliable under conditions of freedom of expression and if no reprisals are feared. On the other hand, incumbents expect party members to defend the government and its policies. This task requires unity in the face of external attacks or political crises rather than internal democracy. If a party is to persuade voters that the government is acting on their behalf even when it betrays electoral promises, what is needed is internal cohesion. "Democratic centralism" was an attempt to combine diversity of opinions (and the task of early warning) with discipline once a decision was adopted. However, the two tasks, early warning via democracy and support via unity, may hardly be compatible. I discuss the trade-off that politicians face if fulfilling one task were to imply costs for the other one.

Finally, when discussing the party, two groups of actors will appear in different occasions. The first group is the public or party officeholders. They share common interests: both to stay in office and to carry out ideological policies. Their differences stem from the varying positions in a hierarchy of power and from their longer or shorter political time horizons. They are all part of the party *nomenklatura*, but some of them will be the potential "political heirs" of the rest. The second group are the party members. Their common interest lies in ideological policies, which compensate the costs of their political commitment; however, they are not indifferent to power as a means to implement such policies. Their internal differences will be expressed in different degrees of activism, related to the intensity of their policy preferences: only if these are strong will party members accept the costs of greater political activism. It is thus possible to distinguish between rank-and-file members and activists: even though both share a long-term political horizon and believe the party is an instrument for policy ideals, activists have greater potential for criticism of their government.

Some conceptual definitions are needed. Internal party democracy refers to the capacity of party members to control their leaders. This control can be prospective: in this case, it refers to the selection of the leaders and the party policies in office. It can also be retrospective: this happens when leaders are accountable to party members for their past actions and are rewarded or punished accordingly (i.e., continue as leaders or be dismissed). Selection and accountability are two different, sometimes contradictory aspects of democracy (Maravall 2007): in this chapter, I assume that a party is democratic when its leaders are internally accountable. This will only happen if members (i) have enough information on the actions of the leadership and (ii) have the instruments to enforce sanctions if policies deviate from the party program. Internal party democracy therefore implies that, if the party holds power, whenever the leaders betray the program, they will need to provide satisfactory explanations to members – otherwise, they may face internal dissent and, perhaps, be thrown out of party office.

The typical institutions to which the national executive committees are held accountable are regular party congresses, more restricted intermediate organs of middle-level elites that meet between congresses, and sometimes the direct vote of party members. These institutions may sometimes be in conflict when disagreements exist within a party: for instance, if militant activists control the local branches and are strongly represented in congresses, the leadership may use the direct vote of party members as a plebiscite to circumvent control by congresses.[1] I assume here that internal party democracy depends on formal rules, not informal practices. Informal rules may be expressed as tolerance or condescendence, but these are a fragile protection for internal dissenters. Critical "voice" (Hirschman 1970) requires the absence of threats and reprisals, and this needs rules. This is why I discuss uninominal constituencies, closed lists, or the decentralized selection of candidates – not "styles of leadership."[2]

---

[1] A substantial number of reforms have increased the participation of party members in the selection of leaders and candidates for office. Primaries for the selection of candidates were, for instance, introduced in the PS (Parti Socialiste) and the UMP (Union pour un Mouvement Populaire) in France; the PSOE (Partido Socialista Obrero Español) in Spain; the SPD (Socialdemokratische Partei Deutschlands) in Germany. Reforms have also given more influence to party members in decisions over policies. This was the case of the British Labour Party under Tony Blair, who held plebiscites in 1995 to suppress "clause 4" of the party manifesto (which declared that nationalization of the means of production was a goal of the party), and in 1996 to validate the program for the elections held in the following year (Webb 2000). The German SPD, the CDU (Christlich-Democratische Union), and the FDP (Freie Demokratische Partei) also increased the use of direct votes by party members (Scarrow 1999). These reforms refer, however, to party democracy as "selection." That they do not necessarily mean greater control over the leaders is reflected in the fact that defeats at the annual conference of the party have become increasingly irrelevant for the leadership of the British Labour Party. Thus, internal accountability by the more informed intermediate organs can be undermined by plebiscites. On the British case, see Mair (1997).

[2] It could be argued that informal rules of tolerance and habits of free speech explain, for instance, differences in the use of "voice" within British and Spanish parties. Thus, when the British parliament voted on February 26, 2003, over the war in Iraq, 124 Labour members of Parliament (MPs; out of 412) stood against war – and against their government. When a similar vote took place in the Spanish Parliament, every PP (Partido Popular) deputy

I similarly assume that governments are accountable when voters can punish or reward them at election time on the grounds of their previous actions. As Key (1966: 10) puts it, "the fear of loss of popular support powerfully disciplines the actions of governments." Governments are representative when they act in the interest of citizens under the constraints of elections and checks and balances. That is, when incumbent politicians are controlled both by voters and by other horizontal institutions of the state.

But for ex post electoral sanctions to be consequential, and thus to induce ex ante representation, citizens must have information about the actions of incumbents. They must be able to monitor what the government does and to establish causal relationships between actions (or nonactions) and outcomes. Voters in search of information about what a government is doing can turn to many sources: the opposition, the press, but also those activists of the party in office who care about policies. On the grounds of this information, citizens will judge whether politicians are consistent with their campaign promises and whether they act in the best interest of voters when they switch from their announced policies. In the first case, voters must have information on policies; in the second, they must have information on outcomes (Stokes 2001: 9–20, 186–90). The crucial information refers to whether the government is representative rather than responsive – that is, whether it acts on behalf of the voters rather than in accordance with their immediate demands (Manin, Przeworski, and Stokes 1999).

Information and monitoring depend on institutional conditions. It has thus been argued that under presidential systems with term limits, the control of incumbents becomes more difficult because the dissuasive effect of future elections on the shirking of politicians will not operate. Also, if mandates are rigid, incompetent and discredited presidents can survive in office. Further, because their electoral support is independent from that of parliamentary majorities, parties cannot control presidents. Cheibub and Przeworski (1999: 231–5) have shown that, of seventy peaceful changes of presidents between 1950 and 1990, only four (4.7 percent) were due to the removal by the party and interim replacements. On the contrary, under parliamentarism, of 310 peaceful changes of prime ministers, 148 (47.7

voted with the government – for war. A more convincing explanation is that British MPs enjoy a much greater political autonomy because of the rules of representation: they are personally elected by their constituency, whereas Spanish deputies are elected within a closed list decided by the party leadership.

percent) were due to internal party politics or the collapse of the ruling coalition. Thus, "in about one half of cases it is not voters who sanction the incumbent prime ministers but politicians" (Cheibub and Przeworski 1999: 232).

Powell and Whitten (1993: 391–414) have also concluded that institutional conditions influence the capacity of voters to attribute responsibility for economic outcomes. Blame can be shifted to others when the policies of a minority government depend on the support of other parties in parliament (Strøm 1990). Further, responsibilities become blurred when several parties share decisions in a coalition. The threat of electoral sanctions is not credible if coalitions can survive a loss of votes by simply coopting new members. In Rosenstone's words (1995: 9), "when a single party governs alone, voters can more easily hold it accountable electorally than when several parties comprise a governing coalition." In parliamentary democracies with proportional representation and fragmented party systems, no relationship may exist between election results and government formation. A party in opposition may lose seats but enter the government; a party in power may win seats but be thrown out of the coalition. Private negotiations within coalitions and internecine struggles within parties often turn politics into an opaque affair for voters.

We know that party systems, parliaments, and the structure of governments influence democratic accountability. However, we know much less about whether parties as institutions can help or hinder the capacity of voters to control politicians. Party politics and internal party democracy have been segregated over a long time from democratic theory. Writing about parties, Sartori (1987: 151) states that "no matter how oligarchic...the result of the competition between them is, on the aggregate, democracy." This segregation cannot stand if the internal politics of parties are relevant for the monitoring of governments and the information of voters. Internal debates and disputes are greater, by definition, in democratic parties: activists and competing politicians can demand information from the leadership and discuss alternative strategies.[3] Whether or not explanations are

---

[3] The 2002 Labour Party conference provides a good example. In September, the Labour government was defending two unpopular policies. On the international front, 65 percent of British voters opposed a unilateral military attack by the United Kingdom and the United States against Iraq, even if Saddam Hussein rejected inspections by the United Nations of his suspected sites of production of chemical and nuclear weapons. On Saturday, 29 September, 350,000 people demonstrated in the streets against the possibility of war. In the party conference, held in the same days, 40.2 percent of delegates rejected an attack against Iraq regardless of the UN Security Council. On the domestic front, the Labour

161

accepted is irrelevant: what matters here is that useful information flows within the party under conditions of internal democracy.

Let us now turn to the political capacity of a government to make decisions and implement them. If citizens want to control the incumbent, it is in order for the latter to carry out the policies for which it was elected, or, if it has switched from policy promises, to ensure that the reason was to improve their welfare. But policies are carried out not just because citizens control the government and this induces its "political will." They also depend on the political capacity to transform this will into decisions and outcomes. Thus, the support of a voter for the policy position of the government will be displaced by a factor that depends on the capacity of the latter. This capacity can be limited by conditions that are external or internal to the government and its party. The external conditions include the opposition in parliament, resistance in society, international difficulties. I do not intend to dwell on these in this chapter.

My concern here is the internal conditions that can influence the political capacity of a government – more particularly, the role of the party in office. To pose the problem in stark terms: a monolithical party, oligarchic and disciplined, can increase the political capacity of its government; a democratic party, with internal debates and disputes over policy, can limit this capacity. But whereas the first can reduce voters' information on what the government does, the second can facilitate it.[4] The political capacity of a government and the information of voters may therefore involve trade-offs. This can conflict with the interests of citizens, who want both a controlled and a capable government.

For trade-offs to exist, rather than sheer incompatibility between information and capacity, open internal debates and challenges to the leadership must not prevent electoral success. Parties in office must be able to debate policy switches and survive if the reasons provided by the

government was proposing to increase private finance of public provision of education and health. This was strongly opposed by public sector unions, was disliked by Labour voters, and was rejected by the conference. Blair was forced to use his speech to the conference on 1 October to provide an array of reasons for military pressure on Iraq and for welfare reform. Information, and rhetoric, reached not only delegates and party members but voters at large. See *The Guardian*, 30 September, 1 and 2 October 2002.

[4] It is obvious that the median voter will prefer a united party, with a single-policy position, to a divided party with multiple positions. The distance with the median voter's ideal position will be easier to assess in the first case, and behavior in office will be more predictable. However, the problem here is different: the party is already in office, and the median voter has incomplete information on the actions of the government.

government are considered to be satisfactory. Examples exist: the British Labour government of Harold Wilson and the Spanish socialist government of Felipe González won popular referenda in 1975 and 1986 on membership in the European Community and in NATO after internal discussions in the parties. If voters see internal debates as a source of information on a justifiable policy switch, the electoral prospects of a party in government need not be harmed. On the contrary, they will be if no reasons are provided for such switch by an internally disciplined and externally opaque party, or if debates are a source of noise, rather than information, and express paralyzing internal struggles.

Thus, voters face trade-offs over internal party politics, between information and political capacity. They may choose different combinations. They may prefer open lists of parliamentary candidates, rather than closed and blocked ones and yet support a more centralized party with closed lists because its political capacity will not be questioned in office. They may think that a party leader is more informative and responsive but vote for another with more authority to keep the party together and avoid confrontations in government.[5] Voters may have to make choices between more authority and capacity or more democracy and information.

Governments in parliamentary democracies depend on the party in office and on voters. Cabinets must be tolerated not just by the electorate but by a parliamentary majority. Prime ministers must cope with the party at large: otherwise, unpopularity within the party is eventually reflected in party congresses and in the parliamentary group. Ramsay MacDonald is a nightmare for prime ministers and parties in parliamentary democracies. We have thus an agent, the government, with two principals: the party and the electorate.

A Triangular Agency Relationship

If democratic representation is seen as a principal–agent relationship, the risk of agency losses exists if the government has interests different

---

[5] In Spain, a survey of Demoscopia (*Barómetro de Primavera* 1992) revealed that a majority of citizens preferred open to closed lists. Yet they did not alter the party list in elections to the Senate where lists were open. In the United Kingdom, voters saw Neil Kinnock as more concerned than Margaret Thatcher about the interests of all groups in society (29.3 percent against 20.6 percent), and Thatcher as more likely to get things done (59.9 percent against 20.3 percent). The outcome was that 42.9 percent voted for Thatcher and only 29.6 percent for Kinnock (Anthony Heath, Roger Jowell, and John Curtice, *British Election Study*, 1992. See Heath, Jowell, and Curtice 1994).

from those of its supporters and if information is asymmetrical. In the relationship of the government with both party and voters, it may be that the latter can increase their information about their agent looking at what happens between the government and the party.

This is a peculiar agency relationship. For one, the two principals are not competing for the agent, although both the party and the electorate want the government to give priority to their respective interests if in contradiction with those of the other principal. For two, the party and the voters stand in different positions vis-à-vis the agent. Voters' instrument of enforcement is, obviously, electoral sanctions and rewards. If the government is not a good agent, it will be thrown out of public office. The instrument of enforcement of the party is sanctions and rewards in internal elections to the leadership of the party or in the nomination of party candidates for public office. Thus, the party previously selects whom voters can choose as their agent.

Voters delegate power to the government in elections, but this delegation to some extent benefits the party, the other principal. Such benefits do not just consist of an array of political appointments that can only benefit a small proportion of party members. They basically involve the implementation of policies on which the party hopes to have some influence. So it is because party activists have preferences regarding particular policies that they want the government to be in office. Their preferences on policies may be different from the voters'; they will also be more intensive. Whereas voters can always replace the government by the opposition, party activists will have a much stronger interest in their candidate remaining in power. There is, however, a threshold to this interest if activists were to believe that the government is not carrying out their policy preferences and is therefore shirking as their agent. When the threshold is reached, the party will be indifferent about its agent surviving in power. It will only want to remain in office replacing the party leader. In Germany, SPD members were largely indifferent about Helmut Schmidt surviving as federal chancellor in the 1982 elections: the party thought that a period in opposition would give new strength to the party's policy preferences after many years of subordination to those of the electorate.[6] Activists will also want to replace the incumbent, whatever their views on the policies being implemented, if

---

[6] Personal interviews with the executive committee of the SPD, 17–20 May 1982. Of course, SPD members could not foresee that, after Schmidt, they would be in opposition for sixteen years.

their value of office is high and the electoral popularity of the government is falling. However, as Cheibub and Przeworski have shown (1999: 232–2), only 30 percent of new leaders who replace incumbents win the next elections. John Major is an exception, not the rule.

The government thus faces demands from two principals and needs the support of both to stay in office. These demands can be very different. Figure 6.1 represents the positions of a government, its party, an opposition, and an electorate in a single dimension space, a simple left–right scale. It is based on Spanish survey data from the mid-1980s, used for illustrative purposes. Here, the ideal policy position of the median activist of the party in office is X_1; that of the median voter is X_2; that of the voters of the government, X_3; that of the opposition median activist, X_4; that of the voters of the opposition, X_5. As Cotta (1999: 10) puts it, "Finding a balance between the preservation of the identity of the party (as required by the rank-and-file) and adapting it to the needs of the national political game is one of the crucial tasks of the party elite. To put it differently: the party elite will pursue the maximization of its goals to the extent that it does not endanger its position within the party." The distance between X_1 and X_3 represents the concessions of the party for the sake of electoralism. What we see in the Spanish case is an overlap between X_2 and X_3: the government was sitting comfortably with an absolute majority, with the opposition far away from X_2, the median voter. González only needed to justify the concessions away from X_1 and stick to his electoral program.

Figure 6.2 represents a similar distribution of preferences, regarding now the role of the government in redistributing income.[7] The data refer to the United Kingdom in 1998: that is, Labour was in office with Tony Blair as prime minister, and the opposition was the Conservative Party under William Hague. The range of preferences goes from 1 to 5: from strong agreement with the proposition that the government should redistribute income between the rich and the poor, to strong disagreement. Positions X_1, X_2, X_3, X_4, and X_5 represent the same preferences as in Figure 6.1. Labour Party activists held more extreme positions than voters. Demands from the electorate are different from demands within the party.

Table 6.1 provides further evidence on the polarized view of politics that party activists can have. The illustration comes from survey data on

---

[7] Note that in Figures 6.1 and 6.2, the distributions of preferences of both party members and the electorate can be considered as exogenous and, on the contrary, the distribution of preferences of government voters as endogenous. That is, the latter would not be static but dependent on the policies carried out by the government.

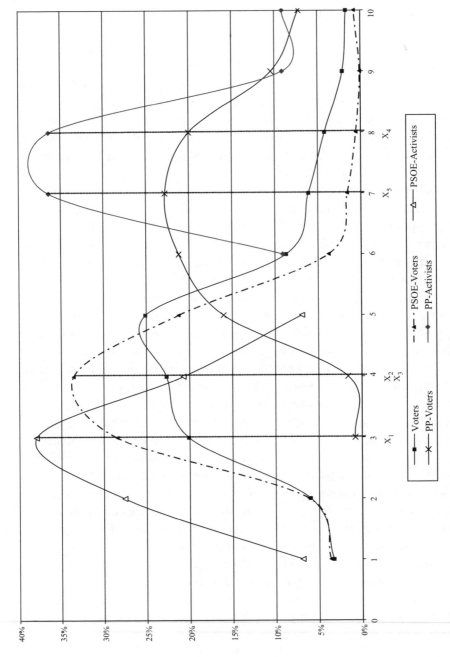

Figure 6.1. Ideological positions (self-attribution), Spain 1986.

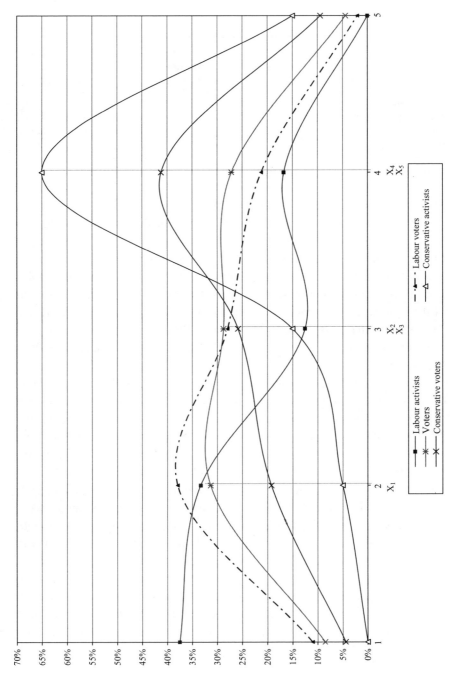

Figure 6.2. Policy positions on redistribution, Great Britain 1998.

Table 6.1. Ideological Positions and Distances (Spain)

	Self-assigned position	Ideological position of the PSOE (diff.)		Ideological position of the PP (diff.)	
According to					
Non-PSOE voters	5.23	3.87	(1.36)	8.27	(3.04)
PSOE voters	3.89	3.69	(0.20)	8.64	(4.75)
PSOE activists	2.93	3.14	(0.21)	8.74	(5.81)

Source: Centro de Investigaciones Sociológicas, survey of February 1986 (N = 2,454).

Spanish politics. If party activists were to disagree with the policies of the socialist government, their polarized view of the opposition (Partido Popular [PP]) would restrain them. Thus, the threshold of tolerance of the party can be manipulated by the government depending on the political polarization and the electoral support of the opposition. The political space is malleable: distances between their own position and that of the opposition are wider for party activists than for voters. If activists care about office, it is because of the value that they attribute to the policies of their government compared with those of the ideologically distant opposition.

The position of the government vis-à-vis these conflicting demands depends on the value it attaches to policies and office. The higher the value of policies relative to the value of office, the less likely the policies of the government will converge with the median voter preferences[8] and the more they will respond to the preferences of the party activists; the contrary will happen the higher the value of office is. As for accountability, if information is asymmetrical between the agent and the two principals, the government will truthfully report its actions if it is behaving as a good agent for both. If it is not behaving as such, it will mislead them – either both simultaneously or only one of them if their policy preferences differ and the government is acting on behalf of one rather than the other because of informational asymmetries between the two principals. If we regard the party as one of the two principals, governments will deploy strategies of concealment if the party does not have information on actions that it would sanction (e.g., corruption in the executive). If this information exists and

[8] This argument rests on several assumptions, among them that the government is perfectly informed about the preferences of voters and that the latter are not distributed over the whole space of political competition in multiparty systems.

concealment is not an available option, governments will turn to strategies of electoralist excuses if the party cares about office, and of party unity if party activists hold a polarized view of political competition. Thus, party unity can be the result of the government acting or not acting on behalf of the party and, furthermore, on that of the voters.

The Control of Governments by Parties

A first argument of why parties control governments goes as follows. Parties provide a "brand name" that facilitates information to voters: judgments about how present leaders behave in office can use as clues past performances of previous leaders. Ever since Downs (1957: 109–11), it has been argued that party labels help voters to summarize past governmental records. Organizational reputations serve as informational shortcuts for retrospective voting (Key 1966; Fiorina 1981; Alt 1984; Popkin 1991; Kiewiet and McCubbins 1991; Achen 1992). A second argument is this: because parties compete in a political market, they must respond to public demand – offer good products and replace bad ones. Parties therefore reduce the scope for opportunism by politicians. For this second argument to stand, parties must have a longer time horizon than politicians. This is a reasonable assumption. Table 6.2 provides information on the average years in office for both heads of government and parties in thirty-eight democracies that lasted over the period 1975–95,[9] with observations for 775 country/years.[10] Parties always lasted longer in office than individual politicians, but this was particularly so in parliamentary systems. If the main difference between both systems affects parties, rather than individual officeholders, then the absence of term limits does not provide a sufficient explanation for such greater longevity of incumbents under parliamentarism. Note that years refer to uninterrupted office: leaders could come back after a period in opposition.

Parties might therefore constrain incumbent politicians "to uphold the party's reputation so that the party's candidates will continue to win in the future" (Wittman 1995: 10). Because various generations coexist in a

[9] The countries are Australia, Austria, Belgium, Bahamas, Barbados, Botswana, Canada, Colombia, Costa Rica, Cyprus, Denmark, Dominican Republic, Finland, France, Germany, Greece, Iceland, India, Ireland, Israel, Italy, Jamaica, Japan, Luxembourg, Malta, Mauritius, Netherlands, New Zealand, Norway, Papua New Guinea, Portugal, Spain, Sweden, Trinidad, United Kingdom, United States, Vanuatu, and Venezuela.

[10] I have excluded those years in which the government was led by an independent, with no party affiliation. Two cases were Cyprus in 1989–93 and Portugal in 1978–9.

169

Table 6.2. Average Period in Office, Democracies between 1975 and 1995

	Total		Parliamentary systems		Presidential systems	
	Years	Months	Years	Months	Years	Months
Heads of government	4	7	4	8	4	2
Parties	7	6	8	1	5	0
N	775		636		139	

party, party politicians have different time horizons: those with the longer ones prevent shirking by the present incumbents. This argument relates to the "overlapping generations" model[11] of Alesina and Spear (1988). Out of office, the politicians' declared ideal policy position is the median voter's; once in office, the positions will not diverge if party members who anticipate running for office in the future want the party to remain credible. In Wittman's (1995: 21) terms, "other members of the party have strong incentives to maintain the reputation of the party since the brand name is valuable in attracting votes." If this model were to fit party politics, internal democracy would serve the interests of voters.

The model, however, faces problems. For one, this internal party democracy is oligarchical: the aspiring "political heirs" are a restricted elite. If the party is to control incumbent politicians so that they will respond to the interests of voters, the internal monitoring and enforcement must be run by the "political heirs," not the activists. For two, the successive generations of politicians must not collude. However, some conditions provide incentives for collusion. Thus, if the incumbent shirks and only the "political heirs" know, they will have no incentives to inform voters unless concealment becomes costly for them. Only if voters are informed by other means will incentives for the "political heirs" to react exist.

An alternative interpretation is that the external accountability of the government depends on party activists rather than on aspiring leaders. If we accept that party activists are hardly in politics for the perks of office, then they must have a strong commitment for policies and think that there is some probability that they will influence the policies of the government.

---

[11] The basic "overlapping generations" model is attributable to Samuelson (1958); it is a discrete-time model of an infinite-horizon economy in which individuals lived two periods and then died and a new generation was born in each period. At any point in time, the population consisted of only two generations, those born at the beginning of the current period (the "young") and at the beginning of the previous period (the "old").

170

The costs of activism are indeed much higher than those of voting: activists must participate in demanding debates, run activities in the local branches, distribute party propaganda, contact potential voters, and so on. Thus, the probability of influence and the party differential (the value attributed to the implementation of the policies of the government compared with those of the opposition) must have a considerable weight in the activists' political commitments. It is therefore plausible to assume that activists will want to monitor the actions of the government as their agent. And, also, that the greater the involvement of activists, the stronger their demands of control of the leaders: there will be different degrees of activism among party members.

Electoral programs are a trade-off for party activists between policies and power: the party will make concessions regarding its ideal policy position (in Figures 6.1 and 6.2, the distance between X_1 and X_3) if they increase electoral possibilities. Voters seldom read political programs; on the contrary, activists debate and scrutinize them intensely because they represent the raison d'être of their efforts. In Stokes's words (1999: 261), "Activists may use party manifestos as a contract between themselves and party leaders, a common understanding of the position they were able to get candidates to adopt in exchange for a quietening of voice." These concessions will be greater if activists fear a victory of the opposition and see the latter as strongly polarized.

Democratic representation may therefore conflict with internal party democracy if the preferences of party members are different and more extreme than those of voters. If the value of policies relative to that of office is greater for activists than for leaders, they will defend policies with less regard to their electoral attraction: contrary to the centripetal influence of the median voter,[12] that of party activists will be centrifugal. If the government tries to be responsive regarding the median voter, it will antagonize the party. This divergence of interests between leaders and activists corresponds to what May (1973: 133–51) called "the law of curvilinear

---

[12] This argument rests on assumptions about available information on the ideal policy position of the median voter. But if there is uncertainty about this position, the information of the government differs from that of the opposition, and parties are not pure office seekers (Ferejohn and Noll 1978), the government is not necessarily drawn to convergence with the opposition and away from party activists. Also, in multiparty systems where the voters' ideal positions are spread across the policy space, the positions of parties will be dispersed in this space and not be attracted to the median voter position (Cox 1987, 1990; Shepsle and Cohen 1990). Under ordinary plurality and proportional representation, the spread of positions will increase with the number of parties (Cox 1990).

disparity." According to this interpretation, if parties control governments, it is no longer to protect the interests of voters and the future electoral prospects of party candidates. The reason is to defend the interests of activists from total subordination to the voters. Thus, whenever the political influence of activists decreases (and internal party democracy becomes limited), on one hand the chances of electoral victory augment and, on the other, governments become more responsive to voters.

The policy positions of party members are usually more extreme than those of party voters. Remember the illustrations of Figures 6.1 and 6.2, and Table 6.1. Iversen (1994a, 1994b), however, contradicts this diagnosis with evidence on voters in seven countries and on delegates to congresses of thirty-seven parties in these countries. He shows that both leaders and delegates to party congresses, on the left as well as on the right, have more radical political views than their voters. Further, he does not find any disparity between the policy positions of leaders and the middle-level elites (the delegates to the congresses). "The overwhelming impression is one of intraparty coherence" (Iversen 1994b: 175). Thus, because no internal differences exist within parties vis-à-vis voters, Iversen indicates that "there does not seem to be any dilemma between internal party democracy and external representation" (Iversen 1994b: 172).

This evidence is not very convincing. Delegates at party congresses, as middle-level elites, can be typical "political heirs" of the incumbent. That is, their interests may correspond to the "overlapping generations" model. To protect their own future electability, they will want the incumbent to be responsive to voters. Were these delegates to be one of the two principals, their interests would be to defend those of the other principal, the median voter.

A problem, therefore, lies in the definition of the party. The control of the incumbent by the party depends on who are the delegates to party congresses. If rank-and-file militants attend them, we can expect their value of being in office to be different than if the delegates come from the party *nomenklatura*. So internal elections to the organs that monitor party leaders and enforce sanctions are important not only for party democracy but also for the responsiveness of the government. If we look at Spanish politics, 67 percent of delegates to the 1990 congress of the Socialist Party (PSOE), when this party was in government, held public office. Internal elections for delegates were ruled by a majoritarian principle and bloc-voting procedures, which resulted in strongly oligarchical congresses in which the policies of the government were generally backed by more than

80 percent of delegates. The proportion of officeholders among delegates to the 2002 congress of the PP, when it was also in government, was 60 percent (*ABC*, 25 January 2002). The control of this congress by the leadership was overwhelming.

The participation of rank-and-file activists in the election of the leadership and in the formulation of policies depends on party institutions. Parties competing in single-member constituencies, selecting their candidates through primaries, and with decentralized campaign resources are likely to have more active internal politics and a polycentric distribution of power; they may also become confederations of powerful and independent barons. On the contrary, parties competing in multimember constituencies, with closed lists and unified campaign resources, will tend to have a powerful central organization, and their internal politics will be much more restricted. The extraparliamentary layer is dominant in mass integration parties; it is much less important in catch-all, cartel, or cadre parties.

Müller (2000: 319) writes that "despite the transformation of European parties in the post-war period, party representatives in public office ultimately remain the agents of the extra-parliamentary party organization." There are important variations, however, in the internal party politics of parliamentary democracies, due to organizational differences. There was a clear contrast, for example, between the British Conservative Party and the Spanish Socialist Party in the 1980s and 1990s. The first consisted of a confederation of notables, with an opaque circle of power, and its candidates competed in single-member districts. The second was run by a strong center that tightly controlled the party; this center had the final decision on the candidates who would be included in closed lists, running in multimember districts. This difference in the control over the party may explain the different end of the incumbency of Felipe González and Margaret Thatcher. Both led long-lasting governments that overlapped greatly in time. But whereas the decline in popularity of González was much more evident, he was never internally challenged and led the party to the electoral defeat of 1996. Thatcher, on the contrary, was replaced by John Major following an internal conspiracy: although she was the incumbent prime minister, party notables believed she had become an electoral handicap.

Internecine party struggles can be due to attempts to reinforce or weaken information, monitoring, and enforcement devices of activists. Formulas for a closer control by rank-and-file members, however, are not clear. For instance, Katz and Mair (1995) have persuasively argued that individual voting may produce greater fragmentation within the party,

173

disorganization of internal opposition, and easier manipulation of activists by leaders. In any case, public office is typically used by incumbents to avoid control by the party. Leaders always demand unity and discipline on the grounds that this is what citizens expect and what competitors try to undermine; they require loyalty, so that any eventual criticism is made internally and "the dirty linen is not washed in public"; they claim that incumbents of public office must always govern for the citizens, not the party; and they dramatize differences with the opposition. If they succeed, dissent between party members and leaders will be limited when the party is in office: only a minority of strongly involved, critical activists will use voice. As Table 6.3 shows,[13] members of the Spanish Socialist Party were more likely to support their government than voters in general, and also more likely than voters of the government. Such support extended to the unemployment record, which increased from 16.3 percent to 21.2 percent between 1982 and 1986 (*Économie Éuropeenne* 60, 1996: 102). Only a small fraction of party members were critical activists: their strongest support was reached in the 1988 congress of the PSOE, when *Izquierda Socialista* had 7 percent of the delegates and obtained 22.5 percent of the congress votes (*El País*, 25 January 1988).

Partisanship induces optimism on future economic performance and exoneration of present policies that are unpopular by nonpartisan voters. Table 6.4 shows how views of the world varied in Great Britain according to partisanship.[14] The stronger the Conservative partisanship, the more likely the optimism about future inflation, unemployment, and industrial performance, and the greater the satisfaction about the National Health Service (NHS; which was under widespread criticism in this final period of the Thatcher government). When education increased, optimism about future

---

[13] In the three logit regression models in Table 6.3, the dependent variable has values of 0 (*bad*), 1 (*good*). The independent variables were coded as follows: (i) PSOE members 1, voters 0; (ii) PSOE members 1, PSOE voters 0; (iii) ideology on a left–right scale of 1 to 10.

[14] The values of the independent variables were as follows: (i) Partisanship: 1, *conservative partisan*; 2, *conservative sympathizer*; 3, *conservative residual identifier*; 4, *other*. (ii) Education: *completed continuous full-time education* – 1, *at nineteen years of age or more*; 2, *at 18. 3, 17. 4, 16. 5, 15 years of age or less*. (iii) Income: 1, *lives comfortably on present income*; 2, *can cope*; 3, *finds it difficult*; 4, *finds it very difficult*. As for the dependent variables, the values were as follows: (i) Inflation a year from now: 0, *will go down (a lot, a little)*; 1, *will go up (a lot, a little) or stay the same*. (ii) Unemployment a year from now: same values as inflation. (iii) Industrial performance a year from now: 0, *improve (a lot, a little)*; 1, *decline (a lot, a little) or stay the same*. (iv) Satisfaction with National Health Service: 0, *satisfied (very, quite)*; 1, *dissatisfied (very, quite) or neither*. Other answers (don't know/not applicable) were excluded.

Table 6.3. Evaluation of the Performance of the Government (González Government in Spain)

	Evaluation of general performance of the government (1986)				Evaluation of governmental performance on unemployment (1993)	
	(1)		(2)		(3)	
	Logit coeffs.	SE	Logit coeffs.	SE	Logit coeffs.	SE
Constant	3.808***	0.209	0.758***	0.180	0.314	0.288
Activists/total voters	1.695**	1.026	1.275**	0.575	–	–
Activists/PSOE voters	–	–	–	–	1.003*	0.622
Ideology	−0.680***	0.042	−0.245***	0.041	−0.185	0.081
Chi²	413.735***		46.870***		8.582**	
−2 log likelihood	1575.805		1010.052		55.095	
Number of cases	1539		1278		489	

*Significant at 10%; **significant at 5%; ***significant at 1% or less.
Sources: Centro de Investigaciones Sociológicas, February 1986. *DATA S.A.*, May–June 1993.

inflation went up, but views on future industrial performance became more pessimistic and satisfaction with the NHS was less likely. Income differences had no statistically significant effects.

That party members, who have strong policy preferences and consider the electoral program as just a transaction, judge their government's policies more favorably than voters is paradoxical. This can be explained by their polarized view of the opposition (see Table 6.1). As a reaction to the threat of the opposition, they defend their government; but if party members see the world with ideological blinkers and the voice of critical activists is limited, the information that parties will provide to voters to control the government will be weak.

Thus, two kinds of parties face problems for the democratic control of their government. In the first, delegates to party congresses belong to the *nomenklatura*. If they are interested in their political careers and learn of hidden actions by the government that would produce electoral sanctions by voters, they will have two options. One is to cover up and perhaps protect their careers; the other, to denounce and probably damage them.

Table 6.4. Partisanship and Policy Evaluations (Thatcher Government in Great Britain)

	Inflation a year from now (1990) (1)		Unemployment a year from now (1990) (2)		Industrial performance a year from now (1990) (3)		Satisfaction with NHS (1990) (4)	
	Logit coeffs.	SE	Logit coeffs.	SE	Logit coeffs.	SE	Logit coeffs.	SE
Constant	1.382***	0.302	0.844***	0.208	0.725***	0.198	−0.013	0.166
Income	0.111	0.115	0.101	0.072	0.060	0.068	0.023	0.055
Education	0.108*	0.059	−0.047	0.040	−0.069*	0.038	−0.113***	0.032
Partisanship	0.263***	0.064	0.247***	0.042	0.261***	0.040	0.316***	0.034
Chi²	26.577***		44.567***		52.714***		106.331***	
−2 log likelihood	1057.570		2073.098		2241.434		2982.555	
Number of cases	2797		2797		2797		2797	

*Significant at 10%; ***significant at 1% or less.
Source: British Social Attitudes, 1990.

They will only denounce (i.e., dissent) if the costs of silence are greater. Parties do not generally police their ranks to deter rent seeking; at best, when they find out about it, they react with internal sanctions of which voters may never learn. The costs of silence will however increase if outside actors (media, judges, the opposition parties) reveal the actions, and voters care and punish. Thus, an oligarchic party collusion between the party and the government means that no information will reach voters except if stimulated by external actors. Forty-one percent of voters who followed the 1990 congress of the Spanish PSOE, held in the middle of a considerable political scandal, thought that it had been a pure propaganda exercise.

Think now of a nonoligarchical party whose activists care about policies but are not indifferent about office. Party candidates for office will not depend on whether they are a clone of the median activist but rather on whether the latter sees them as electable – that is, on how the party interprets the electorate: the expected popularity of a government with the voters influences the support that it will get from the party. Thus, politicians in office may manipulate the party on the grounds of their popularity with voters, as long as activists care about both policies and office.

Support for a leader depends therefore on a utility function of activists that combines electoral prospects and the proximity of policy preferences (Stone and Abramowitz 1984; Abramowitz 1989). The government will try to preserve the support of the party not only with the attraction of its program but also with the argument of its popularity with voters. Manipulation by a popular leader often echoes Michels's words (1962: 82–3): "Whenever an obstacle is encountered, the leaders are apt to offer to resign, professing that they are weary of office, but really aiming to show to the dissentients the indispensability of their own leadership.... The leaders are extremely careful never to admit that the true aim of their threat to resign is the reinforcement of their power over the rank and file. They declare, on the contrary, that their conduct is determined by the purest democratic spirit, that it is a striking proof of their fineness of feeling, of their sense of personal dignity." Only if the political fanaticism of activists makes office irrelevant will such a strategy become useless. Otherwise, the party in general will offer voters little information about the government because of their shared interests with the incumbent and to the strategies of the latter.

There are, of course, endless examples of leaders trying to control critical voice within their party. I briefly examine, for illustrative purpose, the experiences of the British Labour Party, particularly following its electoral defeat in 1979 and until 1997, and of the Spanish PSOE, both in opposition and in government from 1979 to 1996. The two institutional settings were very different: on the one hand, a majoritarian system, with single-member electoral districts; on the other, a system of proportional representation, with closed lists of candidates competing in multimember districts. In the British system, the political position of members of parliament is much stronger, depending on their personal support by voters; a considerable political symbiosis also exists between the Parliamentary Party and the government, so that members of cabinet must be sitting MPs or, occasionally, members of the House of Lords. In the Spanish system, members of parliament are much more dependent on the party; the cabinet is also less connected to the parliamentary group.

Conflict over Control

Leaders think that voters punish undisciplined and divided parties; they must therefore control their party if they want to hold public office. Activists want to control leaders to ensure their faithfulness to the party program. Thus, an important part of politics in parliamentary democracies consists of struggles within parties. Such struggles involve demands for internal party democracy as it has been defined at the beginning of the chapter: accountability of the leaders and capacity of the party members to replace them if they dislike their policies or do not trust their electoral prospects.

In the British Labour Party, according to internal rules, the annual conference of delegates is the supreme policy-making authority. In Clement Attlee's words (1937: 93), the conference "lays down the policy of the Party and issues instructions which must be carried out by the Executive, the affiliated organizations and its representatives in Parliament." Delegates cast their votes in accordance with the prior mandates of the affiliated organizations represented in the conference. Many years later, the opening words of the 1973 program declared that "In the Labour Party policy is made by the members." Over a long time, conflict between the party and the government, the conference and the Parliamentary Labour Party, was avoided: the party was simply an instrument of the government, helping with apologies, propaganda, and electoral mobilization. It hardly acted as a monitoring agency. The conference followed the indications of the National Executive Committee, which in turn obeyed those of the parliamentary leadership. This was the pattern of internal party politics under the Attlee government, and from 1948 to 1960 the official platform was undefeated in the conference.[15] Thus, no conflict existed as long as the party did not question the leadership.

That there were limits to internal democracy was repeatedly indicated by Labour leaders. Sidney Webb described the party branches (the constituency parties) as "unrepresentative groups of nonentities dominated by fanatics and cranks, and extremists."[16] Three episodes revealed this hidden conflict over internal democracy. Two of them followed electoral defeats; the other one was with Labour in office.

The first case was the confrontation between the party conference and Hugh Gaitskell, the party leader, following the overwhelming electoral defeat in 1959. To improve Labour's chances in future elections, Gaitskell tried to drop the traditional party program of economic nationalizations and to stop a policy of unilateral nuclear disarmament in the 1960 Scarborough conference. When he failed, he rejected the verdict of the conference and defended the autonomy of the PLP over policy (Williams 1982: 347–68):

> It is not in dispute that the vast majority of Labour Members of Parliament are utterly opposed to unilateralism and neutralism. So what do you expect them to do?... I do not believe that the Labour MPs are prepared to act as time servers. I do not believe they will do this, and I will tell you why: because they are men of conscience.... What sort of people do you think we are? Do you think we can simply accept a decision of this kind?... How wrong can you be? As wrong as you are about the attitude of the British people.... There are some of us, Mr. Chairman, who will fight and fight and fight again to save the party we love.

Gaitskell eventually managed to change the party's position the following year. The party's electoral appeal improved: from June 1962 onward, Labour won successive by-elections until the party came back to office in 1964. However, the party leadership accepted conference decisions only as far as they reflected its own preferences.

The autonomy of leaders vis-à-vis the party has been defended in the name of democracy. McKenzie has thus argued that party organs cannot supplant the legislature: "[O]ligarchical control by the party leaders of the party organization is indispensable for the well-being of a democratic polity... intra-party democracy, strictly interpreted, is incompatible with democratic government" (1982: 195). And, having stated a few years

---

[15] With the exception of a minor vote in the 1950 annual conference.

[16] According to Beatrice Webb's *Diaries* (18 May 1930: 53–4).

earlier that "the extra-parliamentary party... [was] the final authority on policy issues" (*New Statesman*, 30 June 1961), Crossman wrote: "since these militants tended to be 'extremists,' a constitution was needed which maintained their enthusiasm by apparently creating a full party democracy while excluding them from effective power" (1961; 1963: 41–2).

The second episode was under the Labour governments of Harold Wilson. Between 1964 and 1969, the government suffered twelve defeats in conferences (Howell 1976: 246; Minkin and Seyd 1977: 142 fn. 65). The policies on which the party voted against the government covered employment, prices and income limits, pit closures, prescription charges in the NHS, the Vietnam War, military deployment East of Suez, and the reaction to the military coup in Greece. Two cases were of particular importance: one was the rejection of the white paper *In Place of Strife*[17]; the other, the growing opposition to Britain joining the European Community.[18] Both issues became central in the experience of the Labour governments. Industrial relations and economic policy eventually ended the trade unions–Labour traditional cooperation in the "Winter of Discontent" of 1979, helping Thatcher's electoral victory and the long period of Conservative rule. As for membership in the European Community, it increasingly divided the party. In its spell in opposition from 1970 to 1974, Labour had opposed membership under the terms achieved by the Conservative government of Edward Heath; it promised to renegotiate them and to submit the result to a referendum. Back in office, the Labour government fulfilled both promises: the party, however, rejected the new membership conditions in a special conference held in April 1975. No party discipline existed in the referendum: Labour, as well as Conservatives, campaigned both for a "no" and for a "yes" vote – the latter supported by a majority of Labour leaders, including the prime minister. Debate inside the party on the conditions of membership in the European Community supplied voters with abundant information. The final vote eventually accepted the new conditions of entry.

Thus, in the 1960s and 1970s, Labour became an increasingly divided party over policies. Either in government or in opposition, the leadership

---

[17] The white paper *In Place of Strife* regulated procedures of negotiation and compromise for trade unions. The National Executive Committee voted sixteen to five against legislation based on the document. Fifty-seven MPs voted against the document in a House of Commons debate in March 1969.

[18] Although the leadership supported application for membership to the European Community, thirty-five MPs voted against it in a Commons debate in May 1967.

no longer had its former tight control over the party. The traditional system of internal organization was deeply transformed. The selection of parliamentary candidates had always been closely supervised by the leadership; sitting MPs were not to be replaced as candidates by the constituency parties; intraparty factions were banned. From the mid-1960s, however, factions were allowed to operate; discipline became much less rigid. The *Campaign for Labour Party Democracy* and, later, the *Rank and File Mobilizing Committee* were organized to transfer power away from the parliamentary leadership to the party: the key issues were the election of the party leader and the capacity of the constituency parties to remove as candidates sitting MPs.[19] Therefore, when Labour was in office, activists attempted to win a greater control of politicians by the party.

The third episode of the struggle started with the 1979 elections. The left of the party interpreted the defeat as the result of the uncontrolled autonomy of the leadership, to the lack of accountability toward the rank and file. Demands for greater internal democracy were eventually successful in the 1980 Blackpool conference. Sitting MPs became the subject of mandatory reselection as candidates by the constituency parties; the leader and deputy leader of the party were to be elected by a wider franchise.[20] Activists in the local constituency parties won a much greater political influence.

These reforms in the internal rules were associated with a radicalization of the party's program. At the time of the 1983 general election, 58 percent of voters saw the Labour Party as divided, only 12 percent as moderate, 30 percent as extreme.[21] The electoral results were disastrous: Labour won only 27.6 percent of the vote, its lowest share since 1918. Organizational changes and more radical policy proposals did not attract working-class votes: Labour's share of votes among workers declined from 64 percent in 1974 to 49 percent in 1983 (Richards 1997).

The defeat marked the end of this episode.[22] Neil Kinnock, the new party leader, gradually restored authority and discipline within the party. The Parliamentary Labour Party recovered supremacy over policy; the

---

[19] Between 1973 and 1976, the local constituency parties rejected as candidates several sitting MPs: Dick Taverne in Lincoln, Eddie Griffiths in Sheffield Brightside, Reg Prentice in Newham North East, Frank Tomney in Hammersmith North.

[20] The leader of the party was so far elected by the Parliamentary Labour Party. A special conference, held in January 1981, changed the rules: an electoral college elected the leader and deputy leader. In such, college unions were attributed 40 percent of the votes, the PLP 30 percent, and the constituency parties 30 percent.

[21] According to a MORI survey: http://www.mori.com/polls/trends/party-img-lab.html.

[22] In this narrative, I rely extensively on Richards (1997).

party became again an instrument of support of the leadership. The 1986 conference expelled from the party the Militant Tendency. But the electoral recovery took a long time: in the elections of 1987, Labour's share of the vote increased only 3.2 percentage points. The strategy of greater control by the leadership and moderation of policies continued. On one hand, Kinnock launched in September 1987 the Policy Review, trimming down the more radical proposals of the program. On the other, the leadership was reinforced, against the influence of critical activists, by the introduction of direct balloting and the formula of "one-member-one-vote." Mair (1997: 150) has argued that "democratization on paper may...actually coexist with powerful elite influence in practice." And, from the left of the party, Livingstone complained that "the methods used inside the Labour Party...have been completely Stalinist (*The Guardian*, 24 March 1990). Yet only 15 percent of party members agreed with the statement that "A problem with the Labour Party today is that the leader is too powerful"; 71 percent disagreed (Seyd and Whiteley 1992: 51). Such reforms eventually concluded with the transformation of Labour under Tony Blair and its return to office in the 1997 general election. According to a Market & Opinion Research International (MORI) survey in September 1997, only 3 percent of voters saw Labour as extreme and 8 percent as divided.

The conclusion of the three episodes of the struggle over internal democracy in the Labour Party is paradoxical. For one, direct democracy eventually reinforced the authority of the leaders at the cost of the more demanding activists. This was the result of direct balloting of grassroots members, who supported the leadership against the critical activists. For two, although the reforms that gave power to the latter were presented as an example of organizational democracy (Benn 1992), voters punished the party for its internal disputes and factionalism.

The Spanish PSOE had a long history of factionalism. Internal divisions had been particularly dramatic over the 1934 revolutionary uprising in Asturias and the alliance with the republicans between September 1933 and November 1934. These divisions weakened the democratic experience in the 1930s. The Civil War and Francoism almost destroyed the party, which could only survive in exile and in small, protected enclaves. In the last years of the dictatorship, the PSOE had only 2,000 members inside Spain. However, after a new leadership with Felipe González took over the party in 1974, the number of members increased rapidly: it reached 8,000 in 1976 and 101,000 in 1979. In the first elections of the new democracy, the party won 29.3 percent of the vote, second only to the Unión de Centro Democrático (UCD), the party of the prime minister, Adolfo Suárez.

The expansion of the PSOE absorbed other groups of the left.[23] This contributed much to internal pluralism in the party over several years. But the main organizational concern of PSOE leaders was the unity of the party: an obsession to avoid the fratricidal struggles of the past. Moreover, UCD collapsed because of internecine disputes. Two episodes expressed the conflict between internal democracy and discipline: one with the PSOE in opposition; the other, in government.

The first started in 1979. The PSOE lost again the general elections: its share of the vote hardly changed. The ideological definition of the PSOE as a Marxist party, adopted in 1976, appeared to damage its electoral attraction. But a proposal by González to moderate this ideological rhetoric was rejected by the congress of the party, two months after the election. González then refused to stand for reelection as general secretary of the party. In his speech, he claimed that the resolutions adopted by congress would not appeal to a majority of voters, and that he would not lead the party in a direction with which he disagreed.

> This congress has shown that any Executive Committee, any person whatever his or her position, can lose a democratic debate. ... In this congress Felipe González has suffered a defeat. I have never been a rush pliable by the wind in whichever direction it blows. ... This is a democratic party that wants to transform society. It must therefore count on the support of a majority. [Many men and women] must get from the socialists an answer to their problems. ... The comrades that will have the responsibility of leading the party will not be able to carry out some of the resolutions of this congress.

The congress, however, accepted a reform of the internal rules of the party that increased very much the control of the leadership over the organization. The election of delegates to party congresses changed to a majoritarian, winner-takes-all rule. Delegates no longer represented local branches but rather the much larger provincial organizations. Moreover, this representation was increasingly absorbed by the seventeen regional parties. Due to block-voting, delegates of the different organizations had

---

[23] Former members of the Partido Comunista de España (PCE), Convergencia Socialista, Partido Socialista Popular (PSP), Federación de Partidos Socialistas (FPS), and Frente de Liberación Popular (FLP).

only one voice, that of the regional general secretary.[24] Individual protest votes were thus prevented. The outcome of national congresses became predictable: it was simply the result of oligarchical pacts following the regional congresses. The small executive organ (the Comisión Ejecutiva Federal [CEF]) accumulated vast resources for rewards and sanctions, including the control of closed and blocked lists of electoral candidates (Maravall 1991).

Felipe González was reelected general secretary of a party that was now much more disciplined. The PSOE won the next election in 1982 and remained in office for fourteen years. According to the director of *El País*, the main Spanish newspaper, the socialists were in power not because of "a better program, but because of the greater discipline in their ranks and the stability that they represent" (Cebrián 1989: 9–10). This discipline was a great help for the government when it faced difficult conflicts – over industrial reconversion, educational reforms, or general strikes. Yet to use the party as an instrument for social persuasion, the government had to supply the activists with reasons. This was particularly necessary when a policy appeared to be a volte-face from the electoral program. Thus, when the government switched from an earlier position of the party in opposition over NATO membership, González used the 1984 congress of the party to start providing explanations, first to persuade activists and only later voters in a referendum. He achieved both, and the PSOE won the 1986 general elections with a majority of seats in parliament.

However, internal pluralism became gradually more restricted, debates more inhibited, criticism increasingly irrelevant. The deputy leader of the party, Alfonso Guerra, controlled the organization tightly, with the help of an informal, closely knit network that operated like a party within the party. Weak internal voice meant little monitoring, a poor system of early warning, and growing policy inertias. This first episode consisted, therefore, of a trend toward greater discipline in the party: it started with an internal crisis, and followed with an electoral victory and a long period in government. This discipline was initially helpful in winning elections and in governing. The consequences of the weaker monitoring and warning system were revealed in the second period, which started with the PSOE in government, included scandals and internal divisions, and ended with the socialists in opposition.

---

[24] There were exceptions to these rules. The "political resolution" of congress and part of the members of the Federal Committee of the party (which supervised the politics of the CEF) were voted by individual delegates.

Successive scandals emerged from 1990 onward, provoking demands for political accountability.[25] These demands were expressed within the party's *nomenklatura*: the rank-and-file members were silent, shocked, and uninformed. The reaction to such demands consisted of political reprisals by Guerra,[26] which fueled internal conflict and factionalism. As an editorial of *El País*, sympathetic with the socialists, put it: "That no external explanations have to be given is the main characteristic of the present system of power in the Socialist Party. What is known as *guerrismo*, which served to guarantee the unity of the party when it was valuable, has simultaneously blocked the possibility of internal renovation.... Its main standard-bearers no longer believe in themselves and in their discourse. This has accentuated their authoritarian traits... even at the peril of recklessly destroying everything ("La prueba del nueve," 19 April 1990). Guerra eventually became an electoral liability: he was forced to leave the government in 1991, but tried to increase his control over the party. To quote from an internal document written to González,[27]

> Internal power is often used ruthlessly.... We are ditching a spectacular number of people, generally people that do not belong to the party's machinery and do not accept submission – which is quite different from loyalty.... Nobody, however minoritarian, should be afraid of personal political consequences for dissenting. This is not to defend divisions inside the party: only that internal cohesion can only be the result of debates and of accountability.

The combination of scandals and authoritarianism led to further internal struggles. Whereas in 1990, 66.1 percent of people believed that the PSOE was a united party, the percentage fell to 14.2 percent in 1994.[28] Demands for accountability were dismissed as threats against unity,

---

[25] One of these scandals was the accumulation of wealth by the brother of the deputy leader – the Juan Guerra affair. The other was an illegal system of financing, hidden to the official organs of the party – the Filesa affair.

[26] The two more relevant cases of reprisals were José Rodríguez de la Borbolla, president of the regional government of Andalucía and general secretary of the PSOE in the region (who lost both jobs), and Joaquín Leguina, who had the same positions in Madrid (who remained president of the regional government).

[27] This document is part of a series written by the author to Felipe González while a member of the Cabinet (1982–8) and of the CEF (1979–84, 1988–94). This one is dated 15 September 1990.

[28] Centro de Investigaciones Sociológicas, surveys of November 1990 and February 1994 (N = 2,492 and 2,499). Percentages are calculated excluding people who did not know or did not answer (which represented 23.6 percent and 21.2 percent of the respective samples). The questions were worded differently in the two surveys: in 1990, people were

discipline, and solidarity[29]; their proponents were accused of treason and disloyalty. Yet, although the PSOE was torn by internecine confrontations, González managed to keep vast support: this enabled the party to win the 1993 elections. The new victory did not change the pattern of reaction to the scandals: no explanations were provided either to voters or to party members. The following elections in 1996 brought the years of socialist rule to an end.

This second episode of the PSOE has two conclusions. One is that internal demands for accountability were mostly of elitist origin. Party members contemplated the string of scandals with disbelief, dismay, and political paralysis. They hardly received information relevant to the facts, were manipulated against alleged external and internal enemies, and were eventually drafted into one of the warring factions. The other conclusion has to do with the typical dilemma faced by party leaders when hidden actions are revealed: either to resist or to react. To resist means imposing internal silence and stifling voice; to react, providing explanations and accepting political responsibilities. Both entail political risks, electoral and partisan. To react may indeed split the party. But in the Spanish experience, the outcome of silence was division and defeat.

In the experiences of both Labour and the PSOE, the rules of representation at the parties' conference and congress were crucial for the control of the leadership. The struggles over accountability hardly involved party members at large. These either supported the incumbent leaders against the more ideological activists (in the case of Labour) or were silent and paralyzed in the middle of a political crisis (in the case of the PSOE). The

asked whether the PSOE was united or divided; in 1994, whether divisions existed between the leaders.

[29] A debate in the executive organ of the PSOE (the CEF) may be illustrative. It took place on 12 May 1992. Discussing the Filesa affair of illegal financing, some members attributed to external and internal enemies the fabrication of the scandal, demanded solidarity, and made threats. This was the answer from another member of the CEF: "To react like an ostrich is unacceptable. Nobody must seek refuge in the party to avoid responsibilities at the party's cost. Filesa is not the product of a lack of internal cohesion. Solidarity is a very noble word in socialism, and no abuse or manipulation should be made of it. What solidarity requires is that everyone of us knows, first, what is Filesa, what has happened, who decided it; second, why we seem to put obstacles to the investigation, and whether this is an attempt to put the party beyond the law or to evade personal responsibilities; third, what personal profits have been extracted at the expense of the law and at the expense of the party.... Only if we accept political responsibilities shall we be able to recover ground. The alternative is rejection by vast segments of society and a fratricidal struggle. Some should look at the bottom of this well, because it is a well from which it is difficult to get out."

struggle over the party opposed incumbent leaders either to critical activists or to other members of the party elite. In the first case, such struggle was motivated by disputes over the fulfillment of the program and can be explained by the "law of curvilinear disparity"; in the second, by the discovery of hidden actions that were an electoral liability and fits well with the "overlapping generations model." The "political heirs" were more likely to be successful in their struggle than the critical activists. In the disputes over the program, the leaders (Gaitskell, Kinnock, and González) tried to bring the party closer to voters: they found support for this strategy from the less committed party members and from the elite of "political heirs." The contrast of both cases shows a difference: Kinnock used his support among grassroots members in his struggle against the critical militants; González controlled the party using a more oligarchical organization, added to his immense personal support among grassroots members.

Party Democracy and Electoral Accountability

Voters will be interested in internal party politics if they can extract information on whether the government is a trustworthy agent. Citizens need information to guide their vote at election time. If information and monitoring are costly and if governmental politics are opaque, they will turn to indirect sources. Aldrich (1995: 166) points out that "voters can reasonably assume that nominees will be typical of their parties in platforms, views, and values." On this assumption, voters may use this identity between politicians and parties for informational shortcuts. They will consider that the programs and documents discussed by the party will reveal, at least partly, the preferences and actions of the government, their common agent.

If voters see the party as a "delegated monitor" (Caillaud and Tirole 2002), this is because they believe that it has more information on the government than they do. This is a rational belief: because the costs of political participation are for activists much higher than for voters, and the agency losses potentially much greater, activists will want to know as well as possible what benefits do they draw from their political commitment. In their case, "benefits" mean basically "policies." The preferences of voters and activists may differ, but voters can assume that the electoral program was an acceptable compromise for the party. It preserved policies above a threshold of acceptability while winning electoral support. Thus, voters can conclude that if the party shows acquiescence toward the government, this is because the electoral program is being faithfully implemented. And if the government respects electoral promises, it will defend voters' interests. Otherwise, the government will have to provide good reasons for U-turns in policies. As has been argued, this monitoring by the party requires that its political time horizon be longer than that of the government. When the party cares about the future, in which it will go on competing, it will protect its "reputational capital" with voters. Disagreements within the party about the performance of the government may provide information to voters about what it is that the government is doing. If, after discussions and explanations, a large fraction of the party ends up rejecting the actions of the government, voters may become suspicious of the agent. In such a case, politicians are no longer a reflection of their parties; the government appears unable to preserve the confidence of its closest supporters. If incumbents do not inspire confidence to their own, why should voters trust them?

Voters appear to react in this way following internal disputes of the party in office, or after a confrontation between a government and a trade union that was supposed to support the former's policies. This is why union strikes damage governments of the left but not necessarily conservative ones. For instance, in Great Britain, strikes at the beginning of 1979 put the Conservative Party ahead of the Labour government of James Callaghan by 18–19 percentage points in only eight weeks. At the same time, hostility toward unions was widespread: 85 percent of people favored a legal ban on picketing and 68 percent agreed that troops should be used to maintain essential services in vital industries (Holmes 1985: 152). In France, a vast wave of strikes at the end of 1988 caused a fall of 9 percentage points in the popularity of the socialist prime minister, Michel Rocard. Public opinion was also critical of the Conféderation Générale du Travail (CGT), the trade union that provoked the strikes.[30] In Spain, the general strike called by trade unions against the socialist government of Felipe González in December 1988 caused a drop of 8 percentage points over three months in the vote intention to the PSOE.[31] Contrary to the British and French cases, public opinion sympathized with the unions: only 10 percent attributed to them the responsibility of the confrontation, and 54 percent thought that the government had to change its policies and reach an agreement with the

---

[30] Surveys of IPSOS–*Le Point* and *Figaro*–SOFRES. See *Le Nouvel Observateur*, 1–7 and 8–14 December 1988.

[31] Monthly surveys of the Centro de Investigaciones Sociológicas from July to December 1988.

unions.[32] Fratricidal confrontations erode the credibility of governments as trustworthy agents.

Voters search for signals that might reveal what their agent is doing. Voters will rationally assume that errors are inevitable in their observations of the policies of the government and that they will not be able to assess such errors. If voters believe that activists are more informed about the actions of the government, they will listen to what they say, scrutinize party congresses, and so on. In Spain, 49 percent and 40 percent of voters knew, respectively, about the 1990 and 1994 congresses of the PSOE, then in government.[33] They will listen to statements by activists, in party congresses or elsewhere, about the policy performance of the government, considering that these will be less vulnerable to observation errors and report more accurately on the capacity of the agent. Yet, can signals from party congresses be credible? The policy preferences of voters and activists are likely to differ. Public statements from the party about policies will attempt to maximize its own preferences: the degree to which information from activists will accurately report on the interests of voters will vary. If the results of the political process do not reflect the preferences of the party, the latter will have an incentive to misrepresent, and its reports about the government will not be credible. We also know from deductive models (Lohmann 1998; Grossman and Helpman 2001: 87–95) that, with imperfect information about policy positions, the incumbent will favor the principal that is more informed and has greater monitoring capacity.

Debates in party congresses may show public acquiescence or dissent with the policies of the government. But the reasons for such acquiescence or dissent may be obscure for voters. Acquiescence (i.e., a united party) may be due to (i) the government's faithful implementation of the electoral program or, if it has deviated, its offer of good justifications; (ii) the ignorance by the party of actions of the government, or its acceptance of misleading justifications; or (iii) the internal discipline of the party even if the government has shirked. Discipline and collusion have the same negative effect on voters' information. When dissent rather than acquiescence exists within a party, expressed by a fraction either of the *nomenklatura* or of the activists, the information that voters may extract about the actions

---

[32] Centro de Investigaciones Sociológicas, survey of November 1988 (N = 3,371).

[33] Surveys of Centro de Investigaciones Sociológicas, November 1990 and February 1994 (N = 2,492 and 2,499). When these congresses were organized, two political scandals had a deep impact on public opinion: the Juan Guerra and Luis Roldán affairs of corruption, involving the brother of the vice president and a high official of the ministry of interior.

Table 6.5. Reasons for Internal Disputes within the Spanish PSOE

	1990 (%)	1994 (%)
(i) Due to the personal ambitions of leaders		
A lot	39	68
A little	31	10
Not at all	6	2
DNK/DNA	24	20
(ii) Due to internal democracy		
A lot	40	28
A little	22	27
Not at all	8	11
DNK/DNA	30	34

Source: Centro de Investigaciones Sociológicas, surveys of November 1990 (N = 2,492) and February 1994 (N = 2,499).

of the government will also be difficult to interpret. Dissent may be due to (i) the government shirking from the electoral program beyond a threshold of tolerance of the party; (ii) factional disputes led by purists, with radical demands about the direction of the party; or (iii) political opportunism (i.e., personal ambitions of different party leaders).

Let us examine the last possibility first: that is, political opportunism. Table 6.5 provides evidence from two Spanish surveys of 1990 and 1994.[34] The dates correspond to the last two congresses of the PSOE before losing the 1996 general elections. As I have argued, until 1990, disputes within the party were muted, basically due to the strong leadership of González. They became public in 1990 and increased between the two congresses: political scandals provoked an internal reaction against silence and discipline, imposed by Guerra, the deputy leader with a tight control over the party. Yet voters mostly believed that the increase in disputes was due to personal ambitions and that party democracy had declined. Even in politically turbulent times, when voters were concerned about opaque affairs, internal disputes did not provide them with information. Confrontations were mostly seen as expressions of political opportunism and unrelated to such affairs.

Let us now turn to examine another possibility: factional disputes by purists. These are activists with more intense political preferences and

[34] The surveys are those of footnote 28.

190

lower interest in office than the rest. Thus, they can prevent collusion between the party and the government (Wildavsky 1965). As Aldrich (1995: 193) puts it, "policy-motivated partisan activists are freer than patronage-motivated activists to offer or withhold their support." It may be that in normal times, only a purist fraction of the party may provide information to voters about shirking by the government. If this is the case, then the interests of voters are better protected by the monitoring of the more ideological activists.

Strategies of voice and exit by ideological activists may provide voters with information about the government. This will be the case if the government betrays the electoral program – what the purists see as the threshold of an acceptable trade-off between policies and office. But there are serious limits to such strategies of dissent. For one, the purists are likely to be the more dedicated activists: if they have invested great efforts in the party, then the eventual costs of exit may be very high. For two, the purists are probably the activists more ideologically distant from the voters. We know from formal models that information is credible only if the interests of sender and receiver do not diverge (Austen-Smith 1990: 145; Grossman and Helpman 2001: 195–99, 212–15). Because of the ideological distance between the purists and voters, the government may present their eventual exit as proof that the interests of voters are being taken care of well. Besides, the result of exit may consist in a reduction in the number of those activists more vigilant of the actions of the government, to the benefit of the more disciplined ones. Thus, the government may prefer exit to voice and achieve a greater discipline within the party.

Further, potentially informative debates will happen only in special circumstances: first, when silence may be electorally costly to members of the party's oligarchy; and, second, when criticism by purist activists cannot be dismissed by the leadership. The British and Spanish stories have illustrated both cases. In such debates, incumbents may produce convincing reasons for their actions. However, voters want to control the government because they wish some policies to be implemented or outcomes to be achieved: that is, they care about the capacity of the government to carry out its electoral program or improve their welfare. Internal party debates will interest voters if they are a source of information about what the government is doing but not to the point that such debates undermine its capacity. This capacity requires internal unity, absence of splits and of paralyzing factionalism. Thus, internal party democracy implies for voters a trade-off between debates and capacity. If internal debates do not produce

Table 6.6. The Effect of Internal Unity on Support for the Incumbent Party

	Spain (González government) 1990		United Kingdom (Thatcher government) 1990	
	Logit coeffs.	SE	Logit coeffs.	SE
Constant	−1.712**	0.784	−1.719***	0.422
Past vote	4.305***	0.331	−	−
Nonresponsiveness	−1.090***	0.235	−	−
No corruption	0.662**	0.265	−	−
Support cuts in public health	−	−	0.801***	0.132
Rejection of income redistribution	−	−	0.891***	0.084
Internal division of party	−0.828**	0.275	−1.156***	0.182
χ^2	826.499***		282.617***	
−2 log likelihood	637.049		996.923	
Number of cases	1,056		970	

Sources: Centro de Investigaciones Sociológicas, survey of November 1990; *British Social Attitudes*, 1990. **Significant at 5%; ***significant at 1%.

clear information on the fulfillment of electoral promises, then voters will want to preserve the capacity of the government – that is, the unity of the party. They will support discipline against voice. If disunity is the only indication about what the government is doing, either something is wrong about policies or the capacity of the government is weak.

Table 6.6 shows the effect of different variables on the likelihood of voting for the incumbent. The logit regressions refer to the socialist and conservative governments in Spain and the United Kingdom. The dependent variable is support for the government. The independent variables are, in the Spanish case, past vote and views of responsiveness, corruption, and party unity.[35] All these variables are statistically significant and have the expected sign. Past vote had a very powerful effect on vote intention; perceptions of nonresponsiveness (i.e., no sensitivity to the needs of people), corruption, and lack of unity of the party decreased the probability of voting for the government.

If we turn to the British case, over a long time voters saw the Conservative and Labour parties in very different terms. In 1983, 52 percent of

---

[35] The variables were coded as follows. Vote intention and past vote: 0 (*any other party*), 1 (*PSOE*). Responsiveness: 1 (*yes*), 0 (*no*). Corruption: 1 (*yes*), 0 (*no*). Internal unity: 1 (*yes*), 0 (*no*). Interviewees who did not know or did not answer were excluded from the analyses.

voters thought the Conservatives were united; the percentage for Labour was only 27 percent. In 1992, the difference had grown: 67 percent against 30 percent.[36] Yet Margaret Thatcher had been replaced as party leader and prime minister by a conspiracy of Conservative "barons" in November 1990, while Neil Kinnock had imposed discipline within the Labour Party. These views of the two parties changed rapidly after the 1992 general election. In July 1993, the Conservatives were seen as divided by 30 percent of voters; Labour, by 26 percent; in April 1997, the percentages were 50 percent and 12 percent, respectively.[37] In Table 6.6, the dependent variable is party support. The independent variables are views on whether the government should redistribute income between rich and poor, whether public expenditure in the NHS should be cut down, and whether the Conservative Party was united or divided.[38] Opposition to income redistribution and approval of cuts in the NHS increased the probabilities of support for the Conservatives; views of the party as internally divided reduced them.

Thus, voters reward party unity and punish internal dissent. In addition, they tend to see voice as division, not as a source of information. If the party in office is internally monolithic, the government will have more political capacity, but voters will not receive information from the party about whether the government is carrying out its electoral program or acting on their behalf. That is, the party will not improve by any means the accountability of the government. Paradoxically, voters will limit the contribution that party politics could provide to monitoring.

The government will know that voters punish dissent in the party. Therefore, it will attempt to discipline the party through strategies of persuasion and institutions. The first will rely on the risk of an electoral defeat in the hands of a polarized opposition. As Cotta (1999: 7) writes, "Only when the government seems bound to lose the ensuing election can the

[36] From A. Heath et al., British Election Study 1983 (N = 1,085); A. Heath et al., British General Election Cross-Section Survey 1992 (N = 5,232).

[37] MORI surveys: Conservative and Labour parties' image trends. http://www.mori.com/polls/trends/ party-img-lab.shtml

[38] Support for the government was 0 (*no*), 1 (*yes*); other answers were eliminated from the analysis. Opposition to redistribution of income by the government and acceptance of cuts in public expenditure on the NHS had values of 0 (*no opposition, no acceptance*) and 1 (*opposition, acceptance*). Views on the internal unity of the Conservative Party were coded as 1 (*united*) and 2 (*divided*). In all these variables, those who did not know or did not give an answer were excluded from the analysis.

Table 6.7. Average Period in Office, Parliamentary Democracies (1975–95)

	Prime Minister		Party		
	Years	Months	Years	Months	N (years)
Plurality	4	1	5	6	(95)
PR with open lists	3	7	4	9	(105)
PR with closed lists	3	7	9	4	(246)

parliamentary party regain some autonomy; otherwise loyalty is the rational strategy for the parliamentary party." The government will present party loyalty as the key for electoral success.

Institutions can facilitate the control of the party by the government and also the probability that the latter will survive in office. If resources are decentralized, internal dissent can increase. If politicians have their own local bases of support, their political future will not depend on the sympathy of the center. If individuals with a strong public profile are not filtered out of party lists, the chances of voice inside the party will be greater.[39] Systems of proportional representation with closed lists, on the contrary, favor anonymous candidates obedient to the party leadership. In such systems, the party brand name is what matters, not the popularity of candidates in their constituencies. Closed lists "preclude candidates who have not been prioritized by their party from getting elected" (Müller 2000: 327). Party unity may therefore be reinforced.

Table 6.7 shows that parties survive longer in office under PR with closed lists, compared both with plurality systems and PR with open lists.[40] If PR is the electoral rule, a party that competes with closed lists will enjoy, on average, a period in office 68 percent longer than with open lists. Prime ministers will be indifferent to open or closed lists; only in plurality systems will their average period be 12.2 percent longer. So, closed lists benefit the incumbent party and the "political heirs." Internal party discipline and duration in office are connected; conditions for internal debate run against both.

[39] An example is the crisis of the Liberal Democratic Party in Japan in the 1990s. The autonomy of politicians vis-à-vis the center appears to explain both voice and exit. See Kato (1998).

[40] The countries are Australia, Austria, Belgium, Canada, Denmark, Finland, France, Germany, Greece, Iceland, Ireland, Israel, Italy, Japan, Luxembourg, Netherlands, New Zealand, Norway, Portugal, Spain, Sweden, and the United Kingdom.

Institutions also influence the predictability of losing office. Table 6.8[41] assesses variations in the effect of economic growth, parliamentary majorities, coalitions, and decentralization of candidate selection on the probability that prime ministers will be replaced in government by a politician of another or the same party, in plurality or PR systems with open or closed lists. The dependent variable is a survival time indicator in years. Regressions are a hazard function; negative values of the coefficients mean that as the value of the predictor variable increases, the risk of losing office decreases.

If PR with open lists leads, on average, to shorter periods in office for parties, any reason can make prime ministers vulnerable. As can be seen in Table 6.8, the statistical model is not significant. The lack of parliamentary majorities, bad economic performances, or decentralization of candidate selection offers no explanations. With open lists, alternative variables are not statistically significant either: whether fractionalization of the opposition or the ratio of party activists to party voters. So with open lists, besides shorter political lives, no apparent reasons explain the loss of office.

Plurality systems lead to parties and prime ministers staying longer in office; also, the fate of the latter is somewhat more predictable. Here, economic growth reduces the risk of the prime minister losing power. PR

---

[41] Table 6.8 shows the estimates of a proportional hazard Cox regression model for time-constant variables. It is based on time-to-event data, and the censored cases are years for which the event has not yet occurred. The hazard function is the loss of office at time t: that is, how likely is it to happen, given that the prime minister and the party have survived to that time. If X_1, X_2, X_3, and X_4 are covariates (yearly GNP growth, parliamentary majorities, coalition governments, and decentralized selection of parliamentary candidates), the general model is $h(t) = [h_o(t)]e(B_1X_1 + B_2X_2 + B_3X_3 + B_4X_4)$. In this model, h(t) is the hazard function: an estimate of the potential for a prime minister losing power per unit time at a particular instant, given that he/she has survived until that instant. A high hazard function indicates a high rate of defeat. As for $h_o(t)$, it is the baseline hazard function without the effect of the covariates. B_1, B_2, B_3, and B_4 are the regression coefficients, and e is the base of the natural logarithm. The countries are those of footnote 40.

Data on yearly GNP growth are from OECD, *Economic Outlook*, Paris: OECD, 1992 and 2000. Majority was coded as 0: minority of seats in Parliament, 1: majority of seats. Coalition was coded as 0: single party in government (fractionalization of 0.00), 1: fractionalization between 0.01 and 0.050, 2: fractionalization above 0.050. The correlation coefficient between majority and coalition was 0.078, statistically not significant. The degree of centralized candidate selection is a scale that uses information from Ranney (1981: 75–106), Bille (2001: 366), and Mair and van Biezen (2001: 5–21). The scale is as follows: 1 = *complete control by national organs*; 2 = *subnational organs propose and national ones decide*; 3 = *national organs propose and subnational ones decide*; 4 = *subnational organs decide and national ones ratify*; 5 = *subnational organs decide*; 6 = *direct vote of party members on candidates*.

Table 6.8. Likelihood of the Prime Minister Losing Office (Cox Regressions of Partial Likelihood, Parliamentary Democracies 1975–95)

	Plurality		PR with open lists		PR with closed lists	
Event	81		92		214	
Censored	14		13		34	
Total	95		105		248	
	Coeff.	SE	Coeff.	SE	Coeff.	SE
Yearly GNP growth	−0.094*	0.048	0.005	0.043	−0.005	0.035
Majority	−0.790	1.032	0.210	0.300	−0.651***	0.196
Coalition	0.107	0.275	−0.332*	0.186	0.236**	0.092
Decentralization of candidates	−1.201	0.143	0.072	0.104	0.180***	0.048
Chi^2	8.383*		4.625		21.637***	
−2 log likelihood	581.273		699.723		1992.056	

*Significant at 10%; **significant at 5%; ***significant at 1%.

with closed lists leads to longer periods in office by parties and to greater predictability for prime ministers. Coalitions increase their political risks; parliamentary majorities and decentralized candidate selection help prime ministers to survive. In the latter case, a party may better adapt to the different preferences of constituencies. Apparently, the optimal degree of party unity is the combination of closed lists and a decentralized selection of parliamentary candidates.

Contrary to its effect in plurality systems, economic performance is irrelevant for the likelihood of prime ministers losing office in PR systems, either with open or closed lists. Prime ministers seem to be more vulnerable to voters' sanctions if economic conditions are bad in plurality systems; to weak support in parliament, fragmented governments, or centralized selection of parliamentary candidates in PR systems with closed lists; and to circumstances unrelated to the former ones in PR systems with open lists.

Voters tend to interpret internal discussions in governing parties as signs that something is wrong with the actions of the incumbent or that its capacity to lead is limited. Such signs will undermine their trust on the agent. Institutions can facilitate party discipline, as happens with closed lists. The result in this case is that parties survive longer in office and the prime ministers' future is less uncertain.

Conclusion

Internal party politics may be relevant for democracy if they can contribute to voters' information. The government is an agent with two principals (the party and the electorate), one of which has more information on the agent's actions. The two principals share an interest in the fulfillment of the electoral program. Discussions between party activists and leaders in public office might inform voters on the reasons for policy switches or on hidden actions of the government.

Activists strongly committed to policies will want to monitor the government and so will members of the *nomenklatura* interested in the electoral future of the party. In the first case, political control will be vertical; in the second, horizontal, based on polycentricism and the existence of autonomous positions of power within the party. Incumbents will want their party to inform them on the evolution of public opinion and to serve as an early-warning instrument reporting on the costs of unpopular policies. They will also want to control the party to keep it close to voters' preferences and to avoid potentially damaging information or an external image of disunity. These objectives of the leaders are not easy to combine: they require either internal democracy or discipline. In exceptional occasions, such combination may be achieved: for instance, when a party is about to win power, or in "honeymoons" that may last for a while among leaders, activists, and voters once power has been won. But one objective means control over the government; the other, control over the party. This is why internal partisan struggles are a regular feature of democratic politics.

Voters will be interested in the internal politics of the party in office if they provide information and do not damage the political capacity of the government. In the trade-off between information and capacity, an optimum point may exist: a party that discusses openly the government's policies and actions, a government that contributes with plausible explanations, and a result that is a coherent and united party backing the government. However, discussions within the party may not provide credible information on issues relevant to voters and they can undermine the capacity of the government. In such case, voters will interpret the discussions as a negative signal on the agent. Incumbents will then opt for a party that serves as a disciplined instrument of persuasion rather than for a democratic organization where voice is an early-warning instrument.

Dahl (1970: 5) was right: "If the main reason we need political parties at all is in order for them to facilitate democracy in the *government of the country*, then might not parties that are internally oligarchic serve that purpose just as well as, or maybe better than, parties that are internally more or less democratic?" Voters prefer party unity to internal debates and disputes. They interpret such debates not as expressions of democracy but rather as opportunistic factionalism, as weak political capacity, or as indication that something is wrong with policies. Further, because divided parties are punished, incumbent politicians, their "political heirs," and the majority of party members that support them will introduce discipline. If the party is then seen as united, electoral support will increase. If, to promote discipline, closed lists operate, parties will stay longer in office and the future of prime ministers will be more predictable. Voters can therefore reject "good" agents with parties where voice is actively used and reward "bad" agents with a disciplined party.

Critical activists are the victims. They may only be able to generate incentives for the government to be a good agent when the threat of an internal split is credible (Caillaud and Tirole 2002). The government can then think that such a split is a serious electoral risk. This happens when the dissidents cannot be presented as opportunists or as radicals, distant from the political preferences of voters.

If this is so, parties that can be informative to voters about the actions of the government that they back will be seen as reducing its political capacity; hence, they will increase the probability of losing office. The recipe of a party that facilitates the accountability of its government is likely to be a recipe for electoral defeat.

REFERENCES

Abramowitz, Alan I. 1989. "Viability, Electability, and Candidate Choice in a Presidential Primary Election: A Test of Competing Models." *Journal of Politics* 51 (4): 977–92.

Achen, Christopher H. 1992. "Social Psychology, Demographic Variables, and Linear Regression: Breaking the Iron Triangle in Voting Research." *Political Behavior* 14 (3): 195–212.

Aldrich, John. 1995. *Why Parties?* Chicago: University of Chicago Press.

Alesina, Alberto, and Stephen E. Spear. 1988. "An Overlapping Generation Model of Electoral Competition." *Journal of Public Economics* 37 (3): 359–79.

Alt, James E. 1984. "Dealignment and the Dynamics of Partisanship in Britain." In Russell J. Dalton, Scott C. Flanagan, and Paul. A. Beck (eds.), *Electoral Change in Advanced Industrial Societies*. Princeton: Princeton University Press.

Attlee, Clement. 1937. *The Labour Party in Perspective*. London: Odham.
Austen-Smith, David. 1990. "Information Transmission in Debate." *American Journal of Political Science* 34 (1): 124–52.
Benn, Tony. 1992. *The End of An Era*. London: Hutchinson.
Bille, Lars. 2001. "Democratizing a Democratic Procedure: Myth or Reality? Candidate Selection in Western European Parties, 1960–1990." *Party Politics* 7 (3): 363–80.
Caillaud, Bernard, and Jean Tirole. 2002. "Parties as Political Intermediaries." *Quarterly Journal of Economics* 117 (4): 1453–89.
Cebrián, Juan Luis. 1989. "Reflexiones Electorales." *El País*, 9 October.
Cheibub, José Antonio, and Adam Przeworski. 1999. "Democracy, Elections, and Accountability for Economic Outcomes." In Adam Przeworski, Susan C. Stokes, and Bernard Manin (eds.), *Democracy, Accountability, and Representation*. New York: Cambridge University Press.
Cotta, Maurizio. 1999. "On the Relationship between Party and Government." Occasional Papers 6/1999. Università degli Studi di Siena (published in Jean Blondel and Maurizio Cotta (eds.), *The Nature of Party Government*. London: Macmillan, 2000).
Cox, Gary. 1987. "Electoral Equilibria Under Alternative Voting Institutions." *American Journal of Political Science* 31 (1): 82–108.
Cox, Gary. 1990. "Centripetal and Centrifugal Incentives in Electoral Systems." *American Journal of Political Science* 34 (4): 903–35.
Crossman, Richard. 1961. *The New Statesman*. 30 June.
Crossman, Richard. 1963. Foreword to William Bagehot, *The English Constitution*. London: Fontana.
Dahl, Robert. 1970. *After the Revolution?* New Haven: Yale University Press.
Downs, Anthony. 1957. *An Economic Theory of Democracy*. New York: HarperCollins.
Ferejohn, John, and Roger G. Noll. 1978. "Uncertainty and the Formal Theory of Political Campaigns." *American Political Science Review* 72 (2): 492–505.
Fiorina, Morris P. 1981. *Retrospective Voting in American National Elections*. New Haven: Yale University Press.
Grossman, Gene M., and Elhanan Helpman. 2001. *Special Interest Politics*. Cambridge, MA: MIT Press.
Heath, Anthony, Roger Jowell, and John Curtice. 1994. *Labour's Last Chance? The 1992 Election and Beyond*. Aldershot: Dartmouth Publishing.
Hirschman, Albert. 1970. *Exit, Voice, and Loyalty*. Cambridge, MA: Harvard University Press.
Holmes, Martin. 1985. *The Labour Government, 1974–79*. London: Macmillan.
Howell, David. 1976. *British Social Democracy*. London: Croom Helm.
Iversen, Torben. 1994a. "Political Leadership and Representation in West European Democracies: A Test of Three Models of Voting." *American Journal of Political Science* 38 (1): 45–74.
Iversen, Torben. 1994b. "The Logics of Electoral Politics: Spatial, Directional, and Mobilizational Effects." *Comparative Political Studies* 27 (2): 155–89.
Kato, Junko. 1998. "When the Party Breaks Up. Exit and Voice among Japanese Legislators." *American Political Science Review* 92 (4): 857–70.

Katz, Richard S., and Peter Mair. 1995. "Changing Models of Party Organization and Party Democracy: The Emergence of the Cartel Party." *Party Politics* 1 (1): 5–28.

Key, Vernon O. 1966. *The Responsible Electorate*. New York: Vintage Books.

Kiewiet, Roderick, and Mathew McCubbins. 1991. *The Logic of Delegation*. Chicago: Chicago University Press.

Lohmann, Suzanne. 1998. "An Information Rationale for the Power of Special Interests." *American Political Science Review* 92 (4): 809–27.

Mair, Peter. 1997. *Party System Change*. Oxford: Clarendon Press.

Mair, Peter, and Ingrid van Biezen. 2001. "Party Membership in Twenty European Democracies." *Party Politics* 7 (1): 5–21.

Manin, Bernard, Adam Przeworski, and Susan C. Stokes. 1999. "Elections and Representation." In Adam Przeworski, Susan C. Stokes, and Bernard Manin (eds.), *Democracy, Accountability, and Representation*. New York: Cambridge University Press.

Maravall, José María. 1991. "From Opposition to Government. The Politics and Policies of the PSOE." In José María Maravall et al. (eds.), *Socialist Parties in Europe*. Barcelona: ICPS.

Maravall, José María. 2007. "Accountability and the Survival of Governments." In Carles Boix and Susan Stokes (eds.), *Oxford Handbook of Comparative Politics*. Oxford: Oxford University Press.

May, John D. 1973. "Opinion Structure of Political Parties: The Special Law of Curvilinear Disparity." *Political Studies* 21 (2): 133–51.

McKenzie, Robert. 1982. "Power in the Labour Party: The Issue of Intra-Party Democracy." In Dennis Kavanagh (ed.), *The Politics of the Labour Party*. London: Allen & Unwin.

Michels, Robert. 1962. *Political Parties*. New York: Free Press.

Minkin, Lewis, and Patrick Seyd. 1977. "The British Labour Party." In William E. Patterson and Alastair H. Thomas (eds.), *Social Democratic Parties in Western Europe*. London: Croom Helm.

Müller, Wolfgang. 2000. "Political Parties in Parliamentary Democracies: Making Delegation and Accountability Work." *European Journal of Political Research* 37 (3): 309–33.

Popkin, Samuel L. 1991. *The Reasoning Voter*. Chicago: Chicago University Press.

Powell, G. Bingham, and Guy D. Whitten. 1993. "A Cross-National Analysis of Economic Voting: Taking Account of the Political Context." *American Journal of Political Science* 37 (2): 391–414.

Ranney, Austin. 1981. "Candidate Selection." In David Butler, Howard Penniman, and Austin Ranney (eds.), *Democracy at the Polls*. Washington: American Enterprise Institute.

Richards, Andrew. 1997. *The Life and Soul of the Party: Causes and Consequences of Organizational Change in the British Labour Party, 1979–1997*. Estudio/Working Paper 1997/95. Madrid: Instituto Juan March de Estudios e Investigaciones.

Rosenstone, Steven. 1995. "Electoral Institutions and Democratic Choice." Paper presented at workshop on "The Impact of Institutional Arrangements on Electoral

Behavior." *European Consortium for Political Research*, joint sessions of workshops. Bordeaux, 27 April–2 May.

Samuelson, Paul A. 1958. "An Exact Consumption–Loan Model of Interest with or without the Social Contrivance of Money." *Journal of Political Economy* 66 (6): 467–82.

Sartori, Giovanni. 1987. *The Theory of Democracy Revisited*. Chatham: Chatham House.

Scarrow, Susan. 1999. "Parties and the Expansion of Direct Democracy: Who Benefits?" *Party Politics* 5 (3): 343–62.

Seyd, Patrick, and Paul Whiteley. 1992. *Labour's Grass Roots. The Politics of Party Membership*. Oxford: Clarendon Press.

Shepsle, Kenneth, and Ronald Cohen. 1990. "Multiparty Competition, Entry, and Entry Deterrence in Spatial Models of Elections." In James Enelow and Melvin Hinich (eds.), *Advances in the Spatial Theory of Voting*. Cambridge: Cambridge University Press.

Stokes, Susan C. 1999. "Political Parties and Democracy." *Annual Review of Political Science* 2 (1): 243–67.

Stokes, Susan C. 2001. *Mandates and Democracy*. New York: Cambridge University Press.

Stone, Walter J., and Alan I. Abramowitz. 1984. *Nomination Politics: Party Activists and Presidential Choice*. New York: Praeger.

Strøm, Kaare. 1990. "A Behavioral Theory of Competitive Political Parties." *American Journal of Political Science* 34 (2): 565–98.

Webb, Beatrice. *Diaries*. 19 May 1930. Archives Division, British Library of Political and Economic Science. London: London School of Economics and Political Science.

Webb, Paul. 2000. *The Modern British Party System*. London: Sage Publications.

Wildavsky, Aaron. 1965. "The Goldwater Phenomenon: Purists, Politicians, and the Two-Party System." *Review of Politics* 27 (3): 386–413.

Williams, Philip. 1982. *Hugh Gaitskell*. Oxford: Oxford University Press.

Wittman, Donald. 1995. *The Myth of Democratic Failure*. Chicago: University of Chicago Press.

CHAPTER SEVEN

Choosing Rules for Government: The Institutional Preferences of Early Socialist Parties

Alberto Penadés

Introduction

Electoral institutions bear some effect on the control of governments because they influence the manner in which governments can be made vulnerable. Whatever makes office vulnerable for incumbents makes it accessible for nonincumbents. In this chapter, I propose an explanation of the institutional preferences of the most important newcomer group of parties to early democracies, the socialists, in terms of some of the consequences of electoral rules for government formation. I show that what mattered for the parties was not only how many seats could be expected under different institutional arrangements. For socialist parties, electoral rules had a broader impact on their general participation strategy, including their coalition strategy and the link between electoral success and democratic responsibility in policy making. The choice of electoral rules implied a choice between forging their alliances in the electorate – so as to surpass the majoritarian threshold in the constituencies – and obtaining a potentially very variable ability to influence government, including the responsibility of full control as a result of elections, or forging their alliances in parliament, under proportional rule, and holding a relatively constant but more restrained influence on government. It was the parties more firmly rooted in the working class, understood in terms of unionized voters,

I wish to thank Paloma Aguilar, Sonia Alonso, Belén Barreiro, Carles Boix, and Marta Fraile for their numerous comments to earlier drafts of this chapter. It has greatly benefited from extended discussion with José María Maravall and Ignacio Sánchez-Cuenca, who dismantled all previous versions, and from helpful comments by Adam Przeworski to the penultimate draft. Two anonymous readers made valuable suggestions for improvement on the final draft. In addition, I thank Martha Peach for making hard-to-find books and information easily available, and Stefano Bartolini for kindly storing his data at the Center for Advanced Study in the Social Sciences library.

those who were more willing to commit themselves to an institutional strategy that entailed not only a broader electoral appeal but also a more steadfast, and risky, participation in democratic government. This is the end result of an argument that begins with a simpler and wider question.

Why did different socialist parties support the choice of different electoral institutions? This will be taken as a double question. The first focuses on the intentional aspect of institutional preferences: Why, for what purpose, did parties prefer different rules? The second centers on their origin: Why did parties prefer certain anticipated outcomes of rules? The former question is answered if we can clarify, first, the consequences of rules that may be of particular importance for the parties, and, second, give evidence that their behavior was congruent with their asserted preferences when they are so interpreted. In this sense, preferences, which are observed independently, in the public commitments of the parties, are explained by their ability to predict other kinds of behavior. For the socialist parties, undertaking government responsibility was the last stage of a long process of mobilization, alliances, and divisions. I show that their institutional preferences were consistent with their concern for party unity, their alliances, and, ultimately, their strategy for government participation. The latter question is answered if we can causally explain the disposition of the parties regarding their path toward government and their resulting institutional preferences. I search the origins in the relationship of the socialist parties to the organizations of the workers in the labor market. Social democratic parties that were supported by strong union movements did not face a severe trade-off between their increased participation strategies and the fragmentation of the workers' political movement; when unions were weak or their support was contingent, parties had to countenance the organization of viable dissenting alternatives claiming to represent the working class (Przeworski and Sprague 1986). The first causal link is anticipatory: certain rules were preferred because they favored a pattern of behavior that was preferred. The second causal link explains the origins of preferences; it shows that the choice of strategies was not capricious but rather rooted in the organization of the workers as a class.

Using contemporary data, Maravall shows in this volume that plurality rule makes the survival of prime ministers relatively more contingent on economic conditions, which may be linked to performance, whereas proportional rule makes it more dependent on parliamentary politics – the support and fragmentation of the government – irrespective of the economic conditions. More in general, single-member districts make governments more vulnerable to elections, all else being equal (Maravall, 2007). Thus, by implication, access to government responsibility is more dependent on electoral results with single-member districts, whereas it hinges more on parliamentary politics under proportional representation.

This was not different in early democratic history. By supporting the choice of different electoral rules, the socialist parties were attempting to commit themselves to different participation strategies. Regardless of the electoral system, some parties were more prepared to accept full responsibility in the direction of policy and to tie their fates to the votes obtained in elections, by themselves or together with allies. They chose, when they could, majority-biased systems. Other parties betrayed greater timidity toward government, preferring the parliamentary arena to exercise a more constant, albeit limited, influence over policy, and to be able to decide, in that arena, on the timing and the degree of their commitment to direct responsibility in government, as well as on their choice of allies. Those were the proportionalists. The institutional preferences of parties were almost always revealed before the opportunities to engage in government came forth. The conjecture is that their preferences can be interpreted in the light of those particular features of their ensuing behavior.

Preferences and rules did not always match. The institutional choices were collective choices, and socialist parties often found themselves in the minority. This helps prevent the circularity described in the previous paragraph, which, in part, describes what is the common-wisdom behavior of parties under majority and proportional systems. We observe here that parties preferring the same rules behaved more similarly, under different electoral systems, than parties with opposite preferences competing in similar institutional environments. This lends some support to the view of institutional choices as attempted commitments. Electoral rules were preferred because they suited different long-term mobilization and participation strategies, but those strategies, which had an independent origin, largely imposed themselves in party behavior, at least in the short- to mid-term, even when the institutional constraints were less conducive to them.

The explanation would be on safer grounds if we were able to observe the behavior of the same parties under different systems. Unfortunately, in most cases of rule change, the precedent and subsequent time periods were not comparable in terms of democratic development, and neither was, therefore, the disposition of parties toward government. However, we can observe the evolution of parties in time to assess whether their behavior was consistent with the interpretation of their institutional preferences. For this purpose, I need a wider understanding of those preferences that goes beyond the features of institutions that directly relate to the configuration of governments.

This chapter is a study on the socialist parties that also discusses one basic question on the origins of proportional representation in early advanced democracies. It argues that there was no general rule as to which parties introduced proportional representation (or, for that matter, prevented that choice) during the first wave of democratization: different coalitions of social democrats, liberals, Catholics, or conservatives carried out the reforms. Therefore, it seems reasonable to claim that any explanation of the institutional choices should start by accounting for the actors' preferences in those choices.

The chapter is organized as follows. Section 2 previews the argument. Sections 3 and 4 present an overview of the electoral reform processes in early democracies and of the position of individual parties in those processes. Section 5 discusses some of the existing literature. Section 6 introduces the main empirical regularity: union support predicts the institutional preferences of the parties. Section 7 discusses the mechanisms that explain this regularity. Sections 8 and 9 offer evidence that justifies the proposed explanation; section 8 discusses some of the effects of the trade unions on party behavior and organization that make the choice of rules predictable, whereas section 9 discusses the explanatory power of institutional preferences for government participation. Section 10 briefly concludes.

This is an entirely inductive chapter. The units of analysis are parties. The sample of parties consists in every socialist party exceeding 10 percent of the vote in the interwar period from the sample of twenty-two early democracies for which data are collected in Mackie and Rose (1982). The party of Luxembourg is completely dropped for lack of adequate data, which results in a sample of seventeen parties.

Preview of the Argument

Social democratic parties were shaped across three historical junctures: the decision to participate in representative (and, eventually, democratic) elections, the decision to search for allies to enlarge their electoral support and parliamentary strength, and the decision to participate in democratic government (Przeworski 1985: 7–23). The three decisions can be seen as steps into full participation, and all provoked internal controversies (Przeworski and Sprague 1986, 17). Thus, behaviorally, social democratic parties distinguished themselves from other parties of the left (typically, communists) that resisted full democratic participation.

The last step was the critical one. By the late 1940s, every social democratic party in my sample had had some governing experience, although, by that time, the experience of some parties was decades long, whereas others had spent a very limited amount of time in cabinet, even only a few months. Again, some parties had contributed all-socialist cabinets, whereas others shared their responsibility in coalitions, sometimes serving in leading positions but often in a secondary role. Hence, social democratic parties differed among themselves in the degree and manner into which they reached the final stages of democratic participation.

The branching out of social democracy started before government participation became a possibility. Searching for allies was a task that presented different dilemmas to different parties. Whether the search for allies took the form of electoral cooperation with middle-class parties under majority rule, or it was a strategy directed to attract their voters, or both, this related to different degrees of internal tension within socialist parties. Some parties were more internally divided than others, and divisions were concomitant to the difficulties at expanding their electoral support. Before the First World War, a few parties kept reasonably cohesive while cooperating with liberal forces, whereas others had difficulty in establishing alliances with nonsocialist parties and in attracting votes from outside their core constituency; the latter parties were also more internally divided and, eventually, most of them suffered serious splits. After the First World War, and the attendant Russian Revolution, the dilemmas for parties revolved around government participation and electoral division of the left. The classical treatment of the issue makes it a question of class formation and class coalitions, but this is not necessary for my argument (Przeworski and Sprague 1986). The ultimate source of division among parties claiming to represent the interests of workers is left unexplored here. It suffices to note that government participation entailed different opportunity costs for different parties. The costs can be approximately measured in terms of the votes gained by their challengers from the left.

If full participation (comprising alliances and responsibilities in the executive) imposed electoral and organizational costs in terms of schisms and potential voters lost to rivals, the trade union movement largely determined the size of such costs. This is the key to the analysis of Przeworski and Sprague of the electoral trade-offs faced by the socialist parties. Unions determined the severity of the trade-off. They limited the success of splinters and, for the same reason, the risks of them. When strong unions sided the socialist parties, schisms were moderate to small, almost independently of whatever the party did concerning alliances and government. When unions were weak or did not clearly support the party, splinter parties succeeded, which constrained the socialist parties' strategies in their pursuit of allies and opportunities to influence policy.

This chapter shows that parties with a close relationship with trade unions resisted proportional representation, whereas parties weakly related to trade unions, and often weak themselves, endorsed it. This empirical regularity may be explained in terms of three analytically separable aspects or electoral rules: the consequences for the internal control of the party, the consequences for the pattern of alliances and for electoral growth, and the consequences for government formation.

Proportional representation provided incentive for internal party centralization and also internal proportionality, which suited relatively more divided parties; it also suited parties that found it harder to attract voters from different constituencies or to find electoral allies at the grassroots level because it transferred the coalition game to the parliamentary arena. It also offered the view of a permanent, although possibly limited, influence in policy outcomes from their position in parliament, with an "opting out" clause attached to any direct responsibility in policy making. In sum, proportional rule let the parties graduate their participation to adjust for their opportunity costs, thus flattening the edge of their trade-offs.

Majority-biased systems, in their turn, offered less incentives to the reinforcement of central party organization; they also made it a necessity, to avoid permanent underrepresentation and possible obliteration, either to enlarge the electorate beyond their initial constituency or to find workable alliances at the constituency level; and, last, they imposed stronger variance in the influence over policy, ranging from underrepresentation to the direct responsibility in policy making.

The trade unions, by limiting divisions within the left while reaching toward the right, potentially favored the majoritarian route to full participation. When parties received little support from unions at mobilizing the voters, the internal social and ideological coalition within their electorates was more fragile, and they preferred the proportionalist route to political power. Moreover, if parties could act in coordination with trade unions, they could pursue their ends through the collective-action channel even when their influence in parliament was reduced. Thus, union-based parties should be less risk averse and care less for the variance of electoral results than purely political parties. This should explain the origins of the institutional preferences.

If the reasoning is correct, we should expect proportionalist parties to be relatively more divided, more politically isolated, more stagnated in their electoral growth, and more reluctant to take office. The contrary should be expected of parties that resisted, or tried to resist, proportional rule. This should explain the institutional preferences by showing that they were congruent with the constrained behavior of parties.

I show that proportionalist parties were more internally divided, suffered larger splits, and had a less cooperative relationship with the liberal forces than parties supporting nonproportional methods. Eventually, those constraints imposed larger opportunity costs for participation in government to proportionalist than to nonproportionalist parties, which resulted in the relative political isolation of the former. The latter could more easily pursue a supraclass strategy into participation, including frequent alliances with middle-class parties and a broader electoral appeal, with moderate to negligible losses to their left.

Government participation was the final act of the social democratic mobilization strategy. I show that in the interwar period, parties that had supported majority-biased systems governed more often, started earlier, and took greater responsibility, providing more prime ministers than proportionalist parties. Because government participation was almost inevitable under majority rule, particularly given the successful mobilization strategy of the parties that defended the permanence of such rules, preference for majority rule should anticipate the commitment of the parties. Although the risk of division is part of the explanation for the institutional preferences, once the choice was made, the level of division was partly endogenous to the participation of parties. Participation cost votes lost to the left, but it cost more votes to proportionalist than to nonproportionalist parties. For nonproportionalist parties, the chief obstacle to government participation came from the right: when the parties to their right presented a common front, the social democrats alternated in government with them, usually governing for shorter periods; however, when the right was divided, nonproportionalist socialists governed for prolonged periods. Thus, it can be said that proportionalists preferred rules that allowed for self-restraint, whereas nonproportionalists were restrained, when they were, mostly by the middle-class parties.

The relationship among these regularities is a complex one: there may be more than one causal narrative that connects them. An alternative view, appealing and simplified, might be the following: union-based parties formed wider electoral coalitions, and this increased their opportunities to participate in government. According to this account, majoritarian electoral institutions would be preferred to take advantage of the electoral success. I argue, however, that this picture is an incomplete one. Electoral size did not determine the institutional preferences nor the pattern of government participation. What the early history of socialist parties shows is that moderately sized parties were committed to the conquest of majorities choosing, among other things, majority-biased systems; on the contrary, other parties preferred proportional representation notwithstanding their auspicious electoral prospects. The electoral size of parties bears only a weak relationship with their level of participation in government; this is not surprising, for most parties in my sample had an average size that made them eligible for government in a reasonable amount of the time.

The causal story must be constrained by the timing of events. The union–party links were established before the choice of electoral rules while, generally, the actual potential for electoral mobilization and the level of government participation is observed only after the choices were made. The pattern of alliances and divisions can be observed before and after the setting of the rules, although most serious schisms came only after that. In addition, the union–party links were as durable as the institutions that were the object of choice. Thus, the union movement can safely be placed at the causal origin, whereas the causal connection between government participation and electoral rules must be intentional. Whether the latter was subjectively anticipated or was the inevitable consequence of previous participation choices is not important for my argument. I must indicate, however, that unmitigated radicals were often able to anticipate correctly that the end result of electoral cooperation with the middle class and of broad electoral appeals was the participation in bourgeois governments, even at a time when many moderates would still take that, at least ostensibly, as a form of verbal abuse.

The argument is not deterministic. Trade union support, or the lack of it, facilitated certain courses of action, but parties were agents with the capacity to choose, however divided. They chose their long-term mobilization and participation strategies under constraints. By choosing electoral institutions, they were trying to act on their institutional constraints. Parties that desired the permanence of majority-biased systems were parties that could anticipate that organizational cohesion was a relatively lesser concern, that they would be able to forge the necessary alliances to win substantial representation, and that had relatively less to fear from either temporal underrepresentation or eventual overrepresentation. However, by committing themselves to majority rule, they were also trying to eliminate any alternative course of action. When they did not succeed, they at least signaled their disposition to reach the executive as a majority – or plurality – party and rule.

Overview of Electoral Reform and Democratization

We may say that early representative regimes turned democratic when competitive elections where held with universal-manhood suffrage[1] and when the government was accountable to an elected assembly (save for the peculiarities of presidential regimes). During the nineteenth and early twentieth centuries, both things were often dissociated. In most cases, parliamentary government preceded suffrage extension, but in some cases, universal suffrage was employed to elect assemblies with limited powers (e.g., imperial Germany or Japan). By this criterion, of the twenty-two representative regimes for which electoral data are collected in Mackie and Rose (1982) before 1940, twenty-one (all but Japan) acquired democratic status between 1848 (Switzerland) and 1931 (Spain). Five would break down in the 1930s: Austria, Germany, Greece, Italy, and Spain (plus Japan's involution). Table 7.1 summarizes the data.

Early democracies evolved from nondemocratic representative systems that employed, roughly speaking, nonproportional methods. About two-thirds of the countries that were independent before 1919 and achieved democratic status before 1940 introduced proportional representation, all of them in Europe. Those institutional choices were, by and large, permanent: proportional democracies stayed proportional and majoritarian democracies stayed majoritarian after the Second World War and at least until the 1990s. Perhaps remarkably, those countries in which the system was frequently tinkered with from the start (France and Greece, in particular) had the most frequently changing electoral rules throughout the century.

---

[1] This criterion does not satisfy a true democratic conception of equality, but it would be utterly anachronistic to say that France turned democratic only in the "second wave" (women's suffrage in 1945) and Switzerland in the "third wave" (1971).

Table 7.1. Democratization and Electoral Reform in Early Representatives Regimes (Election Years)

	Parliamentary government[a]	Wide suffrage	Manhood suffrage	Universal suffrage	PR reform	Second PR[b]	Majority reform[c]
AUL	Westminster		1901	1903	No		1919
AUT	1919		1907	1919	1919	1920, 1923	
BEL	1831	1894	1919	1948	1900	1919	
CAN	Westminster	1900		1921	No		
DEN	1849	1848	1901	1918	1918	1920	
FIN	1907			1907	1907		
FRA	1875		1848	1945	No		1919, 1928
GER	1919		1867	1919	1919	1920	
GRC	1924		1844	1956	1926	1932, 1936	1928, 1933
ICE	1904	1908		1916	1934		
IRE	1922			1918	1922		
ITA	1848		1913	1943	1919	1921	
JPN	1946	1920	1928	1946	No		1920, 1928
LUX	1848	1902		1919	1919		
NET	1848		1918	1922	1918	1937	
NZ	Westminster		1879	1893	No		1908, 1914
NOR	1894		1900	1915	1921		1906
SPA	1931		1888	1933	No		1931, 1933
SWE	1907–17		1911	1921	1911	1921	
SWI	1848		1848	1971	1919		
UK	Westminster	1885		1918	No		
US	Presidential	1860		1920	No		

Notes: PR = proportional representation.
[a] Refers not to earliest experiences, when aborted, but to those that either lead to or were coincidental with democracy.
[b] Reforms that turned the systems more proportional, except in the Netherlands (a slightly less proportional formula) and Greece (reintroduction of PR alternating with majority system).
[c] In Greece refers to the reintroduction of the majority system alternating with PR. Other cases are shifts between two majoritarian systems after 1900.
Sources: Compiled with information from Caramani (2000) for European countries, plus the clarification by Cole and Campbell (1989) for the French reform. The sources for non-European countries are Graham (1962) for Australia, Hamer (1987) for New Zealand, and Hayashida (1966) for Japan.

Fourteen countries introduced proportional representation at some point. The earliest experience took place in Belgium, still without full democracy; the latest, in this period, in Iceland. In thirteen cases, the new systems proved fundamentally stable. In six cases, the first proportional reform led to a second one deepening proportionality (often linked to further steps in democratization). In the Netherlands, the most proportional system of all (with a single national district), proportionality was somewhat contained in the second reform. The unstable electoral system was that of Greece, where elections with proportional and majoritarian systems alternated.

The transition from nonproportional to proportional electoral methods was coincidental with the first democratic elections in four cases: Austria, Finland, Germany, and Luxembourg. In Sweden, it was nearly coincidental with democracy, and in Ireland with full independence (which for this purpose can be equated to democracy). Apart from Sweden, Belgium is the only country in this sample to have introduced proportional representation ahead of democracy. In half of the cases, the reform was delayed between two and seventy-one years.

Majoritarian systems were of various kinds. Single-member (sometimes two-member) plurality systems were originally used in Scandinavia and in the Anglophone countries. In Australia, it was substituted by the alternative vote in 1918 and in New Zealand by two-rounds majority in 1908 and 1911, reverting to plurality after that; in Norway, the two-rounds majority method was introduced in 1906. Multimember plurality was the method used in Greece in alternation with different proportional systems. All four Scandinavian countries, plus Ireland, eventually adopted proportional methods.

Two-round majority systems were the rule in the European continent: there were multimember districts in Belgium, Luxembourg, and Switzerland, with predominantly single-member districts in the rest of the countries. Two-round majority systems shifted to proportionality in all cases but France, which by the turn of the century had a tradition in alternating majoritarian systems. The only, but consequential, experiment before the Second World War was a hybrid multimember system in the 1919 and 1924 elections.

Spain and Japan form an unlikely group on their own. In both countries, different systems alternated based on combinations of multimember districts with limited vote and single-member districts (in Spain, sometimes with two rounds). Early democratic Spain generalized the multimember limited vote system, with a second round for candidates not reaching certain thresholds. Perhaps the only country where the predemocratic assembly was further from the parliamentarian ideal than in Japan and Spain was Finland's Estate's Diet, which, however, introduced parliamentary democracy and proportional representation in a single, self-dissolving, constitutional move.

The new proportional systems were characterized by moderate district magnitudes, particularly in the earliest reforms, save for the Netherlands and Germany, and the nearly uniform adoption of the D'Hondt divisors formula, also known as highest averages or as Hagenbach-Bioschoff, for the allocation of seats for parties (quota methods were adopted in Ireland and the Netherlands). Systems allowing for personal vote were not uncommon, in the form of open lists (Finland, Italy, and Switzerland), mixed systems with a personal vote tier (Iceland and rural constituencies in Denmark in 1918 but later abolished), or single transferable vote (Ireland).

The Position of the Parties and Their Initial Electoral Sizes

There is some conspicuous regularity in the patterns of conflict and, broadly speaking, political cultures that associated to different electoral systems. Yet this regularity may be deceiving, for the rules were reformed by collective actors, and their institutional preferences are not easily explained by political cultures or cleavage patterns. Party preferences have not been explored in comparative perspective by the literature and, indeed, the accounts are often imprecise and fragmentary.[2]

The strongest regularity is this: every country where the Catholics (and, in the Netherlands, also the Protestants) had mobilized politically adopted proportional representation. This is a sufficient condition for reform. The second largest group is Scandinavia: all four countries introduced some form of proportional representation. Rokkan (1970) linked this to the rural–urban cleavage in those countries. A third, less compact "group" can be formed with countries in which proportional representation was totally (e.g., Ireland) or at least partially (e.g., Finland) linked to the presence of sizeable "ethnic" or "nationalist" parties. The residual case is Greece.

Socialist mobilization came close to a necessary condition for reform. Apart from Greece and Ireland, the proportional reform processes were

---

[2] I have found information in the following sources: Graham (1962) and Rydon (1956) for Australia; Jelavich (1987), Jenks (1974), and Schambeck (1972) for Austria; Stengers (1990), Goblet d'Alviella (1900), and Glissen (1980) for Belgium; Elklit (2002) for Denmark; Törnudd (1968) for Finland; Bonnefous (1965), Thomson (1964), and Colton (1953) for France; Sperber (1997), Suval (1985), and Berlau (1949) for Germany; Hardarson (2002) for Iceland; Gallagher (1981) and McCracken (1958) for Ireland; Noiret (1994) and Seton-Watson (1967) for Italy; Hamer (1987) and Lipson (1948) for New Zealand; Aardal (2002) for Norway; Verkade (1965) for the Netherlands; Colomer (2004b) for Spain; Lewin (1988), Verney (1957), and Rustow (1955) for Sweden; Lutz (2004) for Switzerland; and Chadwick (1996), Pugh (1980), and Butler (1963) for the United Kingdom.

related to the rise of socialist parties, a fact repeatedly pointed out in the literature. In nearly every country where a significant socialist party appeared, proportional representation was at least considered by some political forces. The socialists' mobilization notwithstanding, it failed to materialize in Australia, Britain, France, New Zealand, and Spain.

As for democracies that did not introduce proportional representation, France and Spain were the only ones outside the Anglophone world (and Ireland the only one in that world) to have diverged. They were also the only Catholic countries (apart from Ireland, nonindependent in the relevant period) where a Catholic party was absent.

The only category of parties that showed little variance in institutional preferences was the Catholic parties. In every case, they contributed to the introduction of proportional representation at some point, although there was diversity in their enthusiasm: the Germans opposed it at least until 1913, and I have not found any record for their support (or opposition) in the Netherlands and Luxemburg beyond the fact that they entered the constitutional consensus that introduced it. The rest were openly in favor and were decisive for the adoption of the new systems.

Secular conservatives (save for internal divisions) opposed proportional representation except in Sweden, Norway, and Denmark, where they indeed championed reform. In Iceland and Finland, they entered a consensual agreement when they could not oppose to it, as many did in Italy. Liberals tended to display the opposite preferences to secular conservatives in each country. They were seldom decisive in the collective choice, although their rejection to proportional representation was as decisive in France as was its endorsement in Italy and, arguably, in the Netherlands. Among failed opponents, the most stubborn were the Scandinavian and the Swiss. In general, many liberal parties turned into supporters of proportional representation between the 1910s and the 1920s. Some, like the British, arrived too late to that policy.

Unlike the other large newcomer group to early democracy, the Catholics, the socialist parties did not have uniform preferences. Table 7.2 summarizes the distribution of the sample of parties that is subsequently analyzed. Of the twenty-two countries in the Mackie and Rose (1982) data set, it includes all social democratic parties that averaged at least 10 percent of the vote in the interwar period except Luxembourg, for which I do not have adequate data. (Luxembourg would be an additional entry in the PR/PR cell of Table 7.2.) The criterion leaves out Canada, Greece, Japan, and the United States.

Table 7.2. Institutional Preferences of Socialist Parties and Early Electoral Systems

	Electoral system during interwar period (N)	
Electoral system defended	PR	Non-PR
PR	Austria, Finland, Germany, Iceland, Ireland, Italy, Netherlands, Norway, Switzerland (9)	France (1)
Non-PR	Belgium, Denmark, Sweden (3)	Australia, New Zealand, Spain, United Kingdom (4)

Note: PR = proportional representation.

The socialist parties opposed proportional representation or, at least, failed to defend it in Australia, Britain, New Zealand, Spain, Belgium, Denmark, and Sweden. In the three latter cases, their opposition was hopeless, and the socialists eventually accepted the accomplished facts and adapted to them. Everywhere else, the socialists consistently stood for proportional representation, and they obtained what they wanted except in France. The French socialists were actively defending proportional rule at least until the mid-1920s.

The influence of the socialist preferences in the final choice varied, but the origin of the electoral institutions cannot be attributed to the parties to the right of the social democrats. Contrary to Boix (1999) or Cusack, Iversen, and Soskice (2003), no model of institutional choice can be solely based on those parties. If we take the most demanding criterion, the social democrats were decisive in five of seventeen cases, and they contributed to the institutional reform, in different degrees, in twelve of seventeen cases. In three cases, the institutional choice was made by provisional transition governments in which socialists had prominent positions (i.e., Spain, Austria, and Germany); in two cases, they failed to support proportional representation in crucial parliamentary votes (i.e., Australia and Britain). It is more difficult to estimate the extent to which the socialists were decisive when proportional representation was introduced with broad parliamentary consensus. Apart from Ireland, they were least relevant in Finland, where they supported the reform mostly from outside the nonrepresentative Diet of Estates; they were most decisive in Switzerland, where they (together with the Catholic right) launched a referendum that curbed the opposition of the liberal majority. The Netherlands, Norway, Italy, and Iceland were intermediate cases. When the socialists opposed the institutional decision, it could be argued that the choice of the bourgeois parties resulted from socialist mobilization; it must, however, be noted that a large part of the liberal current was on the side of the socialists in the Netherlands, Norway, and Italy. Indeed, it was the prospect of a socialist–liberal entente that scared most conservatives, an argument absent in the accounts that attribute the origins of electoral rules to the bourgeois parties.

Were the choices of the social democrats dictated by electoral advantage? To conclude this section, let us briefly look at the initial electoral fortunes of the socialist parties. In the first elections under proportional representation, the socialist parties that had opposed it came third in two cases (Belgium and Sweden) and second in one case (Denmark). The socialist parties that supported the new system won the elections in three cases (Austria, Finland, and Germany), second in five cases, and third in only two cases (Iceland and Ireland). In countries where proportional representation was not adopted, only in Spain were the socialists the most voted party (in a very fragmented election) after having supported a nonproportional system. The opposition to proportional representation by the British has been recorded since early in the period under study, when they were still by far the third party, and the Australians won only the third election after having voted for plurality rule. Thus, as the choices were made, the relative size of socialist parties, vis-à-vis their competitors, did not form a predictable pattern in terms of the maximization of the immediate electoral advantage.

Comparing socialist parties among themselves, as Table 7.3 shows, there is no trace of relationship between party sizes and institutional preferences that may give any clue on the origins of such preferences. For the elections previous to electoral reforms (or failed reforms), the correlation has indeed the wrong sign. The data are limited, however, and so is their comparability because the conditions were not uniformly democratic before the institutional reforms. For the election taking place immediately after reforms (or failed ones), the coefficient is positive but negligible. For purposes of comparison, it may not be clear which is the correct moment of observation for parties in countries in which proportional representation was not adopted. The result of the first elections under new, nonproportional, electoral systems is used in the cases of France and Spain. For Australia and Britain, the observations are taken at times of important

Table 7.3. Electoral Strength and Institutional Preferences – Correlation Coefficients

	Pre-reform elections or vote against in parliament for Australia (1901) and United Kingdom (1923)	Postreform or postvote elections	Socialist vote circa 1919
Preference (PR = 1)	0.20 n.s. (12)	−0.20 n.s. (17)	−0.21 n.s. (17)

Notes: For cases included, see Appendix B. n.s. = nonsignificant; PR = proportional representation.

votes confirming plurality rule. The correlation for all elections around 1919 is introduced for comparison because most electoral reforms were introduced for those elections.

Some Explanations of Party Institutional Preferences

The focus on institutional preferences departs from the main body of existing literature on the electoral reform processes. To pick two recent examples, the role of specific actors is secondary in Blais, Dobrzynska, and Indridason (2005) and in Colomer (2003). The former base their account on previous institutions, and the latter bases his on the fragmentation of the party system. Although the underlying mechanism is, for Colomer, the reaction of parties to fragmentation, there is no indication of specific preferences for specific parties. In Rokkan's (1970) classic but fragmentary remarks, actors are somewhat more prominent. For him, the modal case of proportional reform arise from the interaction of socialist growth and division among the censitaire parties. Old parties feared the overrepresentation of the socialists, to which they could respond either by uniting against them or, when the "tradition of hostility and mistrust," rooted in social cleavages, prevented them from doing so, introducing proportional representation. However, he confusedly adds that socialist parties were also interested in reform to improve their representation, which created a combination of pressure from above and below. Thus, one side feared socialist overrepresentation and socialists feared underrepresentation, a statement that would need a convincing account on the disparity of expectations (which Rokkan does not offer) to make sense.

Boix's (1999) influential article focuses on the parties to the right of socialists and proposes a mechanism, in place of the "traditions of hostility," to explain their institutional choices. Old parties are supposed to have introduced proportional representation when, in the face of socialist electoral growth, their electoral forces were evenly divided. In this situation, fear of a socialist victory due to coordination failure on the part of nonsocialist voters, Boix argues, impelled electoral reform. Cusack, Iversen, and Soskice (2003) introduce a second variation to develop an argument from Rokkan's sketch. It was neither "hostility" nor electoral balance but rather economic divisions other than class that prevented the unity, either by electoral realignment or by fusion of parties, of the non-socialists. They substitute a reasonable typology of economic interests for Rokkan's societal cleavages, but the real strength of their argument seems to rest in the finding (Iversen and Soskice 2002) that proportional representation eventually (after the Second World War) produced more leftist governments and more redistribution than nonproportional systems. Hence, the argument goes, the middle and upper classes, represented by assumption by the parties to the right of the socialists, would have rallied together under some majoritarian system had not economic differences other than class – that is, other than fiscal redistribution – prevented this.

I do not discuss the merits of these arguments here, but I am interested in the imputation of preferences that results from them. For Cusack, Iversen, and Soskice (2003), it is the policy consequences of rules that matters; if they are right, socialist parties should have always advocated proportional representation. In my reading of Boix's argument, what drives the institutional preferences of the right is the minimization of socialist representation. What might motivate the socialist parties' preferences is less clear, but if it is the maximization of their own representation, then, as a rule, socialist parties should have resisted proportional representation whenever the right proposed it. In both cases, the main parties to the right should have agreed on reform when it did take place and, at least for Cusack, Iversen, and Soskice, they should have agreed on nonreform when it did not take place. Yet the stubborn empirical fact is that socialist parties' preferences over electoral systems showed a fair amount of variance, and the pattern was not clearly related to the preferences of the other parties. As for the parties to their right, they agreed on the best institutional strategy as often as they did not.

Referring specifically to socialist parties, it has sometimes been suggested (e.g., Rustow 1950) that socialist preference for proportional
representation was rooted in a socialist belief in equality, which would
translate for this purpose into "electoral justice." It is true, and hardly
surprising, that political arguments defending proportional representation were put in those or similar terms. Yet although socialists advocated
proportional representation more often than not, there is enough variance to make such explanation implausible. One need not be prejudiced
against irrational explanations to question whether, say, the British Labour
Party was less committed to democratic ideals than the German Social
Democrats, or, within those parties, whether Macmillan and Bernstein,
who advocated majoritarian systems, were milder democrats than Snow-
den and Kautsky, who did not.

It may be true (for parties as well as for individual leaders) that ideology
was related to institutional preferences in a different way, for it seems that
moderates tended to have greater reservations toward proportional representation, whereas radicals appear to have been more consistent defenders
of proportionality. The truth of this relationship hinges on how we define
moderation or radicalism, which is not uncontroversial. The explanation,
however, cannot be purely ideological. Ideology matters when it is translated into organization and political strategy, and that is where we should
search for explanations. Even if radicalism were systematically related to
proportionalist preferences, if I show that those preferences were no less
systematically related to weak unionism, the commonsense implication is
that the most fundamental term in the relationship, determining the other
two, is union strength.

A suggestion nearly opposite to considerations of electoral justice is that
socialist parties, as indeed any other party, may be assumed to have different preferences over electoral systems according to their interest in terms
of seat maximization. Hence, smaller parties are expected to prefer proportional representation and larger ones to prefer majoritarian systems. This
is the natural conclusion to extract from the *micromega* principle (Colomer
2004a): smaller parties prefer the large (district magnitudes, electoral quo-
tas, and assemblies) and larger parties prefer the small. However, it was
often the most voted parties that the ones to advocate proportional representation – that is, "large" institutional alternatives – while the success
of some of the parties that opposed reform remained to be seen. There
was no relationship between the electoral strength of the parties and their
preferences.

Institutional Preferences and the Trade Unions

Proportionalist parties were weakly connected to weak unions, whereas nonproportionalist parties held stronger ties with stronger unions. My conjecture is that the multiplicative effect of the organizational link of the party and the mobilization capacity of the union is at the causal origin of the institutional preferences of the social democratic parties. I review the evidence in this section; the mechanisms that explain this pattern are presented in subsequent sections.

When the socialist movement was so organized that the unions (and, in the Belgian case, the cooperatives) were constituent parts of the party, the party rejected, or at least attempted to reject, proportional representation in nearly every case. This happened in Australia, Belgium, Britain, New Zealand, and Sweden. The one clear exception is Ireland. However, this Irish exception is hardly relevant because the decision to adopt proportional representation predates the existence of the party and the union as independent organizations and, in any case, both were rather weak.

It is interesting to note that union–party relations in Norway went along this model except for the break of 1919, when the Labour Party joined the Commintern, leading to a reformist split, whereas the union joined the Amsterdam International. In 1923, relations would be restored, and the two wings of the party (the communists remained as a separate fringe group) were brought together by the union (Esping-Andersen 1985: 67, 80). However, by that time, in 1920, proportional representation had been introduced. In light of the comparative evidence, it seems reasonable to speculate that the Norwegian socialists would have been less favorable to proportional representation had it been proposed at a different time.

Another fairly exceptional case is Iceland. The Labor Party of Iceland was founded in 1916 as the political arm of the Federation of Labour, but the congruence between the two organizations was not enforced until 1930 because members of other parties could be affiliated with the unions. Hence, it was not strictly a case of collective membership. In the 1930 union (and party) congress, it was required of union members to commit to the Labour Party platform. As a result, the communists walked out to set separate unions and a new party (Karlsson 2000: 300, 304–5).

The Danish and the Spanish parties are the only cases of nonproportionalist parties without union collective membership. Esping-Andersen

(1985: 65) stresses that the system of top-level joint representation of both organizations, institutionalized in Denmark in 1890, made the party–union relationships nearly as close as in Sweden and Norway (as long as they were good in the latter case). The Danish trade unions organization did not directly provide affiliates, but it did provide funds and leaders to the party. In the Spanish case, the socialist union and the socialist party were nearly fused at the top from 1920, after the communist split, until 1935, when it was again on the verge of scission. The union took the political direction of the movement during the 1920s, adopting a reformist stance and cooperating with the dictatorship, and it had nearly absorbed the party in the eve of democratization (Juliá 1997: 110–33).

It is difficult to obtain full and systematic comparative evidence on party–union linkages for this period. In his study of the European left, Bartolini (2000) classifies their party–union relationships as "contingent," "interlocking," or "subordinate." However, I do not find this typology completely useful, among other things, because he ignores unionist collective membership in the party as a relevant feature. I assume that some degree of "interlocking relationships" must have been present in nearly every case, except perhaps in the extreme cases of "contingent" relationships, including the cases listed by Bartolini as union-to-party subordination (i.e., Austria, Finland, and Germany), which, in his classification, are lumped together with the cases where he finds party-to-union subordination (i.e., the British and the Irish). Again, whether one of the organizations is more or less subordinate to the other, given "interlocking," must have depended on their relative success.

Using Bartolini's data (supplemented with data for Australia and New Zealand), I have calculated the ratio between socialist voters and unionized workers (in leftist unions) around 1919 (Table 7.4). The observations at this time are comparable in that they are chosen to be previous to the electoral entry of communist parties proper and, at the same time, electorates were greatly mobilized in every country. However, this is the time slice closer to electoral reform in most cases. I assume that this ratio approximately indicates the strength of the unions in the socialist movement, at least provided that relations were not "contingent."

The three cases classified as contingent by Bartolini are cases of proportionalist parties: France, Italy, and Switzerland. Only in the latter case did the union have numerical advantage over the party's electoral mobilization capacity. In the remaining cases for which Bartolini supplies data,

Table 7.4. The Party–Union Link and the Institutional Preferences of Socialist Parties

	Preference	Ratio union to votes ca. 1919	Union members ca. 1919[a]	Union members interwar average	Remarks
Uk	Non-PR	2.36	24.7	17.5	Collective membership
Nz	Non-PR	1.46	11.4	16.1	Collective membership
Swe	Non-PR	1.43	23.5	16.5	Collective membership
Den	Non-PR	1.05	20.5	16.6	
Aul	Non-PR	1.01	23.6	23.3	Collective membership
Bel	Non-PR	0.85	27.4	23.6	Collective membership
Spa	Non-PR	n.a.	n.a.	n.a.	Joint leadership and party subordination 1920–31
Ire	PR	n.a.	n.a.	7.6	Collective membership
Swz	PR	1.25	23.3	17.9	Contingent relationships
Net	PR	0.79	15.4	8.5	
Fra	PR	0.61	8.7	10.7	Contingent relationships
Ita	PR	0.61	11.2	10.5	Contingent relationships
Aut	PR	0.58	20.0	20.4	
Ger	PR	0.47	14.7	13.5	
Nor	PR	0.47	9	9.0	Union/party relations broken 1919–1923
Fin	PR	0.11	2.8	2.9	

Notes: PR = proportional representation.
[a] Percentage of left union members in the electorate. The ca. 1919 observation for New Zealand refers to 1914, and the interwar average is taken from only two observations.
Sources: Author's compilation with data from Bartolini (2000); the Australian Council of Trade Unions: http://www.actu.asn.au/public/about/history.html; and the Northern Amalgamated Workers Union: http://www.awunz.org.nz/. For the sources of the remarks, see the references.

the ratio of unionized workers to socialist voters perfectly matched the institutional preferences of socialists. The lowest ratio of nonproportionalist parties was that of Belgium, the only one below unity, but this figure does not take into account the unique mass cooperative movement that was also a constituent part of the party.

As for sheer union numerical strength within the enfranchised population, nonproportionalist parties were related to stronger unions, whereas the proportionalist parties were sided – if indeed they were – by unions whose membership was lower on average. The correlation coefficient between preferences and union strength circa 1919 is 0.68 ($p < 0.01$) and the correlation with the interwar average is 0.65 ($p < 0.01$).

The Effects of Unions and the Anticipated Consequences of Rules

In this section, I outline the hypothetical mechanisms that link the causal background of union support with the choice of electoral rules and with the behavior of the parties. To explain the empirical pattern that links the trade unions with preference for electoral systems in an agent-based causal narrative, the effects of the trade unions on the socialist parties must be consistent with the intentional choices of the parties concerning the electoral institutions. Unions should contribute to shape the expectations of the parties in such a way that their preferences for electoral systems, given their foreseeable consequences, can be made predictable. Again, given the predictable consequences of rules, the fact that parties preferred them may be taken as an attempted commitment to follow the path favored by them. Thus, on one hand, the institutional preferences are explained by the constraints of unions on party behavior, but, on the other, the institutional preferences contribute to explain part of the subsequent behavior of parties.

To understand for what purpose parties wanted the electoral systems, I suggest singling out three types of effects of electoral rules: the effects on the pattern of coalitions and alliances, including the prospects for electoral growth of the new parties; the consequences on party centralization; and their impact on the variability in policy influence, including the rules of access to government. The list may not be exhaustive, and the three aspects of rules are unlikely to have had equal weight in the institutional choices of the parties. In any case, my argument holds that union support oriented the choices in the same direction on those three accounts.

In summary, unions facilitated the pursuit of a supraclass electoral strategy, and the preference for majority-biased electoral rules was a signal to their commitment to that strategy on the part of some parties. This was, I believe, the main contribution of the trade unions. In addition, unions weakened the incentives for the centralization of the parties. Last, trade union support can be said to have facilitated the transition from supraclass electoral mobilization to democratic government but, because that transition was nearly inevitable under majoritarian electoral systems, the very fact that some parties preferred majoritarian rules should lead us to expect them to be more involved in government.

In a world where there are no natural and permanent majorities, different electoral systems favor different kinds of alliances. In multiparty contests, plurality rule may encourage preelectoral agreements, and we find many in history, but these agreements impose an "organizational contradiction." Plurality fosters relatively decentralized parties, whereas preelectoral pacts are unlikely to easily develop at the local level; on the contrary, they are normally approved and crafted by the central organizations, if only because they require that many local party organizations renounce their candidates. A possible development of this situation is realignment, either by party fusion or by voters' strategic coordination; another is electoral reform. Two-ballot majority allows that electoral agreements be crafted at the local level. Again, agreements need not be preelectoral but may be taken contingently on first-round electoral results. Coalitions may also be needed to form government but, in this case, they are less constrained to match the pattern of electoral alliances than in the case of plurality because the locus of electoral coalition is typically local, often informal, and does not require the commitment to a wide agreement on cooperation set in advance of elections. Last, it is obvious that proportional representation mostly favors postelectoral agreements directed from party headquarters.

Hence, in this connection, for parties to choose a majoritarian system, they had to be confident in their capacity to attract voters outside their main social or ideological constituency, either by realignment or by pact. Voters retain substantial control on the shape of the coalition that may potentially turn into a majority, for pacts wished by leaders need not be honored by voters or even by grassroots activists. Voters may be alienated into abstention, or into opposition, if they reject their constituency candidate when it belongs to a different party to their preferred one, or they may disobey their party instructions for second-ballot pacts. In decentralized parties, militant activists may boycott pacts by launching or failing to withdraw candidates not endorsed by pacts and may fail to mobilize voters into voting for candidates of other parties. Again, the control of voters over coalition politics is minimal with proportional representation because they normally take place after the vote. Any party may substitute parliamentary coalitions for the ability to attract voters from different social groups. If the voters trust their preferred parties, they may also be better off by surrendering the coalition decision to them. Votes are given once and for the entire legislature, and voters may reason that it is better to vote for one's own party and let the party decide with whom and for how long it is going to cooperate, rather than give their vote to a presettled pact when this is locally represented by a candidate of a less preferred party.

The importance of the relationship with the trade unions for socialist parties has been hinted at in several ways in the literature. Without some trade union assistance, socialist electoral mobilization could hardly take off, which has been suggested as a possible explanation to the American exception (Lipset and Marks 2000). Yet even where mobilization took off, Przeworski and Sprague (1986) convincingly argue that the party–union relationship was the basic determinant of the strategic flexibility that allowed certain parties to appeal to nonworker voters while retaining the bulk of the workers' constituency. For Przeworski and Sprague, this also set a limit to a pure supraclass strategy. Precisely because the strategic flexibility derived from a solid collective-action organization of the workers as a class, workers could not be deserted.

When the support of the unions was weak, the supraclass strategy entailed a steep electoral trade-off. In practical terms, this meant that the organization of viable leftist alternatives could only be contained at the price of relative isolation (the Austrian party is a good example of this) or that, more commonly, even a limited amount of cooperation with middle-class parties or the widening of the electoral appeal toward their voters (or both) incited profound conflicts and schisms (the German party is representative of this predicament, shared by many others). When strong unions consistently supported the political movement, splinters ranged from the minimal (in the Labour parties of the Anglophone countries) to the moderate (in Belgium, Denmark, or Sweden).

Not surprisingly, the parties that Przeworski and Sprague (1986) estimate to have faced a more severe electoral trade-off were proportionalist parties (Finland, France, and Germany), whereas, within their sample, the parties for which the supraclass strategy was optimal resisted proportional rule, except Norway – an exception that may be explained by the particular timing of reform (the other cases were Belgium, Denmark, and Sweden).

The direct influence of electoral systems on party organization operates fundamentally through district magnitude and the ballot structure. The effects of magnitude and the number of districts on candidate selection are easily recognized. On one hand, the larger the number of districts, the more difficult to centralize the candidate-selection process. On the other, the larger the size of the units, the easier to accommodate candidates and, under closed lists, the easier to accommodate candidates into safe positions. These connected variables also have a necessary impact on electoral and organizational costs: the larger the size of the district, the more efficient the centralization of campaign resources. Therefore, large and relatively few districts provide manifold incentives for party centralization. These incentives may be partially offset by the effects of open ballots, which allow for personal votes or even for cross-party votes.[3]

Assuming that Przeworski and Sprague (1986) are correct in their argument, it may be argued that a strong union movement siding the socialist party provided a surrogate of party discipline and centralization, precisely because dissidents were unlikely to have much political future without union support, the more so the more the potential dissidents were moved by a class-oriented ideology. At the same time, this might have made internal disagreements within the party much more tolerable because independent-minded leaders were less likely to enter into fissiparous strife. This side effect of union support reduced the incentive to adopt proportional representation that could stem from the concern with internal organization.

The last remarkable effect, for my argument, of majority-biased systems, is that they impose greater variance in the ability of the parties to influence policy. Parties under proportional rule may expect to have a safer representation floor. During the interwar period, the minimal percentage of seats for the twelve parties competing under proportional rule averaged 21.8 percent, whereas for the five parties competing under majoritarian systems, it was 13 percent ($p < 0.05$).[4] Parties under proportional rule may also expect less variability in their representation. The mean range of the seats' percentage for parties in proportional systems was 13.5 points, whereas it was 31.6 points for parties in nonproportional systems ($p < 0.05$).[5]

The unions provided an alternative channel, through collective action, for workers demands. If party and union shared their aims, the risk of political underrepresentation under majority rule was less serious. The socialists were in a position to influence policy via collective action even when the full control of policy rested in the hands of a nonsocialist majority government. When party and union acted in coordination, alternation in government might have been a better result than the more constant, but usually more limited, influence over policy based on proportional representation in the legislature.

---

[3] A detailed comparison of the effects on electoral systems on French and German parties, following those lines, can be found in Kreuzer (2001). For a review of this issue, see Maravall (this volume).

[4] Single-tailed test, not assuming equal variances.

[5] Single-tailed test, not assuming equal variances.

A crucial aspect of the variability imposed by majoritarian rules on policy influence is that those rules and, particularly, plurality rule, make rather unequivocal that winning elections entails assuming the responsibility of government. Proportional representation permits the practice of what Italians later called *conventio ad excludendum*, a convention that may be the excluded's initiative as much as it can be the excluder's. More generally, proportional representation allows for greater control over the desired degree of influence over policy making, whereas plurality rule imposes either little or full capacity to direct policy.

That proportional rule permits parties to restrain their commitment to government does not mean that the parties will choose to do it, particularly, if my argument is correct, the nonproportionalist parties. Thus, in actual fact, socialists governed for longer periods under proportional representation than under majority rule, but this was largely because of the strength of nonproportionalist parties acting in systems contrary to their preference. Hence, it is not possible to determine the exact effects of rules on the behavior of parties without controlling for their preferences.

However, it is worth pausing at a particular effect that it is detectable regardless of preferences, and this is the immediacy of commitment. The link between electoral results and government responsibility was more immediate under majority-biased systems than under proportional rule, and the more so the more serious the responsibility assumed. During the interwar period, different men assumed the office of prime minister 169 times (excluding Switzerland). The socialists were part of the cabinet 35 times, held the prime ministership 20 times, and presided over single party socialist cabinets 10 times. Socialists were part of cabinets in which the prime minister took office as a result of elections – within three months of elections – 43 percent of the time (15 of 35) (the figure for nonsocialists was 27 percent, or 35 of 128). It happened 62 percent of the time (5 of 8) with majoritarian systems and 59 percent (10 of 17) of the time with proportional systems. When the socialists themselves assumed the office of prime minister, they did it as a result of elections 83 percent (5 of 6) and 50 percent (7 of 14) of the time, respectively, with nonproportional and proportional systems; the corresponding proportion for nonsocialists prime ministers was 26 percent (38 of 143), with little difference by electoral systems. Finally, when socialists took office alone, this was a consequence of electoral results in every case (4 of 4) under majoritarian rules, and in half of the cases (3 of 6) under proportional ones.

Hence, if the argument is correct, strong socialist unions made it possible for socialist parties to commit to some form of majority rule rather than to proportional representation. Unions formed the basis of a flexible strategy oriented toward expanding the electorate or at committing voters into electoral alliances, without serious losses; limited the incentives for party centralization; and provided safety against the uncertainties of government based in a majority-biased system. If only for those reasons, unions causally determined institutional preferences. Unions acted as causal constraints that made the choice of the supraclass strategy – signaled by electoral institutional preferences – a nonvoluntary choice. Once a supraclass strategy oriented to a broad electorate was adopted, the decision to participate in government under majority rule could hardly be avoided.

A party choosing a nonproportional system is expected to be a party that could count on its capacity to attract voters from various social constituencies and, by implication, to count on not being deserted by its former voters when trying to attract others. When the party strategy was that of finding electoral partners rather than directly trying to gain their votes, it had to be able to lend and borrow voters to and from contiguous ideological groups. It is also expected, as a rule, to have had less to fear from internal divisions than a proportionalist party. Last, it had to be a party willing to risk underrepresentation in parliament and periods of opposition while also being ready to assume government when on the winning side. This last clause is not superfluous because one gets the impression that what some socialists disliked most of the idea of alternation in government was the governing bits.

Alliances and Divisions

Parties backed by the trade unions and endorsing majoritarian systems were relatively more successful in the pursuit of a supraclass strategy than proportionalist parties. First, during the early period of socialist mobilization, the relations between socialist and liberal parties were supportive, including various kinds of electoral alliances, and in all cases union-supported, nonproportionalist parties. Second, parties supported by the trade unions endured smaller schisms. In addition, nonproportionalist parties may be assumed to have resisted milder organized internal tensions. Presumably, as a result of a successful supraclass strategy, nonproportionalist parties obtained more votes in the long term.

Australia, Britain, and New Zealand, in this chronological order, were parallel and paradigmatic cases of "lib-labism." The labor parties emerged nearly as working-class branches of the liberal movement, with liberals surrendering a number of constituencies to labor candidates in exchange for labor restraint in others. In all three cases, the labor parties eventually overcame the liberals in the electorate, but they kept cooperating until the liberals opted for the right (Overacker 1949, 1955; Loveday 1977; Luebbert 1991). Belgium and Denmark came closest to those cases in their degree of liberal–labor cooperation. Liberal–socialist cartels were present in the first round of Belgian elections in the two elections preceding the introduction of proportional representation in 1900 and continued in four biannual elections between 1906 and 1912, when this strategy culminated in a common electoral platform that was rejected by the electorate (Kossman 1978; Luebbert 1991). The Danish social democrats cooperated electorally with the liberal party from 1877, changing partners to the left–liberal splinters (the Radical Party) from 1906 until the outbreak of the war. The pacts consisted in the allotment of constituencies guided by class composition criteria and were sometimes only narrowly approved by the socialist party conference, which explains their interest in the two-round system (Miller 1996; Elklit 2002). The association between Swedish socialists and liberals was only slightly less formal and continuated: Branting, the socialist leader, was elected in a liberal ticket in 1896 and 1899 and in alliance with liberals in 1902; in 1902–5, the social democrats were informally allied to the liberals, avoiding mutually damaging competition; in 1908, constituencies were explicitly allotted between the parties, and voters' coordination was perfectly successful. Proportional representation was introduced after that, with the significant opposition of both parties, and the electoral pacts ceased, which goes a long way toward explaining why it was introduced by the party of the right (Rustow 1950; Tingsten 1973; Lewin 1988). Events were delayed in Spain but, from 1909 onward, the republican–socialist electoral cartels were also frequent in predemocratic elections and, crucially, it was the electoral victory of that cartel in the 1931 local elections that triggered the transition to democracy and led the cartel into a coalition government (Juliá 1997).

Liberal and socialist cooperation was also significant for three proportionalist parties – the French, the Dutch, and the Swiss – but it was far more intermittent and informal, generally confined to the second round of elections, and always discontinued in parliament. In fact, those three parties, and only those, went into at least partly self-inflicted political isolation after the First World War. The Swiss case is remarkable because the party was entirely "lib-labist" until 1904. Electoral alliances were broken in 1905, later restored, and definitely suspended in 1914. Counting only the most favorable period for cooperation, between 1899 and 1911, there were 146 socialist candidates nonendorsed for 32 endorsed by the liberals in first ballots. When their outburst of "radicalism" passed, proportional representation was already there (Luebbert 1991: 51, 224; Bartolini 2000: 85). The French informal second-round pacts between radicals and socialists were important to both, but the socialists passed resolutions against ministerial cooperation in 1905 and against any kind of formal pacts and first-round support in 1919. Only when proportional representation ceased to be a realistic demand did the moderates attempt a timid rapprochement, although the party rejected an invitation to form government in 1924 and 1929, accepting the Popular Front formula in 1936 (Colton 1953; Judt 1976). In the Netherlands, competition between liberals and socialists in the first round jumped from 23 percent of districts in 1901 to 70 percent in 1905. Although mutual support in the second round was frequent, the socialists rejected an invitation to join the liberal government as early as 1913 and passed a resolution against so doing in the future (Verhoef 1974; Kossman 1978: 516; Verkade 1965: 54).

For most of the other proportionalist parties, the record of early cooperation with liberal parties ranged between poor and nonexistent. It is important to note that cultural or institutional conditions did not determine the outcome. For example, in Norway, in stark contrast with Denmark and Sweden, the socialists self-prohibited any kind of electoral alliances already in 1906, a redundant proclamation because the liberals had consistently rejected them before that date (Luebbert 1991: 121–4). In Germany, the two-ballot system never helped the socialists because they were never able to add any significant support to their votes in the second round. Their attempted electoral pact with the liberals *for the second round* in 1912 was a paradigmatic fiasco, boycotted as it was by liberal voters in the constituencies (and, partly, by socialist radicals as well). This was the perfect example of a pact wished by the elites of the parties but rejected by voters and grassroots activists. The parties found their way into cooperation with proportional representation (Suval 1985; Sperber 1997).

The other side of a successful supraclass mobilization strategy is the containment of losses to parties competing for representation of the workers. As a matter of fact, the level of unionization (in leftist unions) greatly reduced the fragmentation of leftist parties. Figure 7.1 plots the

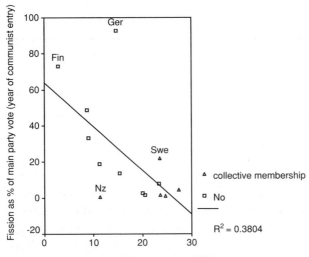

Figure 7.1. Socialists schisms and trade unions.

percentage of union members on the electorate around 1919 against the size of the splinter parties, measured as a percentage of their vote over the main social democratic party vote, in the first elections entered by the communist party. For every point of increase in trade union density, the size of the split was reduced an average of 2.4 points (standard error: 0.89).[6] Taking elections as units, during the entire interwar period, in sixty-three elections contested by communist parties, and for which data on unionization are available in Bartolini's (2000) data set, the correlation coefficient with current union density in the electorate was –0.42 (p < 0.01).

The same conclusion applies for the link between parties and trade unions (Table 7.5). At the year of communist entry into electoral competition, parties without union collective membership (including Norway) endured splits that reached a mean of 28.3 percent as a proportion of their vote, whereas parties with collective union membership had splinters that, on average, amounted to 6.6 percent of their vote. The mean difference stabilized in nearly 14 points along the interwar period.

Because qualitative evidence of internal dissension within parties may be ambiguous, we can take consummated schisms as an indicator of previous (as well as ongoing) organizational division. The organizational

[6] Iceland, Ireland, and Spain are not included in the sample.

Table 7.5. Union Collective Membership in Social Democratic Parties and Size of All Splinter Parties as a Proportion of the Main Party's Vote

Collective membership	Year of communist entry	Interwar average	N
Yes	6.6%	4.3%	6
No	28.3%	20.1%	11
P value for difference	0.12	0.06	–

conflicts not only hindered the success of electoral mobilization, they also provided an incentive to party centralization and, hence, an additional reason to support proportional representation. In fact, as a rule, to the extent that socialist parties defended proportional representation, they defended large districts and closed lists. Open lists or mixed systems allowing for personal vote were arrangements imposed by nonsocialist parties, as documented in the literature for the cases of Denmark (where the socialists turned to demand closed lists once the majority system was abandoned), Iceland, Italy, and Finland. Generally, it was the parties plagued with more severe internal divisions between moderate and radical factions that made this choice. Contrary to common wisdom, it was not proportional representation that aided the communist and other socialist splinter parties; rather, it was the parties that would experience more dramatic breach those who actually preferred proportional representation.

Table 7.6 summarizes the data on the electoral size of communists and other socialist splinter parties in observations taken at the first elections contested by communists. The correlation between leftist schism and institutional preferences is 0.46 (p = 0.056), whereas the correlation between the size of splinters and the electoral system is 0.20 (p = 0.43); the partial correlation coefficient between institutional preferences and schisms, holding the electoral system constant, is 0.43 (p = 0.087).

The pattern of early divisions and cooperation with liberal parties is consistent, in general lines, with the electoral fortunes of the socialist parties in the interwar period. Parties choosing proportional representation were, in the long run, less successful in elections than parties preferring majoritarian systems. For the interwar period, the mean vote for nonproportionalist parties was 10.8 points higher than the mean vote for proportionalist parties (p < 0.01). Holding the electoral system constant, the partial correlation coefficient between the average electoral results and the institutional preferences was 0.63 (p < 0.01).

Table 7.6. Communist and Other Socialist Vote as a Proportion of the Vote for the Main Socialist Party, by Electoral System and Electoral Preferences of the Socialist Parties (Year of Communist Entry)

Socialist preference	Non-PR systems		PR systems		All	
	Mean	N	Mean	N	Mean	N
Non-PR	3.1	4	6.0	3	4.3	7
PR	48.8	1	19.1	10	21.8	11
All	12.2	5	16.1	13	20.3	18

Note: PR = proportional representation.

Thus, proportionalist parties behaved consistently with the interpretation of their institutional preferences: they had more internal problems, more divisions, and more difficulty in establishing electoral coalitions with nonsocialist parties. Nonproportionalist parties, in turn, stayed united while cooperating with nonsocialist parties in the arena closest to the electorate. Those patterns of behavior translated into varying degrees of electoral success in the interwar period but, particularly, as we shall see, translated into different behavior toward government participation.

Government

Nonproportionalist parties are expected to be more ready to enter government than proportionalist parties. In a way, the institutional preferences themselves are an indication to that because they can be seen as an expression of a participation strategy that could only lead to government. Although trade union support was the basis of the success of a supraclass strategy that benefited from a mild electoral trade-off, in this section, I take the strategy, marked by the institutional preferences, to be the explanation for subsequent behavior. By choosing rules, parties sorted themselves out, and this self-classification should be more relevant than any other criterion. The fact that we can explain some of the reasons the parties might have had to choose as they did does not render the choice meaningless.

Most opportunities to enter government came forth after the transition to democracy was completed, during the interwar period, and this is this period in which the behavior of the parties was more clearly comparable. Yet some evidence of their varying attitudes toward government was given even sooner.

To the extent of my knowledge, the only nonproportionalist party to have turned down an early offer to participate in government was the Swedish party in 1911, and this rejection must be qualified. Direct participation was rejected or, better, postponed, on tactical rather than on "principled" grounds, at least by the party leader Hjalmar Branting. The party had nonetheless committed its support to the liberal cabinet already in advance of the 1911 elections, and some informal negotiations concerning its composition were conducted. By 1914, the party officially proclaimed its disposition to enter government, either in coalition with the liberals or alone if necessary (Tingsten 1973: 416–22). The remaining nonproportionalist parties did enter government as soon as their parliamentary majorities or their coalition potential permitted.

This is markedly contrasted with the experience of nonproportionalist parties. For example, when the Dutch party was offered the opportunity to enter government in 1913, the rejection was followed by a party resolution self-prohibiting participation because the leadership was afraid that the party would badly divide as a result. Indeed, the earliest governing experience had to wait to the aftermath of the Second World War (Verkade 1965: 54; Kossmann 1978: 509–10). When individual leaders fell into the temptation of cabinet responsibility, proportionalist parties reacted severely. For example, the Finnish party expelled a veteran party leader in 1906 for accepting a position in the Senate, the predemocratic representative cabinet that should conduct the imminent transition toward democracy (Kirby 1979: 32). As is well known, the earliest cabinet member of socialist affiliation in a national government was Alexandre Millerand in France, but this is known because it triggered a general ban on participation at the Amsterdam Congress of the International in 1904. The French anti-ministerialists persuaded the congress. The French Section Française de l'Internationale Ouvrière (SFIO) incorporated the resolution in its first congress in 1905 and was one of the parties most reluctant to abandon it, with the exception of the brief "sacred union of parties" during part of the First World War, rejecting the possibility of cabinet responsibility until well into the 1930s (Colton 1953; Judt 1976).

Thus, on average, nonproportionalist parties entered "bourgeois" cabinets sooner. Most nonproportionalist parties (all but the Spanish and the New Zealanders) had some cabinet experience by the First World War and well ahead of that in the case of Australia. The only proportionalist parties to have had cabinet experience during the First World War were the French and the Finnish, but the experience was discontinued after the

Table 7.7. Socialist Interwar Government Participation by Electoral System and Institutional Preference (Percentage of Months during Interwar Years; Cases Are Parties)

Socialist electoral preference	Non-PR systems		PR systems		All	
	Average	N	Average	N	Average	N
Non-PR	28.3	4	60.5	3	42.1	7
PR	9.1	1	12.5	9	12.2	10
All	24.4	5	24.5	12	24.5	17

Note: PR = proportional representation.

Table 7.8. Socialist Interwar Prime Minister by Electoral System and Institutional Preference (Percentage of Months during Interwar Years; Cases Are Parties)

Socialist electoral preference	Non-PR systems		PR systems		All	
	Average	N	Average	N	Average	N
Non-PR	16.8	4	39.8	3	26.6	7
PR	5.4	1	6.9	9	6.8	10
All	14.5	5	15.2	12	15.0	17

Note: PR = proportional representation.

war. Appendix A reports the date of first cabinet positions and first prime ministers for my sample of parties.

During the interwar years, as Tables 7.7 and 7.8 show, the parties choosing proportional representation participated in government for much shorter periods, if at all, than parties that had preferred majoritarian systems. They participated in government 12.2 percent of the time, on average, and held the prime minister position 6.8 percent of the time. In contrast, the figures for nonproportionalist parties were 42.1 percent and 26.6 percent, respectively. The difference was even more pronounced for the group of parties competing under proportional systems: the three parties that attempted to resist electoral reform governed 60.5 percent of the time, on average, and held the prime ministership nearly 40 percent of the time.

It might appear that nonproportionalist parties participated more often in government because, for all we know about them, they suffered smaller divisions and were more successful electorally, whereas the contrary

Table 7.9. Socialist Participation in Government in the Interwar Years

Dependent variable: Socialist participation in government (% of months)			
	Coefficient	Robust std. error	p
Constant	34.12	15.0	.059
Socialist preference (1 = PR)	−46.87	9.05	.000
Electoral regime (1 = PR)	25.5	6.82	.003
Communist and other left socialist as % of main party	0.51	.14	.004
Socialist interwar average of votes	−0.28	.477	.562

Notes: $R^2 = 0.71$; N = 17. Minimal predicted value 2.06; maximal predicted value 55.80. PR = proportional representation.

applies to proportionalist parties. According to this, electoral preferences as such would have little or no significant effect in the explanation of government participation, which could be predicted taking into account divisions and votes and, perhaps, actual electoral rules. However, this conclusion would be empirically wrong and theoretically blind to intentional causality.

The element of choice, as opposed to sheer constraints, in the emergence of party divisions and its connection with participation can be illustrated by the opposite experiences of the Swedish and Austrian parties. The Swedish socialists expelled their radicals in 1905 (definitely in 1908, one of the few parties to do so before the Russian Revolution), supported liberal minority governments, governed themselves in minority, and endured a substantial (in the first years) loss of votes to the communist and left socialist parties; yet they consistently grew in the electorate and eventually turned into a party able to win the majority of the vote in 1940 (the only precedents had been in Australia and New Zealand) and the longest governing socialist party in the world. By contrast, the Austrian socialists were already the largest party in the country in 1919 and one of the few European parties that managed to prevent major schisms. However, the official ideology of the party sustained that they had reached their maximal electoral mobilization capacity and preached isolation under the doctrine of the so-called equilibrium of classes, according to which no class could rule over the other. Of course, their vote remained stable. The Austrian socialists exited the postwar coalition with the Catholics precisely to prevent a communist scission and took refuge in municipal socialism (Loewenberg 1985; Sully 1985). Not surprisingly, the Swedish and Austrian parties are clear

APPENDIX A. First Entry in Government by Social Democratic Parties

Country (non-PR party)	Entry	Coalition formula	First Prime Minister
Earliest experiences			
France	1899	One socialist minister in Radical-led cabinet	
Australia	1904	Single-party minority, also in 1908, and majority in 1910	
Parties entering cabinet during First World War or sooner			
Australia	1914	Single-party majority	1904
France	1914	"Sacred Union" of parties	1938
Great Britain	1915	Junior ministers in Liberal–Conservative coalition	1924
Belgium	1916	All-party coalition	1938
Denmark	1916	All-party coalition	1924
Finland	1917	All-party coalition	1926
Sweden	1917	Coalition with Liberals	1920
Parties entering cabinet only after First World War			
Austria	1919	Coalition with Catholics	1919
Germany	1919	Coalition with Catholics and Democrats	1919
Norway	1928	Single-party minority	1928
Spain	1931	Coalition with Liberals and Republicans	1936
Iceland	1934	Coalition with Progressives	1947
New Zealand	1935	Single-party majority	1935
Netherlands	1939	All-party coalition	1948
Parties entering cabinet only after Second World War			
Switzerland	1943	All-party coalition	1949
Italy	1946	All-party coalition	1983
Ireland	1948	All but Fianna Fáil parties minority coalition	–

Note: PR = proportional representation.

outliers in the association between my measurement of party unity and institutional preference (see the table in Appendix B).

Participation in government was a choice, and the style of participation was partly a precommitted choice. Participation *cost* votes lost to leftist rivals; hence, the choice entailed a trade-off. Divisions as such did not diminish the opportunities to participation – on the contrary, we might even say that they enhanced them because we could regard the splits as an observable price paid by socialists to make moderation credible and be accepted for government office. Moreover, the trade-off was different

APPENDIX B. Data

	Preference	System	Reform or realignment		Socialist strength				Socialists in government		
			Vote before	Vote after	Avg. vote	Avg. seats	Peak vote	Left schism as % of soc. vote	% part	% pri. min.	Months of interwar govt.
Aul		PR	36.6	50	40.06	36.9	50.9	1.11	10.5	10.5	248
Aut	PR	PR	25.4	40.8	39.96	41.59	41.1	2.5	12.7	10.1	158
Bel		PR	21.9	22.5	35.17	36.96	39.4	4.06	45.3	3.5	254
Den		PR	29.5	28.7	36.74	36.62	46.1	1.37	81.9	61.6	271
Fin	PR		n.a.	37	33.08	34.67	47.3	72.91	14.9	4.6	262
Fra	PR		16.8	21.2	19.94	18.25	21.2	48.76	9.1	5.4	242
Ger	PR	PR	34.8	37.9	24.51	25.09	37.9	92.59	34.7	22.2	167
Ice	PR	PR	19.2	21.7	16.86	10.01	21.7	18.63	25	0	240
Ire		PR	n.a.	21.3	10.91	8.88	21.3	12.09	0	0	247
Ita	PR	PR	17.6*	32.3	28.48	26.85	32.3	18.68	0	0	39
Lux		PR	n.a.	15.6	23.05	22.97	33.8	5.56	n.a.	n.a.	n.a.
Net		PR	21.5*	30	21.92	22.5	23.8	13.64	0	0	249
Nor		PR	31.6	21.3	31.73	30.42	42.5	33.15	25.4	25.4	244
Nz			26.2	34.3	33.89	33.21	55.8	0.29	33	33	285
Spa			n.a.	24.3[b]	n.a.	19.28	n.a.	n.a.	46	0	63
Swe	PR	PR	14.6[a]	28.5	38.60	41.93	45.9	21.55	54.4	54.4	237
Swz	PR	PR	30.8	23.4	26.04	24.35	30.8	7.73	0	0	240
UK			6.4[a]	22.5	31.50	23.81	37.1	0.67	23.5	23.5	268

Notes: PR = proportional representation.

[a] Restricted suffrage.

[b] Percentage of seats, votes unavailable.

Sources: The first two columns are my own compilation with the literature cited in the text. For electoral results and parliamentary strength, the sources are Ballini (1985) for Italy and Mackie and Rose (1982) for the other cases. The data for government participation (last three columns) come from Flora, Alber et al. (1983) supplemented with Alexander (1967), Delcros (1970), Karlsson (2000), Kirby (1979), Lewin (1988), Lipson (1948), and Verkade (1965).

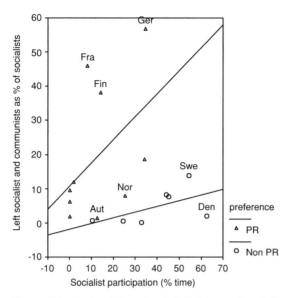

Figure 7.2. Trade-off between left division and socialist government participation.

for different parties, and we can only ascertain it by controlling for the long-term strategies pointed by the institutional preferences of the parties.

Figure 7.2 displays some rough evidence of the various levels of left fragmentation associated with varying levels of participation in government. Without taking into account the institutional preferences and the strategies that, I submit, are revealed with them, the relative success of radical parties shows no apparent connection with the frequency of socialist participation. However, if institutional preferences are controlled for, we must conclude that, first, the fragmentation of the left and socialist governing time were positively related and, second, participation cost more, on average, to proportionalist than to nonproportionalist parties.

Despite the crudeness of the data, it is possible to sustain that this relationship is not an artifact because it holds regardless of the actual electoral system and of party sizes, as Table 7.9 shows. All else being equal, the institutional preference for proportional systems cuts the time of government participation by an average of 47 points, which is the strongest effect of all. Controlling for institutional preferences, the effect of electoral strength disappears,[7] and the effect of party schism is positive. Once the overall strategy is taken into account, parties that stayed united governed less.

---

[7] Electoral results are a significant determinant of government participation in an election-by-election analysis but not in the comparison across parties.

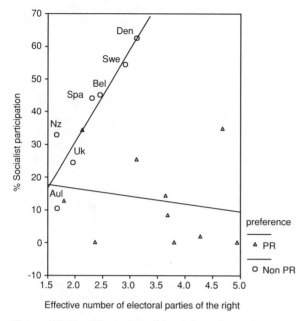

Figure 7.3. Fragmentation of the right and socialist participation.

Because I have argued that the preferences of proportionalist parties may be explained by their interest in restraining and graduating their government responsibility, it may appear that the fact that parties governed more often under proportional representation, even holding their preferences constant, is a disconfirming piece of evidence. It seems as though parties had picked up the wrong institutions. However, the answer lies in the reaction of the parties of the right.

Figure 7.3 plots the fragmentation of the parties to the right of the social democrats and the frequency of socialist participation in government. As we can clearly see, the participation of the proportionalist parties bears no relation to the opportunities opened by the fragmentation of their opponents, whereas for nonproportionalist parties, their participation hinged on the ability of the right to present a united antisocialist front. The paucity of data does not allow for a fully reliable analysis of interactions, but I should note that, controlling for the fragmentation of the right and its interaction with socialist preferences, the effect of the electoral system totally disappears in any equation predicting participation.

Thus, the results are consistent with my explanation: proportionalist parties made their own decision on when to participate, restrained by internal divisions and leftist challengers; nonproportionalist parties participated as much as their opponents to the right allowed them to do so.

Conclusions

The preferences of socialist parties over electoral systems in early democracies provide an interesting puzzle, given that their distribution across a sample of Western parties that were involved in electoral reform defies any straightforward account of them. Only by looking at particular aspects of the electoral systems, which go beyond their mechanical effects on parliamentary parties, can the socialist preferences be understood. I have suggested that the preference for majority-biased systems reflected a commitment to wide electoral mobilization and government participation, perhaps even at the cost of socialist political unity. On the other hand, a preference for proportional representation reflected greater internal tensions, a more isolated electorate, and timidity toward participation in democratic government. Proportionalist parties preferred to be able to restrain their access to government, to ease the electoral and organizational costs that this entailed for them, and they generally restrained it. Nonproportionalist parties preferred to commit themselves to a strategy that would either push them into government responsibility or kept them underrepresented when failed. Those were the purposes of preferred electoral methods. The causal antecedent constraining the choice of strategy was set by the trade unions. At the time of institutional choice, it was union strength rather than party strength that could have predicted the preferences of socialist parties. The choice was made anticipating future events, although the clue to anticipate them had been the strength – and affinity to the party – of the trade union organizations.

In a certain way, it seems that the story of party preferences over electoral systems runs parallel to the story of the fate of the most clearly reformist tendencies within the socialist movement. Indeed, the connection between reformism and institutional preferences has no less illustrious an example than Eduard Bernstein, who, besides preaching the revisionist doctrine, advocated both the permanence of the majority system and the necessity to join the liberals in government, to no avail in his party. Bernstein sometimes complained that only the union leaders saw his points.

REFERENCES

Aardal, Bernt. 2002. "Electoral Systems in Norway." In Bernard Grofman and Arend Lijphart (eds.), *Parties and Electoral Systems in the Nordic Countries* (pp. 167–224). New York: Agathon Press.

Alexander, Fred. 1967. *Australia since Federation: A Narrative and Critical Analysis*. Melbourne: Nelson.

Ballini, Pier Luigi. 1985. "Le elezioni politiche nel Regno d'Italia. Appunti di bibliografia, legislazione e statistiche." *Quaderni dell'osservatorio elettorale* 15: 141–220.

Bartolini, Stefano. 2000. *The Political Mobilization of the European Left, 1860–1890: The Class Cleavage*. New York: Cambridge University Press.

Berlau, Abraham Joseph. 1949. *The German Social Democratic Party 1914–1921*. New York: Columbia University Press.

Blais, André, Agnieszka Dobrzynska, and Indridi H. Indridason. 2005. "To Adopt or Not to Adopt Proportional Representation: The Politics of Institutional Choice." *British Journal of Political Science* 35 (1): 182–90.

Boix, Carles. 1999. "Setting the Rules of the Game: The Choice of Electoral Systems in Advanced Democracies." *American Political Science Review* 93 (3): 609–24.

Bonnefous, Georges. 1965. *Histoire politique de la Troisième République. Tome premier: L'avant-guerre (1906–1914)* (7 vols.). Paris: Presses Universitaires de France.

Butler, David. 1963. *The Electoral System in Britain since 1918*. Oxford: Clarendon Press.

Butler, David (ed.). 1978. *Coalitions in British Politics*. New York: St. Martin Press.

Caramani, Daniele. 2000. *Elections in Western Europe since 1815*. London: Macmillan.

Chadwick, Andrew. 1996. "State and Constitution: Ideologies of the Left and Proportional Representation in Britain, 1900–1924." *Contemporary Political Studies 1996*. Proceedings at the Annual Conference held at the University of Glasgow, Vol. 3: 1551–64.

Cole, Alistair, and Peter Campbell. 1989. *French Electoral Systems and Elections since 1789*. Aldershot: Gower.

Colomer, Josep M. 2003. "Son los partidos los que eligen los sistemas electorales (o las leyes de Duverger cabeza abajo)." *Revista Española de Ciencia Política* 9: 39–63.

Colomer, Josep M. 2004a. "Western Europe: General Overview." In Josep Colomer (ed.), *Handbook of Electoral System Choice* (pp. 179–208). New York: Palgrave.

Colomer, Josep M. 2004b. "Spain: From Civil War to Proportional Representation." In Josep Colomer (ed.), *Handbook of Electoral System Choice* (pp. 265–78). New York: Palgrave.

Colton, Joel. 1953. "Léon Blum and the French Socialists as a Government Party." *Journal of Politics* 15 (4): 517–43.

Cusack, Thomas, Torben Iversen, and David Soskice. 2003. "Specific Interests and the Origins of Electoral Institutions." Paper presented at the Conference of the

Diversity of Politics and Varieties of Capitalism, Wissenschaftszentrum, Berlin, October 2003.

Delcros, Xavier. 1970. *Les majorités de reflux a la chambre des députés de 1918 a 1958*. Paris: Presses Universitaires de France.

Elklit, Jørgen. 1993. "Simpler than Its Reputation: The Electoral System in Denmark since 1920." *Electoral Studies* 12 (1): 41–57.

Elklit, Jørgen. 2002. "The Politics of Electoral System Development and Change: The Danish Case." In Bernard Grofman and Arend Lijphart (eds.), *Parties and Electoral Systems in the Nordic Countries* (pp. 15–66). New York: Agathon Press.

Esping-Andersen, Gøsta. 1985. *Politics against Markets: The Social Democratic Road to Power*. Princeton: Princeton University Press.

Flora, Peter, Jens Alber, et al. 1983. *State, Economy, and Society in Western Europe, 1815–1975. Vol. 1: The Growth of Mass Democracies and Welfare States*. Frankfurt: Campus Verlag.

Gallagher, Michael. 1981. "The Pact General Election of 1922." *Irish Historical Studies* 21: 404–21.

Glissen, John. 1980. "Évolution des systèmes électoraux dans les pays du Benelux, 1814–1921." *Cashiers de Clio* 15: 26–48.

Goblet d'Alviella, Le Comte. 1900. *La représentation proportionnelle en Belgique. Histoire d'une reforme*. Bruxelles: Weissenbruch.

Graham, B. D. 1962. "The Choice of Voting Methods in Federal Politics, 1902–1918." *Australian Journal of Politics and History* 8: 164–81.

Gustafson, Barry. 1986. *The First 50 Years: A History of the New Zealand National Party*. Auckland: Reed Meuthen.

Hamer, David. 1987. "The Second Ballot: A New Zealand Electoral Experiment." *New Zealand Journal of History* 21: 97–111.

Hardarson, Ólafur Th. 2002. "The Icelandic Electoral System 1844–1999." In Bernard Grofman and Arend Lijphart (eds.), *Parties and Electoral Systems in the Nordic Countries* (pp. 101–66). New York: Agathon Press.

Hayashida, K. 1966. "Development of Election Law in Japan." *Jahrbuch des Öffentlichen Rechts der Gegenwart* 15: 471–511.

Hughes, Colin A., and B. D. Graham. 1974. *Voting for the Australian House of Representatives: 1901–1964*. Canberra: Australian National University Press.

Iversen, Torben, and David Soskice. 2002. "Electoral Systems and the Politics of Coalition: Why Some Democracies Redistribute More than Others." Presented at the Annual Meeting of the American Political Science Association, Boston, September 2002.

Jelavich, Barbara. 1987. *Modern Austria: Empire and Republic, 1815–1986*. Cambridge: Cambridge University Press.

Jenks, William Alexander. 1974. *The Austrian Electoral Reform of 1907*. New York: Octagon.

Judt, Tony. 1976. "The French Socialists and the Cartel des Gauches of 1924." *Journal of Contemporary History* 11 (2/3): 199–215.

Juliá, Santos. 1997. *Los socialistas en la política española, 1879–1982*. Madrid: Taurus.

Jutikkala, Eno. 1961. "Political Parties in the Election of Deputies to the Estate of Burgesses and the Estate of Farmers in the Finnish Diet of Estates."

Sitzungberichte der Finnischen Akademie der Wissenschaften 1960 (pp. 167–84). Helsinki.

Karlsson, Gunnar. 2000. *The History of Iceland*. Minneapolis: University of Minnesota Press.

Kirby, D. G. 1979. *Finland in the Twentieth Century*. Minneapolis: University of Minnesota Press.

Kolb, Eberhard. 1988. *The Weimar Republic*. London: Unwin Hyman.

Kossmann, E. H. 1978. *The Low Countries, 1780–1940*. Oxford: Clarendon Press.

Kreuzer, Marcus. 2001. *Institutions and Innovation: Voters, Parties, and Interest Groups in the Consolidation of Democracy – France and Germany, 1870–1939*. Ann Arbor: University of Michigan Press.

Lewin, Leif. 1988. *Ideology and Strategy: A Century of Swedish Politics*. New York: Cambridge University Press.

Lipset, Seymour Martin, and Gary Marks. 2000. *It Didn't Happen Here: Why Socialism Failed in the United States*. New York: Norton.

Lipson, Leslie. 1948. *The Politics of Equality: New Zealand's Adventures in Democracy*. Chicago: University of Chicago Press.

Loewenberg, Peter. 1985. "Otto Bauer as an Ambivalent Party Leader." In Anson Rabinbach (ed.), *The Austrian Socialist Experiment: Social Democracy and Austromarxism, 1918–1934*. Boulder, CO: Westview Press.

Loveday, P. 1977. "The Federal Parties." In P. Loveday, A. W. Martin, and R. S. Parker, (eds.). *The Emergence of the Australian Party System*. Sidney: Hale and Iremonger.

Luebbert, Gregory M. 1991. *Liberalism, Fascism, or Social Democracy: Social Classes and the Political Origins of Regimes in Interwar Europe*. New York: Oxford University Press.

Lutz, George. 2004. "Electoral Reform from Below: The Introduction of Proportional Representation in Switzerland 1918." In Josep M. Colomer (ed.), *The Handbook of Electoral System Choice*. London: Palgrave.

Mackie, Thomas T., and Richard Rose. 1982 (2nd). *The International Almanac of Electoral History*. London: Macmillan.

Maravall, José María. 2007. "Accountability and the Survival of Governments." In Carles Boix and Susan Stokes (eds.), *Handbook of Comparative Politics*. Oxford: Oxford University Press.

Marks, Gary. 1989. *Unions in Politics: Britain, Germany, and the United States in the Nineteenth and Early Twentieth Centuries*. Princeton: Princeton University Press.

Mastropaolo, Alfio. 1980. "Electoral Processes, Political Behavior, and Social Forces in Italy from the Rise of the Left to the Fall of Giolliti, 1876–1913." In Otto Büsch (ed.), *Wählerbewegnung in der Europäischer Gesichte*. Berlin: Coloquim Verlag.

Matthews, Donald R., and Henry Valen. 1999. *Parliamentary Representation: The Case of the Norwegian Storting*. Columbus: Ohio State University Press.

Mavrogordatos, George Th. 1983. *Stillborn Republic: Social Coalitions and Party Strategies in Greece, 1922–1936*. Berkeley: University of California Press.

McCracken, J. L. 1958. *Representative Government In Ireland: A Study of Dáil Éireann 1919–48*. London: Oxford University Press.

Miller, Kenneth E. 1996. *Friends and Rivals: Coalition Politics in Denmark, 1901–1995*. Lanham: University Press of America.

Noiret, Serge. 1994. *La nascita dei partiti nell'Italia contemporanea. La proporzionale del 1919*. Manduria: Piero Lacaita.

Overacker, Louise. 1949. "The Australian Labour Party." *American Political Science Review* 43 (4): 677–703.

Overacker, Louise. 1955. "The New Zealand Labour Party." *American Political Science Review* 49 (3): 708–32.

Przeworski, Adam. 1985. *Capitalism and Social Democracy*. New York: Cambridge University Press.

Przeworski, Adam, and John Sprague. 1986. *Paper Stones: A History of Electoral Socialism*. Chicago: University of Chicago Press.

Pugh, Martin. 1980. "Political Parties and the Campaign for Proportional Representation 1905–1914." *Parliamentary Affairs* 33 (3): 294–307.

Rokkan, Stein. 1970. *Citizens, Elections, Parties: Approaches to the Comparative Study of the Processes of Development*. Oslo: Universitetsforlaget.

Rustow, Dankwart A. 1950. "Some Observations on Proportional Representation." *Journal of Politics* 12 (1): 107–27.

Rustow, Dankwart A. 1955. *The Politics of Compromise: A Study of Parties and Cabinet Government in Sweden*. New York: Greenwood Press.

Rydon, Joan. 1956. "Electoral Methods and the Australian Party System, 1910–1951." *Australian Journal of Politics and History* 11 (1): 68–83.

Scalapino, Robert A. 1953. *Democracy and the Party Movement in Prewar Japan*. Berkeley: University of California Press.

Schambeck, Herbert. 1972. "Die Entwicklung des Österreichischen Whalrechtes." *Jahrbuch des Öffentlichen Rechts des Gegenwarts* 21: 247–308.

Schorske, Carl E. 1955. *German Social Democracy 1905–1917: The Development of the Great Schism*. Cambridge, MA: Harvard University Press.

Seip, Dick. 1979. "The Netherlands." In Geoffrey Hand, Jacques Georgel, and Christoph Sasse (eds.), *European Electoral Systems Handbook*. London: Butterworths.

Seton-Watson, Christopher. 1967. *Italy from Liberalism to Fascism: 1870–1925*. London: Methuen.

Sinclair, Keith. 1988. *A History of New Zealand*. Auckland: Penguin.

Sperber, Jonathan. 1997. *The Kaiser's Voters: Electors and Elections in Imperial Germany*. Cambridge: Cambridge University Press.

Stengers, Jean. 1990. "Histoire de la législation électorale en Belgique." In Serge Noiret (ed.), *Political Strategies and Electoral Reforms: Origins of Voting Systems in Europe in the 19th and 20th Centuries*. Baden-Baden: Nomos Verlagsgesellschaft.

Sully, Melanie A. 1985. "Social Democracy and the Political Culture of the First Republic." In Anson Rabinbach (ed.), *The Austrian Socialist Experiment: Social Democracy and Austromarxism, 1918–1934*. Boulder, CO: Westview Press.

Suval, Stanley. 1985. *Electoral Politics in Wilhemine Germany*. Chapel Hill: The University of North Carolina Press.

Thomson, David. 1964. *Democracy in France since 1870*, 4th ed. London: Oxford University Press.

Tingsten, Herbert. 1973 [1941]. *The Swedish Social Democrats: Their Ideological Development*. Translated by Greta Frankel and Patricia Howard-Rosen. Totowa: Bedminster Press.

Törnudd, Klaus. 1968. *The Electoral System of Finland*. London: Hugh Evelyn.

van den Berghe, Guido. 1979. "Belgium." In Geoffrey Hand, Jacques Georgel, and Christoph Sasse (eds.), *European Electoral Systems Handbook*. London: Butterworths.

Varela-Ortega, José. 1997. "De los orígenes de la democracia en España, 1845–1923." In Salvador Forner (ed.), *Democracia, elecciones y modernización en Europa*. Madrid: Cátedra.

Verhoef, Jan. 1974. "The Rise of National Political Parties in the Netherlands, 1888–1913." *International Journal of Politics*, 207–21.

Verkade, Wilhem. 1965. *Democratic Parties in the Low Countries and Germany: Origins and Historical Developments*. Leyden: Universitaire Pers Leiden.

Verney, Douglas V. 1957. *Parliamentary Reform in Sweden: 1866–1921*. Oxford: Clarendon Press.

CHAPTER EIGHT

Constitutions and Democratic Breakdowns

Alicia Adserà and Carles Boix

Introduction

Ever since the emergence of political theory, political thinkers have debated which political institutions foster democracies, individual freedoms, and good governance. Aristotle's analysis of different types of constitutional regimes and their political effects was retaken and elaborated on by most modern philosophers. Referring to the history of the Roman Republic as well as to contemporary evidence from Venice and other Italian cities, Machiavelli discussed at length the conditions underlying successful republican states in his *Discourses on the First Ten Books of Titus Livy*. In the *Spirit of Laws*, Montesquieu described in painstaking detail the foundations, structures, and operation of monarchies, aristocracies, and democracies and the potential causes of their decay. In turn, John Stuart Mill's *Considerations on Representative Government* examined the constitutional basis of a successful representative democracy.

Contemporary political scientists rekindled the debate on the potential effects of various constitutional structures in response to successive waves of democratic breakdowns across the world in the twentieth century. In an influential essay, Ferdinand Hermens argued that the fall of the Weimar Republic was partly caused by an extremely fragmented party system in turn fostered by proportional representation (Hermens 1942). Linz, among others, identified presidentialism as an important culprit in the instability and fall of several democratic regimes in Latin America (Linz 1994; Linz

Previous versions of this chapter were presented at Waseda University, Tokyo, 2004 Annual Conference of the International Society for New Institutional Economics (ISNIE), 2004 Midwest Political Science Association Meeting, and 2003 American Political Science Association Meeting. The authors thank their participants, particularly James E. Alt and Phil Keefer, for their comments. This material is based on work supported by the Instituto Juan March and the National Science Foundation Grant No. 0339078.

and Valenzuela 1994). More recently, the search for the "right" institutions to strengthen democracy has been bolstered by a growing formal literature stressing the equilibrium-inducing role of institutional rules and searching for "self-enforcing" constitutional norms.

Despite the recent drive to identify the impact that formal rules and constitutions may have on democratic stability, our understanding of their contribution to the eventual survival of democracies is incomplete both theoretically and empirically. From a theoretical point of view, neoinstitutionalist scholars have explored the impact of institutional arrangements without taking into account the preexisting economic and social conditions within which institutions operate. Yet in looking at constitutions as if they were operating in a social vacuum, the institutionalist approach has disregarded the claim, made by a substantial body of democratic theory, connecting democratization to social and economic development (and a correlated set of cultural practices, educational values, and economic structures).[1] From an empirical point of view, studies on the consequences of constitutions are still relatively circumscribed. Most studies have focused on presidentialism and its effects, and they have only looked at the period after the Second World War (Stepan and Skach 1994; Przeworski et al. 2000; Cheibub 2006).

Given the shortcomings of the current literature, the purpose of this chapter is straightforward. Its aim is to assess the impact of various constitutional arrangements (i.e., the type of electoral system employed to choose the legislative body, the relationship between the executive and the legislative branches, and the level of political decentralization) on the stability of democracy, conditional on underlying noninstitutional variables (e.g., the level of development, the distribution of wealth, or the degree of ethnic fractionalization). Accordingly, the chapter is organized as follows. The first part of the chapter offers a theoretical discussion of the mechanisms through which different electoral laws, presidentialism (as opposed to parliamentarism), and federalism may shape the probability of a democratic breakdown. This theoretical discussion is backed up with descriptive

---

[1] See Lipset (1959), Cutright (1963), Przeworski et al. (2000), and Boix and Stokes (2003) on economic development and democratization. On the structure of society and democracy, see, in turn, Moore (1966), Luebbert (1991), Rueschemeyer et al. (1992), and Boix (2003). The neoinstitutionalist literature has been handicapped by a second theoretical flaw. No formal models, which have been abundantly employed to account for varying equilibria within already well-established democratic regimes, have been developed to link various types of constitutions to the stability of regime.

statistics of the distribution of democratic breakdowns for different constitutional structures and social and economic variables. The second part of the chapter employs Cox proportional models to estimate the effects of a country's institutional characteristics and social conditions on the survival of democratic regimes. Our universe of cases encompasses all sovereign countries from the mid-nineteenth century to the end of the twentieth century.

We show that changing the constitutional framework of a country has a moderate to small impact on the stability of a democratic regime. A democracy does not collapse as long as its political actors have no incentives to deviate from complying with its electoral outcomes. Politicians and voters have, in turn, little interest in rejecting an (unfavorable) democratic result when the political decisions the electoral majority adopts differ moderately from the preferred positions of the minority. This only follows when the distribution of wealth and the range of political preferences among voters are relatively homogeneous. In contrast, as the interests and the distribution of assets among voters become more polarized, democracy becomes more difficult to sustain because the electoral minority will grow more alienated from the decisions taken by the majority. In relatively homogeneous, nonpolarized polities, constitutional rules become relatively superfluous to the survival of democracy. Democracy is a self-enforcing mechanism regardless of the constitutional institutions that are employed to govern the country. Unfortunately, in polarized societies, rewriting the constitution to prop up the democratic edifice is likely to be of little help. If it reinforces the position of the majority, it reduces even further the incentives of the minority to comply with the democratic outcome. If particular constitutional guarantees are put in place to protect the minority, the majority also has strong incentives to challenge the legal framework to "democratize" it even further.

Although, generally speaking, democracies survive or collapse as a function of their underlying social conditions, constitutional structures matter in two circumstances. Presidential regimes are less stable in developing countries. Presidents (in contrast with prime ministers, who need the continuous support of a legislative majority in parliamentarian regimes) are endowed with enough institutional tools to increase their hold on power, appropriate assets, and expand their political basis of support without suffering much effective constant control from the legislative branch. Presidents can take particular advantage of their powers in countries where wealth is mostly immobile and therefore unable to flee from state control.

Democracy then collapses through two alternative paths. As presidents expropriate and shift the distribution of assets to their benefit and the benefit of their supporters, democracy weakens and true electoral competition wanes. Alternatively, either the legislative branch or, more often, a third party, such as the army, intervenes to block presidential overreach. This is followed by considerable conflict and the establishment of a dictatorial regime by one of the parties in contention.

Federalism reduces the level of political conflict and bolsters the chances of democratic consolidation for two reasons. First, federalism decentralizes the policy-making process to smaller and generally more homogeneous territories, thereby lessening the differences between electoral winners and losers and raising the incentives of all parties to comply with the electoral outcome. Second, the jurisdictional fragmentation that accompanies federalism reduces the ability of politicians to seek rents and accumulate resources and, therefore, minimizes the likelihood of distorted democratic procedures.

Theory: The Conditional Impact of Political Institutions

To model the impact of various institutional arrangements on democratic stability, we need to describe first the dynamics of democracy. Contemporary democracies can be thought of as the composite of two games. In the first place, a democratic regime is a procedure through which its citizens decide (by casting a vote or a sequence of votes) how to govern themselves. More specifically, it is a procedure through which the majority of the population determines the position (or welfare) of each member of the population (and therefore of the minority that has not agreed with that majority). In the second place, a representative democracy is a game in which the principal – the public – delegates into an agent – the politician or policy maker – a given set of instruments to execute certain goals (generally speaking, those willed by the majority).

Democratic Compliance

Consider in sequential order the ways in which these two dimensions of any democratic procedure relate to its stability. If a democracy is a procedure in which the minority is subject to the will of the majority, a democratic regime will only become possible if the minority nonetheless accepts the electoral outcome. Because the definition and composition of the minority may vary with each issue or decision put to a vote, we can restate the same idea in more general terms. A democracy will only be possible if any participating agent accepts the possibility that the outcome generated by a popular vote may differ from its preferred alternative.

To shed more light on this proposition, consider it in a slightly more specific manner in the context of a representative democracy in which two candidates compete for a given political office such as the presidency of the state. After both candidates engage in an electoral campaign and voters cast their ballots, the candidate with the most votes is proclaimed winner and assumes the presidency. The loser must wait for new elections to be held in the future to have a chance to be elected. In the meantime, he must accept the decisions and the policy program of the elected politician. The electoral process carries no guarantees, in itself, that any of the two politicians will respect the terms and continuity of the procedure. The loser may abide by the election, accept the defeat, and wait till the new electoral contest takes place. However, if it is too unsatisfactory for him to behave well, that is, if the current benefits of the office he is forsaking are too large, he may denounce the results and eventually stage a coup to grab the presidency by nonelectoral means. In turn, the winner may have as well an incentive to use her tenure of the presidency to shift resources in her favor to boost her future electoral chances, to alter the rules of electoral engagement, and even to postpone or cancel the new election.

A stable or successful democracy – that is, the uninterrupted use of free and fair voting mechanisms to reach any political decisions and to select public officials – will only take place if both the winner and the loser have an interest in complying with the outcomes of the periodic votes they employ to decide how to govern themselves.[2] This will be a function of two conditions. First, the smaller the policy differences between majority and minority, the higher the incentives everyone will have to comply with the democratic outcome because the losses experienced by the minority will tend to be negligible. The variance in policy preferences may have different sources. Preferences may vary along redistributive issues. In this case, the distribution of income is likely to determine the heterogeneity of policy preferences: the more unequal a society is, the more heterogeneous its distribution of preferences should be. Preferences may also vary according

---

[2] For a seminal analysis of democracy as an equilibrium resulting from a game in which no one has any incentive to deviate from complying with electoral results, see Przeworski (1991) and Weingast (1997).

to religious and ethnic preferences – as fragmentation along those lines increases, heterogeneity should go up as well. Second, the likelihood of a stable democratic outcome will increase with the costs of overturning democracy – in more general terms, the probability of a stable democracy will rise as the political and organizational resources of both the majority and the minority become more balanced.[3]

Representation and Policy Mandates

In contrast to classical democracies, contemporary democratic regimes are, above all, representative governments. Citizens delegate the capacity to set and implement policies in the hands of professional politicians elected to parliament and the executive. The interests of the principal (the public) and its agent (politicians) are not always identical – in fact, they may often be at odds. Even though partly acting in the interests of their potential electors (the wealthy, the middle class, the workers, or a particular economic sector), policy makers are likely to pursue their own political agenda. Even if they are honest, their ideas about what enhances the welfare of the public may differ from what the public itself wants. In some instances, politicians may simply be interested in enriching themselves while in office. Thus, a lack of information among the public both about the conditions under which politicians take decisions and about the precise nature of the policies they implement opens up the space for significant inefficiencies and corruption among politicians. Moreover, general elections are crude mechanisms to make politicians accountable. Because they only happen from time to time, politicians remain isolated from any credible mechanism to check and correct their behavior. Further, because elections are fought over numerous issues, electors have to decide over the performance of politicians in the context of a very noisy environment. The electoral winner has substantial incentives to use her tenure of the legislative or the executive branch to shift resources in her favor to boost her future electoral chances, to alter the rules of electoral engagement, and even to postpone or cancel the new election. In turn, the losers may respond by challenging the democratic outcome itself.[4]

---

[3] For an exploration of how both preference heterogeneity and organizational conditions sap democracies, see Boix (2003).

[4] On the literature of delegation and political accountability, see Przeworski, Stokes, and Manin (1999), and an empirical test in Adserà, Boix, and Payne (2003).

With this brief description of the mechanisms of democracy, we can now turn to the ways in which different constitutional traits (e.g., presidentialism, electoral systems, and federalism) may affect the incentives of actors to maintain a democratic regime.

Presidentialism

In a groundbreaking essay in the literature on presidentialism, Linz (1994) argues that, other things being equal, a presidential system is more likely to jeopardize democracy than a parliamentarian regime for three main reasons. First, because presidential elections consist in the selection of only one candidate, they generate a sharp zero-sum game in which the winner takes all and the loser is effectively deprived of all power. With political minorities excluded from the political game, any consensual politics are impossible to develop, the legitimacy of the constitutional regime becomes fragile, and democratic breakdowns are more likely. Second, presidential elections raise the stakes of the electoral game excessively, thereby increasing the level of political tension and ideological polarization. Finally, political conflict becomes so intense that the odds that, first, any of the candidates will behave "properly" during the electoral campaign and, second, they will accept the outcome after the elections, will be very low. Electoral manipulation will be rampant, the winner will resort to illicit strategies to secure his reelection in the future, and the loser will be likely to challenge the outcome. Perhaps more important, the institution of the presidency endows its incumbent with substantial means to capture societal resources and to enlarge his power base.[5]

The first two reasons fall under the previous discussion over the extent to which institutions mediate the impact that preference heterogeneity may have on democratic stability. In contrast, the last reason is mainly related to the principal–agent dilemma that comes with representative government. As discussed shortly, neither of the two first claims – that is, that presidentialism generates a system of "majoritarian" politics and that it polarizes both the party system and the electorate – seem to be inherent to presidential regimes. On the contrary, both of them may equally occur in parliamentarian constitutions. As for the third argument, it also seems

---

[5] Linz (1994) also lists several other defective characteristics of presidentialism, such as the presence of a "dual democratic legitimacy" (of both the executive and congress) and the temporal rigidity of the presidential mandate. For the purposes of the discussion that follows, these defects can be subsumed in the three problems already listed.

wrong if we unconditionally apply it to all presidential regimes. Still, it may be valid in those countries that are abundant in immobile assets. Because those assets can be easily taxed and expropriated, presidential regimes may be more likely than parliamentary regimes to engender a dynamic of conflict resulting in a coup. Before we move into the detailed discussion of the effects of presidentialism, we should note that the most recent work on this issue has concluded that presidential systems do not affect the chances of democracy negatively and that any negative correlation between presidentialism and democratic stability is simply a result of the fact that presidential regimes have been most concentrated in countries that had often transited to authoritarianism for other reasons (Cheibub 2006). We come back to this question in our empirical analysis.

Presidential Majorities

To examine whether presidential systems intensify the power of the majority, assume a simple scenario with two candidates running for presidential office and each promising a given policy (e.g., a certain level of taxes and redistribution). In a world with complete information (and full participation), they should converge on the same ideal policy – the one preferred by the median voter. Now, this scenario and the political solution it generates are in no way unique or specific to presidentialism. In parliamentary regimes, the same result will occur for precisely the same reasons. Parliament will end up voting for the median voter ideal point, that is, the policy preferred by the majority.[6]

Whether the policy approved under a presidential system will be a politically stable equilibrium – that is, whether the losers will accept the democratic outcome – will depend on the underlying distribution of interests. If the policy is too extreme (e.g., if taxes are too high) and the political resources at the disposal of the losers considerable, a coup will take place. Otherwise, democracy will remain in place. Yet, once more, the result is in no way different from what will happen under parliamentarianism: whether or not the policy voted by parliament will be acceptable to the losing side will simply be a function of the structural characteristics of the economy and the distribution of political resources.

[6] Naturally, both regimes lead to similar solutions provided that they have the same national median voter – that is, that parliamentarian regimes do not malapportion electoral districts in a way that shifts the parliamentarian median away from the median voter.

Presidentialism and Political Polarization

A similar result emerges when we examine the claim that presidentialism breeds higher levels of political polarization than parliamentarianism. Keeping the distribution of voters' preferences constant, the electoral process leads to polarization if there is either uncertainty about the distribution of voters or reputational problems among politicians. In those circumstances, either the contenders diverge in their policy promises or the winner, once in office, deviates from his electoral promise and imposes a different policy. If that policy is too skewed in relation to the median voter, political turmoil and the probability of an eventual coup should increase. But here again, there is nothing inherent in a presidential regime (vis-à-vis a parliamentarian constitution) that should increase the level of uncertainty or the credibility problems of presidential candidates.

The President as an Expropriator

Consider the nature of the third claim about the dangers of presidentialism – namely, that it both raises the stakes of the game to such levels and gives presidents so much power that it jeopardizes the electoral process. A presidential system makes it easier for a single politician to behave as a harsh rent seeker and, in fact, from the perspective of the owners of the assets, as a bandit, than a parliamentarian regime.

In a parliamentary system, a simple majority suffices to topple the prime minister. Because the prime minister is strongly tied to (and by) the coalition of policy makers that has put her in office, she can only accumulate more power and assets with difficulty. Precisely because an excessive accumulation of resources in her hands would reshape the balance of power between the prime minister and her parliamentary supporters, the latter have an incentive and the capacity (that comes from the prime minister's reliance on parliamentary support) to get rid of her leader.

In contrast, once he has won the presidential election, the presidential incumbent is only partly (or discontinuously) accountable to all the other branches of government. Presidents are elected for fixed terms and can only be removed for exceptional causes and by strong supramajorities. Unencumbered by the opposition, the president has more autonomy to seize assets, to organize extra-legal coalitions, and eventually to impose a dictatorship. In cases of acute political confrontation, the congressional opposition or the armed forces, supposedly behaving as a moderating power, may even decide to launch a coup to preempt the actions of the president. This pattern of a strong presidential structure followed by extra-legal confrontation fits well the experience of most Latin American democratic breakdowns (which represent 70 percent of all crises in presidential democracies), some African cases, and even the Nazi takeover of 1933.

Notice that an additional implication of this hypothesis is that presidential systems will become more threatening the weaker the legislative branch (Congress) is. As Mainwaring and Shugart (1997) have noticed, presidents are more autonomous (and therefore more prone to clashes with the legislature) under at least two circumstances: first, when they are endowed with strong decree powers; and, second, when the legislature's party system is fragmented and therefore unable to build majorities to make the president accountable.

The capacity of the president to accumulate power and properties is, however, conditional on the nature of assets in the country. The threat of presidential expropriation looms large when the existing assets are country-specific – that is, they are hardly movable – and probably when they are concentrated in a few hands. In those circumstances, a strong executive simply gives its holder an excellent opportunity to grab those assets. In contrast, rent appropriation by politicians decreases as assets become more mobile because in response to the threat of distortionary regulation or outright expropriation, their holders can shift them away from the policy maker.[7] Accordingly, mobile capital renders presidential systems pretty harmless. In other words, whereas presidential systems are especially dangerous in underdeveloped countries, they should exhibit similar rates of democratic breakdown than parliamentarian regimes in developed economies. Thus, adopting presidentialism is probably a bad idea in sub-Saharan Africa and a substantial part of Latin America. It may also be an error in postsocialist economies rich in natural resources. However, it should have no deleterious consequences in developed economies with relative equality and highly mobile assets.

To get a first cut at the extent to which democratic stability varies by type of constitutional regime and social and economic conditions, we proceed as follows. First, we calculate the probability of democratic breakdown, that is, the ratio of the total number of cases of democratic breakdown over the total number of annual observations of democracy for a universe of case that roughly extends from the first half of the nineteenth century

---

[7] See Adserà, Boix, and Payne (2003) for a formal discussion and empirical test.

through the end of the twentieth century. The definition of democratic political regime is taken from Boix and Rosato (2001), where all sovereign countries from 1800 to 1999 are coded as either democratic or authoritarian. Countries are coded as democracies if they meet three conditions: elections are free and competitive, the executive is accountable to citizens (either through elections in presidential systems or to the legislative power in parliamentary regimes), and at least 50 percent of the male electorate is enfranchised. Next, we classify regimes as either presidential or parliamentarian. The definition of a regime as "presidential" includes strictly presidential systems as well as semipresidential constitutions.[8] Finally, we compare the rate of democratic failure between presidential and parliamentarian regimes. The comparison is drawn both over all the cases, as well as for various levels of per capita income, for level of industrialization and urbanization, for the extent of inequality, and for the degree of ethnic fractionalization. These four broad measures should approximate our theoretical intuitions about what causes democratic breakdowns (and, hence, the impact of types of constitutional regimes).

As already noted in Stepan and Skach (1994) and Przeworski et al. (2000), among others, presidential systems have a higher rate of failure on average. Whereas the annual probability of democratic breakdown among presidential regimes is 2.9 percent, it is only 1.3 percent among parliamentary regimes. Still, as is apparent from Figure 8.1, in which the probability of democratic breakdown of each type of regime for various income segments is displayed, the distribution of presidential breakdowns is skewed. In line with the recent quantitative literature on democratic crisis, the likelihood of experiencing a democratic breakdown declines with per capita income (Przeworski et al. 2000; Boix and Stokes 2003). Within that trend, presidential regimes have a higher annual rate of failure than parliamentarian regimes in low and medium levels of per capita income. By contrast, for high levels of development (over $8,000), neither presidential nor parliamentary regimes have experienced any democratic crisis (with the exception of Argentina in 1976).[9]

---

[8] The complete definition and sources of the variables that are employed in Figures 8.1 through 8.12 are given in the section on "Empirical Analysis."

[9] Per capita income, which is expressed as Power Purchasing Parity (PPP) $ of 1996, is based on data from Maddison (1995) and Bourguignon and Morrison (2002). We mainly employ Maddison, who reports a continuous series for most countries starting in 1870 and then single-point data for 1820 and 1850. For the period before 1870, we reconstruct the data series by interpolation. For those countries not included in Maddison, we employ the

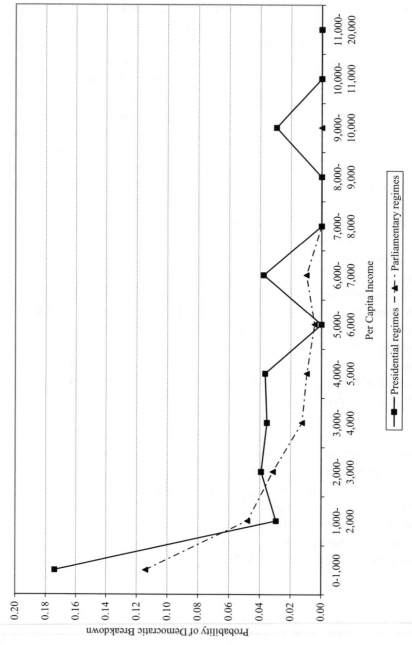

Figure 8.1. Presidentialism, development and democratic breakdowns.

Figure 8.2 reproduces the probability of democratic breakdown for different levels of industrialization and urbanization. As in Figure 8.1, at low levels of industrialization, presidential regimes are more brittle than parliamentarian systems. However, their stability becomes similar as they become highly industrialized.

Figure 8.3 displays the probability of democratic breakdown by the percentage of family farms over the total area of holdings. The percentage of family farms captures the degree of concentration and therefore inequality in the ownership of land.[10] The probability of democratic breakdown declines as rural inequality falls. Presidential regimes are about twice as unstable compared with parliamentarian systems in countries where less than 25 percent of the agricultural land is exploited through family enterprises. The negative impact of presidentialism disappears, however, in relatively equal economies.

Finally, Figure 8.4 shows the performance of presidentialism and parliamentarism by the level of ethnic fractionalization (from the quartile with the lowest level of fractionalization to the one with the highest index) for the period from 1950 to 1999. The yearly probability of democratic breakdowns increases with ethnic fractionalization. Whereas in essentially homogeneous countries it is less than 1 percent, it jumps to around 7 percent in highly fractionalized states. Presidential systems perform worse than parliamentary regimes systematically – the difference, however, is small.

Voting Mechanisms and the Case of Proportional Representation

Compared to the existing work on presidentialism, the theoretical assessment of the impact of electoral systems on democratic stability is much scarcer. In principle, the literature seems to attribute some stabilizing properties to proportional representation rules. The reasons why they should still remain sketchy, however.

On one hand, there are good theoretical reasons to conclude that different electoral systems do not lead to different political outcomes (therefore

estimates supplied by Bourguignon and Morrison (2002) for the world since 1820 (and mostly for every twenty years) to calculate all missing data.

[10] An extensive literature has related the unequal distribution of land to an unbalanced distribution of income. In fact, for the period after 1950, and excluding the cases of socialist economies, the correlation coefficient between the Gini index and the percentage of family farms is −0.66. For countries with a per capita income below $2,000, the correlation coefficient is −0.75.

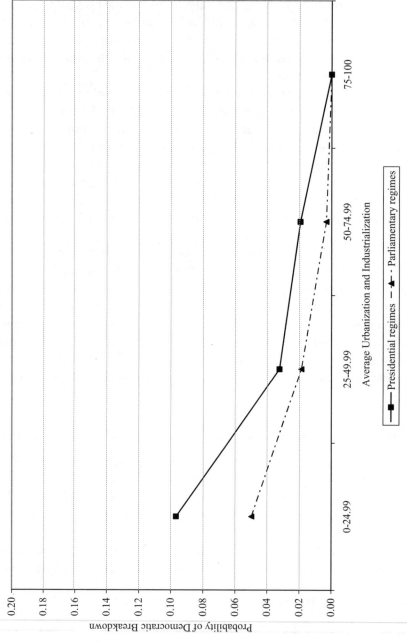

Figure 8.2. Presidentalism, industrialization and democratic breakdowns.

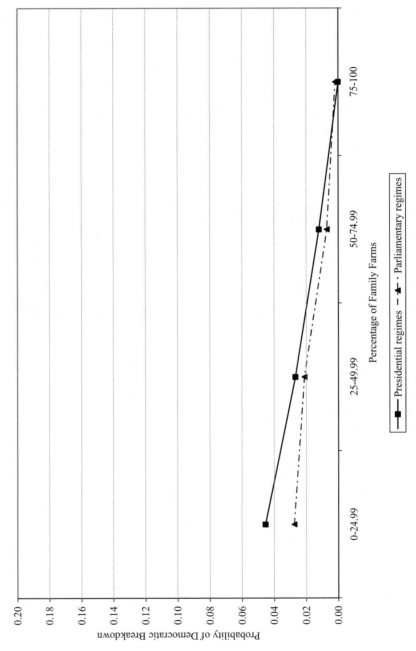

Figure 8.3. Presidentalism, rural inequality and democratic breakdowns.

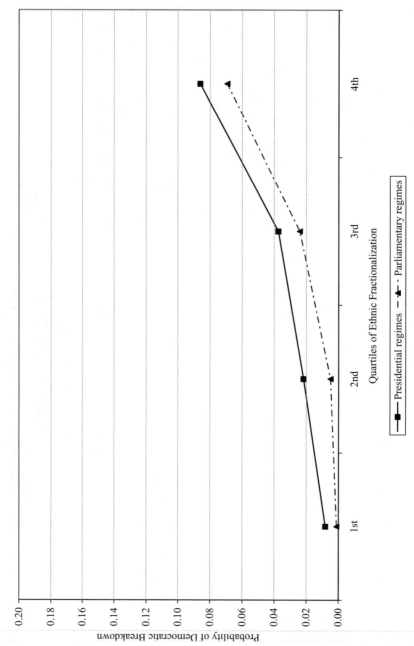

Figure 8.4. Presidentalism, ethnic fractionalization and democratic breakdowns.

affecting the consolidation chances of democratic regimes any differently). Assuming a one-dimensional policy space and well-behaved utility functions, both majoritarian and proportional representation systems will lead to the adoption of the policy preferred by the median voter. In a plurality system, politicians will converge on the median voter's ideal point (Shepsle 1991). In a proportional representation system, although politicians may not converge on the median voter, actual policy (in parliament) will depend on the median parliamentarian (Laver and Schofield 1990). It is also safe to predict that the median parliamentarian will be close to the median voter (Huber and Powell 1994).[11]

On the other hand, one may think of three ways in which different mechanisms of representation may have different effects on the survival of democracies. In the first place, whereas under proportional representation the median parliamentarian (representing the median voter) does not vary over time, in non-PR systems, and given partial divergence among competing parties (Alesina and Rosenthal 1995), the average policy will be equal to the median voter ideal point over time, but it will vary from election to election. Indeed, Powell has shown that "the average legislative median produced by single-member district election rules is about twice as far from the median citizen as the average in the low threshold PR systems" (2000: 226). Now, if the sectors at the two opposite sides in the policy space are risk-averse, the introduction of proportional representation should make a democracy more stable because the agents' expected utility will not be inherently diminished by repeated swings in the outcome.[12]

In the second place, proportional representation increases the likelihood of having multiparty coalitions (Laver and Schofield 1990), therefore raising the number of partners in government. The multiplicity of coalition partners reduces the rent-seeking possibilities of one of those agents at the expense of all others. Although this result may have no consequences in countries rich in mobile assets, in asset-specific countries, proportional representation should reduce the number of regime crises and democratic

---

[11] Notice that the equivalence in policy outcomes under both electoral systems is based on the assumption that electoral districting is such that the national median voter at election time remains so in parliament (through his representative). This is the case if the whole country is a single district (as in the case of direct presidential elections or pure proportional representation elections). The assumption is broken if electoral districts are carved so that the median voter ceases to be decisive in the policy-making process.

[12] If we further assume that risk-aversion declines with per capita income, majoritarian electoral rules should lead to even more instability than proportional representation in poor economies.

breakdowns (in the same way that parliamentarism does vis-à-vis presidentialism).

Finally, imagine that politicians value the intrinsic benefit of office beyond (or in addition to) the implementation of their ideal policies. Proportional representation systems are likely to spread out office benefits across parties more widely than majoritarian systems and, hence, may be better at securing the support of a broader range of public opinion.

Before we look at the empirical evidence, we need to make an additional point. Some scholars wrongly maintain that majoritarian and proportional representation parliaments have different effects over policy and thus democratic stability because they aggregate preferences and coordinate political actors differently. That argument runs approximately as follows. Whereas Westminster regimes produce two parties and solid one-party majorities that govern excluding the rest of social actors, proportional representation structures are more conducive to the representation of minorities (which are left aside in a plurality system) in government through broad ministerial coalitions. Proportional representation systems therefore reduce the incentives anyone may have to stage a coup against democracy. Each electoral system is certainly correlated with a particular party system. But its effects on political representation and governance are much less clear-cut. In other words, that line of argumentation wrongly conflates the institution of proportional representation with the practice of consociationalism (i.e., a system in which several parties belonging to very different political subcultures govern together). Proportional representation may be indeed a necessary condition to have consociationalism. However, it is never a sufficient condition. Once parliament has been elected, proportional representation may well lead (and, indeed, does lead on many occasions) to minority cabinets and minimal winning coalitions. To put it differently, consociational practices may enhance the survival of democracies (a point we do not examine here). But proportional electoral systems alone do not generate any more stability than majority systems through this channel.

To study the impact of electoral rules on democratic stability, we define as proportional representation regimes those cases in which the electoral system employed to elect the main legislative chamber is based on electoral districts that are larger than one seat and use proportional allocation rules. In turn, chambers elected on the basis of plurality or two-round single-member districts are coded as majoritarian systems. In those cases in which the main legislative chamber is elected through a mixed system (with a fraction of the seats allocated through proportional representation and the rest through majoritarian mechanisms), we code them as proportional representation if the majority of the seats are assigned through proportional methods and as majoritarian otherwise. On average, majoritarian regimes exhibit a slightly higher proportion of democratic breakdowns (with an annual rate of 2.3 percent) than proportional representation systems (a yearly rate of 1.5 percent). The underperformance of majoritarian systems is concentrated in very underdeveloped societies. In countries with a per capita income below $1,000, the probability of democratic breakdown is more than twice higher in majoritarian systems than in proportional representation. Above $1,000, the type of electoral system does not seem to have an impact on the survival of a democracy.

Because the impact of electoral regimes may be ultimately mediated by the type of executive in place, Figures 8.5 through 8.8 display the probability of breakdown both by type of electoral law and executive–legislative system. Below $8,000, presidential systems with majoritarian congresses are much worse than any other combination. Above $8,000, the constitutional arrangement does not make any difference. A similar pattern obtains for levels of industrialization (Figure 8.6) and rural inequality (Figure 8.7). A high breakdown rate takes place only in underdeveloped areas under presidential regimes and majoritarian legislatures.

Figure 8.8, which explores the relationship between ethnic fractionalization and electoral system, shows too that the combination of majoritarian legislatures and presidential executive is the worse system by far. Among the top quartile of countries in terms of ethnic fragmentation, proportional representation, and parliamentarism comes second (with a probability of breakdown of over 16 percent). The result changes in the third quartile – majoritarian electoral rules are worse. In the second quartile, all systems except presidentialism jointly with the use of majority rule in the election of congress are stable. Finally, in highly homogeneous countries, none of the four combinations makes any difference.

Political Decentralization

Few studies have examined the relationship between federalism and democratic stability in a systematic manner. Echoing the constitutional debates at the time of the American independence, Tocqueville (1835 [1969]) envisioned federal systems as constitutional structures that could accommodate heterogeneous communities. The most recent

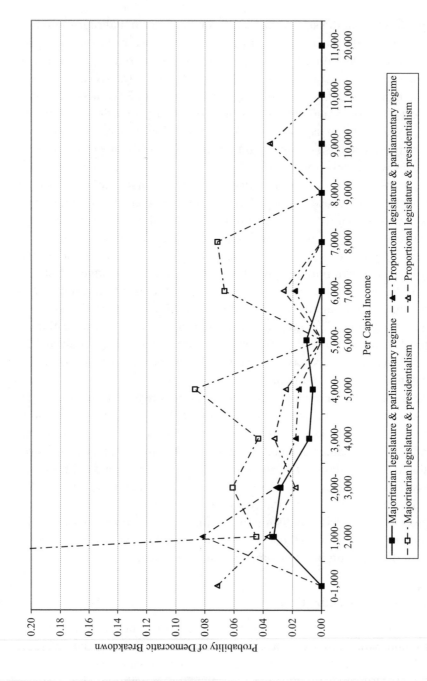

Figure 8.5. Electoral system, development and democratic breakdowns.

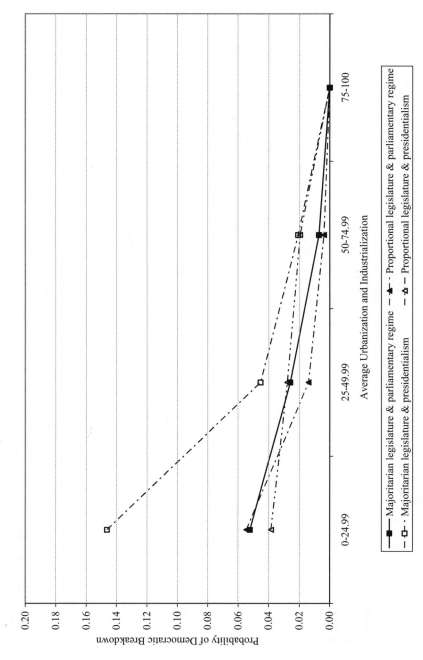

Figure 8.6. Electoral rules, industrialization and democratic breakdowns.

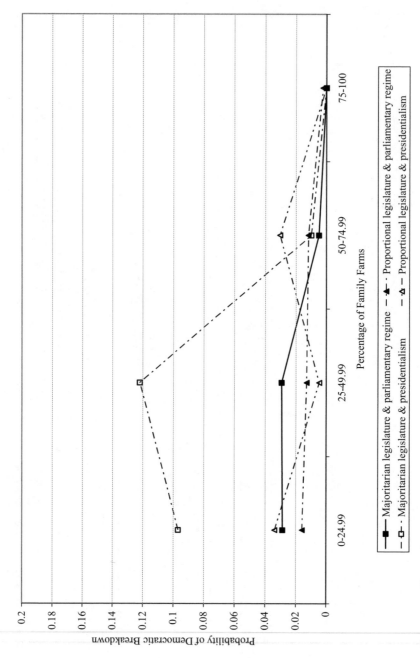

Figure 8.7. Electoral system, rural inequality and democratic breakdowns.

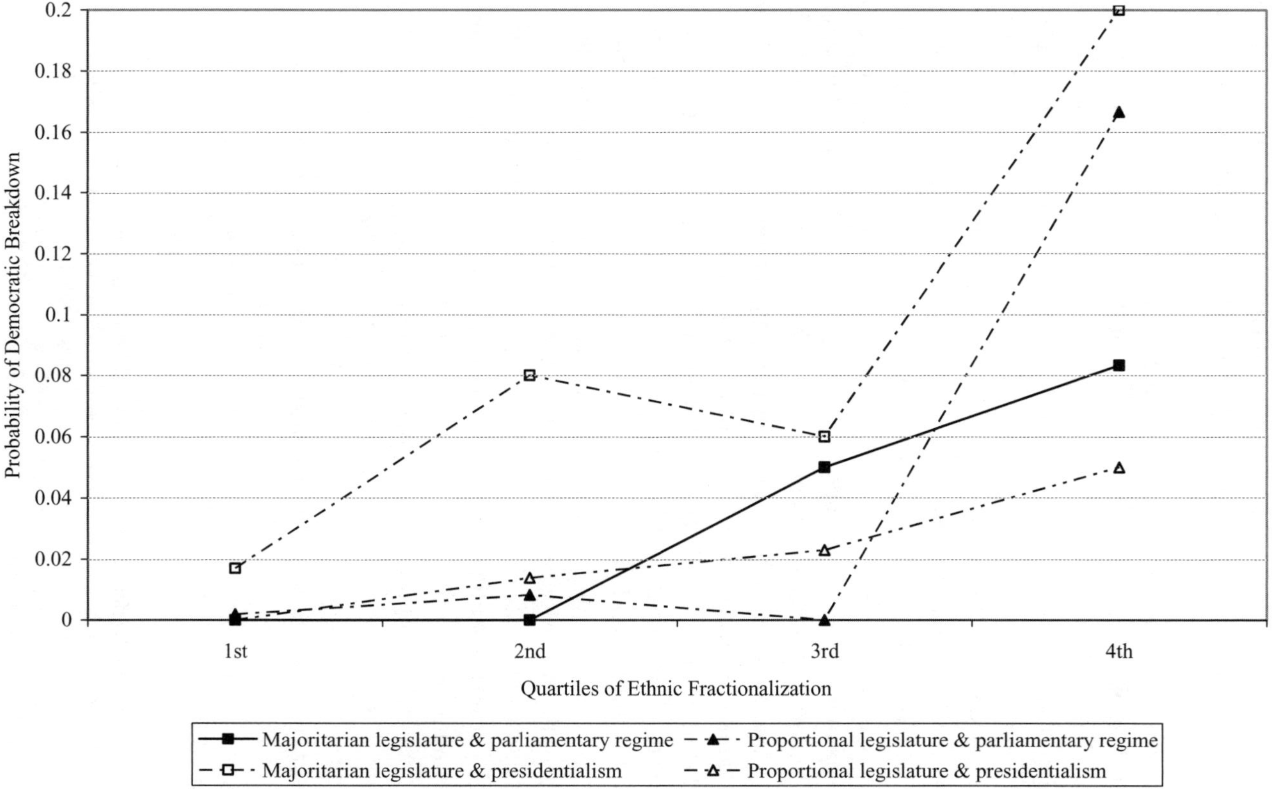
0.2
0.18
0.16
0.14
0.12
0.1
0.08
0.06
0.04
0.02
0
Probability of Democratic Breakdown
1st
2nd
3rd
4th
Quartiles of Ethnic Fractionalization
Majoritarian legislature & parliamentary regime
Proportional legislature & parliamentary regime
Majoritarian legislature & presidentialism
Proportional legislature & presidentialism

Figure 8.8. Electoral system, ethnic fractionalization and democratic breakdowns.

research remains divided, however – probably because it has not moved toward systematic studies of the impact of federalism on democratic survival.[13]

As a mechanism that can accommodate interterritorial heterogeneity, federalism should be able to minimize the level of political conflict and strengthen democracy in the following way. As discussed in the opening section of this chapter, the presence of excessive heterogeneity in preferences and interests jeopardizes the survival of democracy. Consider now the case in which this heterogeneity has a territorial nature; that is, there are several regions or territorial units that differ in terms of their wealth or that have different religious or linguistic practices. Those regions that are in a minority position (in the decision-making process) will only participate in a single and democratic country in which the rest of the country (the majority of regions) sets policy when the benefits that may come from the union, such as trade gains from having a common market and security gains that accrue as a result of a reduction of internal and external military threats, outweigh the set of transfers and regulations that the majority may impose on the minority. If the costs of taxation exceed the benefits of trade and peace, the minority regions will prefer to secede (or to impose a nondemocratic state in which they control the policy levers). In turn, the majority regions may follow two alternative strategies. They may block secession altogether, which generally entails some violence and even a resort to authoritarianism. Alternatively, they may accept giving more autonomy to the regions in the minority block, that is, limiting the degree to which all the regions pool their assets and authority together.[14] To put this more generally, in a situation of high (and/or growing) interterritorial heterogeneity, and holding constant trade and peace gains (high and/or increasing), political decentralization (and, in a related manner, giving stronger guarantees to every territory vis-à-vis the other members of the union) should make democracy more feasible at the national level.[15]

---

[13] Beramendi (2007) offers a review of the existing studies on this question.

[14] Naturally, this is a partial solution because although the low-income regions would rather have this type of weak union to no union at all, they would prefer complete political integration (with tax and transfer powers in the hands of all the union) over any other alternative constitutional arrangement.

[15] It is true that a dispersion of authority may invite more challenges to the authority of the central government, but one has to assess this effect against two other facts: first, the lack of decentralization leads, in heterogeneous territories, to considerable center–periphery tensions; and, second, those challenges probably cancel each other out in a federation in

The United States supplies a good historical example of federalism as a guarantor of democracy. The survival of relatively democratic regimes in the northeastern and western areas of the United States in the nineteenth century was dependent on the maintenance of a de facto confederate system – where states enjoyed nearly complete sovereignty over taxes and the legality of slavery. With a very centralized state, those units would have been affected by the harsh inequalities of the South, and a democratic system would have been harder to sustain. Indeed, it was the assertion of the federal government, under an administration opposed to slavery, that led to the American Civil War. Employing a more extreme example (which, however, follows the same logic), the persistence of democracy in certain parts of the world is only possible because there are many countries, that is, because sovereignty is fragmented. If the world were unified under a single government, its vast inequalities would probably lead to a nondemocratic solution.

Given a federal constitution, the survival of democracy would be further fostered by having a parliamentarian system rather than a strong presidential structure. Federalism probably survives as a result of a self-enforcing equilibrium of the following sort. Federated states accept living in a federal framework to the extent that there are enough guarantees to each one of them that no single state or coalition of states could change the rules of the game unilaterally. This equilibrium requires some dispersion of authority and the corresponding balance of power among states. Federal countries should have enough states to make it difficult for particular coalitions (of states) to coalesce in a permanent basis. Moreover, no state should be too large, have too many resources, or control particular mechanisms that block the decision-making process of the whole federation. To work effectively, any federation has to have – besides a balanced set of federated states – a unified executive (and perhaps a unified legislative branch). The lack of a unified authority makes it impossible for the federation to survive external shocks or to enforce, through credible sanctions, the rules that secure a single market and unified policies across the federation. Yet the executive branch ought not to hold too much power either – partly because this would bolster the president's temptation to encroach on the authority of the federated units and partly because it would allow the president to forge alliances with particular areas and upset the

which the federated units are roughly equivalent in power or where permanent coalitions are difficult to maintain.

self-enforcing equilibrium of the federation. Hence, a robust federation should follow a "Goldilocks" theory of executive–legislative relations: executives should be neither too hot nor too cold. A strong parliamentary cabinet is just right to strengthen the stabilizing properties of federalism.

In addition to its role in lessening any interterritorial tensions, a federal constitution may extend the chances of democracy for reasons that are more closely related to the problem of political accountability and democratic delegation that we explored in the first section of the chapter. The creation of several tiers of government through federalism should contribute to democratic stability by making it harder for any politician to accumulate excessive resources and assets and to rig the electoral process for two reasons. First, the fragmentation of power across several territories is an artificial procedure to increase the mobility of private assets. As territorial jurisdictions multiply in an otherwise unified trade and monetary area, economic agents can escape more easily from the confiscatory policies of any given policy maker. In anticipation of this behavior, politicians restrain themselves accordingly.[16] Second, the fragmentation of authority may multiply the number of examples that allow voters to obtain information about the competence of politicians and hence to monitor them effectively. This effect then reduces the politically induced generation of inequalities and sustains the set of underlying conditions that make democracy stable.

Figures 8.9 through 8.12 display the likelihood of breakdown of federal and nonfederal systems, organized by the same economic indicators employed in previous figures. In addition, they report the same data for federal systems distinguishing between parliamentarian and presidential executive–legislative relationships. On average, federalism has a moderately lower breakdown rate than unitary states. The introduction of federalism reduces the breakdown rate from 3.3 percent to 1.9 percent in presidential systems and from 1.5 percent to 0.4 percent in parliamentary systems.

The combination of parliamentarism and federalism clearly behaves as a democratic stabilizer. Almost no federal parliamentarian system has experienced a democratic breakdown. The results for federal presidential systems are more ambiguous. At low income levels, they behave like unitary systems. At middle income levels, they are better with the glaring

---

[16] See Myerson (2006) for a formal discussion in which federalism encourages good behavior and the electoral selection of "good" politicians.

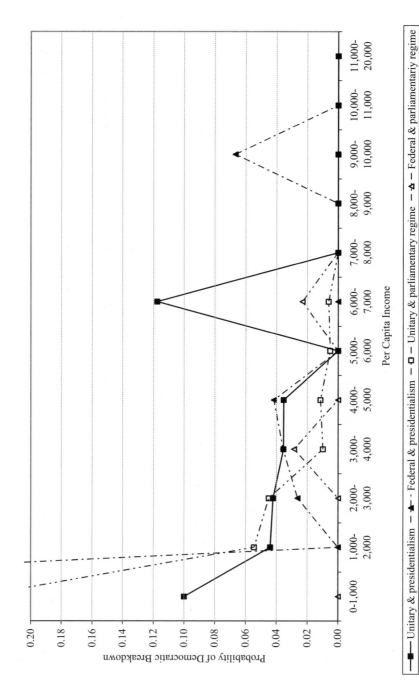

Figure 8.9. Federalism, development and democratic breakdowns.

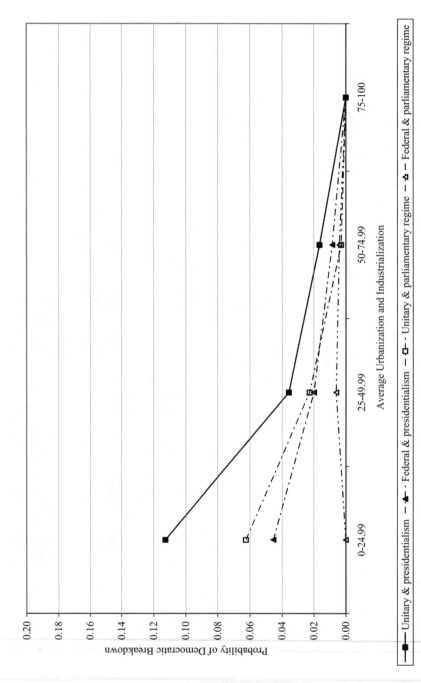

Figure 8.10. Federalism, industrialization and democratic breakdowns.

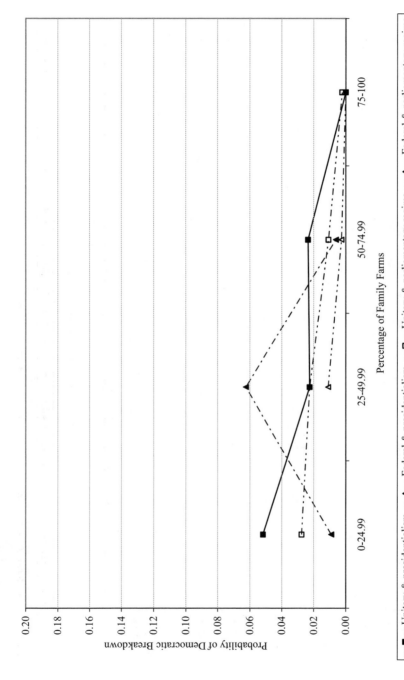

Figure 8.11. Federalism, rural inequality and democratic breakdowns.

— ■ — Unitary & presidentialism — ▲ · · Federal & parliamentary regime — ◻ — Unitary & parliamentary regime — △ — Federal & parliamentary regime

Percentage of Family Farms

Probability of Democratic Breakdown

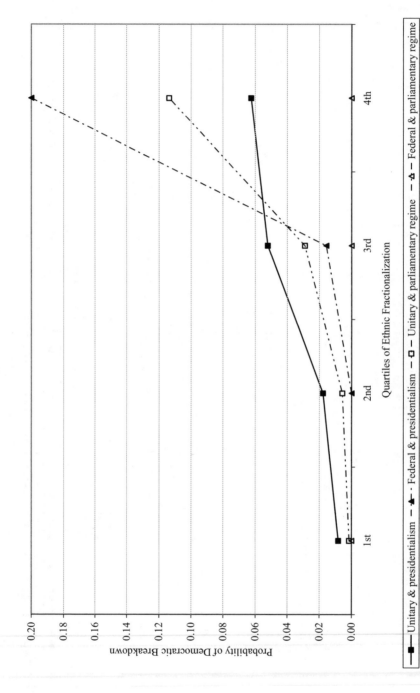

Figure 8.12. Federalism, ethnic fractionalization and democratic breakdowns.

exception of the Argentine crisis of 1976 (Figure 8.9). Federal systems have fewer transitions to authoritarianism for all levels of industrialization and urbanization except one (Figure 8.10). For different levels in the distribution of rural property, the differential impact of federalism is absent or negligible (Figure 8.11). Finally, federal regimes (with presidentialism) are generally much worse in ethnically fragmented countries – but this result is based on just ten observations (Figure 8.12).

Empirical Analysis

Estimation Method

To test the potential impact of different constitutional frameworks on democratic stability, we use Cox proportional hazard models to estimate the effect of a country's institutional characteristics and economic conditions on the survival of democratic regimes. In this model, for countries $i = 1, \ldots, N$, each entering a state (i.e., the starting year of a democratic spell) at time $t = 0$, the (instantaneous) hazard rate function for country i at time $t > 0$ is assumed to take the proportional hazards form:

$$\lambda_{it} = \lambda_0(t) \exp(X'_{it}\beta)\lambda_i,$$

where λ_{it} is the hazard function of the country i at time t; $\lambda_0(t)$ is the baseline hazard function that takes a nonparametric form; $exp(.)$ is the exponential function; X_{it} is a vector of covariates summarizing observed differences between individual countries at t; and β is a vector of parameters to be estimated. Thus, Cox's partial likelihood model allows derivation of the estimates of the coefficients β from a proportional hazard model without placing any restrictions on the shape of the baseline hazard. We incorporate ε_i, a gamma-distributed random covariate with unit mean and variance $\sigma^2 = \mu$, to describe unobserved heterogeneity between countries to account for those countries that undergo more than one transition in our sample. Results are robust to estimate robust errors by clustering on countries, alternatively, and can be obtained from the authors.

Data

The political data set, which encompasses all sovereign countries in the world from 1800 to 1999, includes 68 transitions from democracy into authoritarian regimes out of 174 democratic periods (the remaining

106 cases are democracies still in place in 1999 or disappeared as a result of either foreign occupation, partition, or inclusion in a larger state).

The independent variables are as follows:

1. Proportional representation: a dichotomous variable that takes the value of 1 if the electoral system employed to elect the main legislative chamber is based on proportional representation, 0 otherwise. In those cases in which the main legislative chamber is elected through a mixed system (with a fraction of the seats allocated through proportional representation and the rest through majoritarian mechanisms), we code them as 1 if the majority of the seats are assigned through proportional methods and 0 otherwise.

2. Presidentialism is a dummy variable coded 1 for the presence of presidential and semipresidential systems, and 0 otherwise. Both the proportional representation variable and the parliamentarism variable have been built based on Cox (1997), IDEA (1997), Linz and Valenzuela (1994), Shugart and Carey (1992), and the Keesing's Contemporary Archives.

3. Federalism: a dichotomous variable taken from Downes (2000), coded 1 for federal systems and 0 otherwise.

4. Per capita income expressed as PPP $ of 1996. We employ two data sets for per capita income:

(a) A small data set that includes per capita income as reported in the Penn Wold table 6.1 (Heston, Summers, and Aten 2002), covering the period from 1950 to 1999, plus data from Maddison (1995) – the Maddison data set provides observations for the period previous to 1950, essentially for developed countries and some large Asian and Latin American cases. The Maddison data have been adjusted to make it comparable with the Summers–Heston data set. The combination of both data sets gives us a panel of more than 7,600 country-year observations for the period 1850 to 1999. We call this data set "alpha."

(b) A larger data set that extends the previous data set in two ways: first, it interpolates the data between noncontinuous country-year observations reported by Maddison (who reports, for some countries, data for 1820 and 1850 but in most cases does not start continuous series until 1870). Second, it employs the estimates supplied by Bourguignon and Morrison (2002) for the world since 1820 (and mostly for every twenty years) to calculate all missing data. This second data set, "beta," contains almost 15,000 country-year observations of per capita income – that is, 89 percent of all years of sovereign countries. Although this data set is a fragile one – for example, it does not allow us to calculate yearly growth rates – it overcomes one serious problem of the first data set: the overrepresentation of developed countries. Whereas in the first (smaller) data set, 50 percent of the observations have a per capita income above \$3,371 (in \$ of 1996), in the second (larger) data set, the median per capita income is \$1,732. In other words, about 5,600 country-years with a per capita income lower than \$1,800 are missing in the shorter data set.

5. Percentage of family farms over the total area of holdings, taken from Vanhanen (1997).[17]

6. The index of occupational diversification, also developed by Vanhanen, which is the average of the percentage of nonagricultural population and the percentage of urban population. The urban population is defined as population living in cities of 20,000 or more inhabitants. This index also covers the period from 1850 to 1999. It has a mean of 33 percent and varies from 3 to 99 percent.

7. The level of ethnic fractionalization, computed as 1 minus the Herfindhal index of ethnolinguistic group shares, with new data gathered and calculated in Alesina et al. (2003).[18]

8. Religious fractionalization, also computed as 1 minus the Herfindhal index of religious groups, also taken from Alesina et al. (2003).

9. Percentage of Muslims, Catholics, and Protestants, taken from LaPorta et al. (1999).

10. Economic growth rate (in the year before the observed event).

Per Capita Income and Political Institutions

We first consider the effect of political institutions on the survival of democracies, alone and conditional on per capita income. Table 8.1 reports

---

[17] This measure, gathered and reported by Vanhanen (1997), is based on defining as family farms those "farms that provide employment for not more than four people, including family members, ... that are cultivated by the holder family itself and ... that are owned by the cultivator family or held in ownerlike possession" (p. 48). The definition, which aims at distinguishing "family farms" from large farms cultivated mainly by hired workers, is not dependent on the actual size of the farm – the size of the farm varies with the type of product and the agricultural technology being used.

[18] According to the index of ethnic fractionalization, which measures the probability that two randomly selected people from a given country will not belong to the same ethnic group, ethnic groups are defined in each country according to linguistic or racial characteristics. Which characteristic is employed depends on which cleavage is considered to be dominant in each case.

Table 8.1. A Survival Analysis of Democracies as a Function of Constitutional Structures and Per Capita Income, 1820–1999

	Model 1		Model 2		Model 3 Legislature Elected through		Model 4		Model 5		Model 6	
					Majoritarian	PR						
	DATA α	DATA b	DATA γ	DATA b	DATA γ	DATA b	DATA γ	DATA b	DATA γ	DATA b	DATA γ	DATA b
Per capita income (in thousand $)	−0.611***	−0.480***	−0.539***	−0.532***	−0.622***	−0.603***	−0.479***	−0.466***	−0.375***	−0.401***	−0.739***	−0.554***
	(0.175)	(0.156)	(0.158)	(0.127)	(0.230)	(0.218)	(0.126)	(0.101)	(0.095)	(0.085)	(0.221)	(0.153)
PR[a]	−1.147**	−0.912									−1.209***	−0.633
	(0.435)	(0.633)									(0.419)	(0.612)
PR × per capita income	0.000**	0.171									0.000	0.067
	(0.000)	(0.183)									(0.000)	(0.189)
Presidential sm[b]			−0.412	−0.540	−0.030	−1.412					0.003	−0.008
			(0.622)	(0.514)	(0.825)	(0.913)					(0.739)	(0.591)
Presidential sm × per capita income			0.327**	0.322**	−0.399	0.417					0.237	0.184*
			(0.182)	(0.156)	(0.277)	(0.249)					(0.185)	(0.174)
Federalism[c]							−0.725	−1.307**			0.938	−1.490**
							(0.890)	(0.706)			(0.908)	(0.748)
Federalism × per capita income							0.218*	0.330**			0.176	0.305**
							(0.198)	(0.154)			(0.184)	(0.168)
Federal parliamentarian									−2.112	−2.372**		
									(1.712)	(1.144)		
Federal parliamentarian × per capita income									0.123	0.342*		
									(0.404)	(0.189)		
Log-likelihood	−138.05	−219.89	−170.50	−246.31	−93.97	−81.52	−162.69	−247.28	−171.48	−246.54	−135.47	−215.72
Prob > χ^2	0.0000	0.0002	0.0007	0.0001	0.0119	0.0220	0.0009	0.0000	0.0004	0.0000	0.0007	0.0007
Wald (χ^2)	23.31	21.72	16.91	22.44	10.97	9.63	16.46	23.80	17.95	25.67	25.29	25.23
No. of observations	2870	3344	3114	3636	1427	1909	3105	3637	3114	3636	2870	3336
No. of subjects	108	127	130	146	57	79	128	147	130	146	108	125
No. of failures	38	55	44	60	30	25	42	60	44	60	38	55

Notes: Estimation: Cox Proportional Hazard Model. Standard errors in parentheses. ***p < 0.01; **p < 0.05; *p < 0.10. PR= proportional representation.

[a] Dummy variable. PR = 1.

[b] Dummy variable. Presidentialism = 1.

[c] Dummy variable. Federalism = 1.

the likelihood of transitions from democracy into authoritarianism for electoral systems (Model 1), presidentialism (Models 2 and 3), federal arrangements (Model 4) separately, and for all institutions together (Model 5) for the period 1820 to 1999. For each model (except Model 3), we run two estimations: the first one employing the small alpha data set and the second the beta data set.

Proportional Representation

Model 1 in Table 8.1 shows that both per capita income and the coefficient for proportional representation are negative – they diminish the likelihood of a democratic breakdown – and statistically significant in the alpha data set. In the beta data set, which has seventeen failures more than the estimation with the first data set, the coefficient for proportional representation remains stable in size but loses all statistical significance. To capture the effects of different electoral systems, we simulate the joint effect of per capita income, electoral rules, and their interaction in Figure 8.13.[19] More specifically, we simulate the evolution of the survival rate – that is, the proportion of democracies that will be still in place at each point in time – for majoritarian and proportional representation regimes at three levels of per capita income (i.e., $1,000, $4,000, and $15,000).

Figure 8.13 shows that for low levels of development, the survival rate is very low. Only about 50 percent of democracies reach their sixth year in countries with a per capita income of $1,000 – this level of per capita income corresponds to the twenty-fifth percentile in the sample. By their fifteenth year, the survival rate is about 25 percent. This contrasts with survival rates close to unity in countries with a per capita income of $15,000. Conditional on the effect of per capita income, the impact of different electoral rules is as follows. For low and medium levels of per capita income, the survival rate is higher under proportional representation than under majoritarian systems. Thus, for example, in a country with a per capita income of $1,000, the survival rate stands at 58 percent among proportional representation cases and at 32 percent for majoritarian cases in the tenth year after the transition to democracy. At a per capita income level of $4,000, the difference is much smaller – 80 percent versus 76 percent. In countries with high per capita income, proportional representation is slightly worse, but the difference is negligible.

---

[19] The simulations are done based on the data "beta" column of each model.

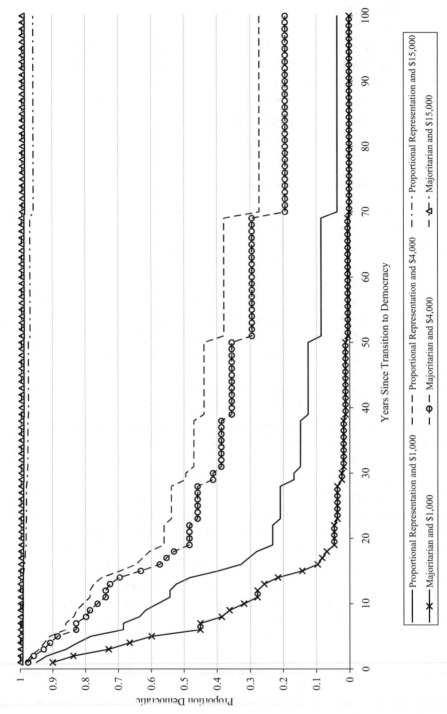

Figure 8.13. Estimated survival for different electoral systems and levels of per capita income.

Presidentialism

Model 2 in Table 8.1 considers, in turn, the effect of presidentialism. Presidential regimes alone have no statistically significant impact on the stability of democratic regimes. The coefficient of presidentialism interacted with development is significant. Still, the results for presidentialism are not robust to the exclusion of a single (and crucial) case: Argentina. They are robust, however, to the introduction of Argentina as a dummy variable.

To facilitate the interpretation of these results, Figure 8.14 simulates the joint effect of per capita income, constitutional rule, and their interaction. Parliamentarian and presidential regimes fare similarly in countries with low per capita income (parliamentary regimes seem to be slightly worse). Noninstitutional factors are here, too, dominant and condemn most cases to failure. Differences are substantial, however, for medium levels of development. Presidential regimes are there much worse than parliamentarian regimes. Ten years after a democratic transition, the survival rate is 86 percent for parliamentary regimes and 72 percent for presidential constitutions. Twenty years after the transition, survival rates are 69 percent and 46 percent, respectively. As per capita income increases, the performance gap between the two types of executives declines.

According to analysis displayed in Figures 8.5 through 8.8, the negative effect of presidentialism (relative to parliamentarian regimes) seemed to vary with the type of electoral regime employed to elect the legislature. Model 3 in Table 8.1 estimates the probability of democratic survival in two separate subsamples: countries with legislatures elected through majoritarian systems and countries with legislatures elected through proportional representation. In the former case, presidentialism reduces the probability of democratic breakdown in conjunction with income. In proportional representation cases, presidentialism alone strengthens democracy but then weakens the latter as countries develop. In neither case, however, are coefficients statistically significant. Figure 8.15 simulates the results for three levels of development. For low and medium levels of per capita income, having a congress elected with proportional representation seems to stabilize democracies, at least in the first years after the transition to democracy. In contrast, presidential systems with majoritarian congresses are better performers in rich countries.

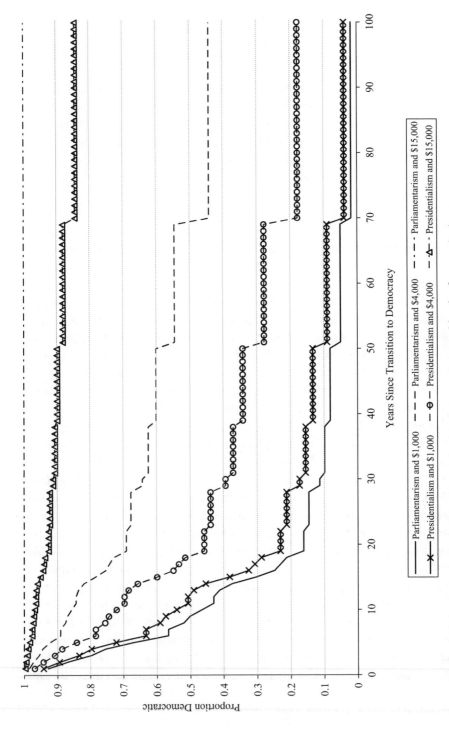

Figure 8.14. Estimated survival for different executive–legislative regimes and levels of per capita income.

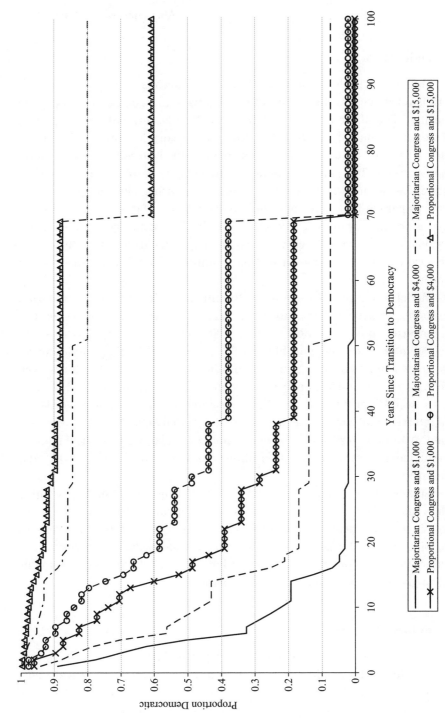

Figure 8.15. Estimated survival for presidential regimes with different electoral rules and levels of per capita income.

Federalism

Model 4 in Table 8.1 tests the impact of federalism. As predicted, federalism reduces the likelihood of breakdown – although according to the positive sign of the interactive term, this effect lessens with development. The simulations of Figure 8.16 show that at very low levels of development ($1,000), unitary democracies are more likely to collapse than federal democracies. The survival rate after fifteen years is 67 percent in federal states yet is only 34 percent in unitary countries. The differences narrow as per capita income goes up. For high levels of development, federal states are slightly more brittle. However, this last result seems to be driven by just one country. Once we exclude Argentina from our estimations, federal and unitary states are equally stable at high levels of per capita income.

Model 5 in Table 8.4 examines the impact of federal parliamentarian systems. As expected from the previous descriptive data, that system has a powerful stabilizing effect on democratic institutions. Figure 8.17 simulates the results. Except for high levels of income, federal parliamentarian regimes are much more stable than other constitutional structures even in very poor countries. Federal parliamentarian regimes are likely to perform so well for two reasons. First, decentralization leads to lower levels of interregional conflict and a more widespread distribution of power. Second, without a president who may topple the balanced territorial equilibrium, federalism retains all its credibility as a guarantor of democracy and minority rights.

Finally, Model 6 tests the impact of all variables together. In the alpha data set, only proportional representation remains significant. Federalism is not statistically significant, although its coefficient is stable relative to Model 4. In the larger beta data set, presidentialism is significant in interaction with per capita income. All in all, it is federalism that remains strongly significant with very stable coefficients.

Robustness Tests

To confirm the validity of the results reported in Table 8.4, we have proceeded to run the models with single-country deletion. Results are robust to the exclusion of single countries – with the (already noted) exception of Argentina for presidential regimes. We have also controlled for land area;

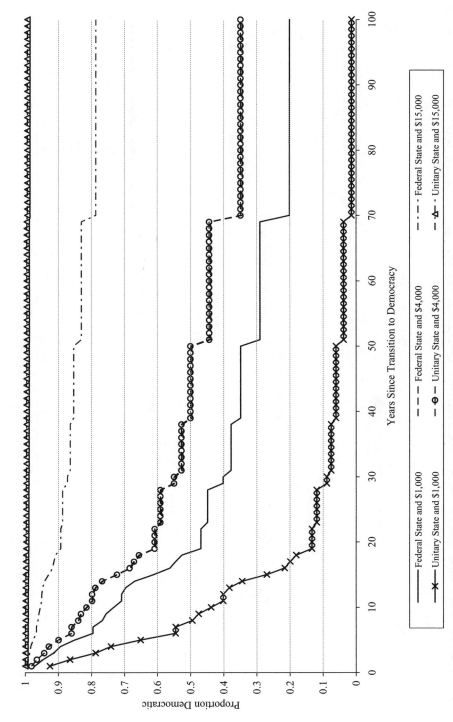

Figure 8.16. Estimated survival for different territorial structures and levels of per capita income.

Years Since Transition to Democracy

Proportion Democratic

Federal State and $1,000
Unitary State and $1,000
Federal State and $4,000
Unitary State and $4,000
Federal State and $15,000
Unitary State and $15,000

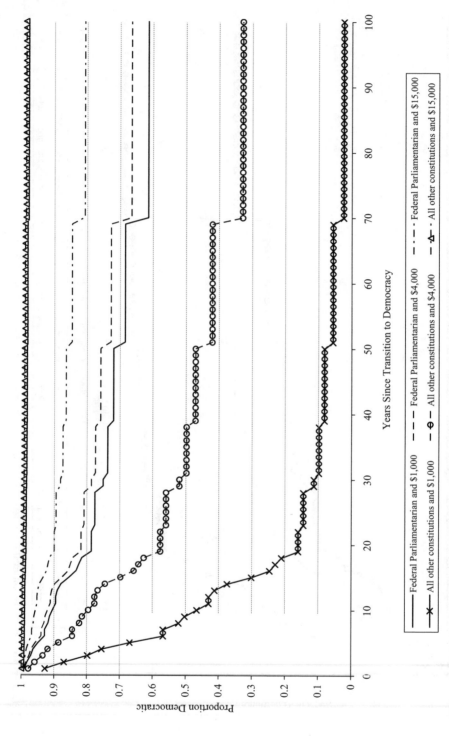

Figure 8.17. Estimated survival for federal parliamentarian regimes and levels of per capita income.

population; ethnic fractionalization; religious fractionalization; the proportion of Catholic, Protestant, and Muslim believers; the lagged growth rate; and regional dummies. Again, the results in Table 8.4 do not vary with the introduction of those controls. Among these control variables, ethnic fractionalization reduces the rate of democratic survival; the growth rate increases it. Population slightly reduces the probability of a democratic breakdown. In the following subsection, we turn to examine ethnic fractionalization in more detail.

Endogeneity

In exploring the role that different constitutional structures may have on the reduction of democratic instability, we need to address the extent to which the existence of particular institutions may not be endogenous to the causes of breakdown. In other words, it may be that it is only countries with certain characteristics that make democracies successful that in turn choose successful institutional rules (e.g., federal parliamentarism).

We tackle this issue by instrumenting our institutional traits for a different set of variables that are arguably exogenous to the success of democratic regimes. For presidentialism, we have identified five variables that explain the choice of executive: the log of the area of the country, year, two dummies for Africa and Latin America, and, particularly, the variable "Presidential Preconditions." This latter variable is built as follows: it predicts presidentialism in noncolonized countries that moved to democracy through violence (i.e., civil wars or revolutions), in former colonies that became independent through violent means, and in former colonies that achieved their independence peacefully from a metropolis governed by presidential regimes. In a probit model to explain the choice of presidentialism, all five variables are significant at the 0.01 level and together result in a pseudo-R^2 equal to 0.58. In turn, federalism is instrumented through the same variables plus being a former British colony – in a probit model, the pseudo-R^2 is 0.34. Electoral systems are instrumented through log of population, year, former French colony, former British colony, and former United States–administered territories – the pseudo-R^2 is 0.39.

Table 8.2 reports the models of Table 8.1 with institutional variables instrumented – that is, we employ the fitted value of electoral systems, presidentialism, and federalism (alone and in the interactive term) obtained through the probit estimations. Income is taken from the beta data set.

Table 8.2. A Survival Analysis of Democracies as a Function of Instrumented Constitutional Structures and Per Capita Income, 1850–1999

	Model 1	Model 2	Model 3	Model 4
Per capita income (in	−0.802***	−0.613***	−0.425**	−1.025***
thousand $)	(0.248)	(0.164)	(0.107)	(0.236)
PR[a]	−0.989			−1.133
	(0.763)			(0.797)
PR × per capita income	0.619**			0.487
	(0.297)			(0.305)
Presidentialism[b]		−1.224**		−0.730
		(0.551)		(0.692)
Presidentialism × per	0.571**			0.429**
capita income	(0.187)			(0.204)
Federalism[c]			−1.605	−2.106*
			(1.096)	(1.095)
Federalism × per capita			0.427	0.580*
income			(0.282)	(0.348)
Log-likelihood	−243.13	−237.97	−244.55	−236.62
Prob >χ^2	0.0000	0.0002	0.0003	0.0001
Wald (χ^2)	22.56	14.06	18.68	29.18
No. of observations	3309	3309	3309	3309
No. of subjects	144	144	144	144
No. of failures	59	59	59	59

Notes: Per capita income taken from the beta data set. Estimation: Cox Proportional Hazard Model. Model 4 has been estimated without parametric frailty test. Standard errors in parentheses. ***$p < 0.01$; **$p < 0.05$; *$p < 0.10$. PR = proportional representation.
[a] Dummy variable. PR = 1.
[b] Dummy variable. Presidentialism = 1.
[c] Dummy variable. Federalism = 1.

Generally, the coefficients do not change relative to the estimations in Table 8.1, with the exception of the interactive term of electoral system and per capita income, which becomes much larger. The statistical significance of the electoral systems and presidentialism variables goes up. In contrast, federalism and its interactive term become statistically insignificant in Model 3, although they border the significance test at 10 percent. When all constitutional rules are regressed, federalism, alone and in interaction with income, is significant. Presidentialism is only significant in the interactive term. All in all, the results in Table 8.1 (particularly for federalism) seem to hold up to the instrumentation of constitutional rules.

Ethnic Fractionalization and Political Institutions

As discussed in the theory section, preference heterogeneity, fed by ethnic differences, may jeopardize democracy. In the robustness tests performed on the models of Table 8.1, ethnic fractionalization alone was never statistically significant. Still, Table 8.3 displays a set of models that add a measure of ethnic fractionalization and its interaction with constitutional structures to the basic setup of Table 8.1 (where we employed income and institutions as independent variables).

Because the measure of ethnic fractionalization starts only in 1950, the sample shrinks by about 40 percent and the number of democratic failures by more than a third. Moreover, the covariates seem to be plagued by collinearity problems. Hence, results should be interpreted with caution. In all models, ethnic fractionalization has a strong negative impact on democratic survival. Model 1 shows that proportional representation stabilizes democracies, although (according to simulated results not shown here) not to the point of overcoming the effects of ethnic divisions: the estimate of electoral system alone completely counteracts the slightly negative coefficient of the interaction of fragmentation and electoral rules. In contrast, presidential regimes minimize the negative impact of ethnic fractionalization considerably: the negative coefficient of the interactive term "presidentialism × ethnic fractionalization" cancels out any negative effects of ethnic fragmentation. Finally, contrary to theoretical expectations, Model 3 shows that federalism does not mediate in any way in ethnically diverse societies: the coefficient of the interactive term of federalism and ethnic fractionalization turns out to be positive.

Political Institutions, Property Distribution, and Industrialization

Table 8.4 extends the same analysis to the period 1850 to 1997, now interacting the type of constitution with the percentage of family farms and with the index of occupational diversification, which is the average of nonagricultural population and urban population. These estimations have two advantages. First, they employ variables that go beyond per capita income and thus proxy, even though in an imperfect manner, the underlying conditions we pointed to in the theoretical discussion. Second, they cover almost all democratic breakdowns.

Table 8.3. A Survival Analysis of Democracies as a Function of Instrumented Constitutional Structures and Ethnic Fractionalization, 1950–99

	Model 4	Model 5	Model 6
Per capita income (in thousand $)	−0.387**	−0.317**	−0.380***
	(0.160)	(0.134)	(0.111)
Ethnic fractionalization	2.084⌢	−3.733***	1.453*
	(1.293)	(1.372)	(0.847)
PR[a]	−2.084⌢		
	(1.546)		
PR × per capita income	0.216⌢		
	(0.208)		
PR × ethnic fractionalization	0.357⌢		
	(2.028)		
Presidentialism[b]		1.558⌢	
		(0.274)	
Presidentialism × per capita income		0.079⌢⌢	
		(0.175)	
Presidentialism × ethnic fractionalization		−3.171*	
		(1.675)	
Federalism[c]			−4.196⌢
			(2.729)
Federalism × per capita income			0.370**
			(0.221)
Federalism × ethnic fractionalization			4.520⌢
			(3.417)
Log-likelihood	−119.95	−147.07	−148.15
Prob >χ^2	0.0000	0.0000	0.0001
Wald (χ^2)	28.89	29.29	26.18
No. of observations	2051	2279	2280
No. of subjects	105	123	124
No. of failures	36	41	41

Notes: Estimation: Cox Proportional Hazard Model. Standard errors in parentheses. ***$p < 0.01$; **$p < 0.05$; *$p < 0.10$. ⌢⌢$p < 0.01$ in joint test with variables of interactive term; ⌢$p < 0.05$ in joint test with variables of interactive term. PR = proportional representation.
[a] Dummy variable. PR = 1.
[b] Dummy variable. Presidentialism = 1.
[c] Dummy variable. Federalism = 1.

In line with previous research, more equally distributed land and higher rates of industrialization and urbanization contribute substantially to the survival of a democratic regime (Boix 2003). In countries where the agrarian property is concentrated in few hands and the level of industrialization is low, democracies break down quickly. Conversely, in countries with a

Table 8.4. Annual Probability of a Democratic Breakdown as a Function of Constitutional Structures, 1850–97

	Model 1	Model 2	Model 3
Percentage of family farms[a]	−0.034***	−0.029**	−0.029**
	(0.011)	(0.012)	(0.009)
Index of occupational	−0.054***	−0.058***	−0.0544***
diversification[b]	(0.016)	(0.012)	(0.010)
PR[c]	−1.357$^{\frown\frown\frown}$		
	(0.941)		
PR × percentage of family farms	0.015$^{\frown\frown\frown}$		
	(0.015)		
PR × index of occupational	0.013$^{\frown\frown\frown}$		
diversification	(0.020)		
Presidentialism[d]		−0.788$^{\frown\frown\frown}$	
		(0.857)	
Presidentialism × percentage of		0.006$^{\frown}$	
family farms		(0.016)	
Presidentialism × index of		0.022*	
occupational diversification		(0.017)	
Federalism[e]			−1.780$^{\frown\frown\frown}$
			(1.239)
Federalism × percentage of			0.006$^{\frown\frown\frown}$
family farms			(0.018)
Federalism × index of			0.036**
occupational			(0.021)
diversification			
Log-likelihood	−211.04	−248.70	−248.24
Prob >χ^2	0.0000	0.0000	0.0000
LR (χ^2)	34.25	33.18	36.77
No. of observations	3070	3341	3342
No. of subjects	126	146	147
No. of failures	55	62	62

Notes: Estimation: Cox Proportional Hazard Model. Standard errors in parentheses. ***$p < 0.01$; **$p < 0.05$; *$p < 0.10$. $^{\frown\frown\frown}p < 0.01$ in joint test with variables of interactive term; $^{\frown}p < 0.05$ in joint test with variables of interactive term. PR = proportional representation.

[a] Area of family farms as a percentage of the total area of holdings. *Source:* Vanhanen (1997).

[b] Arithmetic mean of percentage of nonagricultural population and percentage of urban population. Urban population is defined as population living in cities of 20,000 or more inhabitants. *Source:* Vanhanen (1997).

[c] Dummy variable. PR = 1.

[d] Dummy variable. Presidentialism = 1.

[e] Dummy variable. Federalism = 1.

high proportion of family farms or high levels of industrialization, democracies survive independently of the constitutional structure in place.

Model 1 in Table 8.4 examines the impact of the type of electoral rule on the survival of a democratic regime. Models 2 and 3 do so for presidentialism and federalism, respectively. Their impact conditional on the distribution of land is minimal. Their effect in interaction with the level of industrialization and urbanization is stronger and requires its simulation. This is done in Figures 8.18 through 8.20.

Figure 8.18 simulates the effect of different electoral systems for different patterns of industrialization and urbanization (and a fixed proportion of family farms at its mean value). For the lowest levels of industrialization and urbanization, majoritarian electoral rules are correlated with more fragile democracies. Otherwise – that is, at high levels of development – the negative effect of majoritarian electoral rules declines.

The impact of the type of executive–legislative relations turns out to be marginal according to Figure 8.19. Underdeveloped economies break down early on, regardless of the executive in place. Developed countries are much more stable – within them, presidential regimes exhibit a slightly higher rate of authoritarian transitions.

Finally, Figure 8.20 simulates the impact of unitary and federal systems. Unitary states are much worse among agrarian countries. Their survival rate is about half the survival rate among federal cases. In contrast, federal states perform worse among industrialized and urbanized countries. As before, however, this result is mostly driven by Argentina – once this country is excluded from the sample, federal and unitary states perform equally well at high levels of development.

Conclusions

To date, political science has explored the consequences of different constitutional settings, such as proportional representation, parliamentarism, or federalism, without controlling for the distribution of interests and the levels of political mobilization in the countries under study. Yet the consequences of institutions can only be determined in the context of a fully specified model, that is, a model in which preferences are described (and then allowed to vary for different types of constitutional designs). Accordingly, this chapter examines the conditions under which institutions, given an underlying distribution of preferences, may reduce democratic

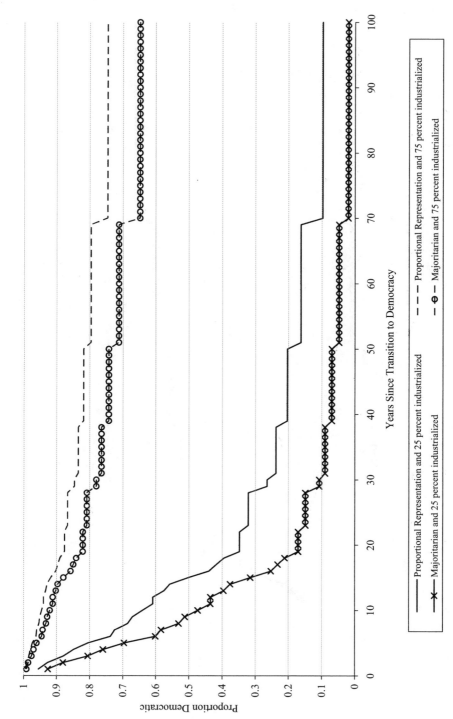

Figure 8.18. Estimated survival for different electoral systems and levels of industrialization.

Proportion Democratic

Years Since Transition to Democracy

Proportional Representation and 25 percent industrialized

Proportional Representation and 75 percent industrialized

Majoritarian and 25 percent industrialized

Majoritarian and 75 percent industrialized

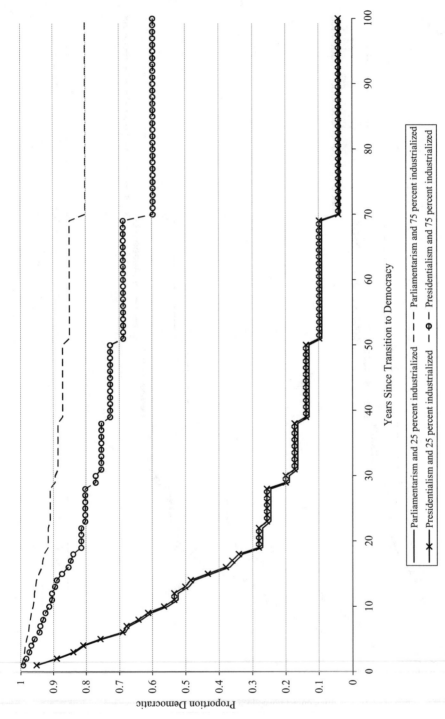

Figure 8.19. Estimated survival for different executive–legislative regimes and levels of industrialization.

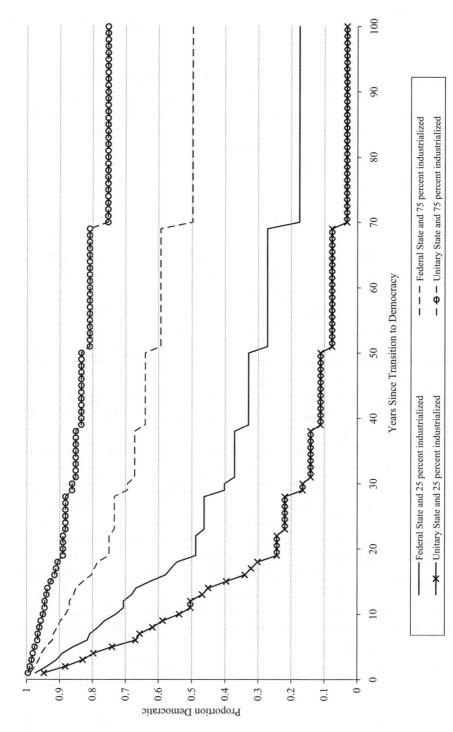

Figure 8.20. Estimated survival for different territorial structures and levels of industrialization.

breakdowns. It then tests the theory by estimating the probability of democratic breakdowns in a sample that extends from 1820 to 1999.

Underlying economic and social conditions play a dominant role in the stability of democratic regimes. For any given constitutional structure, the probability of a democracy surviving for at least fifty years rises from less than 10 percent with a per capita income of $1,000 or a marginal industrial economy to 40 percent with a per capita income of $4,000, 80 percent for a per capita income of $8,000, and close to 100 percent for $15,000 or complete development.

Within the strictures imposed by social and economic factors, constitutional structures play a relatively marginal role in most cases. The probability of democratic breakdown is about 10 percent lower in poor countries under proportional representation systems. This small difference disappears for highly developed countries.

Parliamentary systems have a bigger stabilizing effect (relative to presidential systems) but only in developing countries. In very poor countries (with per capita income of $1,000), parliamentary and presidential systems are equally doomed. In turn, in developed countries, the likelihood of survival is minimally affected by the type of executive system. For middle-income countries, however, parliamentary regimes slash by two the probability of democratic breakdown (i.e., from 70 percent to 40 percent at the fiftieth year).

Why should parliamentary regimes be safer for democracy in low- to middle-income countries? Contemporary democracies are a game in which the principal (the public) delegates into an agent (the politician or policy maker) a given set of instruments to execute certain goals (generally speaking, those willed by the majority). Given self-interested politicians, the delegation of decision making and policy implementation inherent to representative democracies may open up the space for significant inefficiencies and corruption among politicians. The electoral winner may also have an incentive to use her tenure to shift resources in her favor to boost her future electoral chances, to alter the rules of electoral engagement, and even to postpone or cancel the new election. In turn, the losers may respond by challenging the democratic outcome itself. Parliamentary mechanisms may then restrain the ability of rent seekers and therefore reduce the instability of democratic regimes because the executive is subject to a confidence requirement of *continued* support from a majority in the legislature. As a result, the space for unchecked appropriation of wealth and power by the prime minister is much smaller. Presidential systems instead give much more autonomy to their incumbents through temporally rigid mandates, the use of veto powers, and the need for large majorities to impeach them. All these presidential tools became especially dangerous in economic settings in which economic assets are immobile and relatively concentrated and therefore easy to grab. In short, it is difficult to envision many prime ministers acting as expropriators (unless their grip on their own parliamentary supporters is very tight). In contrast, we can name many presidents acting as expropriators – just think of Juan Perón, Ferdinand Marcos, and Hugo Chávez. Compare them with Indira Ghandi's flirt with a state of emergency in the mid-1970s.

Federalism also reduces the probability of democratic breakdown, but it only does so in a consistent manner in combination with parliamentarism. The positive impact of federal parliamentarism is extremely powerful – to the point that it seems to be the only institutional mechanism that stabilizes democracy regardless of nonconstitutional conditions in the country. Since the mid-nineteenth century, there have been only two breakdowns among federal parliamentarian systems – amounting to a breakdown rate of 0.4 percent. The estimated probability that a federal parliamentarian regime survives after fifty years of democracy is above 70 percent even for $1,000-per-income nations. Federalism matters because it creates relatively homogeneous subnational territories, thus minimizing the losses of the minority defeated in an electoral contest and bolstering the chances the latter will accept its defeat. Federalism may also strengthen democracy by creating a decentralized decision-making process in which a large number of actors are needed to take decisions and no actor can act easily as a monopolist rent seeker. The success of federal parliamentarism (as opposed to presidentialism in a federal system) seems to be related to the fact that parliamentary regimes sustain in a credible manner the federal pact made among regions to overcome their territorial differences. Once again, in most cases, presidents are too powerful to guarantee the respect for the minorities enshrined in the constitution.

REFERENCES

Adserà, Alicia, Carles Boix, and Mark Payne. 2003. "Are You Being Served? Political Accountability and Governmental Performance." *Journal of Law, Economics and Organization* 19 (Fall): 445–90.

Alesina, Alberto, Arnaud Devleeschauwer, William Easterly, Sergio Kurlat, and Romain Wacziarg. 2003. "Fractionalization," *Journal of Economic Growth* 8: 155–94.

Alesina, Alberto, and Howard Rosenthal. 1995. *Political Parties, Divided Government, and the Economy.* Cambridge: Cambridge University Press.

Beramendi, Pablo. 2007. "Federalism." In Carles Boix and Susan Stokes (eds.), *Oxford Handbook of Comparative Politics.* Oxford: Oxford University Press.

Boix, Carles. 2003. *Democracy and Redistribution.* New York: Cambridge University Press.

Boix, Carles, and Sebastian Rosato. 2001. "A Complete Data Set of Political Regimes, 1800–1999." Chicago: University of Chicago.

Boix, Carles, and Susan Stokes. 2003. "Endogenous Democratization." *World Politics* 55 (July): 517–49.

Bourguignon, François, and Christian Morrison. 2002. "Inequality among World Citizens: 1820–1992," *American Economic Review* 92 (September): 727–744.

Cheibub, José A. 2006. *Presidentialism, Parliamentarism, and Democracy.* New York: Cambridge University Press.

Cox, Gary. 1997. *Making Votes Count: Strategic Coordination in the World's Electoral Systems.* New York: Cambridge University Press.

Cutright, Phillips. 1963. "National Political Development: Measurement and Analysis." *American Sociological Review* 78: 253–64.

Cutright, Phillips. 1965. "Political Structure, Economic Development, and National Social Security Programs." *American Journal of Sociology* 70: 537–50.

Downes, Alexander. 2000. "Federalism and Ethnic Conflict" [mimeograph]. Chicago: University of Chicago.

Hermens, Ferdinand A. 1941. *Democracy or Anarchy? A Study of Proportional Representation.* Notre Dame: University of Notre Dame.

Heston, Alan, Robert Summers, and Bettina Aten. 2002. *Penn World Table Version 6.1.* Center for International Comparisons at the University of Pennsylvania (CICUP).

Huber, John D., and G. Bingham Powell, Jr. 1994. "Congruence between Citizens and Policymakers in Two Visions of Liberal Democracy." *World Politics* 46 (April): 291–326.

IDEA. 1997. *Voter Turnout from 1945 to 1997: A Global Report on Political Participation.* Stockholm: International Institute for Democracy and Electoral Assistance.

LaPorta, Rafael, Florencio Lopez de Silanes, Andrei Shleifer, and Robert Vishny. 1999. "The Quality of Government," *Journal of Law, Economics and Organization,* 15 (April): 222–79.

Laver, Michael, and Norman Schofield. 1990. *Multiparty Government. The Politics of Coalition in Europe.* Oxford: Oxford University Press.

Linz, Juan. 1994. "Presidential or Parliamentary Democracy: Does It Make a Difference?" In Juan J. Linz and Arturo Valenzuela (eds.), *The Failure of Presidential Democracy: Comparative Perspectives.* Baltimore: Johns Hopkins University Press.

Linz, Juan J., and Arturo Valenzuela (eds.). 1994. *The Failure of Presidential Democracy: Comparative Perspectives.* Baltimore: Johns Hopkins University Press.

Lipset, Seymour M. 1959. "Some Social Requisites of Democracy: Economic Development and Political Legitimacy." *American Political Science Review* 53: 69–105.

Luebbert, Gregory M. 1991. *Liberalism, Fascism, or Social Democracy: Social Classes and the Political Origins of Regimes in Interwar Europe*. Oxford: Oxford University Press.

Maddison, Angus. 1995. *Monitoring the World Economy, 1820–1992*. Paris: Organization for Economic Cooperation and Development, 1995.

Mainwaring, Scott, and Matthew S. Shugart. 1997. "Juan Linz, Presidentialism, and Democracy: A Critical Appraisal." *Comparative Politics* 29 (July): 449–71.

Moore, Barrington. 1966. *Social Origins of Dictatorship and Democracy: Lord and Peasant in the Making of the Modern World*. Boston: Beacon Press.

Myerson, Roger B. 2006. "Federalism and Incentives for Success of Democracy," *Quarterly Journal of Political Science*: 1 (January): 3–23.

Powell, G. Bingham. 2000. *Elections as Instruments of Democracy: Majoritarian and Proportional Visions*. New Haven: Yale University Press.

Przeworski, Adam. 1991. *Democracy and the Market: Political and Economic Reforms in Eastern Europe and Latin America*. New York: Cambridge University Press.

Przeworski, Adam, Michael E. Alvarez, José Antonio Cheibub, and Fernando Limongi. 2000. *Democracy and Development: Political Institutions and Well-Being in the World, 1950–1990*. New York: Cambridge University Press.

Przeworski, Adam, Susan C. Stokes, and Bernard Manin (eds.). 1999. *Democracy, Accountability, and Representation*. New York: Cambridge University Press.

Rueschemeyer, Dietrich, Evelyne Huber Stephens, and John D. Stephens. 1992. *Capitalist Development and Democracy*. Chicago: University of Chicago Press.

Shepsle, Kenneth. 1991. *Models of Multiparty Electoral Competition*. Chur: Harwood Academic.

Shugart, Matthew S., and John M. Carey. 1992. *Presidents and Assemblies. Constitutional Design and Electoral Dynamics*. New York: Cambridge University Press.

Stepan, Alfred, and Cindy Skach. 1994. "Presidentialism and Parliamentarism in Comparative Perspective." In Juan J. Linz and Arturo Valenzuela (eds.), *The Failure of Presidential Democracy: Comparative Perspectives*. Baltimore: Johns Hopkins University Press.

Tocqueville, Alexis de. 1835 [1969]. *Democracy in America*. New York: Doubleday.

Vanhanen, Tatu. 1997. *Prospects of Democracy: A Study of 172 Countries*. London: Routledge.

Weingast, Barry R. 1997. "The Political Foundations of Democracy and the Rule of Law," *American Political Science Review* 91 (June): 245–63.

Wolf, Eric R. 1969. *Peasant Wars in the Twentieth Century*. New York: Harper.

Author Index

Author Index

Subject Index